FINDINGS KEI

Ralph Russell is best known as one of the foremost western scholars of Urdu literature. For over fifty years his teaching, translations and writings have made this rich literature accessible to readers with no knowledge of the language, and earned him a high reputation among fellow Urdu scholars. For thirty years at the School of Oriental and African Studies, and afterwards in Asian communities in British cities, he pioneered the teaching of Urdu as a means of bringing closer understanding between people and bridging cultural divisions. His honesty, humour and unusual insight have won him a unique place in the affections of lovers of Urdu worldwide.

This delightful first volume of his autobiography gives an insight into the formative years of an unusual man. An absorbing picture of three decades and a world war seen through the eyes of a child, boy and young man of warm affections, high ideals, and refreshing honesty.

RALPH RUSSELL

Findings, Keepings

Life, communism and everything

AN AUTOBIOGRAPHY

PART 1 · 1918–1946

SHOLA
BOOKS

LONDON

FINDINGS, KEEPINGS
published by Shola Books
copyright © Ralph Russell, 2001

cover design by Andrew Corbett
printed and bound in Great Britain by
Biddles Ltd, Guildford
distributed by Shola Books,
33 Theatre Street, London SW11 5ND

ISBN 0 9519752 2 6

Foreword

The present form of this autobiography has evolved from earlier writing about my life, some of which goes back more than fifty years. I have been told that I have an exceptionally vivid memory, and that may be so, but in the chapters on my wartime years in India I have been able to draw also on letters and an account of these years which I wrote in 1945-6, immediately after my return to Britain. I have similar records of some other experiences.

I am grateful to my brother Rex for reminding me of things I had forgotten, and for his help with some of the maps and diagrams; to Sharon Molteno for transcribing the music of the songs; to Andrew Corbett for the cover design, and help beyond the line of duty with illustrations and production; and to Greg Lanning, Terry Byres, my son Ian, and others who read various drafts and made very helpful comments. But my greatest debt by far is to Marion Molteno whose constant urging enabled me to transform into a proper autobiography what was originally simply an account, written as long ago as 1973, of the development of my political ideas. I had come to realise that this was of real interest only to those who had, like myself, been actively engaged in Communist political activity since the 30s, and for several years her questioning, her suggestions, and her constant encouragement elicited all the material that a true autobiography needs to include. Often when I recalled some incident of my life she would say, 'Put that in the book', and I did; and her outstanding editorial skills produced the narrative which is now before you. She has alerted me to what readers of a different generation need to have explained, and convinced me that the book would be enlivened by illustrations; she herself prepared most of the maps, selected the photographs, and pressed me to include the songs. For more than a year now she has postponed her own writing projects to give every hour she could spare to the preparation of this book, and if all the writing is mine, it is she who is responsible for its present shape.

LOSSINGS, SEEKINGS

FINDINGS, KEEPINGS

A YORKSHIRE SAYING

1

Some people think that only famous and important people should write their autobiographies. I'm not famous, except within the small circle of people who study Urdu, and among those of you reading this there will be some who don't even know what Urdu is. I'm not important either, in the sense in which 'important' goes along with 'famous', though I may be important to a small number of people who know me personally. So why am I writing this?

First, because I think that every human being is important, and that includes me. And second, because anyone who has thought seriously about how they want to live – what they want to live for, if you like – could, and in many cases should, write their autobiography. Whether they do so or not, they are likely to be interested in the experience of others who have lived like that, and can learn things valuable to them through reading about it. So that is why I am writing mine.

I have recorded all that I regard as significant in my life experience and haven't regarded anything as too 'private' to be written about. My belief, which I don't expect others to share, is that there ought to be no subject whatever which mature adults should not be able to talk about to each other.

∞

I was born on 21st May 1918 in a workhouse in Homerton, where I eventually learned my parents were master and matron. I have only fragmentary memories of the place. Of a nurse-maid, a black woman called Louie, who my mother told me I used to call Woolly and who would give me my feeding bottle on the command of 'Bokla, Woolly, bokla' … Of looking out of our first floor window down the long workhouse yard … Of watching men carrying great sides of beef on their shoulders down the steps to the kitchen or pantry or wherever. I remember burying one of my milk teeth and getting a coin – I think it was a sixpence – from the tooth fairy. And of the time I had diphtheria and was in hospital – probably the infirmary attached to the workhouse. My older brother Noel was also there and in the same ward. We had bread and butter and boiled egg for breakfast, and I would chew up a mouthful, take it out of my mouth, roll it into a ball between my hands, and then put it back into my mouth again.

Then we moved away, to the village of Holme on Spalding Moor in East Yorkshire. It never occurred to me to wonder why we moved to the village. My father did not come with us – 'we' was my mother and us children, four boys. I must have been about four at the time, so Noel would have been nine, Rex six, and Wilfred about two. My mother's mother lived in the village and I suppose I had some sense of being in a place that was just as much home as Homerton had been. It was here that I first came to continuous awareness of my surroundings, and I have always felt about it as other people feel about their birthplace.

My grandmother had married again in her old age, a saddler and harness maker named George Finch. I am told that eyebrows were raised when they married, village opinion being that old people should be above such things as sexual desire. Until recently I had thought that we lived with them when we first came to Holme, but Rex tells me that this wasn't so. But we were certainly there often and I remember it, and them, very warmly.

I realise now that grandfather Finch's property occupied quite a substantial piece of land, with a frontage extending for about forty yards. Their house was one of two in a row, but the second was never occupied except for one musty-smelling room which was used one day a week by a bank from the nearest small town of Market Weighton, five miles away. On the other side of the house was a stable and loft, and across a broad drive was grandfather Finch's saddler's shop, a wooden structure raised on low stilts above the ground. I have a photo of him sitting on the steps holding a horse collar. Behind that was grass and apple trees and a big chicken-run for my grandmother's hens. Opposite the back of the house was a washhouse (for clothes) and behind that an outside lavatory and a pig sty, the smell of each vying with the other. Beyond was a stretch of land with fruit bushes – red currants mainly – and apple trees that bore a delicious fruit with pink streaks in the flesh. Many years later I discovered its name but I've now forgotten it again. And beyond all that was a big field where grandfather Finch kept his pony Kitty and a cow. For some reason he was always nervous of Kitty, and of course the nervousness communicated itself to her and made her nervous too. He kept both a buggy and a trap. The buggy was low to the ground, with a square body with seats along each side so that people sat facing each other – I guess at a pinch it could seat three on each side. The trap stood very high, with wheels higher than I was, and the only

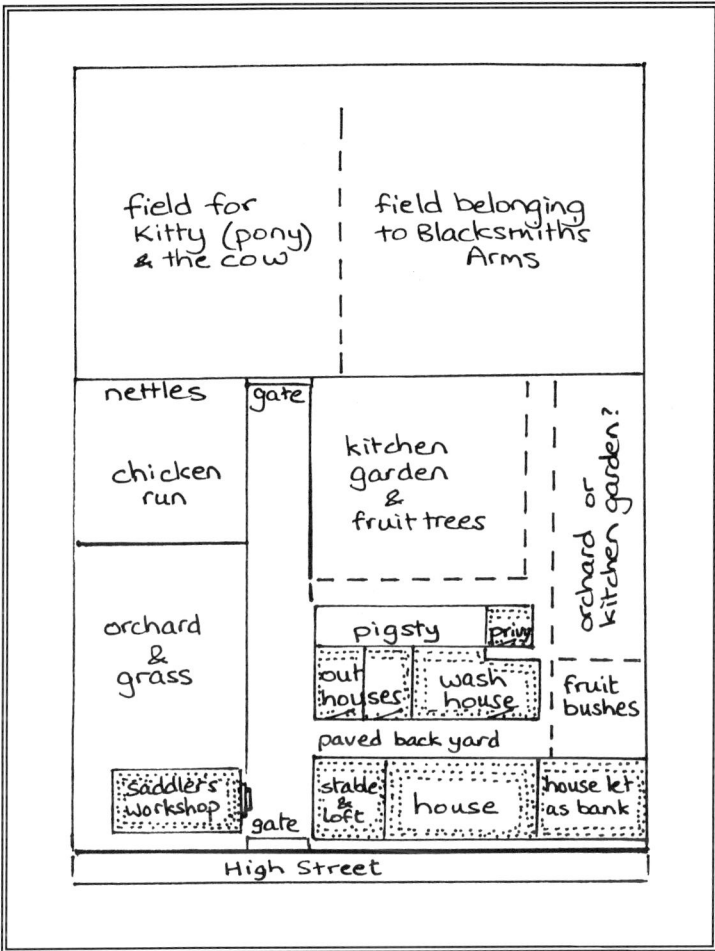

Grandfather Finch's land

Grandfather Finch and his saddler's shop

seating was one cross-seat on top just wide enough for grandfather and at most two of us children. I'm not sure what purpose it was designed for, but I imagine the rest of the space could be used for loading things like sacks of potatoes. There wasn't a lot of motor traffic on the road but grandfather Finch was made nervous by whatever there was and would shout abuse at drivers of approaching vehicles. 'Get over, squeer 'ead [squarehead]. D'you want *all* t'road?'

You will have gathered that he and grandma produced a lot of their own food. The hens gave eggs and an occasional fowl for roasting. The pig was killed every year for ham and bacon, lard, and scraps fished out of the lard that we loved to eat. In Holme they were *called* scraps, but in Lancashire, I believe, 'chitterlings'. Grandma had a baking day once a week on the huge blackleaded kitchen range. We would eat bread cakes, like a large bap, straight off the hot baking tray and soaked in golden syrup. Delicious! We children had a fine time and felt entirely at home, so though many of our experiences were new, none of them seemed strange.

They didn't have a dog but kept a number of cats – strictly working cats, expected to find their own food. Grandma often used to have the outside door open as she worked and had a whip handy to flick the cats if ever they ventured in. This room was a sort of outer kitchen where she prepared food and washed dishes. Beyond was the room where practically everything else happened. The huge kitchen range occupied the largest part of one wall, and filling the middle of the room was a big table at which people sat to eat. The window looked out on the street. Another room – rarely used – opened out from it, with a harmonium and something in a glass case that I think was a corncrake but Rex thinks was a peewit which nodded its head when the harmonium played. I don't remember anyone ever playing the harmonium but I liked the sound it made when you pulled the *vox humana* stop, without of course knowing what *vox humana* meant.

Both grandma and grandfather Finch were kind and loving, although grandma was less demonstrative than he was. When he was milking the cow he would sometimes turn the teat in our direction and squirt us with milk and laugh with us as we squealed. His own children had long been grown up and he loved having us. He used to call us 'honey' – or more precisely, '*oony*, dropping the 'h' and pronouncing the 'o' to rhyme with the 'oo' in 'wood'. He had a close-cropped grey beard and would sit us on his knee and rub it round our faces, saying that it would make our whiskers grow. He taught us some Yorkshire sayings, for example,

'Lossings, seekings; findings, keepings'

– which seems to me now a good summary of what this book is about.

For us grandfather and grandma's house was the centre of the village, of which we knew a quite limited area. Next door on one side was a smithy, and Mr Harrison the blacksmith was indeed all that a child who read Longfellow's poem would imagine a blacksmith to be –

The smith a mighty man is he,
And the muscles of his brawny arms
Are strong as iron bands.

Across a large yard came the appropriately named Blacksmith's Arms. Then a green, on which stood the old school house, no longer used as such, where we learnt that my mother's grandfather Thomas Amos had been the master-cum-teacher-trainer. To one side of the green was the post office, and further along a field ending at Rush Corner, the main road junction of the village, and the police station around the corner. Going the other way there was a pub, the Hare and Hounds, and beyond that the yard and house of the Burleys who owned a threshing machine pulled by a big steam engine – Puffing Billy we called it, or in Wilfred's version, puffer billy shrakshan (traction) – that they used to hire out to go the rounds at harvest time.

It was a village of farms, with only a few other buildings and shops. One, or perhaps both, of its two butcher's shops belonged to men who were also farmers. Two of the main shops of the village were almost directly opposite us – Bailey's, a hardware and clothing store, and Harrison's, the old-established grocery run by Willie Harrison and his two unmarried sisters. Rex tells me that people called him Half-prune Willie because he would cut a prune in half rather than have the packet go overweight. Beyond the shops on one side was a field, at the back of which stood The Beeches. It was one of the few really big houses in the village, named after the tall copper beech trees that stood at the side of it, and belonged to the headteacher. In the other direction was Holme Institute, a large wooden building, and behind it a field where every September Holme Feast was held, with swings and roundabouts and coconut shies and all the rest of the traditional fairground attractions. Beyond that was the nursery, supplying plants and so on, and then the farm of grandfather Finch's son Harry. Not far from there was the village school and near it Mrs Mason's shop – in fact just a room in a house on a little triangular patch of land.

6

Though I know now that we were quite poor, I never realised it at the time and did not feel the contrast that there must have been between the way we had lived in Homerton and how we were living now. We moved to a succession of rented houses, with furniture of broken chairs repaired and given new seats by grandfather Finch, or orange-boxes draped at the front with a piece of cloth and used as shelves and cupboards. One was a house in Stocks Hill, so called because nearby were stocks (the remains still identifiable) into which malefactors used to be put. One memory of Stocks Hill is that I had boils on my legs for quite a long time, but they eventually went away. Another is that we had a well from which we had to draw our water – unusual, for most houses in the village had a pump. My mother did not know how to get water out of the well. She would throw in the bucket on the end of the rope but it would just float on the top of the water. Grandfather Finch told her to throw it in so that the open end of the bucket hit the water first. When she did, the bucket turned over – full of water – and gave her a jerk which nearly pulled her into the well.

Rex and I used to take cans to get our milk from a farm nearby, belonging to one known in the village as Crafty Ward. Rex was a mischievous boy, and often quite malicious. One day he was carrying the milk can and swung it round over his head and demonstrated that the milk didn't fall out. He then handed it to me and told me to do the same – and the milk spilt all over the road, at which he laughed delightedly.

Another move was to a cottage that stood in the large garden of a house where one of the school teachers, Miss Davison lived. While we were there I had a toy monkey which I called Munno, and later another larger one which I called Munno More. At one time Munno disappeared and for a long time could not be found. We ultimately found him up a tree where I must have forgotten I'd put him.

We finally settled in a house next to the school, in an area called Runner End. I still have some photos of my mother and us children at that house. I remember planting some nasturtiums outside our loo, which like all the loos in the village at that time was an earth closet some way from the house, and I remember also that I was afraid to shut the door when I was in it. A woman called Mrs Raper used to come to do our washing and I was once covered in confusion when she passed by while I was sitting on the loo, door ajar. Mrs Raper had a very good opinion of me and once said to my mother, 'Ee Mrs Russell, you'll never rear that bairn, he's too good for this world' – which as we know proved not to be the case.

It was from here that I started school. It was the only one in the village, so children of all classes went there, from farm labourers to farmers. I don't think there was much sense of class distinction, though I do remember Clive Finch making sure everyone knew he was a *farmer's* son – not that that impressed anybody much. I remember how in the reception class we were taught to count using mottled pink and black beans, and I later realised the significance of the saying 'He knows how many beans make five.'

The reception class had two teachers, Mrs Ward and, under her, Amy Hurd, who was grandfather Finch's daughter. I think they co-taught the class. Mrs Ward lived – alone I think – in a thatched cottage, and I liked her. We didn't like Mrs Hurd, though I don't quite know why. She always wore unattractive knitted clothes of khaki wool. She had a husband, Jim, but no children, and they lived in a big house opposite the school. Amy was the breadwinner, but if Jim didn't take a job it may have been because he had some other source of income. Jim was a soft-spoken, constantly smiling man who somehow always gave me the creeps, though again I couldn't say why. By village standards there were things that must have constituted a black mark against them – the fact that she and not he was the breadwinner and that they were childless. It was also said that Jim's behaviour towards women was not all that it should have been. Amy, besides her teaching, also did dress-making, and it was said that when ladies came to try on the dresses Amy made for them they did so in Jim's presence. 'Jim won't mind,' Amy would say – and he would cast surreptitious but lascivious eyes upon them. It may well have been that I unconsciously absorbed the village's negative feelings about them.

The teacher I remember best was Miss Davison, who taught the next class up from the reception class. Rex tells me that she had trained as a teacher under my mother's grandfather. I remember with great pleasure how she used to read to us. It was through her readings that I first made the acquaintance of Grimm's fairy tale 'The shoes that were danced to pieces' and some of Kipling's *Just So Stories*. Years later I was fascinated by the fact that when my elder daughter Sarah was little 'The shoes that were danced to pieces' was *her* favourite story too.

Being read to was one of the two things about school in Holme that I liked very much. The other was the singing. I think it must have been in Miss Davison's class that we all sang

This old man, he played one
He played knick knack on my drum.

Later I learnt a song I have never encountered since, which begins

8

My father died & I do not know how. He left me 6 horses to follow the plough with a wing-wang waddle-o, Jack sold his saddle-o, blossy boys, bubble-o, under the broom.

It goes on to

I sold my six horses and bought me a cow …

and so on, with something valuable being sold and something less valuable bought instead until there is nothing valuable left. Many years later I heard Burl Ives singing one on a similar pattern – but not this one. And seventy-five years later I found in a selection of songs collected by Cecil Sharp something very close, though neither the words nor the tune are exactly the same.

The class above Miss Davison's was, I think, co-taught by the head teacher Samson Feather and his wife Lucy. Rex must have been in their class – he was two years older than me – but I have no recollection of any contact with him in the school context. My younger brother Wilfred didn't go until later, and when he did there was an unexpected problem to face. After I had started school he was the only one of us left at home and he told my mother that he wanted to go to school too. Though two years younger than me he was already taller than me, and he could already read quite fluently. He had an amusing fondness for the books my mother read although he certainly could not have understood them. Anyway, my mother went to the headmaster who said, 'Let him come when he feels like it. He can sit in with the children in the infants' class.' When he came of school age he wanted to continue this pattern and couldn't understand why he now had to go to school every day. But he liked school, and the problem was soon sorted out.

My oldest brother Noel was away at boarding school and we saw little of him except during school holidays. At the time we had left Homerton he had already been at school for several years, and in the classy kind of school, moreover, to which it was considered appropriate for somebody of my father's status to send his children. Now, after a short stay at the village school he won a scholarship to Bridlington School. I have a photo of him wearing his surplice for the choir, and another of him with his two pet rabbits.

Of the girls in the school I remember only that there were four whom I thought very pretty, Ivy Wincup, Marion Southgate and Lena and Marie Sherwood. Ivy was the daughter of the roadsweeper, and

With my mother and brothers, probably 1923 L-R: Rex, Noel, Wilfred, Ralph

With Wilfred

Ralph, aged about 5

Lena and her elder sister Marie (pronounced Marry) were daughters of the man who delivered the Co-op groceries on his horse and cart. Lena told me decades later that she remembered me as a little curly-headed boy who 'always got all his sums right' – an ability which I no longer retain.

Our closest contacts were with our neighbours the Finches – grandfather Finch's son Harry and his family. They had a farm only about a hundred yards from our house at Runner End, and we used to go there for milk, butter and eggs. Harry's wife Edie was a big stout woman who always used to wear a man's cloth cap. We liked both her and Harry. There were four children – Clive, the oldest, then Edgar, Mildred and Cecil. Cecil, like the youngest in many families, was a spoiled brat, but we got on well enough with the others. Clive became very fond of my mother and would often come to our house. He once told her that he had worked out that she was his step-aunt. Another thing about him which amused my mother was that when our alarm clock went off he said 'Dawn't it ding in your ears, Mrs Russell!'

Mildred Finch has the distinction of being the person who first gave me any indication that boys' and girls' bodies were different. Up till that time I had not had the least idea of this, since we were a family of boys, and my mother – like most mothers until quite recent times – would never have dreamed of allowing herself to be seen naked. But I can remember clearly the development of a feeling of the attractiveness of women and girls (young women more than girls of my own age). One of the publicans in Holme had three beautiful daughters and I was strongly attracted to one of them, Eileen Burke, who must have been eighteen or nineteen years old at the time. I remember imagining how nice it would be to see her naked and to admire her beautiful white penis.*

I must have been about seven when Mildred invited me into a sandpit in her father's field with the suggestion that we should 'have a bit of bod', which I discovered meant playing with each other's genitals. I remember vividly the pleasant feeling of having an erection and trying to get my willy into the entrance of her slit – either I knew instinctively that this was what I was to do or else she told me – and also feeling that I wanted to pee but couldn't. And I remember too the attractive smell of Mildred's genitals. When we emerged from the sandpit into the Finches' orchard we were greeted with a broad grin by Ozzie Burley, sitting on the Burleys' gate on the other side of the road. I remember thinking that he almost certainly knew what we'd been up to, and that he had probably had the same delightful experience with Mildred before I had. But this was a one-off experience and I don't recall any desire either to repeat it or not to repeat it. Nor do I think that this experience affected my vision of Eileen, whom I probably still imagined to be the possessor of a lovely white penis.

Neither with Mildred nor anyone else during our years in Holme did I develop a close friendship. Nor, I think, did my mother. If we ever wondered what my father was doing or why he wasn't with us I guess we assumed that he was doing something or other 'down south', as Yorkshire people say. He came on occasional brief visits such as at Christmas time and we were always glad to see him. Although Holme had a railway station he chose to walk the nine miles from Howden, a feat which impressed us greatly.

There wasn't much visiting of one another's homes. The exceptions were the houses of people related to us. One of these was my mother's uncle John and his wife Lizzie. Uncle John was either owner or tenant farmer (I think owner) of two farms, Chapel Farm opposite the Wesleyan Chapel, which he farmed himself, and Hasholme, a farm way out in the outskirts of the village. He had a very deep voice and was quite deaf, while Auntie Lizzie had a high piping voice so that she had to repeat everything she said to him. Uncle John, and everyone else of his generation, spoke much broader Yorkshire than most younger people – for example saying 'wee'ant' and 'dee'ant' instead of 'won't' and 'don't', 'tiv' instead of 'to', 'oil' for 'hole', 'I'm not off to' for 'I'm not going to' along with other Yorkshire usages that were still current, such as 'starved', meaning 'cold' and 'scelp' meaning 'smack', 'lug-oil', meaning 'earhole'. My mother used to tell us things they had said. Once when Uncle John was ill in bed he was given one of those cups with a spout so that he didn't have to sit up to drink. He was asked how he liked it and said, 'Ah think nowt tiv it. It ods [holds] nowt.' And once when Auntie Lizzie opened the door to Willie Harrison ('half-prune Willy', the grocer) someone called out to ask who it was. Auntie Lizzie said, still standing facing him at the door, 'Oah, it's only Willie with a wheel off.'

Uncle John used to ride a bike and, being unable to hear such little traffic as there was in those days, used to ignore it, relying on others to get out of his way. He was also colour-blind and could see, as he put it, only 'rid and yella'. They had a lawn in front of their farmhouse which Lizzie used to cut with a pair of scissors.

Hasholme was farmed by John and Lizzie's two sons and one daughter, Arthur, Clarence and Elsie. We often took a trip out there, sometimes in grandfather Finch's buggy, though at other times we walked. All three were unmarried in my childhood (and as far as I remember only Clarence ever did marry), and Elsie kept house for them. She had been courted by someone for years and years and I later learnt that he used to bring her chocolate. She didn't like chocolate but never told him so and there were stacks of bars of chocolate in her chest of drawers.

Uncle John was rather remote from us children and we warmed more towards his brother Tom and his wife Polly. We never saw any sign that Uncle Tom did any work on his farm, and such little work as was done seemed to be done by his tall lugubrious son Sidney. Two other sons had 'bettered themselves' and gone off somewhere else and rarely visited their parents. My mother once told me that Polly didn't like Lizzie, and when she heard of Lizzie doing anything she disapproved of would remark, contemptuously, 'Why, she's a Clough' – Clough being Lizzie's maiden name. Anyway both she and Lizzie used to give us a good tea when we visited, including buttered spicebread and, in accordance with local custom, bits of cheese – though as far as I recall only the adults ate the cheese. Spicebread figured in a rhyme children recited at New Year :

Lucky bod, lucky bod, chuck, chuck, chuck
Master and missis it's time to get up
Your feathered flocks and your new calved coo [cow]
Master and Missis, how do you do?
A little bit of spicebread, a little bit of cheese
A cup of cold water and a penny if you please
If you haven't got a penny a halfpenny will do
If you haven't got a halfpenny, God bless you!

In September 1925 when I was seven we suddenly (to us children's way of thinking) left Holme and moved to Loughton in Essex, about twelve miles from London. But though this changed our lives completely the bond with Holme remained, and I kept going back.

When I picture the village now I see it set in its surrounding landscape. It lies in flat country in the Vale of York. Towards one end of it is the only hill for miles around, quite a high one, on which the church stands. It is a long village, essentially Y-shaped, and grandfather Finch's house was indeed almost at its centre as we had thought it was. In one direction houses and farms run out to the west towards Selby, the nearest reasonably big town, twelve miles away. At an angle to that another road runs towards Howden, nine miles away, and the stem of the Y goes

The village

The house at Runner End, with the school next door

Church Hill

towards Market Weighton, five miles away.

There are things that I never thought about at the time but that now interest me. Names like Rush Corner, Runner End and Water End suggest that there was once a lot of water about the place. The name of the village itself is a curious one. According to two place-name dictionaries I have consulted it is associated in some way with the tribe of the Spaldingas, although Spalding, miles away in Lincolnshire, is the nearest other place named after them.

Though as a child I was largely oblivious of it, it is clear looking back that there was a clear social stratification. A handful of the educated, of whom the headmaster and the doctor seemed to be the core, the farmers (not particularly well-educated), and the farm labourers. I guess the shopkeepers ranked with the farmers. Each had their own religious affiliations – as in other parts of rural England the cultured were C of E, the farmers Wesleyan Methodists, and the labourers Primitive Methodists – and these certainly represented social class rather than religious difference. Rex tells me that grandfather Finch was a Wesleyan Methodist and an occasional lay preacher, and that on Sundays he wore highly polished leather leggings. Church and chapel attendance was sufficiently large to keep the buildings in reasonably good shape, but I don't recall any kind of religious fervour in the village.

The village was fairly self-contained. There were buses on certain days of the week to York and Selby, and a railway station, but except for the farmers who used Selby market people didn't travel out of the village much. I remember being told that there were Holme people who had never been out of the village all their lives. I sometimes think that if I had lived there all my life I too would never have wanted to.

15

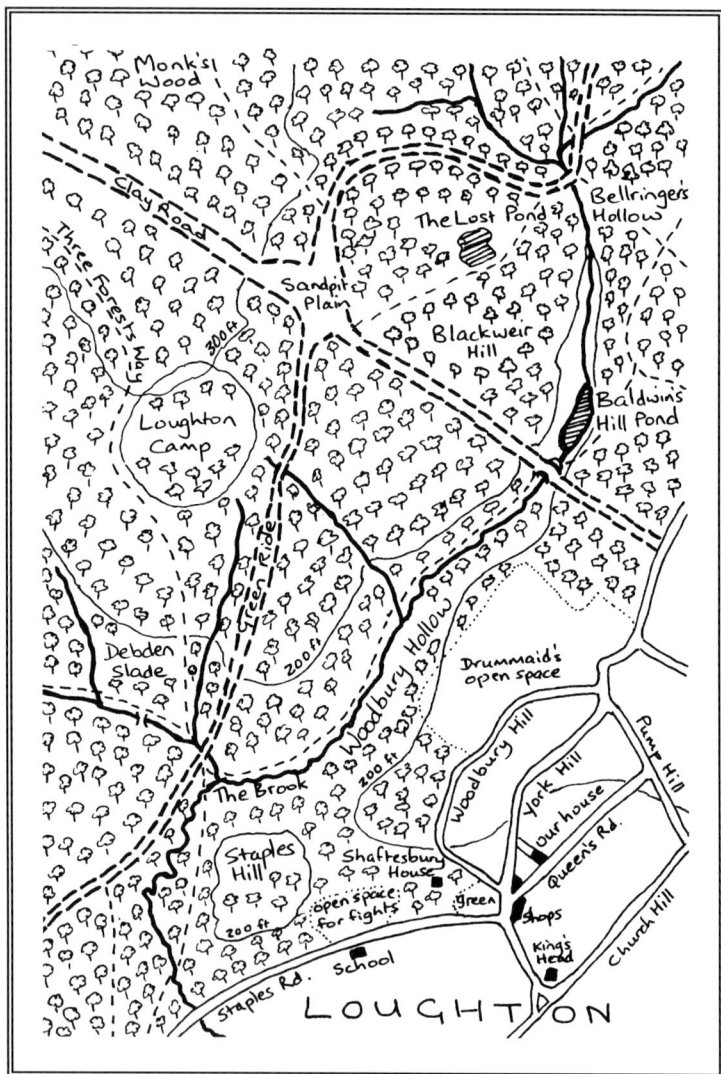

Loughton: home, school & forest

2

I remember every detail of the evening we arrived in Loughton and the events of the following morning. My father met us at the station and we made the short journey to the house that was now going to be our home in a four-wheeled horse-drawn carriage. (I don't know the English name for it, nor do I remember when it vanished from the scene in England, but years later I encountered it again in Bombay where it was called a Victoria.) At the house tea was ready for us, prepared by our auntie Kath, the wife of my father's brother Harry. We had blackcurrant jam, and when evening came she lighted a gas-light – something we had never seen before, for in Holme lighting was oil lamps. Upstairs there was a WC – again a thing we had never seen. The sound of the rushing water when we pulled the chain scared us, and we used to pull it and then dash downstairs as fast as we could.

The morning after our arrival we were eager to go out and explore the neighbourhood. Rex and Wilfred and I went to the corner shop and caused considerable, but not unkind, amusement by asking for a sweet called a 'Blackjack', pronouncing it in a pure Yorkshire accent. We then walked up the the quite steep road our house was in, and were fascinated to find that the houses were numbered and had names – ours was Roseley, 6 Queens Road – which again was something entirely strange to us. There was street lighting – there had been none in Holme – and we would see the lamplighter come round on his bike with his long pole to light the gaslights. But by that time we had ceased to be impressed by new things, and took this discovery in our stride.

As with our move to Holme we neither knew nor felt any curiosity to know the reasons for our move. We just accepted that we had a new home, that our father was now part of it, and that he used to go to work every day in London, at a place called St George's in the East, Stepney. Noel was transferred from Bridlington School to a tinpot private secondary school, inferior in every way to Bridlington, and he never ceased to feel bitter about it. The three younger of us children went to the local council school that catered for the great majority of Loughton boys.

The transition from life in Holme was easier than it might have been because our house was no more than five minutes' walk from the edge

Epping Forest: Monk's Wood, with old pollarded beeches

of Epping Forest. It was an ancient forest, about half a mile deep and running north and south more miles than we could explore, sometimes dense wood, sometimes open glades, rising over a series of small hills and dipping into hollows with ponds. Rex and I would collect acorns which we loaded in an old pram and sold for next to nothing to Mr Gould in a shop in the High Road that supplied animal feeds. We would follow the course of a brook and jump across it at frequent intervals. The broadest part, and the deepest water, were at a place we called the well, and for me it was a proud achievement to jump across it without falling in.

School was only a short walk from our house. We passed a green with a huge hollow tree-trunk lying on it, big enough for us children to crawl through. Then along Staples Road, with buildings only on the lefthand side and on the other, Epping Forest. Right opposite the school was an open area with no trees, and here there would occasionally be fights after school between some school kid and another one he had fallen out with. These used to be announced in whispers round the class. 'Fight tonight!' 'Who?' 'Jack and Tom.' Some joker would sometimes whisper to the boy next to him, 'Fight tonight' and when asked 'Who?' would say 'Me and my tea.' Fights had to be started and finished before the headmaster got wind of them; otherwise he would come out and stop them. Occasionally the boy who had been challenged would get cold feet and back out, whereupon the spectators would call out, 'Give him a coward's blow!'

There was a much greater awareness of class than there had been in Holme. At one end of Loughton was a road called Smarts Lane where in those days the poorest of the Loughton population lived. There was a certain fear of the Smarts Lane people among the rest of the population and other children took care not to upset the Smarts Lane children. I seem to have had a kind of cherubic air which for some reason made them like me. I remember a boy called Stubbings who wore short trousers worn to a sizeable hole over each of his buttocks taking it upon himself to act as my protector.

We were even more afraid of (as we saw it) the wild and savage children who every summer were brought for a holiday in the forest from the East End of London. They were accomodated in a building called Shaftesbury House, just inside the forest a little way beyond the green. They really were a wild lot, and the bane of the forest keepers because they would tear branches from the trees just for the hell of it. When we walked in the forest we gave them a wide berth.

We all used to go home from school for our midday meal. When we returned in the afternoon the headmaster would stand at the door and cane (once, on the hand) any straggler who came in late. Once *I* was late – I can't remember why – and entered the school in fear and trembling. But perhaps the same air of innocence that led the Smarts Lane boy to protect me operated with the teachers, for the headmaster looked straight through me and let me pass.

We rented our house from Mr Bosworth, who had a butcher's shop in Church Hill. The house was quite big. On the ground floor was a hallway, one large and one smaller sitting room, a kitchen with a scullery beyond it and a pantry. Upstairs was a bathroom, a lavatory, two medium sized bedrooms and a smaller one. A narrow staircase led up to a third floor with a small L-shaped landing, lit by a skylight, and a large attic room, which we three younger boys shared. At the far end of it was a window from which we could look up the whole length of Queen's Road, which rose quite steeply.

Our house too stood on rising ground. A front garden with peonies and Chinese lanterns sloped up to broad steps that led up to the front door. At the back was a paved yard and about four feet above that, a large lawn. There was an apple tree that never produced anything worth writing home about, and some plum trees that produced a good crop of small, sweet, yellow plums. My mother said they were probably not plums but bullaces but I now know that they couldn't have been, because bullaces are black. There was a coal house and an area for the dust bin, over which at one time was the web of a large and beautiful spider. We used to catch flies, throw them on the net and watch the spider dash out and wrap them up.

The atmosphere in our house was – I now realise – rather extraordinary. My mother was not cut out for the role of full-time mother and housewife and the house was always an absolute tip. Every flat surface was piled with old newspapers so that you could not sit down anywhere without first moving them off a chair. She was also a terrible planner. She would buy a huge joint of beef (which I believe is called H-bone) and after we had had one meal of it, leave it in the pantry and forget it until it was covered in mould. For dirty dishes she had her own system. In the scullery was a large copper, a boiler of iron set in a squat brick tower, maybe three feet high and three feet in diameter. At the bottom was a small fireplace where you would light a fire to heat the water in the boiler, to boil clothes in. I would guess that in suburban Loughton as opposed to rural Holme it was a piece of household equipment that was already obsolete. Certainly the use to which our copper was put was quite different from that for which it was designed. We had an enormous quantity of plates, dishes and cutlery, and the copper was a convenient place on which to stack the dirty ones. My mother would pile them up until they practically reached the ceiling. It was then usually my father who, very complainingly, did the washing up.*

There were regular duties allotted to each of us. My father used to empty all the chamber pots on a Sunday morning. He also used to clean all the shoes and never learnt that putting them in front of the fire after they had been cleaned would transform the shine into a sort of dull matt. He never ceased to express his annoyance at this but neither did he learn not to do it. We children had no duties during the week, but definite tasks to perform every Saturday morning. I can't remember what all of these were, but one was to clean the cutlery – this being before the days of stainless steel.

Just up the road from us lived the Brady family. The father was a self-important character, a bus driver who liked to be called Major Brady. He may indeed have been a major, though some people said he'd only been a sergeant-major, which was not the same thing at all. There were two boys and a pretty girl called Rosalind, about five years old at the time of this memory. I discovered that I could lift her up by putting my hands between her legs – I liked doing this, but I remember no sexual feeling about it and did not connect it with my earlier experience with Mildred Finch. I am pretty sure that my mother and her mother had consultation about this and I expect I was told not to do it again.

Another near neighbour was a school friend, Jack Bloy. My mother was on quite close terms with the Bradys (who were genteel) but didn't know the Bloy parents (who weren't). Mr Bloy was a policeman, with a regional accent of some kind. In those days it was common practice to recruit policemen from areas other than that in which they were to serve. Jack invited me to tea once and I remember being a bit disconcerted by his father's blunt manner. At one point he said of someone whom he thought a habitual liar, 'I wouldn't believe him if he told me today was Thursday' – and that day *was* Thursday. I was both embarrassed and amused by this statement and often recalled it later, aware that not every statement by a habitual liar is necessarily a lie.

It never entered my head that I should get my mother to return the Bloys' invitation. Evidently it never entered *her* head either. I can't in fact remember anyone being invited to our house, and no one except relatives visited us. I assumed that this was the normal state of affairs – that the house was somewhere we lived and had our meals and slept, and nobody else came. Years later Noel told me that my mother had suggested to my father that instead of meeting his friends in the pub he should bring them home. Noel does not remember my father's reply, but said, 'I knew bloody well why he wouldn't. The house was never in a state you'd want to bring anybody else into.'

I quite quickly won a reputation for excellence in my schoolwork. I felt a great pride in this, nourished among other things by my father's extravagant admiration. We used to write from time to time what in later years in my daughter's school was called 'News', and my father always used to read what I wrote. I must have expected always to get everything right, for I remember to this day how mortified I felt when I had written 'We are aloud to' and my father corrected the 'aloud' to 'allowed.'

In those days it was common for children to be expected to stand up and recite poems for other people's entertainment, drawn mostly from books dating from the late nineteenth century and bearing titles like 'Children's Reciter'. I remember one piece of doggerel I was called upon to recite called 'Tommy's Errand', in which Tommy was sent shopping and got everything wrong, asking, for example, for a pint of jam and six rashers of eggs or whatever. A favourite of my parents was one about Sir Ralph the Rover and the Inchcape Rock (by Southey, I recently discovered.) This dastardly character used to sail the seven seas delighting in making difficulties for others. The Inchcape Rock was covered by shallow water and a bell was fixed there to warn ships of the danger. Sir Ralph thought it would be a great joke to cut the fastening of the bell. He did so, and it 'sank with a gurgling sound.' He paid the penalty. Sailing that way his own ship struck the rock, and though

> *Sir Ralph the Rover tore his hair*
> *And curst himself in his despair*

it didn't do him any good, and that was the end of him. My mother sometimes called me Ralph the Rover. When Wilfred was little he picked it up from her and transformed it into Ralphy Rover.

The teacher I remember best was Mr Lebbon, whom for some reason all the kids called Cods. He was a remarkable teacher, and I think I sensed this at the time although it was not until years later that I made a proper estimate of him. I remember with great pleasure that under him singing rated the same importance it had in Holme school. The whole class would sing in unison – songs like the pilgrims' chorus from Tannhauser, and what I thought until quite recently was Mendelssohn's 'Spring Song' but have since discovered to be words someone had set to a melody by Rubenstein★:

Win-ter has gone & the springtime is here, whispering glad-ly to the tall tree-s,

Other songs I remember are a chauvinistic one beginning

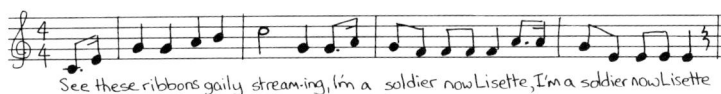

See these ribbons gaily stream-ing, I'm a soldier now Lisette, I'm a soldier now Lisette

one which included the words

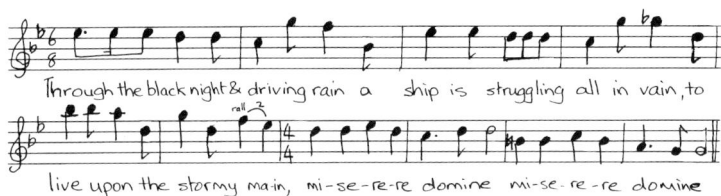

Through the black night & driving rain a ship is struggling all in vain, to
live upon the stormy main, mi-se-re-re domine mi-se-re-re domine

and an appropriate one which began

Gone is the winter gone is the snow, off to the forest gaily we go.

– appropriate because directly opposite our classroom was Epping Forest, where we did indeed go gaily to play. We also sang songs taught in the traditional way, in which we were not expected to understand the words and it never occurred to us to think that we needed to. 'Drink to me only' is a good example. It wasn't until I was an adult that I had the slightest idea of what the first verse was all about. I didn't know what 'drink to me' meant, or how you could drink with your eyes, or what 'I will pledge' meant, or what on earth 'Jove's nectar' was. I'm still not sure what I think about this method, but I'm not sorry I learnt to sing the song even if it didn't occur to me to wonder what it meant.

It was Lebbon too, I think, who organised the yearly singing of Christmas carols. It was in these carol concerts that I learnt one of my favourite carols, 'Love came down at Christmas.' The pleasure I felt in singing has continued with me all my life, and I still sing a lot, both on my own and in the company of others who like it (as not everybody does!)

Lebbon also fostered my love of reading. In the last period on Friday we were allowed to read, and I loved it. I was in the middle of *Nat the Naturalist* when to my great regret I had to leave council school to go to Chigwell School. Only a few years ago I found a copy of it in some junk shop and was shocked to learn that the boy Nat's response to every bird or animal that interested him was to shoot it to add to his collection.★ Lebbon lent me books to read out of school too, one of which was Mark Twain's *Huckleberry Finn*. He was a great fan of Mark Twain, but I

Staples Road School, about 1927: part of a class photo, with the headmaster;
Ralph front, 2nd R

Lebbon's violin class

should have thought that he would have realised that I was far too young to appreciate it properly (I was only nine or ten when he lent it to me.) But I enjoyed it simply at the level of an exciting story and I am ashamed to say that for some reason I decided to keep the book and swore blind that I had returned it to him. I still have no idea why I did this and have always been aware that it was a disgraceful thing to do.

He took a great interest in local history. He told us that Loughton stood in a sort of saucer surrounded by low hills, but with a bit broken off where the station was and flat fields led from there to the River Roding. He told us the history of Epping Forest and of the 19th century struggle to preserve 'lopping rights'. Since medieval times people who lived near the forest had maintained – against the resistance of the landowners – their traditional right to cut branches of trees for fuel. When in the mid nineteenth century the lord of the Loughton manor enclosed forest land, a man called Willingale continued to lop in defiance. Lebbon quoted to us a poem about it which relates Willingale's response when told to stop:

And Willingale said several things
And Willingale went on.

He was fined, and when he refused to pay was sent to prison. Eventually higher authority intervened on the side of the poor. The enclosures were countermanded, and Epping Forest was from then on administered by London Corporation for common use.*

Lebbon had an odd sense of humour and told us jokes that amused him without bothering to think whether they meant anything to us – I imagine he thought it no more important that his jokes should be intelligible to us than that the words of 'Drink to me only' should. Two I remember were about Handel's Messiah. I'm sure that most of the class had no idea who or what Handel or the Messiah were, and thinking about it now, I'm surprised that *I* did. He said there is a piece which begins 'All we like sheep' and, smiling all over his face, went on, 'Not true, of course; we *don't* all like sheep.' And at another point, he said, a chorus sings 'Unto us a child is born' and a lot of women reply 'Wonderful! Wonderful!'

On at least two occasions he had what I imagine was an epileptic fit. He fell to the floor and lay there with his legs jerking about. The class would panic, and rush to the door into the next room where the head master taught, and he would take things in hand. Another vivid memory is of an occasion when I let out a silent but exceptionally potent fart – so potent that it could be smelt all over the classroom where about forty boys were assembled. Lebbon peered anxiously up at the gas light as though he thought there was a leak, although I'm sure he knew what it really was (and, quite probably, who was responsible for it). I was sitting next to a boy I liked called Laurie Tomlin. He certainly knew it was me but he kept silent, and when the smell dispersed that was that.

He was unfailingly kind to me and sometimes expressed this kindness in somewhat inappropriate ways. To my intense embarrassment he once took me out to a meal at the smart Trocadero Hotel near Piccadilly Circus. I had never been in such a situation before (and for that matter have rarely been in such a situation since) and felt intensely embarrassed throughout the whole proceedings, for example when the waiter wheeled up a joint on a trolley and proceeded to carve it according to our instructions in our presence.

It was in Loughton that we first learnt who our relatives were, and through that gradually came to know about our parents' backgrounds.

My father was an orphan, or to be more precise, his father had died when he and his two brothers were children. His mother survived for many years after that. After his father's death he and his brothers were sent to a kind of orphanage where they received the training that would fit them to take clerical jobs when they grew up. At least, I think that was the objective, and where my father and his older brother were concerned this was achieved.

My father's attitude to his older brother Will was one of amused contempt. Will was some sort of superior clerk and had become a freemason. I don't think my father had any serious objection to freemasonry but he thought that the paraphernalia which accompanied it and Will's self-importance about it were ridiculous. Will was quite short in stature and my father used to refer to him as the LOMCD, 'Little Old Man Cut Down.' Like many more or less self-educated people Uncle Will was immensely proud of his knowledge. We saw little of him and we shared our father's attitude towards him. But we did quite like Auntie Nelly, his wife, mainly because she was totally unimpressed by the pompousness of her husband. She had a peculiar gesture which I have never seen in anybody else – when he got cross with her she would put her hands to her temples with the thumbs touching her head and wiggle her fingers back and forth and say 'Scissors, scissors!'

Father's younger brother Harry never made the clerical grade and spent all his working life working in some capacity which I never discovered in Woolwich Arsenal. We children all liked Uncle Harry, and I think my father did too, though in a rather condescending way. My mother was fond of him but objected strongly to a habit he had of licking his lips before he kissed her. My recollection is that he generally came alone, without his wife Kath. He was infinitely obliging, and would climb our plum trees and at horrifying danger to himself crawl out along the slender branches to pick plums for us.

I guess the reason why Auntie Kath rarely accompanied him was that my mother didn't like her. She always used to say that Kath had married Harry only because she couldn't marry my father. (This was because he was already engaged to my mother and in those days breaking your engagement was quite a scandalous thing.) We children too didn't like Auntie Kath, although I can't say why. I still remember with annoyance how she would greet us. ''Allo, dear? 'Ow are you dear? Alright? *That's* right' – all delivered without a pause. It is she who is probably to blame (so to speak) for an irrational dislike of the London accent (other than cockney) which I feel strongly to this day.

My father's mother also came to stay occasionally, though never, I think, for very long. The last I remember of her was her saying she would come again 'when the plums are out,' but I don't think she ever did. I have no idea where she lived or who looked after her. I guess it was in Plumstead, which was where she came from and where Harry and Kath lived. They had no children and it was, I guess, they who took care of her. I can't remember my father ever speaking of her and he never seemed to think much about her, although he was kind and thoughtful to her whenever she came to our house. This was typical of him. He was a kind and affectionate man but on the whole it was out of sight, out of mind.

I know a little more about my mother's family, partly from living in Holme. Our grandma came from a farming family in that area, and Uncle John and Uncle Tom were her brothers. My mother's father and his father had both been schoolmasters – her grandfather Thomas Amos had been the schoolmaster in Holme for thirty-seven years. I never knew my mother's father, Amos Frank Amos, for he had died before any of us were born, and maybe even before my mother's marriage. But I know that as a schoolmaster he was posted to Essex or found a job there, and so for the best part of my mother's childhood she lived in Lawford, near Manningtree. Later on she moved to somewhere in the Sutton area in Surrey and worked for some time as a shop assistant. I have an idea that she 'lived in' for a while in the house of the woman who owned the shop where she worked, because she used to talk about having breakfast there and quoted with amusement the words of the woman in charge that porridge filled you up but 'didn't stand by you.'

It must have been during her years in Sutton that she met my father, who had risen through clerical grades to administrative ones and at one time, I think, worked in the lunatic asylum at Banstead. When they got married he was appointed master of the workhouse in Homerton, London, and that made her the matron. That was probably in 1912 when he was about thirty-eight and my mother thirty. They remained there for ten years.

We knew most of my mother's siblings. (As in many families of that period several had died in childhood.) The oldest was Charles – full name Charles Leslie Amos. Then there was Amos Ralph Amos and a sister, Clara Emily Amos. But they all had pet names – I do not know whether this was common at that period. So Charlie was always called Chick, Amos Ralph Amos was always called Rack and Clara Emily Amos was always called Tats.

Auntie Tats is the one Rex and I remember best, and with real affection. She never married and there were rumours that she had been jilted and decided never again to have anything to do with men. She was two years younger than my mother, who always treated her rather as a glorified servant. In our earliest years when my mother was immersed in her administrative duties as workhouse matron, Auntie Tats was a sort of nanny to us, and always very nice with us. In later years we became aware of the unwarrantedly superior attitude which my mother always adopted towards her. For example, whenever Tats made a statement my mother was likely to correct her. Rex's favourite memory of this kind is of when they visited a house and Tats remarked that the rooms were bigger than the rooms in our house. My mother said, 'Not bigger, dear, just more room'!

Uncle Chick and his wife Auntie Maudie we would visit now and then in Sutton, where Auntie Maudie was manageress of the Darleydale Laundry. Chick owned a car – something quite unusual for a person of his class at that time. I remember him taking us in it to Eastbourne where I played with a ball on the top of a cliff, ran after it and was stopped just in time before falling over Beachy Head. Uncle Chick had been in the Royal Horse Artillery in the war. I remember us visiting him soon after I had gone to secondary school and had begun to learn Latin, and feeling proud of myself because I could translate the Royal Horse Artillery's motto, Ubique quo jus et gloria ducunt – Everywhere where right and glory lead. He had been awarded the DCM (Distinguished Conduct Medal), the other ranks' equivalent of the Officers' DSO (Distinguished Service Order) – but he would never tell us what he had been awarded it for.

Uncle Rack was a jolly man and we all liked him. He was a bachelor and I think as gay a bachelor as circumstances permitted – not gay in the sense it bears now but in the sense that he was, or would have liked to be, a gay dog with the women.

28

Loughton: the corner of our road and York Hill

The butcher shop of Mr Bosworth, our landlord

There was one other brother, Reg, a sort of black sheep or at any rate rather dark grey sheep of the family. A rather portly man with a handsome face and a curly black beard, who hardly figures in my childhood memories. He spent most of his life as a seaman and I seem to remember that during one voyage he was operated on for appendicitis, without anaesthetic.

For several years after we came to Loughton we boys were sent back to Holme to spend some of the summer holidays at grandfather Finch's house. Rex tells me that the last time was in 1931 when I would have been thirteen. We would spend all day at Crafty Ward's, the farm where we once used to get our milk. The Wards had a son Eric and three daughters, Betty, Kathleen and Mary, each a year or two older than Rex, me and Wilfred, and we spent our time with the girls. I can't remember Noel being there though I know he must have been. The girls had two docile ponies that we used to ride bareback. But my main memory is of my delicious childlike love for Kathleen, who would let me lie with my head in her lap and comb my hair with her fingers.*

Then grandfather Finch died and our grandma came to live with us in Loughton. We all liked her, and her gruff autocratic manner couldn't disguise the fact that she liked us too. With my father she sometimes *was* autocratic, to the amusement of my mother and us children. But he certainly asked for it. He was always concerned to show what a considerate son-in-law he was and every now and then would ask her if there was anything he could do for her. If there was, she had no inhibitions about telling him. She used to bring up a lot of phlegm and had a spittoon, a thick white china mug with a funnel on top of it, which she used to refer to as 'ma mug thing.' In winter she would sit in her chair by the open fire and her 'mug thing' would sit in the corner of the fireplace, doubtless filling the warm air with germs. In summer she would often sit on the lawn. One afternoon Daddy came out to her and asked his usual question, and she at once replied, 'Yes, fetch me ma mug thing.' He had no choice but to go into the house and fetch it, grumbling all the time he was out of earshot. It was clear that he didn't think *that* was the right answer to his question, and that he had expected something like, 'No thank you, dear. I'm alright.'

I think now that we boys used to give her quite a hard time, but although she scolded us for it she never got really cross. We used to take her out in a bath chair – for those who don't know, this was a sort of reclining wheel chair made of basketwork, with two large wheels under the seat and two small ones under the feet. Rex, Wilfred and I would take her out in this. From our house Queens Road rises steeply towards the top and leads into Pump Hill, which descends equally steeply down to Church Hill. We often used to bowl our iron hoops at great speed up the first hill, down the next, right into Church Hill, right again up York Hill, and then right again to bring us back to where we had started. We would whizz grandma in her bath chair along the same route at something like the same speed, ignoring her protests, and I feel sure now that she must have been really frightened, poor woman. Noel didn't take part in this particular operation but he used to tease her a lot, mocking her by imitating her Yorkshire accent, at which she would laugh and call him a 'fond' something – I can't remember what – using fond in the dialect (and once standard English) sense of 'foolish.' I had at that time recently acquired a secondhand copy of the works of Rabelais, illustrated by Gustave Doré – I wish I still had it – and Noel held it up to her and said, 'Look grandma. The works of Rabelais, by John Bunyan.' 'Oh,' she said, 'by 'im, is it,' her tone indicating clearly that if it was 'by 'im' she had no desire to read it.

I guess her time with us can't have lasted more than a year or two. In her last days her mind began to wander. Opposite our house was a line of one-storey flats allocated to policemen, and she somehow got it into her head that Noel was a police inspector and began calling him Inspector Noel.

She died while she was living with us, though not in our house but after a short stay in hospital.

All this was the setting in which I began to observe my father and mother and draw conclusions about what I saw. In fact it was only in the Loughton years that I began to get any sense not only of my parents' relationship to each other but of any relationships between adults. Until now my assessment of adults had been simply of their attitude to me – I was not concerned with their attitudes to one another. I was older now of course, but perhaps more important was the fact that in Holme I had lived in a home where the father was missing. Now for the first time I saw my parents together.

I quickly learnt that my father was an irresponsible husband and father. Like most men of his generation he assumed that he was lord and master in his family and that his wife and children should be subservient to him, and if possible love him. His life outside the family was his own affair. He was a stupidly generous man and when he was in the pub and felt in the mood would stand drinks to everybody in the bar. My mother once told me that he would sometimes come home and say to her, 'I'm sorry I can't give you any housekeeping this week. I can't tell you why.' My mother would have to cope as best she could. I also remem-

31

ber one occasion when my mother was summoned to appear in court for some unstated and still unknown reason which I think probably had something to do with a debt my father had run up. She on her side accepted the convention of subservience to her husband, I think simply because it never occurred to her that there was any alternative.

It was some years before I came to know the historical background of their current situation. They had been master and matron of the workhouse for about ten years when my father was dismissed for taking money out of the till – in all probability the consequence of his absurd lord-of-the-manor generosity. Rex thinks it was a subordinate of Daddy's who was guilty but that he accepted responsibility, but I had never heard this version. Noel, who being older understood more of what was happening, told me that their dismissal was a terrible blow to my mother. She had been an excellent administrator and had made drastic reforms in the antiquated workhouse regulations, and Noel thought she never really recovered from this blow. (If my father ever felt such grief over it I never saw it.) It was his dismissal that had caused our migration to Holme, while he, during all the years we were there, was allegedly looking for another job. My own guess would be that he didn't look very hard and was quite glad to be free of marital and family ties. Meanwhile I think other people with a more responsible attitude looked for and ultimately found him a job, which he had to take.

Leaving the workhouse had deprived my mother for ever of the satisfaction of exercising her considerable administrative skills. Rex has seen the testimonial which the guardians gave her at the time of their dismissal and it was in glowing terms. It is not difficult to understand that to be relegated to the status of a sort of domestic drudge must have been very painful for her. Her inadequacies in that role no doubt derived from that.

In the Loughton days all this was beyond the ken of us younger children, and our relationship to our father was a warmer and closer one than our relationship to our mother. His irresponsibility didn't register much with us. We knew that he loved us and we were amused rather than annoyed by his selfishness. When my mother had cooked a meal he particularly liked he would serve himself a second helping, remarking as he did so, 'Your mother's a good cook, isn't she, boys,' – which indeed she was. If any of us did the same he would look anxious and would say, 'Remember there's others to follow.' He would sometimes follow us up the stairs as we went to bed, crawling on all fours and pretending to be a tiger, and of course we loved it. But appreciation of his affection didn't mean that I didn't live in awe of him. Once he was doing a crossword and needed a rubber and asked me for one. I hadn't got one. He reacted

Master and Matron of the workhouse: my parents the year before my birth, with Noel & Rex

as if this was a remarkable and regrettable thing – a schoolboy not having a rubber. I felt this was unjust. Greatly daring and greatly embarrassed I said, 'Pot calling kettle black.' To my astonishment this moved my mother to delighted laughter.

There were other times when my mother surprised me. I had never thought that she would speak of anything sexual at all, let alone speak of it light-heartedly. Yet I remember three occasions when she did. Once I came across a song called 'The Spotted Cow' in *British Songs for British Boys*. I can't read music and asked Wilfred to play the tune for me on his violin so I could learn to sing it. It tells the story of a young man who meets a young woman lamenting because she's lost her spotted cow. He says:

No more compla-in no longer mourn, your cow's not lost my dear,
I saw her down in yonder bourne. Come love I'll show you where.

He does so and evidently shows her other things besides, because thereafter whenever she encounters him she begins to wail that she's lost her spotted cow. My mother thought this terribly funny.

On another occasion she sang a snippet of a song in which the singer is supposedly a husband:

And all the pret-ty girls there were dressed up in tights
my-y mis-sus she won't let me look at such sights.

And another she once sang was

My friend E-liz-a-beth's out of temper, out of breath
Ever since she found skirts must trail upon the ground

same tune: She's got a nicer set of legs than even Mistinguette
Now she has to hide what was once her joy & pride

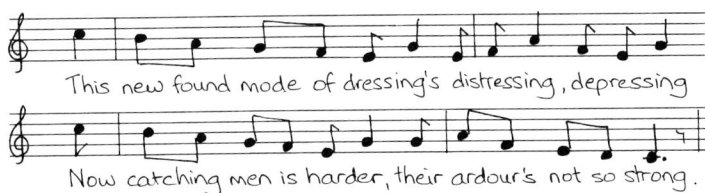

This new found mode of dressing's distressing, depressing

Now catching men is harder, their ardour's not so strong.

For my mother anything as frivolous as pretending to be a tiger would have been quite unthinkable. She behaved responsibly towards us and looked after our physical needs but I never felt that she loved us as our father did. Looking back I think she loved Noel after a fashion, and looked to him (as he looked to himself) as the one who would one day regain the social position his parents had once held; and in due course that did indeed happen. For Rex and me I don't think she had any very affectionate feeling. For Wilfred, the youngest, she felt a real love.

The realisation that my mother loved Wilfred much more than she did me never made me feel jealous, because I too thought him a very lovable child. My mother once told me that the reverse was not always true and that Wilfred sometimes felt jealous of me. She said that once when he was very little I was lying in bed next to her and he said, 'You farver mover, you Ralphy Rover; that's *my* mamma.'

In our earliest years he was the brother I was closest to. On Sunday mornings he and I would join our father and mother in their big double bed and all of us would sit up and talk. I imagine Noel and Rex were considered too old to participate in this assembly. Wilfred used to make up stories to tell us. He already shared my father's interest in cricket, which none of the rest of us did, and one of his stories was about someone digging down and down until he had got right through to Australia and came up in the middle of the cricket pitch where a test match was being played. One curious incident I recall is of news being brought to us there that our dog Pat had been run over and killed. I was in tears, and my father laughed at me; but for some reason I didn't feel hurt by this.

Contact between us four brothers was on the whole minimal. Noel went to a different school. I have a few fragmentary but vivid memories of him at this period in my life. One is of his instructing me how to peel an orange – in his standard tone of disdainful superiority which implied, without saying anything, 'I can hardly believe that you don't know these elementary things.' He said you start at the top and make sure that the first bit of peel you take off brings with it the sort of pith stalk that goes down the middle of the orange. This enables you to remove all the rest of the peel and pith together. Before that I used to take off the peel bit by bit but couldn't shift the pith. Rex, Wilfred and I all went to the council school but our ages put us in different classes. School in fact increased the distance between Wilfred and me. He had from childhood a quality of, so to speak, merging himself completely with those he associated with. I remember once in Epping Forest seeing him some distance away with a gang of kids of his own age, speaking in exactly the same mode as they did and with exactly the same accent. Rex and I had never achieved, nor wanted to achieve, this complete identification.

Rex and I got on amicably enough but I remember mainly his mischievousness. Once we were playing some game in which he tied me up so that I could move neither my hands nor feet. He then pushed me over. It was in the paved yard, and I remember vividly the feeling of helplessness as I crashed to the ground. He was also very good at getting his own way, generally by a silent, unavowed refusal to do anything he didn't want to do. I can remember standing by myself at the side of the house fuming because *I* had to run an errand which I knew perfectly well that *he* should have been sent on, and which my mother ought to have insisted on sending him on. She never did, sensing, I think, that it would have taken a major confrontation to make him do what he didn't want to do. So it was always I who did the errands. About this time someone – Auntie Tats, I think – told me that the name Ralph meant 'helpful.' Whether it does or not I've no idea, but I believed her and comforted myself with the contemplation of my own virtue, which, as everybody knew, is its own reward.

I don't remember either my mother or father showing any particular interest in what we children felt or thought. I wouldn't now think it a good example for parents to follow, but I don't think any of us minded at the time. And their mildly indifferent attitude did give us a freedom and an emotional independence that, looking back, I feel was very valuable to us.

When I try to recall what early influences might have shaped the development of my political ideas or personal values, I feel that essentially there was very little there to draw on. My parents' mild indifference applied in most areas of life. Politically they were a sort of inert Tory. My father took an incomprehensible pride in knowing all about which aristocrat's son married which aristocrat's daughter. My mother was not interested in such things, or indeed in politics at all, or at any rate in anything which she would have called politics. Such political prejudices as they had were conservative ones, although conservative with a small c.

Outings with Auntie Tats: the bus to London via Woodford

On holiday in Holme, in Grandfather Finch's buggy

There were examples of this whose significance I only understood later, looking back. One was at the time of the General Strike, the only one in British trade union history, which began in May 1926, eight months after our moving to Loughton.* Of course I had no idea what the strike was about and knew only that the buses had stopped running, and that the big gate to the station approach was closed. My father went to work throughout the strike, walking the twelve miles to work and the twelve miles back every day.

Despite his interest in aristocratic marriage alliances Daddy was not in the least snobbish in his personal relationships and would mix freely and relaxedly with the 'hoi polloi.' Not so my mother. She would say of people, 'She's common', with an expression on her face which I always called her camel face because it so strikingly resembled the camel's supercilious look. None of us children (except maybe Noel?) thought of this attitude as anything but ridiculous. Rex remembers that she would sometimes add, 'But some common people are nice' – and maybe that was in response to our not going along with her.

Not long after our move to Loughton our contact with adults outside the family expanded through my mother taking in lodgers. It must have been her idea, though I never heard that my father objected. He was probably aware that his provision of housekeeping money was so erratic that she needed a more regular and dependable source. I remember three sets of lodgers. The first were a couple, Mr and Mrs Hart and their children May and Vi. I think they had had some connection with my parents during Homerton days. The main things I remember about them was their cockney accent, their lack of control of their children, who would wipe their marmalady fingers on the wallpaper, and the absurd baby-language which Mrs Hart used with their younger daughter ('All-y fall-y Vi Vi Go to Mi Mi', for example, meaning 'Mind you don't fall, Vi. Go to May.') Another was one J E C Vecqueray, called (by himself) Jec Vec, who was what was called in those days a commercial traveller. Noel, his face already set towards social climbing, much admired him because he had a small car.

The longest lasting were the Walker brothers, or rather the older of the two, because the younger didn't get on with his elder brother and soon moved out. The elder was a nice old boy, some sort of civil servant, and a conventionally well-educated man who had learnt Latin and Greek at school. This was enough to earn deferential behaviour from my mother, to which he responded as a gentleman should, with courtesy and consideration. This didn't always please my father, who contrasted her care to keep Mr Walker's rooms clean and tidy and to serve him well-prepared meals on time, with her far more lackadaisical attention to our needs. But she probably felt that Mr Walker did more to merit such attention than my father did and that she could rely on him, as she could not on my father, to provide her with regular income.

He was a whisky drinker and not infrequently overdid it, particularly in his last years with us. This never made him boisterous but he would get a bit hazy about where he was and what he was doing. One morning we found that he had peed in the hatstand in the hallway. When Noel had reached something approaching adulthood Walker would sometimes confide in him. He once encountered Noel coming home late at night and said conspiratorially, 'Been a naughty boy tonight Noel. Not a word to your mother. Dear old soul, dear old soul!' I don't know whether it was the whisky or something else, but when he went to the loo in the morning he made the most God Almighty stink, which pervaded the whole house.

There was no family religious influence worth speaking of. Just as my parents were inert Tories, they were inert members of the Church of England. We boys were sent to Sunday school, at one time both in the morning and again in the afternoon, but I'm sure this wasn't done out of religious duty but simply to give them a bit of peace. I cannot recall that my father ever went to church even on the occasions when my mother did, and he never showed any interest in religion – which didn't stop him saying, when Noel once made some anti-religious remark, 'I prefer the simple faith myself.' Noel was moved to loud and irreverent laughter (which, to my surprise, caused my father no resentment). Daddy had a great fondness for short set phrases like this, to be brought out upon suitable occasions. For example, 'An appointment is a sacred thing,' brought out when he thought that any of us was not going to be ready in time to keep one punctually. Or 'A woman's crowning glory is her hair' – this a rather nostalgic one, because I don't think any of the women among his contemporaries had long hair. (One older woman did – Mrs Mason, who had been the matron of the master-matron couple that had preceded my parents at the workhouse. People used to say of her that her hair was so long she could sit on it.) Like many largely self-educated men Daddy liked pompous language. At Christmas time, encountering in the street people he knew, he would never say 'Merry Christmas', always 'Compliments of the season to you, sir!' One of his favourite authors was Frank Bullen, who wrote mainly about the sea and would never write 'whales' when he could write 'denizens of the deep.'

My mother did not share Daddy's alleged enthusiasm for 'the simple faith' and had things to say about the Bible and the prayer book which I recall with enjoyment. She took a poor view of the prophet Elisha, who when the children jeered at him ('Go up, thou bald head') called two bears to come and eat them up. (My mother didn't tell me the full story, but II Kings 11, verses 23-24, tells us that the two she-bears 'tare forty and two children of them.') And she thought that when the priest intoned, 'Give peace in our time, O Lord' and the congregation responded, 'Because there is none other that fighteth for us but only Thou, O God,' this was hardly complimentary to the Lord God, because the logic of it was, 'If you're the only one we can rely on when fighting breaks out then let us hope devoutly that it *won't* break out.'

For me, Sunday school and church attendance had no religious significance. I liked some of my Sunday school teachers and I liked singing some of the hymns, but what I looked forward to most was borrowing books – particularly those of R M Ballantyne – that Sunday school made available to me.⋆ I was also in the Boy Scouts – woodpigeon patrol – run by an ex-army officer (Major, I think) Chater. He had the scar of a sword-wound on his face. He'd been to Harrow and was a wealthy man, living in a large house on the edge of Epping Forest at the top of a long grassy slope called Drummaid's which ran down to the brook. (Lebbon told us that it was said to be a shortened form of 'Drummer Maynard's' – one Drummer Maynard having at one time had some connection with the place.) Chater's manner was that of an aristocratic patron carrying out his *noblesse oblige* duty towards the lower orders, presiding in a rather aloof manner over their activities. It was in Scouts that I made the acquaintance of the *Hackney Scouts' Song Book,* which has some very jolly songs in it. He also taught us some remarkably inappropriate ones –'Forty Years On' (the Harrow school song) and the one which begins:

He asks

Whose hat is that? Whose can it be?
My wife she said 'It's the baby's hat' that's what she said to me.
Miles I have travelled, ten thousand miles or more
But a bowler on a baby's head I never have seen before.

And so on for several verses, including

Whiskers on a baby's face I never have seen before.

The risqué implications didn't dawn on me until many years later.

One summer the Scouts went camping at Dunwich, and I loved it, not least because I fell happily in love, silently and at a distance, with a girl called May, the daughter of a local shopkeeper. I have a vivid memory of walking along a footpath just behind her in the company of my patrol leader Roger Free, who was carrying on a mild flirtation with her. I was holding in front of me a bendy stick I had got from somewhere, with its end pushing along the ground. At one point it jumped up and lifted the back of May's skirt. I was terribly embarrassed, but she only smiled.

Roger Free I remember also as one of two men who made homosexual advances to me. In his case I can't remember exactly what they were, and I don't think he can have pursued them very far. The other was a bus conductor called Don Wilson. He had been a soldier in the war and had been infected with a taste for spit and polish. I never encountered any other bus conductor who polished to a brilliant shine the leather strap of the bag into which he dropped the fares. We Russell boys – or me and Wilfred, at any rate – were among those he used to take for walks in Epping Forest. He would call at the house and ask us out, and it seems never to have occurred to my mother any more than it did to us that he harboured any improper designs upon us. He used occasionally to sing army songs to us, like this one to the tune of 'What a friend we have in Jesus':

When this wicked war is over, oh how happy I shall be

When I get my civvy clothes on, no more soldiering for me.

No more church parades on Sunday, no more waiting for a pass

We shall tell the sergeant major to keep his passes to hisself.

We could see of course that the last line didn't rhyme but it wasn't until I was in the army myself many years later that I learnt that the correct version was 'to stick his passes up his arse.'

Once when he was out with me in the forest he suggested that we

The story of Lopping Rights: 1859 woodcut showing start of annual lop

Alfred Willingale, imprisoned for defending lopping rights

lie down together, and then clamped his thigh over mine. But when he could see I didn't like it he abandoned any plan he may have had for taking things further.

It was during these years that I had my first experience of intense love. That is undoubtedly the proper word for it, and it was a feeling unconnected with anything else that I remember before. I was about nine, and what I experienced was a deep adoration for another boy, the Laurie Tomlin whom I mentioned earlier. I remember particularly that when he cut his finger I wanted to suck the blood from it to make it clean. He was amused and tolerant. I did not expect any return from him beyond permission to love him. I just felt an intense pleasure in loving.

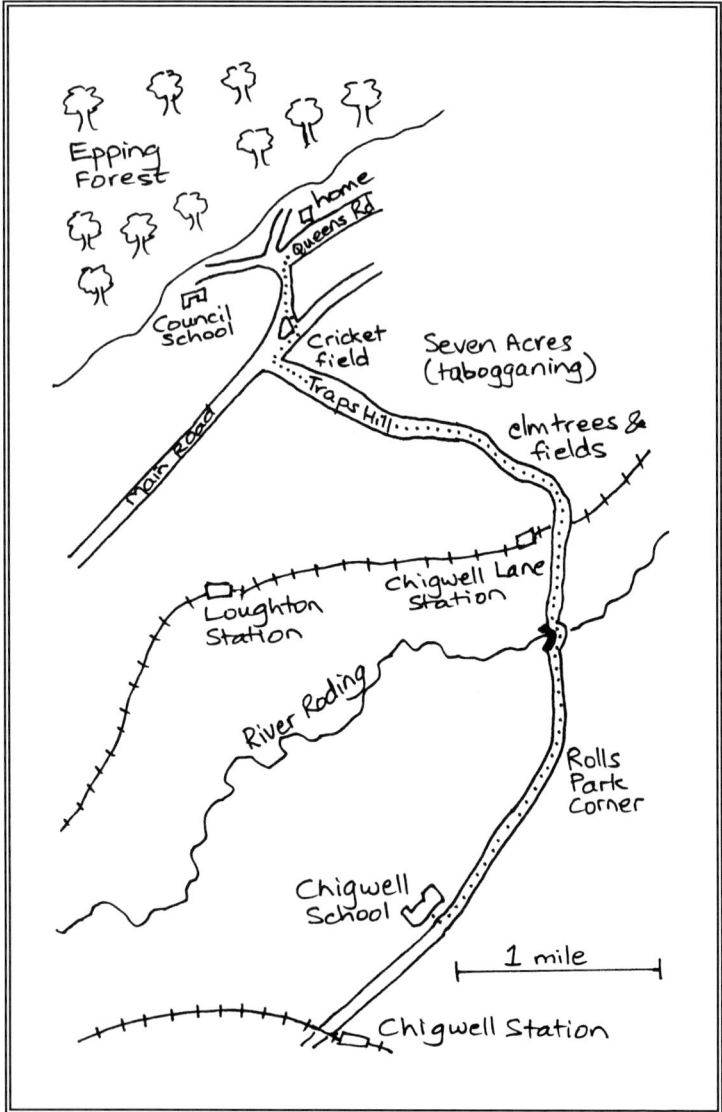

Epping Forest

home
Queens Rd

Council School

Cricket field

Seven Acres
(tabogganing)

Traps Hill

elm trees & fields

Main Road

Chigwell Lane Station

Loughton Station

River Roding

Rolls Park Corner

Chigwell School

1 mile

Chigwell Station

The road to Chigwell

3

I was not yet ten when I was entered for a scholarship exam. I am not very knowledgeable about the state of the British school system at that time, but I know that the school leaving age was fourteen, and children whose parents didn't aspire to getting them a secondary education left them in council school until that age. For those who did aspire there were scholarships, and in Loughton the council school teachers kept their eyes open for children who they thought could pass the scholarship exam. Who set the exam I do not know, and what its content was I do not remember.

I must have been regarded as unusually bright because I was entered for the exam at the same time as Rex, despite being two years younger. We both won places, I in Chigwell School and he in Bancrofts School in Woodford. I think there was a pecking order in which Chigwell got first pick of the boys who passed the scholarship exam. It was a (very minor) public school and its students and staff intended that nobody should forget this – or rather, they could forget the 'minor' but not the 'public.' Rex's was a school founded by one of what I think are called livery companies – in this case the Drapers' Company. I think the quality of education at Bancrofts was in many respects a good deal better than that at Chigwell, and in some respects I know it was.

Noel continued at his tinpot school in Loughton, and Wilfred at the council school until it was his turn to take the scholarship exam. He failed it. I feel sure that he had been discouraged from working hard at school by my father's idiot infatuation with my brilliance. Lebbon, who was as kind to him as he had always been to me, came to his rescue. He had taught Wilfred the violin and had once composed a tune for him set to the words

Wilfred Russell went to school
Down beside a reedy pool.

(Quite untrue. There was no reedy pool anywhere near.)

There he was so wise and sane
That he never got the cane.

(Clearly his poetic talent did not match his kindness.)

45

When Wilfred failed the exam Lebbon got him awarded a choir scholarship at the posh West End church school of All Saints, Margaret Street. He was a boarder there all the years until his voice broke, and the rest of us saw even less of him than before.

My pleasure at winning the scholarship was accompanied by relief at not having to move up from Lebbon's class to the next one. I knew that there I would have had to learn about things called debentures and I had absolutely no desire to. (I still, more than seventy years later, don't know what they are.)

But anyway I was off to Chigwell and didn't give much thought to anything else.

Chigwell School was four miles from Loughton. At first I used to walk there, only later doing the journey by bike. It was a very pleasant journey, almost all of it along open spaces and country roads. I would turn right out of our front gate and down to the junction, then left down the hill to a triangular green with a war memorial, a pub called the Kings Head on one side, and across the road on the far side, a cricket field. I walked along the main road until I reached Traps Hill, running off to the left. This was a steep hill, with a large field on the left called Seven Acres or, by some, Eleven Acres. One winter when we had snow for quite a number of days we used to go tobogganing on it. The diagonal run was quite a long one, longer than that on Drummaid's where we also went tobogganing. At the top of Traps Hill there were some big houses. Beyond that for a while there were no houses at all and the road was lined on both sides by tall elm trees. Then the line of trees on the right came to an end and was succeeded by an open grass field. The road turned and went downhill to a railway station then called Chigwell Lane (now called Debden) with a few houses, and beyond that to a hump-backed bridge over the river Roding. Then it rose again between green fields, up to Rolls Park Corner. For a little way after this a high wall ran for some distance. I still have no idea what lay behind it. Then the road ran again through open country until, near the point where Chigwell village begins, it reached the school. The school was a long, one-storey building with tall windows standing behind a gravelled open space. At right angles to one end of it was the headmaster's house and attached to that the boarders' dormitories. Running from the back of the other end were the classrooms, and beyond the buildings, two large playing fields. At some distance from the main school buildings was a row of rather unsavoury lavatories. In my early days I was too shy to go to the loo, and I would try and keep my bowels tightly closed until I got home in the evening. Predictably, disaster befell me one day. I had not got beyond

Chigwell School

'Apparelled in celestial light'
on the walk to school, just after Traps Hill

Rolls Park Corner when I could no longer hold on, and for the rest of the walk home tried, without success, to conceal the shit that ran down my leg – I was still in short trousers, otherwise concealment might just about have been possible. My mother found it impossible to wash my trousers thoroughly enough to banish the smell completely. (I remembered this in later years in the army, when my soldier-comrades used to speak of 'sticking like shit to a blanket'.)

The quality of my experience of school now changed very markedly. I was a year and a half younger than the average age of boys in the class, and small for my age – for years now Wilfred had been taller than me. But more important than size or age, it was evident from the start that scholarship boys were regarded as constituting a lesser breed without the law. The children in the elementary school just over the road were referred to as the 'Nips', and an attitude of contempt towards them and the social class they came from was the norm. I did not object to this attitude but I took a poor view of any suggestion that *I* was a Nip, particularly since my school-fellows were often far less bright than I was. I guess it was my awareness of my intelligence that made me feel that I was not a Nip and need not feel any respect for Nips. I reacted with vigorous contempt of both my schoolfellows and the teachers when they made it clear that they thought the boys from well-to-do homes were *of course* my superiors. Once in a lesson about Roman Britain the teacher asked whether any of us knew the name of the flooring of Roman villas heated from underneath. I was the only one who did know and said it was called a 'tessilited pivement.' I was full of indignation both at my fellow pupils and the teacher whose only response was to mock me for my pronunciation.

I remember one other unpleasant experience in the early days. There was a bad-tempered English teacher called Mr Thurston who set us to write a poem on Sports Day and then called on some of us to recite what we had written. I was very pleased with my lines

> *The day is done, the races run*
> *All good things to an end must come*

but my recitation of it was a disaster. In those days the fashion was to recite verse as though it was prose and I just couldn't do that (and I'm glad to say still can't.) Thurston was furious and bellowed at me, 'Stand on the form!' The form was the seat of a long desk; this was a standard punishment, the equivalent of the by now obsolete one of making a boy put on a dunce's cap and stand in the corner.

The school week ran from Monday to Saturday – in Loughton it had been Monday to Friday – finishing at 4 pm. It began with an assembly, which in Chigwell was a two-part affair. The first part was for administrative purposes – school announcements and so on – though the headmaster often pontificated at us about something or other. Then our names were called and as we answered we filed out of the hall up a short passage, then through the school library and out across a space of about five yards and into the chapel for the religious part of assembly. It was a substantial service with hymn-singing and psalm-singing, and extended substantially my repertoire of hymns. My favourite memory of chapel is the discovery that completely united mass action is invincible. In the hymn

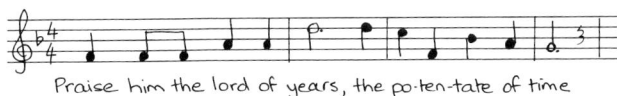

Praise him the lord of years, the po-ten-tate of time

we would all with one accord belt out 'the potentate of time' with tremendous emphasis on the t's. The headmaster would glare furiously but there was absolutely nothing he could do about it.

Following in my mother's footsteps, although perhaps not consciously, I began to ridicule some of the things that the Bible, prayer book and hymn book said. In one hymn come the lines

When the earth shall be filled with the glory of God
As the waters cover the sea.

The waters don't cover the sea – in the context the waters *are* the sea. Another was the 'potentate of time' hymn, beginning 'Crown him with many crowns' – an absurd concept – and later with these lines

Fruit of the mystic rose, as of that rose the stem,
The root whence mercy ever flows, the babe of Bethlehem.

What on earth does it mean?★

After chapel there were classes until mid-morning break. During break we were allowed a minimal time to go to the tuck shop to buy a packet of crisps or a 'penny Turkish' or even (extravagantly) a 'twopenny Turkish' – i.e. chocolate covered rectangles of Turkish delight – or a penny or twopenny marshmallow. But most of the break was taken up by a combination of physical exercise and military drill for which we were divided into squads commanded by a prefect. The drill included the military exercise (soon to become obsolete) of forming fours. The squad formed two lines, the second standing at a suitable distance behind the first. You were then commanded to 'number' and the boy on the extreme right shouted 'One' and the others 'two, three, four', etc to the end of the line. Then came the command, 'Form fours' and the even numbers took one pace back and one to the right, thus transforming the two ranks into four. Our squad commander was a handsome red-haired youngster called Shillito, and I liked him. He would march us at the double down the road and back again just in time for break to end.

Then more classes until lunch time, when we all assembled in a hall at long tables, each presided over by a master who served out the food. On a raised platform at one end was high table, where the head and those masters not serving food sat. Proceedings were initiated by the head saying grace – '*Benedictus benedicat, per Jesum Christum Dominum Nostrum, Amen.*' – May the blessed one bless, through Jesus Christ our Lord, Amen. Grace after the meal was '*Benedicto benedicatur, per Jesum*' etc – May the blessed one be blessed, etc.

Classes again in the afternoon, except for Mondays, Wednesdays and Saturdays when we had compulsory games – football in the Michaelmas term, crosscountry running in the Lent term, and cricket in the summer term.

I quickly lost my initial shyness and was happy at school. I started Latin, did well at it, and loved it. We were taught it by Mr Kay, a strict but fair teacher. He used to announce from time to time in his rather nasal voice, 'Three things I will not tolerate – nominative for accusative' – and two others which I cannot now remember. He lived in a house called Harsnett's, belonging to the school and a hundred yards or so up the road, and had an old chain-driven Trojan car which we used to smile at when we saw him chugging around in it. He was always dressed in black.

Lebbon, though I was no longer at his school, continued to take an active interest in me. Soon after I'd started learning Latin he played a trick on me, giving me a piece of paper on which were written four lines of Latin and asking if I could translate them. To my disappointment I couldn't. They ran:

Is ab ille ers ago
Fortibus es in aro
O nobile, themis trux
Vatis inem pis et dux

He sat grinning while I struggled with them and then said, 'What they say is:

I say, Billy, ere's a go
Forty buses in a row
O no Billy, them is trucks

I didn't have any particular friends in those middle years, but I don't remember at the time being conscious of this as something that bothered me. School was about lessons, and I enjoyed almost everything we learnt in class. The highpoint was those with Mr Fellows, our teacher for both Latin and English. He was an excellent teacher, kind, humorous and encouraging. Chigwell worked on the valid assumption that at the age of eleven you were capable of appreciating and being inspired by some of the great classics of English literature, and accordingly Fellows introduced us to Shakespeare. We read *Julius Caesar*, which I loved, and then *Henry V*, which I didn't like, and still don't much like because of its English chauvinism and contempt for the French simply because they were French. I can't think why at so early an age I felt such hatred for this kind of chauvinism, but I know I did. I also disliked the scene in which Alice teaches Katharine some English. Shakespeare seems to be showing off, pointlessly, his knowledge of French and his lofty amusement at Katharine's pronunciation of 'the' as 'de.' But I thrilled to the lines in Julius Caesar which I have never forgotten –

But I am constant as the northern star
Of whose true fixed and resting quality
There is no fellow in the firmament

and felt with tremendous satisfaction, 'Yes, that's me.'

At the same age we read a book in two volumes called *Clarendon Readers in Literature and Science*, designed, the editor tells us, for 'pupils between twelve and fifteen.' I still have it. It includes an excellent retelling of the story of Homer's Iliad, and J A Froude's account of the martyrdom of Ridley and Latimer, who were burnt at the stake in 1555. I learnt by heart Latimer's wonderful words, 'Master Ridley, play the man. We shall this day light such a candle by God's grace as I trust shall never be put out.' Whether anybody else felt as inspired by these things as I did, I don't know.

Fellows encouraged us to write in lively, colourful styles. He once said 'You could call Liverpool Street Station a filthy cavern,' adding at once with a grin, 'But if I set you to write an essay on Liverpool Street Station you're not to call it a filthy cavern.' Essay writing was in fact the only thing I didn't like about his classes. I could see the point in writing when I had something to say but I had no desire to write about things that didn't interest me, and couldn't do it. I remember one essay shortly after we had read a selection from the writings of the naturalist W H Hudson, entitled *Birds of Wing and other Wild Creatures*, in which I particularly liked his vivid account of gannets fishing, and a passage on pigs. Fellows subsequently set us an essay on pigs. I wrote a few lines and then quoted W H Hudson at length. When Fellows handed it back he had written 'I liked the essay and the quotation, but isn't the latter rather long in relation to the former?'

I think Fellows felt a personal interest in me from the start. In my reports for the first year he taught me Latin he described me as 'in a class of his own for reliability,' and in English, 'easily the best stylist and most thoughtful worker.' For some obscure reason I never used to call him 'Sir' – a certain shyness had reduced my 'Sir' first to its initial 'S' and then to nothing – but he was not put out by this, and was rather amused by it.

Singing was one of our subjects, to my great delight. I remember a song which began

In Hans' old mill his 3 black cats watch the bins for the thieving rats

Whisker and claw they crouch in the night, their 5 eyes shining green & bright

But mostly we learnt songs like Handel's 'Let the bright seraphim' and 'O had I Jubal's lyre', Schubert's 'Who is Sylvia?' and 'Hark, hark the lark', and Papageno's song in Mozart's *The Magic Flute*. Our teacher had a genuine enthusiasm for his subject and took a real pleasure in helping us develop a taste for good music. He had in his charge a collection of gramophone records which we would borrow. I borrowed, and loved, Beethoven's Fifth and Fourth symphonies and the early volume of the Columbia *History of Music* – from which I can still sing *Summer is icumen in* and *Veni sancte spiritus*. I also sang in the Glee Club, after the end of the school day. I remember that among the things we sang were Coleridge Taylor's 'Hiawatha's Wedding' and Bach's 'Peasant Cantata' –

If fortune had made me the master, and riches & castle were mine

I'd always get up in the morning, provided the weather was fine

We occasionally gave public performances, at which Fellows, who had a good tenor voice, was the star turn. It was from his singing that I first learnt 'Greensleeves' and (in a much sanitised version) 'The Derby Ram'. I remember vividly how at Glee Club he would show, silently but unmistakably, his contempt for Mrs Grant, wife of Rev D.P. Grant, the school chaplain, who used to accompany us on the piano.

I had to face the fact that I was no good at science, maths and carpentry. The science lab was at the other side of the road from the main school building, and we were taught by Mr Dyball. He knew I could not cope, and it saddened him. I think he couldn't understand why, and I don't think *I* could either. We did experiments showing that putting zinc into H_2SO_4 produced H_2O and $ZnSO_4$ (if this is the correct formula for zinc sulphate), while putting it into hydrochloric acid or nitric acid produced parallel results, and we had to record this as 'an effervescence took place and a gas was given off.' We weren't told to record what gas this was and this didn't bother me, but I remember that one of these processes – I can't remember which – produced an exceptionally vigorous bubbling and a beautiful blue liquid, and I felt that this ought to have been explained and recorded too. I don't know either why I was so bad at maths, but have an idea that things were taken faster than I could easily follow. It was taught by Mr Doouss (strange name), a handsome man with dark wavy hair. He too, like Dyball, was uncomprehending but kind. 'He thinks things out, though rather slowly' says the comment on an early report; and later, still hopeful, 'If allowed to take his own slow pace, is generally accurate'; but eventually a blunt admission, 'Not at home in this subject.' Carpentry classes – I think once a week – were taught by Mr Radley, the owner of a carpentry shop just up the street. I could never manage the simplest operation, and took evasive action whenever possible so that Mr Radley wouldn't discover this. (But I think he did.)

Nor was I any good at games – except for cross country running, which I liked. But while I regretted my poor performance at science, maths and carpentry I never felt like that about games. I could never see any good reason why those who didn't like them should be forced to play them and my dislike was enhanced by my contempt for the absurd public school admiration for those who were good at them, no matter what clots they might be at anything else. (I was later to learn that this was even more true at university level.) An additional bind was that those who were not playing had to stand and watch those who were. I rejoiced whenever we were rained off and I could go home. At football I always did my best to be allowed to play full-back. Usually it is the heftiest who play full-back and I was far from that, but I reckoned that since there were two full-backs, when the ball got as far as us I could always leave it to the other one to do whatever backs were supposed do. In cricket I was never called up to bowl because I could never throw a ball overarm. There was one physical thing I *could* do more easily than the other boys. A long rope hung from a high branch of an acacia tree in the school grounds, and I found I could quickly pull myself up to the top using only my arms. But this rare talent didn't get me far because it wasn't needed in any of the official school games.

In addition to the playing fields behind the main school building there was a second lot further up the road, reached by a drive that ran between Harsnett's where Mr Kay lived and Hainault House, which housed the prep school. The first of these fields had a line of tall trees on the far side. I found these trees amazingly beautiful, and when, quite early on at Chigwell I read Wordsworth's 'Ode on Intimations of Immortality from Recollections of Early Childhood', I responded immediately to its first lines

> *There was a time when meadow, grove and stream*
> *The earth and every common sight*
> *To me did seem*
> *Apparelled in celestial light*
> *The glory and the freshness of a dream.*

Life at school and at home rarely overlapped, and this was just as I wanted it to be. I was leading two separate lives, of which school was by far the more important. At 8.15 I left the house to set off on the four mile journey to school and I didn't get back until about five in the afternoon. As the years went by I would stay on at school later and later, until quite late in the evening. The mild indifference of my parents towards their children expressed itself in complete unconcern as to where I was and what I was doing all this time.

Like many boys I felt acute embarrassment on occasions like Speech Day when parents visited the school. They were not 'out of the top drawer' like the parents of the other boys and I felt ashamed of anything about them that was different. I never felt *myself* to be inferior to the other boys, but my inner defence against their assumption of superiority was that I was academically superior to them, and that didn't apply to my parents who were not intellectuals. They were also embarrassingly unfamiliar with the rigid norms of minor public school life. Once when I needed a warm winter coat my mother made me one out of a rather rough material of airforce blue crisscrossed with orange lines. The standard style in Chigwell was a sober navy blue, and I knew that if I wore this coat to school I would be laughed at. In fact the occasion never

54

arose. At that time I was going to school by train and had to change trains at Woodford. The first day I had my new coat I was carrying it, not wearing it. The first train got into Woodford late and when I got to the other platform to catch the Chigwell train, it was already moving out. I opened the door and threw the coat into the compartment, thinking to get in after it. But the train was already going too fast for me to do this safely. I never saw the coat again and I felt very bad that all my mother's labour had been lost. Despite the ridicule I would have been subjected to I would have worn it, and I am sure I didn't deliberately lose it. But I still remember vividly the look on my mother's face when I told her what had happened.

Speech Day, apart from the unwelcome participation of parents, was an exciting and enjoyable day. There were no lessons. We all had to get dressed up in stiff collars and Eton jackets that only came down to the waist – bum-freezers as we used to call them. There was a service in the church across the road at which we sang St Patrick's Breastplate – a hymn I still like a lot – and Blake's Jerusalem. The lesson was 'Let us now praise famous men.' I especially remember the 1929 speech day, when we celebrated the tercentenary of the school's foundation by Archbishop Harsnett. We sang the ludicrous school song which incorporated an English version of the school's Latin motto, *aut viam inveniam aut faciam* – I will either find a way or make a way. It ran

Which is the way to be happy? Not only for self to take care

To be sound in your mind & your body, and loving to do & to dare

[chorus] Find a way or make a way, brave old Harsnett's son

The upward way, the onward way, the way the founder's gone.

We boys were appropriately irreverent about it, and accompanied 'the upward way' with pointing upwards, 'the onward way' with pointing forwards – and 'the way the founder's gone' by pointing downwards. The line 'Brave old Harsnett's son' always made my father laugh heartily.

We also sang a Latin school song of which both the words and the quite attractive tune were by the headmaster. It began *stirps alma nostra, moenia bracchio*

I once knew the words that followed but could never quite work out what they meant because the phrasing was so convoluted. In Latin word order is not particularly important in establishing meaning because the relationships of the words are clear from the case endings. But here the first three words could be either nominative or vocative, the fourth either nominative or accusative and the fifth could mean either to, or for, or by, with or from 'arm'. The only way to work it out would have been to follow the words through to the end of the sentence, and I didn't have the patience.

It was in Chigwell that I had my first encounter with theology. All of us who were sons of Church of England parents were required each year to take something called the Diocesan Examination, in which one had to answer such questions as 'How may the baptism of infants be justified?' (This was a regularly recurring one.) We were prepared by the school chaplain, the Rev D P Grant, who also taught geography. He taught both subjects exceedingly badly. His favourite method was to dictate notes. At the time my only objection to this process was that it was so boring. His list of the arguments to justify infant baptism began
    '(a) The analogy of circumcision'
and we duly reproduced this in the exam. Only years later did it dawn on me that I didn't know what either 'analogy' or 'circumcision' meant. By the second year I had learnt that the results of these exams counted for nothing in one's school record. I therefore wrote on my paper in answer to this hardy annual, 'In my opinion the baptism of infants cannot be justified,' and without bothering about any of the other questions handed my paper in, left the hall and enjoyed the period of leisure this gained me.

My favourite memory of D P Grant dates from a year or two later when some bible passage we were reading mentioned eunuchs. A plump boy called Papineau asked Grant what a eunuch was. (He knew perfectly well what it was.) Grant said, 'Well, he was a sort of major domo, and' (stroking his bald patch with an attempted appearance of nonchalance) 'I believe he was usually celibate.' Papineau was in some ways a rather obnoxious boy, contemptuous of anything old-fashioned and conventional, and would probably have been more unpopular but for the fact that he was an excellent swimmer. He exercised quite an influence on me. He told me that the kind of novels one ought to read were David Garnett's *Lady into Fox* and Eimar O'Duffy's *King Goshawk and the Birds*. I did read both, finding them rather odd but quite interesting.

Though I was uninterested in theological arguments of the Diocesan exam kind, I had early on in my time at Chigwell a fervent religious phase. Its main feature was a belief that I needed an all-understanding, all-supportive friend, and that Jesus was he. It was all very vague – I don't recall that it aroused in me any desire to study what the gospels reported Jesus as saying – and the phase was short-lived. Then for a while I belonged to a sort of advanced level Sunday school in Loughton run by an organisation called Crusaders. It was led by a well-to-do gentleman called Mr Charles and met in the upper storey of a building behind his big house. We used to sing choruses of a breezy, jolly Christian kind. One was

Build on the rock, the rock that ever stands. Build on the rock, & not upon the sands

You need not fear the storm, nor the earthquake's shock

You're safe forever more if you build on the rock.

When we came to the word 'shock' we would all stamp our feet on the floor. Another song was

I'm eating of the living bread, I'm drinking at the fountain's head

And whoso drinketh, Jesus said, shall never never thirst again.

What? Never thirst again? No, never thirst again!

What? Never thirst again? No, NEVER thirst again!
etc

But Mr Charles got more and more fervent as time went by and would literally foam at the mouth as he exclaimed, 'Oh boys, if only you knew Jesus as I do.' He also introduced a drill. We all had to tuck our Bibles under our armpits and on his command, 'Draw swords!', would 'draw' the Bible and hold it aloft crying, 'The sword of the spirit, which

Holidays in Holme: playing draughts with Wilfred

On Wards' Farm with Mary Ward

is the Word of God!' All of this got a bit too much for me, and I stopped going.

Looking back, my feeling that I needed a perfect friend seems hardly surprising. As a scholarship boy I was still someone apart. I had no idea what went on in the lives of the other boys outside the school. I was also much younger than most of them. By my second year – called for some reason 'Lower Middle' – I was coming first in the class and was given a double promotion, missing out 'Upper Middle' and going straight to 'Remove', where I was now a small twelve year old in a class of large fifteen year olds.

But I was increasingly happy at Chigwell as the years went by, and developed a real love of the place. I still don't know why I should have been so *very* happy, but I can recognize some of the things that contributed to that. There were some teachers who appreciated my exceptional prowess, and I must say that I also appreciated it myself. Even after skipping a class I was soon coming near the top again in most academic subjects (except for maths and science in which I had slipped even further back.) My mother later told me how mortified I was on one occasion when I only came second in Greek. My father was immensely proud of me, which I am sure was not at all good for my brothers, and especially for Wilfred. I still have a sheet my father wrote, headed in his characteristically pompous phrasing, 'Scholastic Achievements', in which he set out my excellent qualities to display to his colleagues in the office, who must have been bored to tears.

I have a couple of memories from these years of clear feelings of love. One was for Kathleen Ward, the farmer's daughter in Holme who used to run her fingers through my hair. Then early on at Chigwell I formed an attachment to a boy my own age (I guess we were about twelve years old.) It was less intense than what I had felt for Laurie Tomlin, but still quite strong. I remember telling him to his embarrassment that I thought we should get married when we grew up. He told me rather sharply that this was not possible, that men did not marry each other. Since he said so, I accepted it and didn't think it necessary to ask why not.

I was unaware of any connection between these experiences of loving and my gradually developing sexual awareness, of which I have only fragmentary memories. At a certain point I discovered the pleasurable sensation of lying on my belly and rubbing myself up and down on the bed sheet. As with earlier experiences, I don't remember feeling that this related to anything else, nor feeling any shame about doing it. I also remember enjoying a picture which Mr Fellows had put up in the classroom. He now taught history and was very good at visual displays. This particular picture was a medieval one of people being cast into hell. The women were all naked and, to my delight, were shown with a black slit at the joint of their thighs.

It was not until I was about fourteen that I learnt the facts of life from another schoolfellow. My reaction I guess was a common one in those days, and maybe still is. I was indignant at the suggestion that my mother and father did the things that I was being told about. I still can't work out why I felt that way. I enjoyed my own sexual activity, such as it was, and felt no shame about it, so why should I have felt any shame about theirs? I thought at one stage it was because my activity concerned only me, whereas theirs involved their doing things to each other. But my tentative explorations with Mildred Finch had involved that. Or perhaps it was because I saw my parents' life only as it related to us? They were there to provide for us, to take care of us, and the idea that they had lives of their own to live and were seeking pleasure just for themselves had never entered my head, and so was a shock. But who knows? There may well have been more to it than that.

4

There are some fragmentary memories that indicate that despite my apparent happiness at school I was in some way troubled. My slowness at Maths and Science had now become an issue. We had to take an exam called School Certificate and could not be promoted into the VIth form unless we passed in one or both of these subjects (I can't remember which). I didn't and so had to stay in the Vth form another year. I don't remember feeling this as a particular hardship, nor do I remember being bored by repeating, for I think we read different books the second time round. But there were things about how I behaved at this time which I didn't understand and which adversely affected my self-image.

One is that I began regularly not to do my homework – why, I have no idea. In class the next day I would sit anxiously trying to catch up and so not be caught out. I usually succeeded, but I was always anxious just the same. Homework meant preparing the next bit of Latin or Greek that we were reading in class and I was desperate to make sure that I could translate my bit when my turn came. I could nearly always manage this, because our texts had vocabularies and I could surreptitiously look up in them such words as I did not know. But once I *was* caught out, and when my turn came to translate I couldn't. The master asked me why I hadn't prepared it and, greatly embarrassed, I told the lie that I hadn't been well last night. The master, who I think was as embarrassed as I was, because he guessed I was lying but didn't want to rebuke someone of my well-known academic ability, turned to the class and asked if anyone could name the figure of speech that I had just used. I can't remember if anyone could, but I think it was *litotes* – 'not well' being an understatement for 'ill'.

More troubling was a moral issue – I occasionally stole books from our classroom library. One was called *Ancient Peoples* by (if I remember rightly) Helen Corke. I have no idea why I stole it, just as I had not understood why I had kept a book of Lebbon's and denied that I had it. I had always wanted to possess books, but I knew that was no justification for stealing them.

My brief encounters with organised religion of various kinds had ended up with my becoming an atheist. Agnosticism never appealed to me much, and when in later years I heard that Marx had called it 'shamefaced atheism' I felt that this completely accorded with my own feeling. I think it was Fellows who once told us of the man who, when asked why he didn't believe in God, replied, 'I have no need of this hypothesis.'⋆ But abandonment of belief in God brought its own problems.

I was in my fifth year at Chigwell, aged fourteen or fifteen, when I went through a great spiritual crisis. I shall have the utmost difficulty in describing it. I don't know how or why or exactly when it started; I remember almost nothing about the course of events while it lasted, and only one detail of the way in which it was resolved. I think it lasted only a relatively short time, though at the time it felt for ever. The main thing I remember is how desperate I felt. I could no longer accept the religious doctrines that I had been taught and felt that, lacking a religion – a religion in the sense of what every religion professes to be, namely a sure guide to conduct in every area of life – I lacked any means of determining right and wrong: and without such a means I could not live. Why I should suddenly have felt this desperate need, I do not know. Nobody else seemed to be feeling it, and not only then but for ten years afterwards I assumed that I must be a very peculiar sort of person. But I did feel this need, and that too very acutely. I felt that to live meant to act, and to act with the feeling that for all I knew my every act might be a deadly sin, was a burden that I could not bear.

I have no recollection of anything remarkable occurring in the course of day to day events, and must conclude that the turmoil I was feeling had no visible impact upon them. Certainly nothing was apparent to the other boys – except one, and he too one who was not particularly close to me. He was a rather owlish boy called Fotheringham and one morning on our way into chapel after I had been telling him something of what I was feeling he looked at me and said solemnly, using the words of a song popular at the time, 'You're heading for the last round-up', i.e. it looks as though you're heading for suicide. This gave me a jolt, and I think I must have thought that now I must do something about it and decide something. So I did. In Greek I had met the concept of 'man as the measure of all things' and somewhere, perhaps from Fellows, had heard of 'the greatest good of the greatest number' and I thought that these two concepts together formed a good and adequate basis for a practical morality. In short I embraced the doctrines of humanism, though I didn't know the word at the time in the sense of a coherent system of morality. And this restored to me the mental and emotional peace I had lost.

It is obvious that something well beyond rationality was involved both in the start of the crisis and its resolution, but rationality now took

Aged about 15, the time of the 'crisis'

over, and has continued to govern my approach to life ever since, so far as I can make it do so. Perhaps because my newly-discovered principles came to me as the result of a profound spiritual crisis they became in effect a replacement for religion, and something better than religion because based solely on rationality. At all events they became for me what religion is to those deeply religious people who make their religion their guide in every aspect of their lives.

It was a while before I began to explore how to apply my new-found principles. This was, I now realise, characteristic of the way I approached things. In my early school reports the words that recur are 'thoughtful', 'careful', 'steady'. At fourteen, 'He works intelligently but rather slowly.' Five months later, coinciding with the time of my inner crisis, there is a definite shift – 'He is rapidly maturing' – 'Shows quickness and developing taste' – until, as I approached sixteen, 'He thinks and writes extraordinarily clearly.' Without knowing the details the teachers who knew me best charted an inner process that I myself did not understand, and in which – finally – my slow pondering led me to some clear conclusions about the world around me, and what my place in it should be.

There had been nothing in my background either at home or at school to awaken an interest in current events, either national and international. The school establishment's attitude towards politics was decidedly ambiguous. There was a repeated insistence that the values of ancient Athens were the ideal values, and in the classic expression of these, in his speech over the Athenian dead, Pericles says:

> Here each individual is interested not only in his own affairs but in the affairs of the state as well: well-informed on general politics. This is a peculiarity of ours – we do not say that a man who takes no interest in politics is a man who minds his own business; we say that he has no business here at all!★

It is quite likely that the teachers who read this with us were unaware that this wasn't a view they agreed with. In fact the school's dominant ethos was exactly the opposite. The unstated assumption was that every right-thinking boy would think as the school establishment did, and the establishment was uncompromisingly Tory – no less so because its Toryism was unavowed, disguised as a gentlemanly lack of interest in anything so vulgar as politics. Any tendency to develop an active interest in politics was regarded as distinctly bad form.

It was in fact a long time before I did develop any such interest. I had listened to the headmaster's recurrent pontifications at school assembly on what, years later, I realised was the great crisis of 1929 and its aftermath; but at the time I hadn't the slightest idea what he was talking about. All I gathered was that we all needed to feel very concerned about something or other. Of the victory of fascism in Germany early in 1933, which happened when I was nearly fifteen, I remained unaware for more than a year.

What first led me towards political awareness was concern at the looming danger of a second world war, less than two decades after the appalling slaughter of the first had ended. During these years, thoughts about this greatly exercised my mind and my emotions. The school anthologies at this time were still giving prominence to such pieces as Julian Grenfell's 'Into Battle'* which expressed an establishment-approved, 'patriotic' point of view. But a great change in public opinion was now taking place, mainly because concern about the danger of war had now become very general. The *real* poetry of the war, that of Siegfried Sassoon, Wilfred Owen and others, was beginning to make an impact. I was at this time spending most of my pocket money in the bookshop in Loughton and it was probably there that I picked up Erich Maria Remarque's *All Quiet on the Western Front*. Its effect on me was like a thunderbolt – and though at the time I was unaware of it, it had made the same kind of impact on hundreds of thousands of other English readers. It was as though someone had at last expressed boldly what millions had been feeling, but had been afraid to express. My own edition of *All Quiet* gives its early printing history. The original German book was published in January, 1929. Within three months the English translation had appeared – five years before I discovered it – and this was reprinted no less than eight times in April and three times in May, eventually selling 260,000 copies. Within eighteen months of publication the book had sold 2,500,000 copies in twenty-five languages.

Reading *All Quiet* turned me almost instantly into a pacifist. I wanted passionately to expose what war really meant. I knew its foreword by heart:

> This book is to be neither an accusation nor a confession, and least of all an adventure, for death is not an adventure to those who stand face to face with it. It will try simply to tell of a generation of men who, even though they may have escaped its shells, were destroyed by the war.

I was determined never myself to participate in a war, and eager to persuade others to share my point of view. Pacifism seemed now the obvious form through which my humanist principles should be expressed; and finding a cause I could so fully believe in created a focus for the intense feelings that had been building up throughout the period of spiritual turmoil.

The first outcome of this newfound conviction was a clash with the school establishment. I was now in the VIth form, having passed the School Certificate exams second time round – or, as I now think more likely, having again failed in maths and science but been promoted anyway because I was good at Greek and Latin, the only subjects that mattered in the canons of the school. There was at this time in public schools an institution called the OTC, which every young British gentleman was expected to join. To readers of the present generation who have no experience of the phenomenon I should explain that these letters stand for Officers' Training Corps – described by its opponents, with some exaggeration but much truth, as the British equivalent of the Hitler Youth. It operated after school hours and since even young British gentlemen often regarded it as a chore, it was what these unwilling recruits called 'voluntary compulsory', voluntary in theory, compulsory in practice. At Chigwell when you reached the age of sixteen you were summoned to a meeting after school and told by the master in charge of the OTC that you were now of an age to join. He would then ask which boys were medically unfit. Their names were noted and they were told that they must produce a medical certificate to this effect. Next he asked which boys had parents who had conscientious objections to their joining. Their names too were noted and they were told that there would be communication with their parents about it. The rest of us were then told that our first parade would be on such and such a day and at such and such a time. I stood up and said I wasn't going to join. Why? the master asked. Had my parents got conscientious objections? I said No, they hadn't, but I had. There was a lot of kerfuffle about this, and I had to have two interviews with the school chaplain, d P Grant, who was also the deputy head. I told him that in my opinion a true Christian must be a pacifist (without, I think, saying whether *I* was a true Christian) and lent him a copy of *The Psalms for Modern Life*, with an introduction by Dick Sheppard who at that time was Dean of St Martins-in-the- Fields and well-known for his pacifist convictions.★ Grant looked at it, and expressed his respect for, but disagreement with, the pacifist interpretation of Christianity; and when I maintained my stand the matter was dropped.

This turn of events marked a profound change for me. One of the most striking features of *All Quiet* was its expression of the anger of ordinary honest people against the stifling, hypocritical, bullying attitudes of the establishment in the 1914-1918 war. I began now to see these features, in somewhat muted form, still in evidence in the establishment of the world around me, including the school establishment. And just as important, I had discovered in myself an ability to stand firmly for what I believed, without thought of the consequence. I took strength from the knowledge that I had, as I felt, 'The courage never to submit or yield.'

In the summer of that year, 1934, something happened out of school that brought a sharp focus to this growing political awareness. Rex was friendly with a boy at Bancroft's whose father was a convinced socialist. Rex and I were both curious to find out what socialism was all about. This was linked with our deep concern about the danger of war. To be against war was fine, but shouldn't we try to find out why wars happen? So we attended a street corner meeting opposite the Napier Arms in Woodford, four miles from Loughton, organised by the Labour League of Youth, the youth organisation of the Labour Party. We listened to the speaker, Nat Whine, argue that the cause of war was capitalism and that until capitalism was abolished the danger of war, and indeed the inevitability of war, would still be there. We were convinced, and we both joined the Labour League of Youth.

Having concluded that modern wars were caused by capitalism, it was obvious that capitalism should be destroyed and a socialist system should replace it. I had expected that my fellows in the Labour League of Youth would have something to teach me about how one set about this task. I was both puzzled and disappointed to find that most of them didn't have any clear ideas about this and weren't particularly interested. But now a communist, George Miles, appeared upon the scene. As a Communist Party member he wasn't allowed to be also a member of the Labour League of Youth, because the comprehensive proscription of communists from membership of Labour Party organisations had by then long been in force. But the Party at that time had numbers of its members conceal their membership in order to be able to work in the Labour Party and its ancillary organisations.* George was not only interested in the question of replacing capitalism by socialism but was quite clear how to do it. It had to be done by revolution. George's arguments convinced me, and I became a communist.

My speedy journey through humanism, pacifism, socialism and into communism had opened up a world of issues to explore. Through that summer I eagerly devoted as much time as I could to the activities the Party was engaged in, and began to realise that momentous events were happening all around me. Mosley's British Union of Fascists had recently been formed, and there was evidence that quite influential political figures were ready to encourage it, though a little disapproving of its ungentlemanly flamboyance. The *Daily Mail* which in those days used to announce itself immediately under its title as being 'For King and Empire', regularly (every Thursday, if I remember aright) used to give Mosley the hospitality of its columns.★ The communists thought that the fascist threat should be taken seriously. The Labour leaders on the other hand thought that an attitude of lofty respectable democratic disdain, or alternatively, of light-hearted ridicule, was the appropriate treatment for these upstarts. In the now-defunct *Daily Herald,* which was then the main mouthpiece of right-wing Labour opinion, Hannen Swaffer, a leading Labour publicist, recommended that fascist street-corner speakers should be hailed with cries of 'Mickey Mouse'! Even when Mosley's overt anti-semitism had won him something like a mass following in the East End of London, the Labour Party did not encourage any vigorous action against him.

Unemployment stood at something like 2,000,000, and the state's treatment of the unemployed was so inhuman that you cannot read detailed accounts of it even now without feeling a raging indignation at the class that prescribed this treatment, and hatred for the mean, squalid men who applied it at the lowest level – vividly portrayed in Walter Greenwood's novel of 1933, *Love on the Dole*. But the Labour Party did nothing to inspire and organise the unemployed, or the employed workers, to fight back. It was the communists who organised the National Unemployed Workers' Movement and the now legendary hunger marches of the early thirties.

All this strengthened my sense of oneness with the communists. Each new thing I learnt made me feel more and more that the policies of the British Labour leaders and of their defenders were, politically, intellectually and morally contemptible. The Communist Party called for a united front, for common policies and common action on issues of this kind, but the Labour leaders did not want to dirty their hands by co-operating with a party which it classed with the fascists as 'enemies of democracy.' By contrast the communisits were people who were not afraid to think rigorously, to accept the conclusions to which their thought led them, and then to act upon their conclusions and devise the forms of organisation and activity best suited to achieve their aims.

Naturally, I wanted to join the Party. I knew it was organised on different principles from other parties, including one of which I strongly approved, that membership was open only to those who *worked* in a basic unit of the Party. I wanted to be one of these people who worked for what they believed in. But I was still two years too young – the Party rules said eighteen was the minimum age. It was also made clear to me that I was expected to prove myself worthy of admission into the Party – an attitude I fully approved of.

During this 'probationary' period I took part in the great demonstration of September 9th, 1934, called jointly by the Communist Party and the ILP – Independent Labour Party (now, so far as I know, long defunct.) We were to converge on Hyde Park where the fascists were holding a rally, and 'drown them in a sea of working class activity.' It was one of the first demonstrations I had taken part in and I still remember it as the most impressive of any I have experienced. Whenever I stepped out of the ranks to look at those who were marching behind me there was no end of the column in sight. What happened in Hyde Park appeared most clearly from an aerial photograph which appeared in the *Daily Sketch* the next day. It showed the Blackshirt rally, surrounded by a solid ring of police standing shoulder to shoulder, and a great mass of people pressing in upon it from all sides. The numbers in the antifascist demonstration were estimated at 150,000. I don't remember whose estimate this was. If it was the communist *Daily Worker's* it was certainly not a reliable one, since the communists of those days applied the pseudo-communist principle that you report things as being more favourable to you than they are in the hope that this will help to make them so. But whatever the correct figure may have been, there is no doubt of the enormous success of the demonstration or of the fact that many thousands of Labour Party supporters must have disregarded the advice of their leaders in order to take part in it.

I went back to school that autumn with a dramatically different world view from only a year earlier. My hatred of the values of the school establishment had intensified, but somehow this did not make me feel at odds with the school, which I still loved. One reason must have been that there were a few teachers who did not share the dominant illiberal ethos. They helped to create an environment in which I could pursue my by now passionate need to enlarge my understanding, and to define my own set of values.

One was the excellent Mr Fellows. He was remarkable because he was not content to pay occasional lip service to the idea that we should think for ourselves, but constantly encouraged us to do so. Now he persuaded the headmaster (who I guessed even then must have agreed without enthusiasm) to let him take one period a week for what would later have been called current affairs, general studies, liberal studies, or something like that. Only in these was anything remotely connected with modern political theories discussed in class at school. It was from

Police protecting a fascist demonstration in Trafalgar Square

Fellows that I borrowed Fred Henderson's *The Case for Socialism* (a book which I should like to read again now). I remember how enthusiastically I agreed with it and equally well how, when I expressed that agreement in class, he froze me off.

Another was W D Wells, who taught us French. I am not quite sure how the situation arose, but at some stage when I had to see him in his room about some of the exercises I had done for him, I noticed books in his bookcase that interested me and asked if I might borrow them. I remember him refusing with a smile to lend me a book called *In Defence of Sensuality,* but he did lend me Shaw's *Intelligent Woman's Guide to Socialism,* and later Laski's *Communism.* Unlike Fellows, W D Wells never expressed in class any view which could have suggested that he was not at one with the school establishment, but the fact that he possessed such books and was willing to lend them to me was clear evidence that he was not 'one of them.' I enjoyed *An Intelligent Woman's Guide,* and Laski's *Communism* inspired me in a way which Laski certainly would not have wished it to. I remember especially the great appeal which his account of the Communist International – the Comintern – made to me. Here was a worldwide brotherhood of men and women working in unity, in all countries and at all times, bound to each other by the strongest tie that can unite you with your fellow humans – the desire for a world in which war, poverty and inhuman exploitation would be ended. I found this a profoundly inspiring vision, and the book contributed a lot to my communist ardour.

While Fellows and Wells helped me in my political development, the teacher who without any inhibition behaved as a friend to me was the Reverend R K Roper, who had succeeded D P Grant as the school chaplain. He was a remarkable man, quite markedly learned in his knowledge of the Bible and of Christian doctrine, but also completely unbigoted. He had a completely open and entirely unashamed admiration for young boys, which as far as I know (and I would feel quite certain about this) never led him to do or attempt anything undesirable with them. Although I had by that time become an atheist and a communist and he knew this, he was not in the least disconcerted by it. I used to spend long evenings in his room in Harsnett's which was about five minutes' walk up the street from the main school building. He wasn't interested in politics, but didn't think it reprehensible that I was. I once assailed him vigorously for taking no stand against the Japanese invasion of China which was going on at the time and asking him how on earth he could justify on Christian grounds an ignorance of and indifference towards what was happening there. The next day I received a little note enclosing a five pound note, which was quite a

71

large sum at that time, and saying that it was a *'pignus amoris'*, a pledge of love. (These words are quoted from a famous passage in Lucretius which he knew that I had read.) On the next occasion when we met he told me with some humility that he was not the kind of person who felt himself qualified to make judgment upon large political questions.

In December 1934 at the age of sixteen and a half I was finally accepted as a member of the Party. I was told that I had been granted a special dispensation to enable me to join a year and a half below the official age. I became a member of a local cell, as the basic unit of the Party was then called, and began now to live two equally real lives – life at school, and life in the evenings and at weekends. I was in the same cell as George Miles, in South Woodford, meeting in a room above a shop – I forget how often, but perhaps once a week. George's influence on me now increased. He was a man who exemplified some of the best features of the old-style British communists of those days. He insisted on the interests of communism as the sole standard by which your every action must be judged, and on the principle that your belief in communism must mould and direct your whole life. His revolutionary morale was proof against every discouragement, and he inspired me with the same spirit. One of the first duties assigned to me was to stand in the street shouting the virtues of the Party's daily paper, the *Daily Worker*, as I offered it for sale. In George's philosophy, you did whatever the interests of communism required you to do, and if you felt awkward or embarrassed about doing it, that was neither here nor there. You might feel reluctant because you were doing something which most of the great public disapproved of. Or you might want to rebel against participating in proceedings where 'bourgeois' behaviour was expected of you. In neither case did his standards permit you to feel that your feelings had the slightest relevance to the situation. He used to tell a story of the early days of Soviet rule when Chicherin, the first People's Commissar for Foreign Affairs protested to Lenin against being expected to wear a top hat at some diplomatic function. Lenin, said George, replied that if the interests of the revolution had required it he would have had to wear a nightgown. I don't know where he got this story from, but I accepted the attitude it expresses.

It was in response to George's pressure, and the pressure of my own communist conscience, that I forced myself to do things which I didn't like doing – like public speaking (which I came to enjoy) and selling papers in the street and canvassing from door to door (which I hated, and later, for reasons that I considered valid, gave up.) He taught me the absolute equality within the party of every individual party member, from the most exalted to the newest recruit, and the duty – not just the right, but the duty – of every communist to 'fight for your line' – that is, to do your utmost to convince your comrades of the correctness of your views until either you did convince them or they convinced you, or until it became necessary to take a decision one way or the other and bind all members to action upon the majority view. He more than once rebuked me for not having put forward in the cell a view which I later expressed to him. He used to study the proceedings and resolutions of earlier Communist Party congresses, and once quoted with great approval a statement in an early document that 'in a Communist Party there is no rank and file'* meaning that it was a party of leaders, of men and women who would be able individually, even in situations when consultation with other communists was impossible, to assess a situation correctly, decide what should be done, and proceed to do it.

There were things I strongly approved of in the way our cell ran. The first was that self-criticism was genuinely practised – and I assumed that this was the same throughout the world communist movement. Its importance is summed up in a statement of Lenin.

The attitude of a political party towards its own mistakes is one of the most important and surest criteria of the seriousness of the party … To admit a mistake openly, to disclose its reasons, to analyse the conditions which gave rise to it, to study attentively the means of correcting it – these are the signs of a serious party; this means the performance of its duties.*

I also learnt the importance of the serious study of Marxism, following Stalin's dictum, 'theory without practice is sterile; practice without theory is blind.'* We used to read together the Marxist classics – first the *Communist Manifesto* of Marx and Engels, and later the 1928 *Programme of the Communist International*. We read aloud, turn by turn, and paused at the end of every paragraph to discuss it before going on to the next one. One consequence of this weighing of every paragraph was that we – or at any rate I – could remember key passages almost word for word or, failing that, knew exactly where to find them. One of my school reports at the time said 'What he learns, he learns with praiseworthy thoroughness' – and it certainly applied to what I was learning here. I don't know whether anyone these days reads with the full concentration with which we read these things, and perhaps I should try to explain why we did.

The discovery of the communist explanation of the world was a revelation to me of the path I needed to follow in every aspect of my life. I and many others had discovered it at a time when a repetition of the terrible experience of a world war seemed to be looming on the horizon. If we could not avert war, millions and millions of people would again be killed or mutilated. It was a time too when German fascism, the most ruthless and inhuman force in modern history, was driving towards world conquest. We believed that if the drive to fascism and war could be defeated, we would go on to bring about in the near future the greatest change in the history of humankind for thousands of years, and establish at last a world in which all humankind's best potentialities would be developed to the full. So everything that fed our understanding of these things needed to be studied and assimilated – the historical process which had brought us to where we were now, and the continuing trend of that process which would make it possible to achieve our aim. We felt that we needed to learn absolutely everything that those whose life-work it had been to formulate our guiding theory had to tell us. A passage in a short article of Lenin on the state written in 1919 expresses very well what we all thought. He speaks of 'the fundamental works of modern socialism, every sentence of which can be accepted with confidence, in the assurance that it has not been said at random but is based on immense historical and political material.'

We nevertheless had a healthily irreverent attitude to at any rate the style of some of the things we read. I remember Alan Winnington, the only member of our cell who later achieved international fame, reading a paragraph in the *Programme of the Communist International* which contained a sentence beginning 'It [the proletariat] has inscribed on its banner' … and continued with a text which ran to sixty-five words before it reached even the first full-stop.* Alan read to the end of it, paused, and remarked with a grin, 'Bloody big banner!' This didn't prevent us, however, from taking very seriously the content of what we read.

I enjoyed this reading all the more because Marx's splendid rhetoric in the *Communist Manifesto* made a strong appeal to my youthful craving for splendidly sweeping, decisive pronouncements. I learnt whole stretches of it by heart, and I think, with an effort, I could still recall word for word its opening and closing paragraphs. Not only those. I always liked the bit that begins 'The dangerous class, the social scum, that passively rotting mass thrown off from the lower layers of the old society' – I hope I've got it right; I am quoting it from memory. And another towards the end of the *Manifesto,* where Marx and Engels poured contempt on other brands of socialism, and especially one they labelled 'feudal socialism'. Its proponents were members of the aristocracy of France and England who presented themselves as champions of the exploited working class – but, said Marx and Engels, were motivated primarily by hatred of the bourgeoisie who were replacing them in power:

> The aristocracy took their revenge by singing lampoons on their new master, and whispering in his ears sinister prophecies of coming catastrophe. In this way arose feudal socialism: half lamentation, half lampoon; half echo of the past, half menace of the future; at times, by its bitter, witty and incisive criticism, striking the bourgeoisie to the very heart's core, but always ludicrous in its effect, through total incapacity to comprehend the march of modern history.
>
> The aristocracy, in order to rally the people to them, waved the proletarian alms-bag in front for a banner. But the people so often as it joined them, saw on their hindquarters the old feudal coats of arms, and deserted with loud and irreverent laughter.

I now think this is a grossly exaggerated piece of writing. Its tone would have been justified only if the ideas being so treated had *really* ceased to have any hold on any important section of the people whom Marx and Engels wished to influence. And the last line either reflects an extreme kind of wishful thinking or is an example of what Lenin later called 'Communist lying' (though so far as I know he was never so impious as to accuse the founding fathers of it) – that is, making statements which you know to be untrue in the hope that your making them will speed the day when they will *become* true.★

Besides joint study in the cell meetings I devoted quite a lot of time to reading on my own. There was no shortage of materials –there was a daily, a weekly, a fortnightly and two monthly journals, all of which we were expected to read. The daily was, of course, the *Daily Worker*. The weekly bore the inoffensive name of *International Press Correspondence* – abridged in characteristic communist style to *Inprecorr* – but was in fact a weekly newsletter of the Comintern. The fortnightly was the *Communist International*, the Comintern's official organ, and the monthlies were *Communist Review* and *Labour Monthly*. I read substantial amounts of all of these.

I also began to read some of the shorter works of Lenin, then available in a series called the Little Lenin Library. (The twelve bright orange volumes of Lenin's selected works had not yet been published.) Still preoccupied with the menace of war, I gave priority to what Lenin had to say about the 1914-18 war. I knew that Socialism had always been an internationalist doctrine, aiming at uniting the people of all countries and believing that the true interests of the people of one country could never conflict with the true interests of the people of any other country.

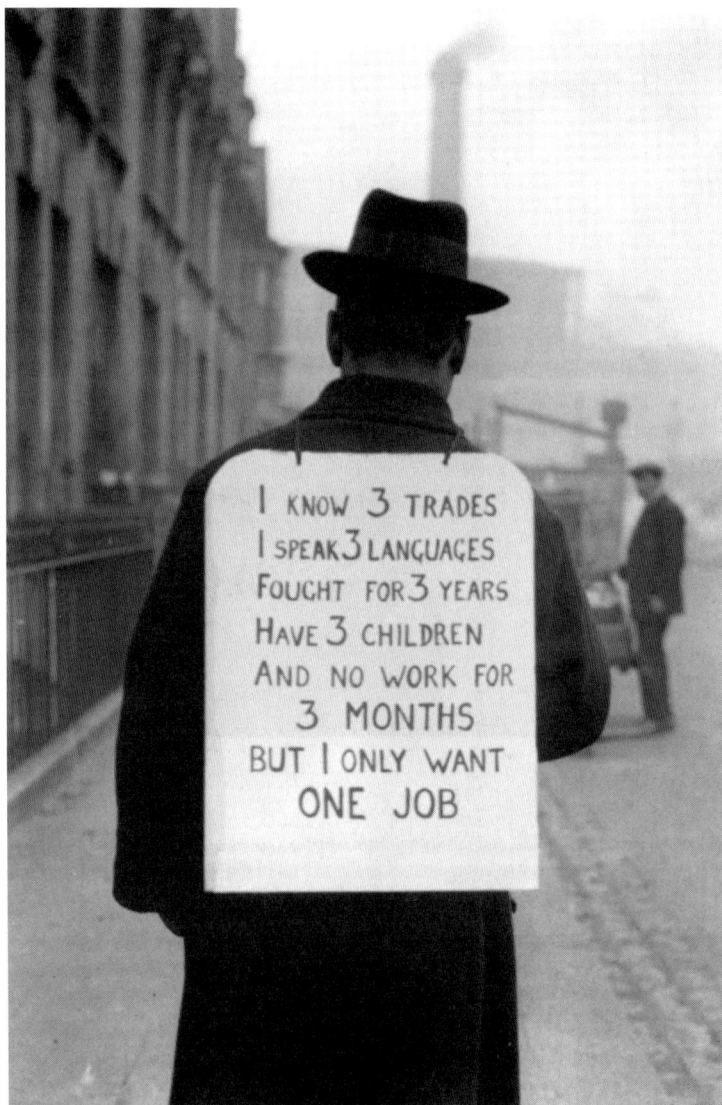

Unemployment made visible

I now learnt that before 1914 all socialist parties had taken this stand, and that only just before 1914 their international organisation, the Second International, had resolved that if war broke out they would take united international action to bring it to an end. Yet when war broke out only the communists (and a few others) stood firm, and all the others betrayed it. The British Labour leaders, with few exceptions, had declared that Britain was fighting in a just cause. The German Socialists, again with few exceptions, had supported German imperialism. It was this great betrayal that had caused the communists, who until then had been members of the Second International, to break with it and eventually form the Third, Communist International.

Now in a period when another war was clearly threatening, surely all serious socialists would be looking back to the 1914-18 war, analysing what it had all been about, and drawing conclusions for their own future guidance? And if they did so, they would see that one of the three following propositions must be correct. Either the aims of the British and their allies were consistent with the aims of socialism – so socialists in all countries should have supported them. Or the aims of the Germans and their allies were consistent with the aims of socialism – so socialists in all countries should have supported *them*. Or the War was an inter-imperialist war – so for a socialist there was nothing to choose between the conflicting parties. The German and the British socialists in 1914 could both have been wrong; what was sure was that they could not both have been right. The reception of *All Quiet* had shown that millions of people, unequipped with the greater understanding which socialists possessed, had been able to see that the War had been a battle between rival imperialists which brought nothing but unprecedented suffering to the peoples of their countries. Surely one could expect that socialists would now conclude that neither side in 1914-18 had pursued aims which any socialist could support, and draw a practical conclusion for their own course of action accordingly? But I found to my surprise that neither Labour supporters nor their leaders were particularly interested in this problem, or indeed in any really rigorous examination of any other problem of this sort of magnitude. The communists, by contrast, paid proper attention to these problems and drew logical conclusions for future action.

Then there was the question of how capitalist society could be transformed into socialist society. The communists argued that this could only take place by revolution. For non-Marxists I should explain that 'revolution' in communist terminology means the ending of the rule of one class and its replacement by the rule of another. In our time this meant destroying the power of the capitalist class and the establishment of the rule of the working class. We assumed that this could not be achieved without the use of armed force. The Labour Party theorists were ardent supporters of social change through the processes of constitutional democracy, but they had no convincing answer to the communist argument that the capitalist class would never allow democracy to develop to the point where it threatened the existence of capitalist power. At school I had written a longish essay on this theme which I still have, and for which, to my great amusement, I was awarded a the Montford Essay Prize. I was equally amused when I won the Powell Greek Testament Prize, since by that time everyone knew that I was a convinced atheist. I hasten to add that this didn't involve any guile on my part, because most of the marks were awarded for accurate translation of the Greek passages set.

I regret to say that in my early days in the Party I was a very fanatical communist. I generally use this word reluctantly, because in common usage, people are often called fanatics simply because they stand firmly by the principles in which they believe regardless of any trouble this may get them into; and such people deserve not contempt but admiration. But I guess it is the right word to describe the Ralph Russell of 1934-5. George Miles drove me hard, and I eagerly accepted all the tasks he allotted me. Every Saturday I used to stand at the bus terminus in Loughton selling the *Daily Worker* to the very small numbers of people who would buy it. I also sold the *Busman's Punch*, the paper of the communist-led rank and file movement in the Transport and General Workers Union. ('Don't say 'comrade' when you're selling this,' George told me. 'This is a trade union paper. Call them 'brother'. That's how union members address each other.') This was much more enjoyable, because there was wide support for the rank and file movement and I sold quite a lot of its paper. Then I would cycle the six miles from Loughton to Epping to sell it outside the bus garage there.

George sang a lot, and I learnt a lot of revolutionary songs from him, and from a book called *The Workers Song Book*. Some I loved, both for their tunes and the energy of their words, like

Whirlwinds of danger are raging around us, o'erwhelming forces of darkness assail

Still in the fight see advancing before us red flag of liberty that yet shall prevail.

Then forward ye workers, freedom awaits you, o'er all the world on the land & the sea

On with the fight for the cause of humanity

March, march ye toilers & the world shall be free.

But there were others which even in my revolutionary enthusiasm I privately thought had ridiculous words. In 'The Comintern' one verse ran

> *Betrayed where we trusted, our wages adjusted*
> *The richer ever richer while millions are starving*
> *With nothing to lose but our hunger and chains*
> *We'll fight for our country and all it contains*
> *And all it contai-ains, and all it contains!*

I immediately found myself thinking that I must sternly repress the feeling, and try to think that since what the songs said was unexceptionable it was totally unacceptable to criticise the manner in which they said it.

I also felt guilty if I ever gave myself up, however briefly, to enjoyable occupations when I should have been devoting every moment to the service of communism. I can well remember sitting on one sunny afternoon on the grass at Woodford Green. I was in the sixth form and sixth formers had the privilege of not having to play what had hitherto been compulsory games three afternoons a week (unless they wanted to, and I most certainly didn't.) So, rejoicing in my new-found leisure, I lay back and thought how wonderful it was to be able to lie there and enjoy the lovely sunshine. But this soon gave way to a sense of guilt, a feeling that I ought to be ashamed of myself lying back like this when I ought to be doing something to right the wrongs of the world.

I now began to discover that my political views were going to bring me into conflict with people I liked. All through these years I had continued to walk in Epping Forest and had become friendly with the son of a forest keeper – Mr Woolley, I think his name was. I once laboured with him and others to put out a fire – probably deliberately started – in a part of the forest called Long Running, and learnt how difficult it is to put out such a fire, because it travels below the leaf mould where it can't be seen. The keeper's cottage was not far away from the scene of the fire,

Epping Forest, not far from the keeper's house

One of the offending booklets

near an old pub called the Wake Arms; I used sometimes to go there, and Mrs Woolley would feed me a delicious concoction of sausage meat mixed with egg and fried. They were always warm and welcoming – until, probably from something I myself said, they discovered that I had become a communist. Nothing was said, but there was an immediate change in atmosphere; when I next arrived at the house they were civil, but the warmth and ease had gone.

The greater part of my days were spent at school, and it was mainly with my school-fellows that I used to argue my views. On my journey home from school I went a bit out of my way to cycle with another boy named Douglas Ambrose. He used to argue what I can briefly describe as the *Daily Mail* point of view, and I never saw any signs that I was making any impression upon him. After some weeks I discovered that he had been urging my arguments on his parents, and that this had so incensed them that they had written to the headmaster complaining about my pernicious influence on their son. (I can't remember now how I got to know of this. I think it was Douglas himself who, much later, told me about it.) Nothing was said about it at the time, but things were building up to a head-on clash.

The real crisis came a bit later. At George Miles's suggestion I took a lot of anti-war pamphlets to school and sold them to anyone who would buy them. (Actually it was not only anti-war pamphlets that I sold. In those days tins of Lyle's Golden Syrup carried a recipe for making toffee, and I used to make it and sell that too.) Two of the pamphlets that I remember well carried photographs of men horribly mutilated in the war, and in another crude cartoons slammed home the point that for capitalists of all countries war was a terribly profitable business. Authority's reaction to this was swift and drastic. All of these pamphlets that could be found were confiscated. I was ordered to collect in any I had sold, hand them in to the headmaster, and refund the money to boys who had bought them. Further, I was forbidden to bring any such material to school again, even for my own reading. The headmaster then assembled the whole school and lectured it on the enormity of my crime. He was a dignified, imposing man called Ernest Herman Stewart Walde, and all of us – including me – were in awe of him. He never mentioned my name from start to finish, but then he didn't need to – everyone knew perfectly well who he was talking about. He remarked that there was 'really no place in this school for a boy who refused to join the OTC.' But he took no further action after that. Some weeks later I went to him and asked him to return to me the pamphlets he had confiscated, saying that they were not mine, that I had taken them on a sale or return basis and that if I didn't return them I should have to pay for it all out of my pocket money. He did return it, on the understanding that I would remove it from the school forthwith.

I have one other memory of confronting the school authorities. I discovered that one of the members of my cell, Alan Winnington, was an old boy of Chigwell. He told me that he had presented to the school library a copy of R Palme Dutt's *Fascism and Social Revolution*. My enquiries revealed, not unexpectedly, that it had never been put on the shelves, and I thereupon demanded, successfully, that it should be. I don't think anyone read it, and in fact it wasn't until a good many years later that I read it myself. But at times when I seethed helplessly under the bigoted, illiberal dictatorship of these guardians of tolerant, liberal values I used to take the book down and gain comfort from Lenin's fiery words quoted opposite the title page:

> The bourgeoisie sees in Bolshevism almost only one side – insurrection, violence, terror; it endeavours, therefore, to prepare itself especially for resistance and opposition on *this* field. It is possible that, for more or less short periods, they will succeed. There is absolutely nothing dreadful to us in [this]. Communism 'springs up' from positively all sides of social life, its sprouts are everywhere. Let the bourgeoisie take vengeance in advance on the Bolsheviks, and endeavour to exterminate in India, Hungary, Germany, etc., more hundreds, thousands, and hundreds of thousands of the Bolsheviks of yesterday or those of tomorrow. The communists must know that the future at any rate is theirs. In all countries communism grows; its roots are so deep that persecution neither weakens, nor debilitates, but rather strengthens it.★

It wasn't until years later that my friend Chris Freeman, who more than anyone else has contributed to my education in political honesty, pointed out to me that if – *if* – that had been a correct judgement when Lenin wrote it, it had long ceased to be so, and that savage persecution was a very effective means of stemming the advance of communism.

5

There came a time when the headmaster seemed to conclude that there was no need to continue punishing me for my sins. Each of us had made his position clear, and we could now leave it at that. Almost certainly what made this possible was my academic record and my genuine enthusiasm for Latin and, even more, for Greek literature. In these final years of school everything we studied was literature – Greek, Latin, English and a bit of French. I enjoyed it all and didn't regret the wholly disproportionate place which I realised even then that the classics occupied in the school syllabus. The headmaster's own love for the Latin and Greek classics was unmistakable, and he taught them extremely well. So despite the real revulsion which he felt at my political views there was a bond between us, and at this level we genuinely appreciated each other.

My admiration for our French teacher, W D Wells, was tempered by a disapproval of some of the texts he chose for us to read. Some I liked – some of de Maupassant's stories, and his very moving *Deux Amis* – Two Friends – made me want to read more. (A good many years later I did, in English translation, and thought his best work excellent and his worst unbelievably bad.) But I disapproved of his choice of Andre Maurois's 'Colonel Bramble' books (chosen early on because his French idiom is strikingly close to English) because they managed to write humorously about the 1914-1918 war. Even more I disapproved, on orthodox communist grounds, of his choice of Andre Gide's *Retour de l'URSS* – Return from the USSR – because it records his disillusion with the wonderful Soviet Union. I expected better of someone who I guessed was a good socialist. Besides the liberal Fellows, the socialist-inclined Wells and the friendly Roper, the other teachers as far as I could see weren't interested in what I thought or did, or didn't think or do, outside the classroom in which they taught me. One such was Mr Doouss, who in my early years in Chigwell had been unable to understand my incapacity at maths. He now took us for English, and here we had a shared enthusiasm. I remember with pleasure the breadth of our reading – Chaucer's *Prologue to the Canterbury Tales*, Marlowe's *Dr Faustus*, Sidney's *Apology for Poetry*, Shakespeare's *Twelfth Night*, *A Winter's Tale*, *Hamlet* and *Lear*, Milton's *Comus*, *Samson Agonistes* and *Areopagitica*, Johnson's *Rasselas*, selections from Lamb, Dickens' *Barnaby Rudge*, and a lot of Palgrave's *Golden Treasury*. We were also encouraged to read more widely on our own, and given E H Blakeney, *A Rapid Survey of English Literature* (first published in 1918 but still useful) which gives brief details of the major English writers in chronological order, with brief extracts from their writing. It was Doouss who told us of Macaulay's vitriolic review of Robert Montgomery's verse:

> We have no enmity to Mr Robert Montgomery ... We select him because his works have received more enthusiastic praise, and have deserved more unmixed contempt, than any which, as far as our knowledge extends, have appeared within the last three or four years.

The vigour of Macaulay's rhetoric appealed to me much as Lenin's did. I particularly enjoyed the sentence, 'We take this to be, upon the whole, the worst similitude in the world.' And I loved Samuel Johnson's scathing letter to Lord Chesterfield, which was included in a book called *Pages of English Prose*. Chesterfield had held out hopes that he would support Johnson while he was compiling the first English dictionary but had done absolutely nothing. When the dictionary was finished Chesterfield wrote articles praising it and, it seems, hoped that Johnson would dedicate the dictionary to him. In Johnson's sarcastic response he says,

> Such treatment I did not expect, for I never had a patron before. Is not a patron, my lord, one who looks with unconcern on a man struggling for life in the water, and, when he has reached ground, encumbers him with help?

Doouss had an exceptionally high opinion of me and called me 'homo russelliensis' as though I constituted a distinct species of the human race. He was quite free and easy in his manner and liked to pontificate. He would announce that '*Tom Jones* is the greatest novel in the English language' or 'Respectability is a deadly sin' – statements which he never elaborated. He used to pride himself, quite legitimately, on his clear, legible handwriting, and liked to quote the lines from Hamlet

> *I once did think it as our statists do*
> *A baseness to write fair*

and express his hearty agreement with those who ridiculed this attitude. He once said that the hymn which included the verse

> *They climbed the steep ascent to heaven*
> *In peril toil and pain*
> *Oh Lord to us may grace be given*
> *To follow in their train*

would be more appealing if instead of 'in their train' it had been 'in the train.'

Another master who was neither shocked by nor even interested in my political views was Mr Stott, nicknamed for some reason Gobi, who was one of those who taught us classics. He spoke with a slow, solemn, very nasal accent. He once informed us that the word '*cruentus*', which occurred frequently in Vergil's *Aeneid*, meant 'bloody,' but this was in its literal sense and was 'not to be confused with the word that so often falls from the lips of uneducated men' – all this in complete solemnity. I once wrote for him an essay on the reforms of the early Athenian statesman Solon, quoting Lenin's contemptuous words on 'that lackey of the moneybags, Lloyd George' and saying that Solon had been a comparable figure. Whether Stott knew who Lenin was I doubt, but he took no offence at his being quoted and simply noted on the essay, 'Aren't you rather hard on Solon?' He often used to quote, a propos of nothing, somebody's judgement that the three greatest love poets were 'Sappho, Catullus, and pure Robbie Burns.' By this time we had read some Catullus and I loved his passionate expressions of his love. In fact I liked *all* love poetry and love stories. Shakespeare's sonnets especially appealed to me. In later years I wondered whether Stott had ever read the three poets he cited, because a person as conventional as he was would have felt some difficulty in according them such high praise. Sappho was Lesbian (indeed the word derives from her, because she came from Lesbos), Catullus and Burns were both adulterers, and Burns, by conventional standards, far from pure.

My study of Greek literature had led me to develop an interest in verse translation into English in a way which conveys the rhythm of the original, though where Greek and a number of other languages are concerned this involves substituting a stress-based metre for the quantity-based metre of the original. I decided to read Homer's *Odyssey*, and chose to read it in the English hexameter translation of H B Cotterill. This I did, and felt surprised when Stott regarded this as a remarkable feat.

Reading Cotterill's translation produced an unexpected by-product. My edition was a large-format, illustrated one and there was a picture of Circe, portrayed as a tall, beautiful, full-figured woman dressed in diaphanous clothes surveying the swine into which she has transformed Odysseus's comrades. I associated this picture with Circe asking Odysseus to come to bed with her:

Come let us hasten
On to my couch to ascend, and folded in tender embracement
Revel in love and in sleep, and trust each other for ever.

I found this picture incredibly arousing, and masturbating over it, for the first time ever ejaculated – into the chamber-pot, where I observed with mild curiosity the bits of white stuff floating in the pee. I know my father saw them too, because it was a Sunday, and one of his Sunday chores was to empty the chamber pots. (I think on other days of the week we emptied them ourselves.) He certainly knew what they were, but made no comment.

It was my communist life out of school that continued to dominate my thoughts. It was now becoming increasingly evident to me that the admirable George Miles was not so wholly admirable as I had thought, and that he had qualities, and practised methods, which were not consistent with the communist standards which he himself had done so much to instil in me. His 'communist lying' was one of the things that made me feel uneasy. I remember one instance in relation to a meeting Winston Churchill was coming to speak at. We took this meeting very seriously, and made preparations which now strike me as comic rather than anything else. We decided that before the meeting we should paint a slogan along the wall outside the building where it was to be held. George proposed, and we accepted, the slogan 'Indian workers get 4d a day – less if Churchill had his way!' And this was duly painted up. When the meeting took place we attended it, prepared to heckle and to ask unanswerable questions. I don't think that in the event we did heckle, and I am pretty sure that there was no provision made for questions. What I do remember is that, at an indication from George, we rose in a body (all five or six of us) and left the hall, and that George then drafted a report to the *Daily Worker* saying that before Churchill could finished his speech the indignant workers rose to their feet and marched out in a body, drowning the conclusion of the speech with the stamping of their feet.* Whether he ever sent in the report, and if so, whether the *Worker* ever printed it, I don't know.

I can't think that the time and energy which we spent on all this were justified by any result we may have achieved. The meeting was a small one, attended, presumably, mainly by the most convinced and devoted Tories, and if our actions had any effect on them at all I guess it would have made them think the communists used even more dastardly methods than they had supposed, and were prepared even to go to the lengths of washing, shaving and wearing normal clothes in order to make themselves appear just like ordinary people. And my misgivings about George's report gave rise to wider ones. I couldn't help wondering how many other reports in the *Daily Worker* bore about the same relationship to the truth as George's.

The illustration of Circe

Churchill as parliamentary candidate for Epping

George always behaved as though he only had to appeal to the revolutionary instinct lurking just below the surface of everyone's consciousness to get an immediate response. He once called at my house at a time when I wasn't there, and got talking to my mother. She told me afterwards, with great amusement, that when for some reason the headmaster of Chigwell was mentioned George said, 'Oh, he's a well-known reactionary.' Reactionary was a word rarely used at that time outside communist circles, and I don't think I myself had ever heard it until I joined the Party. On another occasion I was with him on the upper deck of a bus when he began to sing loudly

Poor old Lord Ashfield, pity Lord Ashfield, starving to death on 5 million a year

Poor old Lord Ashfield, pity Lord Ashfield, pity Lord Ashfield the underfed peer.

Lord Ashfield was the boss of London Transport (at the time called the London Passenger Transport Board) so George no doubt felt it particularly appropriate to sing this while travelling on a London bus, as a sure means of stimulating the desired class hatred against aristocratic bosses. I am sure that most people on the bus had never heard of Lord Ashfield, let alone knowing who or what he was.

I did sometimes wonder whether the prospects for revolution in Britain were so bright and so imminent as we told ourselves they were, but George had no such misgivings. Once when I suggested diffidently that a party of about 5000 (as the Communist Party then was) was perhaps rather a small one to bring about a revolution he told me to remember that the Bolsheviks had been only a tiny minority of the population when they conquered power. And I think that this more or less satisfied me at the time, or, more accurately perhaps, enabled me to push this feeling to the back of my mind.

I was now spending a lot of my time in the home of a couple called Jake and Mike Hubbard. They were not members of the party but were close sympathisers. I took to going to there almost every evening after school, and quite often stayed overnight. My parents never seemed bothered about this. By that time my younger brother Wilfred was at Chigwell, for the arrangement with his choir school was that he would be sent there when his voice broke. When Wilfred got home in the evening my mother would ask him whether he had seen me at school that day, he would say that he had, and they never asked any further.

I liked Jake and Mike's house, which was new, comfortably furnished, and tidy. They kept a fairly open house, and a number of regulars were often there. All of them were Party sympathisers, but none of them members, and most of them were happy to mock at Party activities which they found ridiculous. Dick Miles, George Miles's brother, was one of them. He owned a Riley car which he always called his 'racing Riley.' Once when George, with typically absurd optimism, suggested that we should run a communist candidate in the local elections and needed an appealing slogan, Dick suggested 'Bums for buggers!' Two others were the Fitzgerald brothers, Gerald and Justin, and Justin was as impressively handsome as I felt that someone so named should be. There were two women, who were sort of rivals for Alan Winnington's sexual attentions, a very nice one called, if I remember rightly, Kay, and a not very nice one called Vee. Kate was committed to Alan no matter what, and had had to have several abortions because Alan would turn up drunk late at night and make her pregnant. Vee was a highly made-up woman, justly (as far as I could judge) detested by Jake, who used to say that the lines in *The Beggar's Opera* song

'Tis most certain, by their flirting, women oft have envy shown

Pleas'd to ruin others' wooing; never happy in their own.

might have been written specially for her. But I don't think Vee really cared a toss either about Alan or about Kay.

I think it was Jake and Mike who first introduced me to the great Soviet films, Eisenstein's *Battleship Potemkin*, about the 1905 revolt of the sailors in the Black Sea fleet, and *Mother*, based Gorki's novel. I also remember Pudovkin's *Storm over Asia*. These used to be shown at a small cinema whose name I can't now remember on the right as you went downhill in the little street, Villiers Street, next to Charing Cross station. It was under the railway, and you could hear the sound of the trains passing above. I remember what is probably the best-known scene in *Battleship Potemkin*, which, after the firing on the mutinous sailors and their supporters, shows an abandoned pram lurching down the steps. Another was the scene on the battleship where the sailors, having been served meat crawling with maggots, seized their officers and threw them overboard. The final scene of *Mother* too, also set in 1905, was very vivid. The triumph of Tsarist forces is symbolised by the Russian flag

At Jake's house: Ralph 2nd L, with Bunty Hammond

flying above the Winter Palace, at the side of the river frozen over with thick ice. As you watch, a wind gets up, blowing more and more fiercely, and the flag, straining at the mast, becomes the red flag. The ice on the river cracks and breaks up and is jostled along on the now rushing torrent of the river.

Jake and Mike had a lot of gramophone records, and it was there that I got to know, amongst other things, Beethoven's *Emperor Concerto*, Ravel's *Bolero*, and all the songs of the *Beggar's Opera*. I also liked the songs of the Boswell Sisters, especially 'Shuffle off to Buffalo'. But I strongly objected to the lines

Some day the stork may pay a visit & leave a little souvenir

Just a little cute 'what is it' – but we'll discuss that later dear

I thought, Christ, here's a couple off on their honeymoon and presumably planning a life-long partnership, and they haven't yet discussed whether they want children or not. How could they be such fools? There was another song Jake particularly liked, that expressed the feeling of the many women who, regrettably, believe what their lovers tell them though they know perfectly well it is probably false –

So you think that I'm terrific & you love my company

I bet you tell that to all the girls – it still sounds good to me.

So you think I fit the picture of the good old family tree... (etc)

One thing Jake did for me was to free me, at any rate to some extent, from a feeling of guilt when I ventured to question the appropriateness of the words of our songs. Here was she, not a Party member it was true, but a warm sympathiser of the Party, freely ridiculing some of the things we sang. There was a Red Air Force song which included the words 'We drop them leaflets while we bomb their bosses' and Jake pointed out to George Miles that this was likely to be a totally impracticable operation. (Thinking about it now I realise that her objection was not valid. She clearly hadn't realised that the two operations weren't neces-

91

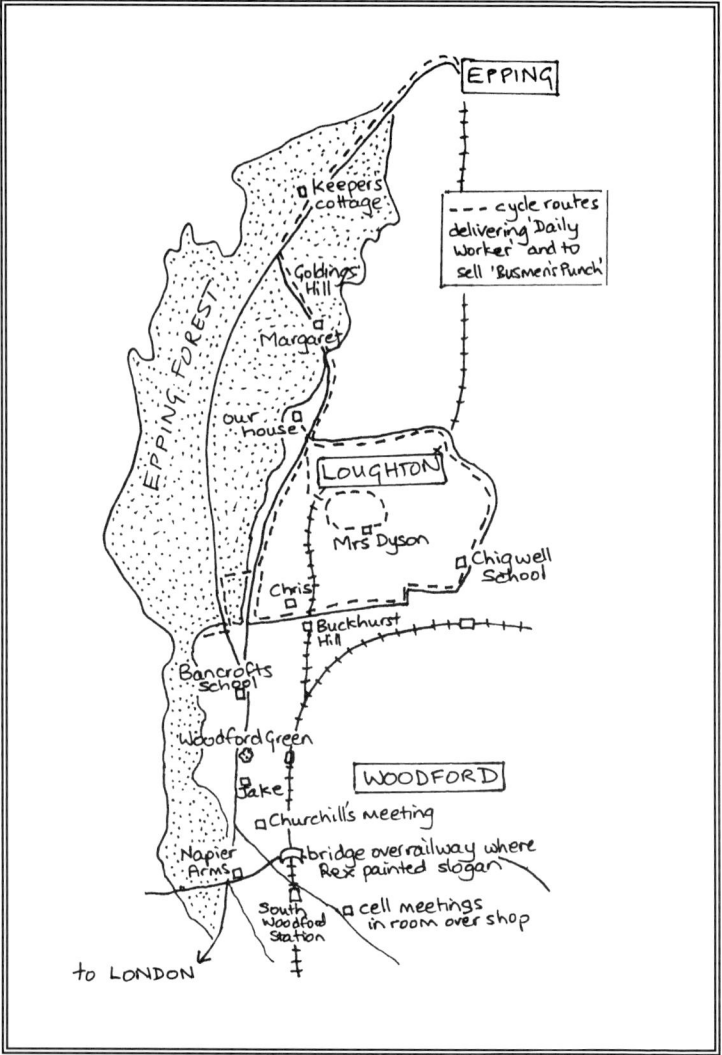

EPPING

□ Keepers cottage

- - - cycle routes delivering 'Daily Worker' and to sell 'Busmen's Punch'

Goldings Hill

□ Margaret

□ our house

EPPING FOREST

LOUGHTON

□ Mrs Dyson

□ Chigwell School

Chris □

□ Buckhurst Hill

Bancrofts School □

Woodford Green ✪

Jake □

WOODFORD

□ Churchill's meeting

Napier Arms □

□ bridge over railway where Rex painted slogan

South Woodford Station

□ cell meetings in room over shop

to LONDON

Woodford to Epping: life out of school

92

sarily envisaged as being carried out in the same raid.) She also ridiculed the line of The Internationale, 'And so farewell to spirits craven' saying that it conjured up a picture – and here she suited the actions to the words – of our merrily waving our hand and saying with a cheerful smile, 'Tata, spirits craven!' But I can't claim that she completely banished my misgivings on this point, and it was with a feeling of relief a good many years later that I encountered Engels' remark that the words of many famous revolutionary songs are ridiculous.★

Jake performed another service for me. She thought that George Miles was overloading me with Party work, and ticked him off for it. She was quite right, and I was pleased to go along with her. So I took it upon myself to act accordingly. One argument that both Jake and I used was that I was preparing to go to Cambridge. But to do this I would need to win a scholarship; and to do that I would have to pay more attention to my school work. To some extent I did this. Jake would sit me down in a room on my own and I would study J B Bury's *History of Greece*. (My essay on Solon was a product of this study.) But I must admit that I did so only in fits and starts, reducing the volume of my communist work to make room for my studies, but not in fact using anything like all the time that this gave me to get on with them.

Jake's house also provided one vital missing ingredient in my life – contact with women. Except for holidays in Holme, which had stopped a couple of years ago, I had lived in a world inhabited almost entirely by the males of the species. Now, at sixteen, I was full of constant, intense sexual desire, which attached itself enthusiastically to a series of women. Jake was the first, and the fact that she was married didn't do much to discourage my interest. I correctly sensed that she had a very healthy sexual appetite and an absence of any inhibitions about it. I remember seeing her one day when she was wearing wide-legged shorts sitting on a chair with her feet up on the chair seat and showing, as the phrase goes, 'all she'd got.' She was clearly aware of this and quite unembarrassed. But it was my own desire rather than any encouragement from her that brought about some minimal sexual contact with her. When I was in their car with her and her husband, he would be driving, she sitting next to him, and I in the back seat immediately behind her. I would lean forward over her seat and fondle her breasts. Neither she nor her husband made any attempt to discourage this, but I wouldn't conclude from that that she (and he) had no misgivings about it. They probably thought, 'Well, we communists aren't bound by bourgeois conventions. Here is a young comrade with a vigorous sexual appetite. Why should we discourage him?' Anyway, I never attempted to take things further, much though I would have liked to – liked to in the abstract, so to speak, because I would have considered it impermissible to break up a fellow-communist's marriage. In any case I soon learnt that she was in love with someone else, for whom she eventually left her husband.

With the coming and going in Jake's open house there were other women I found attractive, like Bunty Hammond. She wasn't particularly interested in me – she actually had her eye on Jake's husband Mike – but she was kind to me, and quite willing to be physically affectionate. But Jake's successor in my love life was another married woman, Chris Dickinson. She was a working class girl – before her marriage she had been employed as a shop assistant – with an intellectual husband, Jack, who was a party member. I often looked in on her on my way home from school. Her house was a bit further on my route home than Douglas Ambrose's. My desire for her was more chastely expressed. She obviously didn't feel about me as I did about her, but she liked me, told me a lot about herself and, among other things, taught me the song, 'A Farmer's Boy'. I never touched her in any amorous way and I was very happy simply to feel that I was in love with her.

At one stage Chris and her husband felt that they should attempt to get me interested in unmarried girls of my own age, but there was absolutely no prospect of their succeeding. I thought that girls of my own age were a silly, giggly, frivolous lot, and I didn't want to have anything to do with them. I never approved of the theory, held by communists as firmly as others, that classified people of eighteen to the middle twenties as 'youth' who allegedly had to be distinguished from adults over that age. As far as I was concerned, at eighteen you were an adult and should expect yourself, and should be expected by others, to behave like one and take life seriously. That didn't rule out all kinds of enjoyment that did not hurt other people, or experimenting with different ways of life, but then this should have been seen as equally permissible for people of *any* age. In my own case I didn't know why the Party potentates never insisted that I should join the Young Communist League instead of going straight into the Party, but I was heartily glad that they didn't.

The summer after I turned seventeen, 1935, was a momentous time for me. The Seventh World Congress of the Comintern was taking place, the first world congress since 1928. I can't hope to convey the immense pride, and joy, and satisfaction which this event brought me. We had studied the *Programme of the Communist International* and believed the picture that emerged. I thought that the leadership of the Communist International must comprise the finest revolutionary communists that the whole world could produce, and that for the Congress now in session in Moscow every Communist Party would have chosen its best members to represent it. Here, I thought, was the cream of the world communist movement, devising policies which would guide all of us in concerted revolutionary activity throughout the world for years to come.

I eagerly awaited the arrival every week of *Inprecorr* – International Press Correspondence – the world-wide weekly paper of the Comintern – which carried summaries of the Congress sessions, and I read these avidly. After a week or two special supplements, each the size of a full issue, began to appear, carrying the full texts of the main reports, extended summaries of the main contributions to discussion, and the full texts of the resolutions adopted. I think I read almost all of this material, and certainly all the main reports and most of the contributions to discussion. Nothing that I had read since I had become a communist roughly a year before had impressed me so profoundly. I saw the world communist movement carefully taking stock of the world situation as it was here and now, and showing in terms of practical action what being a communist must mean. I began to feel for the first time that I was getting a picture of the world around me that made sense all along the line.

The profound satisfaction which this brought me at the time was enhanced by the sense of relief I felt. For the Congress had declared, in effect, that the revolutionary overthrow of capitalism was not immediately on the agenda. I no longer had to try and convince myself that the final decisive battle for the overthrow of capitalism was imminent. It wasn't – the highest body of the world communist movement had *said* that it wasn't. Instead, it had presented a recognisable picture of current reality, in which the urgent and immediate tasks of revolutionaries were to halt the advance of fascism and, if possible, prevent the outbreak of another world war. To do this communisits would need to ally with all forces which could be won for cooperation for these specific aims. Ultimately they would carry with them as many as possible in a counter-offensive which would in due course develop the character of a socialist revolution. I was inspired with a new confidence in communism and an increased zeal to work for it.

I was also inspired by what I saw as the truly international character of the Congress. The four main reports presented to it were given by Pieck, a German, Dimitrov, a Bulgarian, Ercoli, an Italian (Ercoli being as we learnt later the pseudonym of Togliatti) and Manuilsky, a Ukrainian. For the first time I learnt something of the characteristic names of people of different countries – for example that the names of all the Polish delegates seemed to end in 'ski'. There was an Esthonian delegate called Kuus, and I wondered whether my English teacher Mr Doouss originated from Esthonia.

Manuilsky's report presented an inspiring picture of the international role of the Soviet Union. The Soviet party was shown as an integral part of the world communist movement, a party of exceptional importance but one whose policies must be determined by the interests of the whole international movement and not simply by those of the Soviet Union. He quoted Stalin's words:

> The working class of the USSR is part of the world working class. We have triumphed not only as a result of the efforts of the working class of the USSR, but also as a result of the support of the working class of the world. Without this support we would long ago have been torn to pieces.

Manuilsky continued:

> Our strength and our achievements belong not only to the peoples of the USSR, not only to the communist vanguard, but to the working class of all countries … Our socialist achievements belong to the toiling population of Chapei, to the Negroes of Liberia, to the Chinese, the Hindus, the Malayans: they belong to the toilers of the whole world irrespective of nation and race, language and colour, to all those who are fighting exploitation and oppression.*

In both Pieck's and Dimitrov's reports there was what appeared to me to be bold and far-reaching self-criticism. Dimitrov spoke of the 'Left-Wing Communism' against which Lenin had written in 1920 – the sort of immature conviction that you made a revolution by keeping your revolutionary purity unsullied by compromises with other groupings. He said that this was no longer the 'infantile disorder' which Lenin had called it, but a 'deeply rooted vice.' In George Miles's communism there was more than a touch of this 'deeply rooted vice' and it was a relief and a pleasure to see it so thoroughly condemned. In fact, one of the things which the Congress did was to make communists all over the world once more study *Left Wing Communism*. In it Lenin had written

> It is possible to conquer the more powerful enemy only by exerting the utmost effort, and by taking advantage of even the smallest 'fissure' among the enemies, of every antagonism of interest among the bourgeoisie of the various countries, of the smallest opportunity of gaining a mass ally, even though this ally be temporary, vacillating, unstable, unreliable and conditional.*

One example of 'antagonism of interest among the bourgeoisie of the various countries' was happening right then, for in 1935 France broke

Dimitrov, drawing by Rex, 1939

the common capitalist front against the Soviet Union by signing the Franco-Soviet Pact of Mutual Assistance. An earlier statement of the need to take advantage of such events to find allies was given in Lenin's 1918 *Letter to American Workers*. It was now re-published because of its obvious relevance to the current situation. He had written

> When, in February 1918, the German imperialist vultures hurled their forces against unarmed, demobilised Russia, I did not hesitate to enter into an 'agreement' with the French monarchists … concerning certain services that French army officers, experts in explosives, were ready to render us by blowing up railroad tracks to hinder the German invasion … The French monarchist and I shook hands, although we knew that each of us would willingly hang his 'partner.' But for a time our interests coincided. Against the advancing rapacious Germans, we in the interests of the Russian and the international socialist revolution, utilized the equally rapacious counter-interests of other imperialists. I will not hesitate to enter in a similar 'agreement' with the German imperialist vultures if an attack upon Russia by Anglo-French troops calls for it.★

The alliances which the Congress reports envisaged – both the alliances of the socialist state for limited purposes with imperialist powers like France, and the alliances within individual countries as exemplified by the socialist-communist united front only recently formed in France, the People's Fronts later (1936) formed in France and Spain, and the Kuomintang-Communist united front later formed in China – were conceived of as principled alliances which in no way curtailed the independence of the parties to them. For instance, the French communists were not bound to inhibit their attacks upon the French imperialist government by the agreement which the Soviet government had concluded with it. In 'common front' alliances the communist parties could continue to advocate their views, and could criticise their allies whenever they disagreed with them at the same time as working unitedly with them in the pursuit of commonly agreed goals. I was disturbed that one French communist leader was reported as saying that the Communist Party and the Socialist Party would henceforth cease criticising each other, but I can't now trace the speech and many have told myself that the report was not accurate.

It was through studying the Congress reports that I found a hero, a model for how I thought a communist should live. The secretary of the Comintern was the Bulgarian Dimitrov – Georgi Dimitrov – who had won international fame by his conduct in the Reichstag fire trial in 1933. It was only now that I learnt the story of this, and it made an enormous impression on me.

Shortly after the Nazis came to power, there was a great fire at the Reichstag – the German counterpart of the Houses of Parliament. The Nazis immediately declared that the communists had set fire to it as a signal for a revolutionary rising, and Torgler (the leader of the group of communist MPs) and three Bulgarians, Popov, Tanev and Dimitrov who were working in Germany at the time, were brought to trial on charges that they were implicated. The trial took place against the background of a wave of terror against the German communists. The communist accused were kept in such conditions that one of them, (Tanev, as far as I can remember) attempted (unsuccessfully) to commit suicide by cutting his veins with glass. Neither he nor Popov made any effective attempt to rebut the charges or accuse the Nazis. Torgler confined himself, in effect, to a purely 'legal' defence, raising none of the broader political implications, not replying to political attacks upon him and his Party, and accepting the services of the 'defence' counsel, a certain Dr Sack, nominated for him by the court. 'I do not wish to insult my party comrade Torgler,' said Dimitrov in his closing speech. 'He has already been sufficiently insulted by his defence, in my opinion. But I should prefer to be innocently condemned to death … than to take advantage of a defence such as the closing speech of Dr Sack.'

Dimitrov alone elected to conduct his own defence, and from start to finish fought the trial as a great political battle against the Nazis, making headlines in the world press and turning what the Nazis had planned as a great triumph into a signal defeat, for the court felt obliged to acquit the accused 'for lack of evidence.' A highlight was his cross-examination of Goering, which put Goering in such a rage that he shouted in open court, in the presence of representatives of the world press, 'Wait till I get you out of the power of this Court!' He fought in the face of every kind of difficulty, of which I would rate his virtual desertion by his communist fellow-accused as perhaps the worst. He was for a long time handcuffed day and night; his knowledge of German was imperfect and his knowledge of German law more imperfect still. He was long denied the books and the other materials that he needed for preparing his defence. While he was in prison his wife died. And in spite of all this his spirit was absolutely unbroken. He dominated the trial, towering above everyone else – the judges, the lawyers and the big Nazi leaders – and in speeches full of vigour, humour and irony, held them up to ridicule and contempt. His closing speech is deeply moving and profoundly inspiring. I quote only the words which inspired me most, words which I believed every communist worthy of the name ought to be able to speak and to mean:

I am not a lawyer, whose profession it is to defend. I am defending my political and revolutionary honour, my communist outlook, my ideals, the whole meaning and content of my life. Every sentence I utter is my blood, every sentence is the truth.*

When I came to know of all this it made him a heroic figure in my eyes. His conduct was beyond all praise. The difficulties he faced and the courage with which he overcame them were immense, and the contribution he made, at a time when he stood almost alone, to the development of the world revolutionary movement, was unforgettable. His report to the 7th World Congress, and his almost equally important reply to the discussion, now impressed me as having the same burning sincerity, and carrying the same conviction.

∞

In the aftermath of the Congress a three-way split developed in my Party branch – no longer called a cell – between George Miles, Alan Winnington and Jack Dickinson. All of them, of course, declared their fervent support for the view that the 7th World Congress had brought a new understanding to the world communist movement. But George was in fact an unregenerate, pre-7th World Congress communist, whose understanding of the 7th Congress was that it was a gigantic and fiendishly cunning hoax designed to lure socialists and others into our embrace and smother them to death. The other two, Alan and Jack, in my opinion understood the new line well, but Jack was poised, often in masterly diplomatic silence, between the other two. I think that perhaps the major concern of each of the three was to establish himself as the undisputed leader of the branch as the first step towards a position of greater power in the Party. I was annoyed and repelled by the way in which all of them schemed and manoeuvred against one another instead of fighting in the branch for their line in honest, principled discussion.

I was also very much repelled by the way in which two of the three treated women. I had known of George's exploits almost from the time I had first met him about a year earlier. The ease with which he lured women into his bed (or said he did) on the one hand excited my envy and increased my own sexual desires and on the other aroused my misgivings about whether communists really ought to do that sort of thing. By mid-1935 I had heard – from others, and perhaps inaccurately – enough of his, and Alan's, doings to be quite certain that they shouldn't.

They were indeed men 'only after one thing', as the traditional form of words has it; and I didn't think that was consistent with being a true communist, for whom it should have been impermissible to treat a woman simply as the means of his own sexual satisfaction. But that's what George and Alan both did, and if only a half of only half the stories were true, they sometimes went to outrageous lengths to be rid of the woman afterwards. Of course the 'one thing' was important to me as it is to everyone, but I never thought I would be justified in going for it regardless of the means by which I got it.

My certainty that George and Alan were wrong was strengthened when I read an extract from Clara Zetkin's *Reminiscences of Lenin*, produced as a pamphlet under the solemn title *Lenin on the Woman Question*.* But I had already reached much the same conclusions as his before I became a communist. I already believed that women had the same rights as men, should be treated as the full equals of men, and should not be exploited by men in any way. About sex outside marriage I thought what most people thought in those days, that a man and a woman should have sexual intercourse only if they both intended to marry each other, and that the aim of marriage should be a life-long partnership – though I also thought that divorce should be freely given to a partner who had decided that a continuing happy marriage was impossible. I now also thought that my intended wife would need be a communist too, or have the potentiality to become one, because only such a wife would be ready to face with me the tribulations which working as a communist was sure to bring.

That same summer something happened that took my sexual experience a stage further. In Loughton there was no Party branch but there was a branch of the Labour Party League of Youth, and I was drafted by my Party branch to go and convert it to the communist cause. There I met a sixteen-year-old girl, Iris Dyson, who fancied me and took me home to meet her mother. It soon became clear that her mother fancied me even more than she did and her interest was very warmly returned. Her name (I think!) was Elsie, but I never called her by it and never spoke of her except as Mrs Dyson, probably because, unlike Jake and Chris, she was getting on for twice my age and, as yet, not a communist comrade.

We had plenty of opportunity to be alone together because her husband was on shift work, and I had a great deal of free time, especially now that I was freed from the compulsory games on Monday and Wednesday afternoons. I learnt early on that she had entered into sexual manoevres with others than her husband (or perhaps only one other) before I appeared on the scene. My predecessor had had mild sadistic tendencies, which, it seemed, she hadn't objected to. She once showed me quite a nasty burn on her bare arm which he had inflicted on her by keeping a lighted cigarette pressed on it. But she dropped him when I arrived.

It was she who made the running but she knew how to make it appear that it was me. I was once hugging her with my erect penis pressed against her pubic mound. I said, 'Can I see it?' She said, 'No, you can't see it. But you can feel it,' which I at once proceeded to do. We were soon lying together in a bedroom upstairs. The house was overlooked by others and if we had drawn the bedroom curtains people would have wondered what was going on. But there was a cupboard next to the window, and she opened its door to block the window and then lay on her back and asked me to take off my trousers and lie on her. Then she gradually edged herself up the bed until my penis fell to the entrance of her vagina, whereupon I pushed it in. I remember the feeling of surprise and delight at how warm it was. She clearly expected that a further stage would follow, but it didn't – I had said from the start that she must first do something about contraception. I thought she should do so even with her husband, as she didn't want to be pregnant. By the next time she had bought some Rendells, a contraceptive with a cocoa-butter base. (Does it still exist?) The instructions said that you must wait for the cocoa-butter to melt before proceeding to intercourse, and against her urgings I insisted on doing this. Then one day, quite by chance, I learnt from Noel that Rendells on their own were not a reliable contraceptive. So I then made her go to a clinic and get herself fitted with a cap.

I used to tell her emphatically that bourgeois conventions about sex and nakedness were ridiculous, but she didn't at first believe that I would disregard them. She once sent me to Woolworth's to buy her a sanitary belt, thinking that I would not have the courage to ask a female shop assistant for such a thing, but I did. Another time (with Iris's permission) I went to see Iris lying in the bath – but that misfired because it made Mrs Dyson jealous. (She never let me see *her* completely naked.) I made another mistake when I first discovered Shakespeare's sonnet, 'My mistress' eyes are nothing like the sun' and read it out to her. She didn't like that at all.

In those days I was working as a paper-boy on the estate where she lived, and her house was one at which I delivered a daily paper. I had to get to the newsagent's by 5.15 am. On days when her husband was at work I would begin to push the paper through the letter box and the door would at once swing open and there she would be, dressed only in her nightie and ready for immediate love-making. I fondly believed that

102

the time it took was negligible, but soon learned from my employer that it wasn't, and he repeatedly asked me why I had been so long.

After I had finished the round I went to the railway station, took delivery of a bundle of the *Daily Worker,* which in those days the wholesalers refused to handle, and delivered them over quite a wide area (not less than five or six miles cycling). And then I got ready to cycle to school. I had a convenient hole in my right-hand trouser pocket, through which during the course of the day I would remind myself of the pleasures with which the day had begun. I always left my penis unwashed after intercourse so I could put my fingers through the hole, and then smell on them the attractive combination of coconut butter and sexual juices.

It would have been against my principles to enter into a relationship based purely on the mutual satisfaction of lust. I was convinced that I sincerely loved her. Her husband liked me and seemed to know nothing of our sexual relationship, but he must have seen that while his wife was happy and relaxed in my company, she was glum and unhappy in his. The unhappiness of her marriage seemed to me to be 90% her husband's fault and I wanted her to break with him and marry me. I was (very unrealistically!) perfectly ready to take on responsibility both for her daughter Iris and for her younger, ten-year-old daughter, who was very fond of me.

And naturally, I wanted to convert her to communism, and was confident that I could. She went along with me in this and I remember her going with me from door to door selling a penny pamphlet on Abyssinia (as Ethiopia was then called) issued by the League Against Imperialism, which was a sort of satellite organisation of the Communist International.* The Italian invasion was then under way, and was very widely condemned.

Our sexual relationship was highly satisfactory to me, and I assumed it was to her too, since she never gave any indication that it was not. The belief in those days (is it still?) was that the ideal in sexual intercourse was to come at the same time as your partner, and I assumed that we achieved this. Now I have no idea whether we did, because I feel sure that she would have faked it to make me happy. Many years later Noel pointed out to me that this kind of affair between an experienced woman and an inexperienced lad can lead to an illusion on his part that the eminent satisfaction is all his work, whereas it is more likely that, unknown to him, it is the work of his experienced partner.

Though so much older than me she was in some respects a good deal more ignorant of sexual things. She must have been born in 1903, twenty-one years later than my mother. My mother had not known until after her marriage how babies were made. Mrs Dyson knew how babies were made, but not how they were born, being under the impression that the doctor at the appropriate time cut your belly open and took the baby out. It was not until she was heavily pregnant with her first child that her mother enlightened her, telling her with a laugh, 'It comes out of the same place as it was put in.'

I feel sure that the feeling for me was more lust than love, but there were moments when at the level of fantasy at least, love did enter into it. On one occasion I was sucking her nipples and stopped to say, 'Are these for my baby to suck on?' and she burst into tears.

I don't know what difficulties the affair would have led to if it had not come to a sudden and dramatic end in the summer of 1936, about a year after it had started. Her husband had, unknown to me, grown very jealous of me. One evening she and I were sitting on the sofa as he set off for work. She said after he'd gone, 'Don't do anything yet. I think he may come back.' And so he did, bursting into the house and yelling at us both and then physically pushing me out of the house.

I went home and soon took to my bed with what was probably as much a psychosomatic illness as a physical one. She came to see me a few days later. Her husband regretted what he had done, and both he and she wanted me to resume visiting them. I had the sense not to do any such thing, which suggests that on my side too, whether I was aware of it or not, it had been lust more than love.

And that was the end of that. Except that my mother, suspecting that something scandalous had happened which could bring the fair name of Russell into disrepute, went to see my newsagent employer to see what he had to say about me. He, it appears, had a golden opinion of me, despite the longer than usual time it had recently been taking me to do my rounds. So honour was satisfied.

Twice during those last summer holidays in Loughton I visited Holme upon Spalding Moor. I cycled all the way, up the Great North Road, passing through eight counties – about 180 miles. The first time I decided I couldn't do the whole journey in a day, and so broke journey on the way up at a youth hostel near Doncaster. But I didn't feel at ease in the youth hostel, and on the way back did the whole ride in one day. The second time I did the whole ride there and the whole ride back in one day. I reckoned I could average twelve miles an hour, stopping for two eggs on chips at a transport cafe whenever I felt hungry. So that meant fifteen hours' cycling.

In Holme I stayed with Auntie Lizzie and Uncle John. Uncle John asked me each time which way I'd come, and when I told him, said, 'So

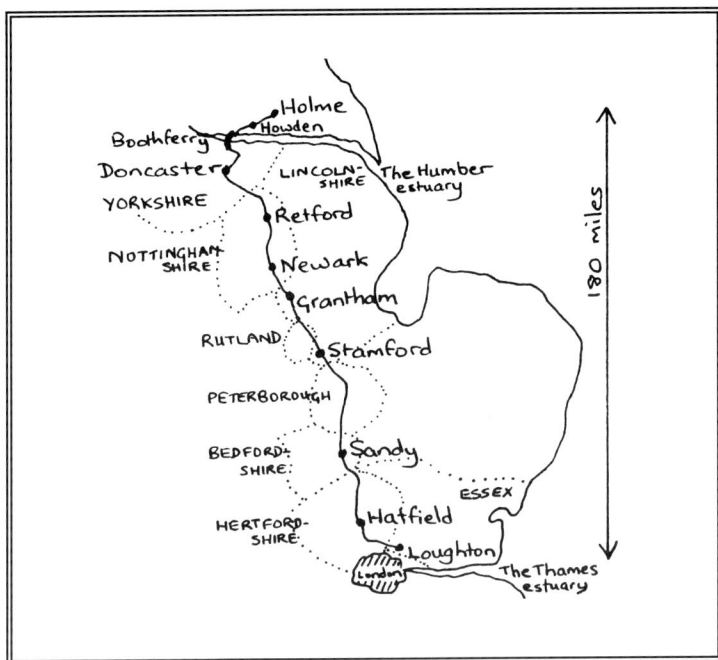

The cycle route to Holme

you'd come o'er Boothferry.' The building of the Boothferry Bridge had been a big event in the twenties, and not to be forgotten. At the dinner table there used to be a regular exchange between Lizzie and John, which went as follows.

> *Lizzie: (in her high piping voice) Do you want any more*
> *meat (pronounced mee'at) John?*
> *John: (very deaf) Mmm? (a deep interrogative growl)*
> *Lizzie: Ah say, Do you want any more mee'at, John?*
> *John: Noa, I've 'ad plenty*

One of these visits was made during the Mrs Dyson episode. I can neither remember nor even surmise why going to Holme seemed important enough to abandon the few days of sexual delights with her. But I deprived myself of them for no more than four days – one day's ride to Holme, two days there, and one day's ride back. Uncle John and Auntie Lizzie were, understandably, amazed at my insistence that having come all this way I could not stay longer.

105

Things at home didn't interest me, and I have only the haziest recollection of who was doing what. By my last year in school Wilfred was sixteen. In the two years he had been at Chigwell I had had little to do with him. To the extent that I thought about him at all I got the impression that he took little interest in anything except cricket, at which he excelled enough to win Fellows' admiration. My mother reinforced this picture by telling me that Wilfred was badly affected by my father's ignoring him in his preoccupation with me. Only recently I came across Wilfred's school reports and discovered that the picture was more complicated than that. He had at first done very well academically – his reports, no less than mine, were full of glowing comments, including for his violin playing, which he kept going throughout. But when he reached sixteen things seemed to slip. Perhaps he had his own version of a personal crisis, about which I noticed nothing.

Noel had left school at sixteen, and though never abandoning his determination to make his way into the upper classes, had been employed in undistinguished clerical jobs – one I remember was in Fenchurch Street. At home he had always behaved as though he already *was* someone of social distinction. Rex and I both remember with distaste how he treated my mother as though she were his servant, and with equal distaste how she seemed to feel that this was appropriate for one with his ambitions. He was always late leaving for work and would eat only the yolk of the poached egg she had set before him before rushing off. Then he married, a woman called Margot from a distinctly better-off family than ours, and I think went to live with them. I hardly remember seeing him in those years.

Rex was the one with whom I had most in common, for he had joined the Party at the same time I did. He had always been very good at art, and he used it among other things to express his political sympathies. On the ceiling of the attic room which he, Wilfred and I shared he had painted a huge picture of a worker carrying a red flag, inspired by the Spanish uprising of October 1934, in which the miners of Asturias held out for fifteen days before the uprising was bloodily suppressed. But it says something about my intense preoccupation with my own development during these years that I have very little recollection of what he was doing. I had the impression that he was not nearly as active as I in the local Party branch, but he now tells me that he too stood in the street selling the *Daily Worker* and that before the Churchill meeting I have spoken of he was one of those who hung over the side of the railway bridge that crossed Southend Road painting the slogan we had decided on – something I wouldn't have had the courage to do.

He was eighteen when he joined the Party and left school soon after.

He won a scholarship from Essex County Council to the Royal College of Art, but it was not enough to cover the cost of his fees, his fares to London, and the art books and materials that he would have needed, so he found a job as a commercial artist – first a badly paid one in a firm off Fleet Street, where Noel's wife also worked, and then in another that paid better but demanded very long hours. I now know what happened to his hopes of studying art, but I am not at all sure how much I was aware of at the time. Initially he managed to persuade Essex County Council to let him use his grant to pay the fees for evening classes. But the hours he had to work were so long that he often had to miss classes. Essex Council asked him to explain his poor attendance. He did, and this time asked if he could use his grant to buy art books and materials so that he could continue working on his own. But the Council couldn't see its way to doing this and he was stuck with having to repay the grant, at a rate of half a crown (one eighth of a pound) a month.

The things I remember doing with Rex would mostly have been during the summer holidays of my last years at school, 1936 and 1937. In early 1936 the Left Book Club was formed, and this became the focus of his political energies. The Club included many people who weren't in the Party, but Party members were its guiding force. Rex ran one of its many local discussion groups, and I had the impression that this suited him better than working as part of a basic party unit. By now he had got together with a woman whom he and everyone else called by her maiden name, Froude (her first name was Eleanor) and she too was part of this circle.

It was probably through Rex that I got to know Ron Horton and his wife Margaret. They were foundation members of the Party – that is, they had been in the Party since 1920 – and were looked up to accordingly. Ron, like Rex, was an artist. They lived in a cottage at the top of Goldings Hill, the hill leading out of Loughton on the road to Epping, and we were quite often there. I remember a Sunday afternoon sitting in the garden with Margaret, Rex, and other communist comrades, reading aloud, turn by turn, the Soviet writer Fiodor Panferov's novel *And then the Harvest*. Margaret and Ron also had a country cottage at a place called Cherry Green, where I stayed on a couple of occasions with Rex.

It was Margaret we got to know best. She and I shared an enthusiasm for English literature, and her judgements were always very refreshing. They were very strikingly her own, and a thing that I always liked very much about her was that she was totally unpretentious about them, never expressing contempt for other people's judgements and never vaunting her own great originality. Like many such people, she ought to

In Margaret's garden, probably 1937: L-R Ron, Froude, Margaret, Rex

have written about these things, but never did. She used to like me singing, and would sometimes ask me to sing 'The Rose of Tralee' or 'The Mountains of Mourne'. She knew other words to one of these – I can't now remember which – because to her it had a title which, for some extraordinary reason, included the words 'Queen Victoria.' Years later Margaret laughingly told a friend that she and others in our circle used to call me 'the gadfly', because I would always challenge them to justify anything they did or said which I thought was wrong.

In the summer of 1936 I decided I would like to spend my last year at school as a boarder. My parents discussed the idea with the head and he agreed, and my memory is that he excused them the extra fees which this would normally have involved.

It's difficult now to work out why I chose to do this. Becoming a boarder removed me during term time from political activity outside school – and equally from the possibility of partnered sex, leaving masturbation as the only practicable form of release. Perhaps, after an emotionally tumultuous period, I was unconsciously choosing a situation with less freedom. But that was certainly not how I explained it to myself.

I enjoyed that last year at Chigwell more than ever. The unresolved and unresolvable conflict between the establishment's values and mine had been pushed into the background. I was made a prefect, and eventually head boy, and could foregather with the other prefects for the best part of the evening in the prefects' room. My fellow-prefects liked me, and to the extent that my being a communist interested them, thought that it was some inexplicable lunacy which need not concern them.

The evenings which we prefects spent together in the prefects' room were very enjoyable. Among topics of conversation was masturbation and we compared notes as to who had done it how many times in a day. One boy asserted that he had never masturbated. I think this may have been true – he always struck me as somebody who was incapable of feeling intense pleasure in anything, and quite unaware that he was missing out on anything.

Scholarship boys had ceased to be regarded with the contempt with which I had been regarded when I had started at Chigwell, eight years earlier. There was a boy called Peel who spoke with a quite non-U accent, which people occasionally mocked, but without any marked hostility. He once brought a note to school from his mother explaining why he had been absent the previous day. A prefect called Crabbe saw this note and noticed that it was signed 'Agatha Peel', after which he always called Peel 'Agatha's boy', but all of this was quite lighthearted.

My own relations with Peel were quite amicable but there was a thing about him which I intensely disliked. He was one of those people who can excel at their schoolwork without ever having an original idea in their head. These people know what to say in order to get top marks and they say it, and that is that. I expect I also felt some resentment against him because by this method, without having any thoughts of his own, he could score marks almost as high as mine.

By now an even more disproportionate amount of the timetable was devoted to studying classics, which was regarded as the only *really* important subject. We were taught by the head, in the school library, a long, narrow room with several light oak tables arranged end to end and stretching almost the whole length of the room. He sat in a chair at the head of the table and I was always next to him sitting on his left at the top of the first table. He always read from the Oxford Classical Texts, which gave the authentic text without any kind of annotation, but we, of course, used annotated editions. He always assumed that we could not be expected to prepare more than about five lines of Homer although in fact we could easily have prepared twenty or more. We all used 'cribs' in preparing our work, that is, English translations of the work we were reading. There was a definite pecking order in these cribs. First there was Giles, and the use of Giles was very much frowned upon because the help he gave his readers was considered grossly excessive and very bad for their morale. Next came Kelly's *Keys to the Classics*, which were just about tolerated. But the approved translations were the proper literary ones, Butcher and Lang for *The Odyssey* and Lang, Leaf and Myers for *The Iliad*. Since these were much in demand, not all of us were always able to get hold of them and one very urbane character called Bird used instead the Earl of Derby's blank verse translation published in the Everyman Library. This was anything but literal, but Bird read it out word for word and the headmaster never noticed that he was doing this. At one point he interrupted Bird and said with great delight, 'Bird, you are translating into blank verse. Can you continue?' On another occasion however, Bird came unstuck. The Earl of Derby's translation included the words 'on the sand' which had no equivalent in Homer's original. The headmaster asked, 'Bird, which word means 'on the sand'?' and Bird replied '*Pusei*.' I can't remember what *pusei* actually means but it was part of a verb and of course had nothing to do with sand.

Thinking back on it, the sheer volume of Greek literature we read was astonishing. A lot of Homer's *Iliad* and some of *The Odyssey*, of which I still know the opening lines by heart. Then one tragedy each of Aeschylus, Sophocles and Euripides, a comedy of Aristophanes, and at least one of the pastoral poems of Theocritus, Bion and Moschus. In prose, some Herodotus, more than one book of Thucydides (including that which gives a vivid and harrowing account of the failure of the Athenians' Sicilian expedition), more than one of the shorter dialogues of Plato and a substantial amount of *The Republic*, and a speech of Demosthenes. And this list is almost certainly not complete. Our reading Latin was equally wide.

That I would go to Cambridge seems to have been regarded as some sort of natural phenomenon, no more requiring thought or comment than the fact that summer follows spring. At Chigwell it had always been the assumption that if you were bright enough to win a scholarship to Cambridge that's what you would do, and at home I guess that the school's assumption was simply echoed. I was duly entered for the scholarship and won a place at St John's College.

I expect my father felt his usual pride at my achievement. What anyone else in the family thought I don't know. But when I left school, Wilfred did too, without waiting the last year to complete the sixth form. He took a job as a shop assistant in Loughton, in a shop that sold electrical goods. It was within walking distance of home, and a neighbour who worked there had got him taken on. He appeared to have no ambition except to coast along and get by with the minimum of exertion, taking advantage of my parents' willingness to give him food and shelter and, I believe, contributing nothing to the cost of it.

I left for Cambridge in October 1937. I was not particularly excited at the thought, but neither did I feel any reluctance to go. I simply accepted that this was the next step in life.

It can't have been long after that my parents retired, leaving Loughton and moving to Holme on Spalding Moor, where life was considerably cheaper. So I didn't have any call to go back to Loughton. I occasionally wrote to Roper, the chaplain who had also become a friend, but I made no attempt to keep in touch with my fellow students at Chigwell. Rex stayed on in Loughton. He and Froude married and set up in a house of their own, and in later years it was from Froude that I would hear news about what had become of our mutual friends in the Woodford branch of the Party. The one I stayed closest to was Margaret Horton. For years afterwards we wrote to each other, continuing by letter the lively conversations about literature that had started in her garden.

Wilfred moved to Holme with my parents. By then I was absorbed in my new life and I hardly registered that the move was happening, but

I later discovered that he had supervised the moving of my books. They had been steadily accumulating over the years, and were the only possession I cared about. Wilfred carefully marked each with a shelf position number, so that in the new house he could reassemble them in the right order.

6

My first impression of Cambridge was of the physical beauty of the colleges. I thought St John's gateway the most beautiful in Cambridge, and its first, second and third courts too were lovely, despite one side of the first being spoilt by the incongruously huge and unlovely college chapel. But there was not enough room for all the students to have rooms in the college, so I was put into university licensed lodgings in Hertford Street, not far from the college.

In those days it was thought that a Cambridge student would be able to live comfortably on £200 a year, but I could raise only £160. Of this £80 came from Essex County Council and the rest was probably from an 'exhibition' awarded by the college on the results of the entrance exam. If I had done better in the entrance exam I would have been awarded a major scholarship, and my headmaster thought, probably correctly, that I could have won one if I had worked harder. These exams were still quite archaic. At one time candidates had to write Greek verse, and in my day you could still do this but were given the option of doing a second piece of prose instead. My college tutor later told me that one of the things that went against me was that I wrote my Greek without accents. All Greek texts were printed with accents, which I had been told at school had been devised long after classical times to show how the words would have been pronounced. But in reading Greek neither we nor our teachers took any notice of them, and they were also disregarded in working out the scansion of Greek poetry. So I had decided from the start not to bother to learn them. Anyway, I managed on my £160 and I don't remember the material side of student life causing me any distress. College regulations required us to have our evening meal in the college not less often, if I remember rightly, than three nights a week, and since Cambridge was a university for gentlemen, the food was good, probably enough to compensate for living as cheaply as possible the rest of the time.

I also felt quite confident academically. I knew I hadn't done myself justice in the last couple of years at Chigwell, and I arrived in Cambridge determined that for the next three years I would not let myself get deeply involved in party activity but would apply myself to my studies and achieve the academic standards of which I was capable.

St John's College gateway

It should have been easy enough to do, for once again I was doing Classics, and Chigwell had already given me a thorough grounding. But for reasons that I did not at first clearly understand I found it impossible to settle to work. Partly it was the problem common to many students in their first year at university, that after years spent according to a timetable prescribed for every hour of the day, I didn't now on any particular day *have* to do *anything*. But there was another reason, and in my case a more powerful one – I was in a state of emotional rejection. Far more than at Chigwell I was surrounded by an atmosphere of class privilege, and it disgusted me. We moved within a set of prescribed rituals, idiocies considered essential to make Cambridge Cambridge. I had to buy a gown and an absurdity which elsewhere is called a mortarboard but in Cambridge a 'square'. Gowns were of two kinds – undergraduate gowns came down to just below the knee and graduate gowns went down to the ankles. The tassel on the square the graduates wore hung down over the edge, but the undergraduates' tassel extended only as far as the edge, and when I went to buy it the supplier took a graduate square and in my presence solemnly cut off the overhanging bit. We had to wear gowns to lectures, tutorials and to 'hall' – the college dining hall – and this too was accompanied by its own invariable rituals. Before the meal, grace was said (I think by a graduate) and was, of course, in Latin – *Oculi omnium in te expectant, domine, et tu das eis cibum in tempore* – though it could perfectly well have been recited in the prayer book's English – 'The eyes of all wait upon thee, O Lord, and thou givest them their meat in due season.' There was no pretence of any genuine feeling, and the thing to do was to gabble it at the greatest possible speed, each reciter aiming to do it at greater speed than the last. There was a special vocabulary for the most ordinary features of student life constantly reminding us that we were different from students at lesser universities. We had 'dons' not teachers, we did not 'study' but 'read', our degree was not a degree but a Tripos, we came 'up' to Cambridge though the land around was completely flat. There was a code about how 'gentlemen' behaved which one was supposed to know instinctively. If we were out after dark we were supposed to wear both gown and square, and university officials called proctors, accompanied by college porters called bulldogs, roved the streets at night to make sure we did. So we carried our squares but only put them on if we saw proctors coming. If you were spotted not wearing it a bulldog would approach you and ask, 'Are you a member of the university, sir?' If you were, he would take your name. If you made a run for it the bulldogs were there to run after you. (The proctors couldn't do anything so undignified.) Undergraduates paid a fine of six shillings eight pence for such a lapse, and graduates thirteen shillings four pence. It was all ridiculous.

The university population seemed to me universally phoney. The students were only too eager to receive the priceless gift that an Oxbridge education confers – the invincible conviction that Oxbridge men are superior to all other mortals. The dons appeared on the surface to be open, friendly, helpful, and interested in you personally, but if you were naive enough to act as if they meant all this, they rapidly drew back. They had not the least understanding of the life of ordinary people nor any desire to acquire such an understanding. Quite soon after my arrival my tutor raised the question of what I would be doing during the long vacation. If I liked to travel in Greece and Italy, he said, the College would pay my expenses. I explained that I would have to get work in the vacations so that I could pay my parents for my keep. If the College was willing to help, it would be far more useful if they could make me a grant so that I would not have to work and could devote my time to study. But such considerations didn't fit into their scheme of things.

I felt alien from it all, not belonging and definitely not wanting to. I felt increasingly desperate, and took defence in a fierce pride in being a communist, in being able to see through the worthless social attitudes that surrounded me, in knowing there was a powerful movement for change in the world, and that I was part of it. My resolution not to get involved in political activity didn't last.

The manner of my being re-connected with the Party organisation was this. Before I had come to Cambridge George Miles had spoken of me to a Cambridge student communist he knew* who had just taken his degree. This student mentioned me to Ram Nahum, who was in those days the leading student communist at Cambridge. Ram wrote to me saying they looked forward to seeing me in the Cambridge student branch, but because of my resolution I made no attempt to find him once I arrived. Still, I used to go to the Party bookshop to buy communist literature, and one day I was in there buying, among other things, the fortnightly journal of the Comintern, *The Communist International*, when another student came up to talk to me. It was Ram – he had guessed that the unknown buyer of *The Communist International* might be me.

Having been identified, I had to promise Ram to go and meet him and his fellow-members of the branch secretariat – the branch didn't have a one-person secretary – in his room at Pembroke College. This in itself was a shock. In their upper-class ways – indefinable, but unmistakable – they seemed no different from the all the rest of the Cambridge students. When I arrived they were making coffee in one of those things consisting mainly of a clamp, a glass retort sort of thing, and a spirit lamp. I'd never in my life drunk coffee with anyone who possessed one of these things, and felt an inadequacy and an embarrassment which I am sure that they sensed and almost equally sure they were quite at a loss to comprehend. Obviously, there's nothing uncommunist in owning a percolator (if that is what it's called) and nothing communist in feeling acutely embarrassed in the company of someone who does; but there it was.

The members of the secretariat then began to question me. A good reputation had preceded me – they had clearly been told that they were about to receive a valuable addition to their forces – but the conclusion they seemed to have drawn from this was that I must be well-read in the works of Lenin. I wasn't, and said so. I had read little more than the things I have already mentioned reading. I got the impression that they thought that all this was very elementary, light-weight stuff, and that the works of Lenin were the real thing. Their obvious disappointment in me, plus the fact that as far as I remember they never even asked what practical communist *activity* I had done, disconcerted me and made me feel uncomfortable. I was very glad when our interview was over and I could get away.

In my isolation I had held on to my sense of what it was to be a communist, and comforted myself by feeling connected in spirit if not in daily life to people who shared those high ideals. Now I had found these Cambridge fellow communists, and they were far from what I regarded as true communists. Most of them weren't, as people, substantially different from the other students. All seemed to be from upper class homes – from the aristocracy, the bourgeoisie, and the professional and upper middle classes. All were from public schools or the highest grade of grammar schools. None of them had any contact with people of classes below their own, nor had it occurred to them that there was any reason why they *should* have such contacts. The everyday social conventions of their milieu were the norm, and where they encountered (in people like me for example) conventions which did not match theirs they found them quaint and laughable. Ram, who seemed better than the rest, was from a family of wealthy industrialists and had the same upper-class ease. He took his responsibilities in the branch seriously but he and the others were strictly *university* communists – most had become communists at university and all their communist activity was conducted there. When the small number of us who had been members of local units of the Party urged that they should be communists for fifty-two, and not just thirty, weeks of the year, and should, during the generous university vacations, work in the Communist Party branches in the places where they lived, this was an idea that had never occurred to them. Meanwhile, in the world outside fascism was growing and the threat of war loomed nearer.

A Jesuit friend of mine would say that it was providential that at this stage I met among my fellow communists one who was recognisably human, Bob Hone. If I had not met Bob and rapidly become close friends with him, I doubt whether I could have stood Cambridge for more than a term. He was the son of a militant socialist bricklayer – I never knew of anyone else there who was of working class origin, and he was the only one I think in our communist student branch. I felt immensely relieved to find someone whose understanding of what it meant to be a communist was the same as mine. He understood and shared the feelings that had been inspired in me by the life of Georgi Dimitrov, the conviction that communism was 'the whole meaning and content' of his life. And it was a great comfort to find that he too felt less than satisfied with the quality of our student fellow communists. Bob once said at a branch meeting that most of our members led double lives; in purely political activity they were communists, but in the rest of their lives they weren't communists at all. The remark, of course, was greeted with superior amusement.

I spent all the time I could in his company, and began to feel less desperate. Bob liked music a lot and I would often sit in his room listening with him to the records he played. I remember being delighted with Bach's Brandenburg Concerto no. 6 and with the song from Gluck's *Orpheus and Eurydice* in which Orpheus laments her loss. On one occasion he put me painfully in my place. A record was playing and I started to say something to him. He took absolutely no notice, and after the record was finished told me that when you listen to music you listen to music and don't talk.

I was once there when his father came to visit him. He had had a hard time during the worst days of mass unemployment, because in those days when jobs were scarce militant trade unionists didn't usually stand much chance of getting one. Bob admired his father's ability to see through the appalling jargon which the Comintern then used – e.g. calling people 'counter-revolutionary spiders' (!) – to the essence of what was being said. On one occasion he picked up a copy of the *Communist International* that Bob had in his room, read a page or two of it, and then said 'This seems to be a good book, Bob.' (Like many working class people he called magazines and periodicals books.)

Bob used to enjoy telling me of the odd behaviour or outrageous sayings of some of his friends and acquaintances. One, confronted with a dish of something he'd not encountered before, would first stare at it, then smell it, and then put it to his ear to listen to it. Another used to make what Bob considered an absurd distinction between 'clean dirt' and 'dirty dirt.' Another used to announce that Milton's *Lycidas* was the most insincere poem in the English language. He used to laugh at some of the words of revolutionary songs. Someone had set communist words to the Nazi Horst Wessel song (which celebrated Horst Wessel as a martyr to the Nazi cause). It went, in part

We march along the road to revolution, while Hitler rants & Mussolini howls

We workers have grown weary of their ravings

We'll thrust their lies back down their filthy jowls

He thought this last line was especially laughable. I asked him who had written it, and to my surprise, still laughing, he said '*I did.*'

Through Bob I got to know two others in the branch who, like him and me, had experience of life in the real world, so to speak, that is, of work in an ordinary local branch of the Party. As a group we began to exercise a belligerent pressure upon the branch, and I became fired with zeal to convert these part-communists into proper communists. One of our targets was the rating of knowledge of theory above experience of practical work. This had been evident in my first interview with the secretariat and was quite general. When the time came to elect a new branch committee the outgoing committee would, in accordance with general communist practice, present a list of its recommended candidates. This list always included the names of comrades who were said to have a 'high political level'. Typical of those so described were comrades who would remark after someone had made a report on the political situation that 'the comrade failed to mention the revolutionary upsurge in the Philippines' – or wherever. (*Inprecorr,* the Comintern weekly of those days, was always discovering revolutionary upsurges in different parts of the world.) Included on the outgoing committee's list was the name of Eric Hobsbawm, who was a year senior to me and widely considered to have a high political level. Our group would oppose this nomination on the ground that his high political level didn't find any significant expression in the practical work of the branch.★

As a group we considered ourselves the true, proletarian element in the branch, but only Bob had much justification for this view. It was true that we were free of the upper-class limitations of most of our fellow-members of the student branch, and this did make us, in that respect, better communists than they; but the qualification is an important one. In other respects Ram, for example, was a better communist than at any rate I was, though I wasn't very willing to recognise it at the time. In my own 'proletarian' attitude there was a good deal that was phoney. It was not until at least nine to ten years later that I got rid of the inverted snobbery which made me allow people to think that I was a true son of the industrial proletariat, and made me reticent about the fact that although up to the age of ten I had grown up with mainly working class children, my parents were 'non-political' Tories; that my mother was a great snob, descended on her mother's side from farmers and on her father's side from schoolmasters, and that my father, though the son of working class parents, came from the 'respectable', know-your-place section of the working class.

I can't claim that my neglect of my studies was due to immersion in political activity all day and every day – and even if it had been, this would not have been a sufficient justification. Harry Pollitt, then (and for nineteen years thereafter) General Secretary of the Party, had announced that for a communist student it was a duty to be 'first a good student', and theoretically I accepted this. I have pleasant memories of what little studying I did do. I enjoyed the lectures of T R Glover, which covered the same ground as his book *The Ancient World*.★ I liked him as a man too. He always spoke with a humorous directness which I guess owed something to his Canadian background. He was for a time a sort of academic tutor to a group of which I was a member, and in line with Cambridge practice, set me to write essays on subjects not related to the subject we were reading. I still have a short essay which I wrote for him under this dispensation on Wordsworth's canons of poetry, which he liked and which I still think is OK. I also liked the lectures of Angus on pre-Socratic Greek philosophy. He once remarked that there are two kinds of philosophy – a kind that asks 'How?' and another that asks 'Why?' – and that the latter kind is useless. I have always agreed with this, with the reservation that I realise that the question 'Why?' can sometimes be equated with 'How?'

But it was a difficult time to curtail political activity and concentrate on ancient Greece. The need to fight the rise of Fascism was ever more urgent, for we knew that if we did not succeed, Europe was almost certainly headed for war. I and thousands of others were fired by the conviction that if enough people took action, we could change history. If we could persuade our fellow students of the magnitude of the issues facing the world, we could not only halt the spread of fascism and prevent the outbreak of another terrible world war, but also build a broad movement to demand an end to exploitation by the powerful over the rest, and bring about the kind of society in which all human beings would be valued.

It was an inspiring vision, and large sections of the population shared it with us. Everywhere around us there was a sense of the urgency of political issues. This was perhaps most strikingly demonstrated in the widespread public sympathy for the Spanish Republic's battle against Franco. In February 1936, the year before I went up to Cambridge, there had been elections in Spain in which the parties of the People's Front had won 256 seats, while the parties of the right won only 143. In July Franco and his generals had staged a right-wing revolt against the legitimate People's Front government, and a war broke out which would last the best part of three years.

The fight of the Spanish republicans caught the imagination of thousands of young people from many countries, and many gave up their studies or jobs to go and to fight alongside the Spanish in the International Brigade. But this was simply the most colourful manifestation of a significant shift in political attitudes. For me personally the most remarkable evidence of it was the change in my mother. She had shown no signs at all of interest in contemporary politics, but now, without any prompting from Rex and me, she became a fervent supporter of Republican Spain and was full of indignant contempt for right-wing British 'democrats' who supported rebellious generals who had to resort to using colonial troops against a democratically elected government. She wrote a letter in this vein to our Tory MP, one Major Carver, with a result which I shall relate in due course.

There was also a widespread admiration for what was being achieved in the Soviet Union. In America and Europe the great economic crisis of 1929, set off by the Wall Street crash of that year, had shaken people's confidence in capitalism. The socialist economy of the Soviet Union experienced no such crash, and people were naturally interested to find out why. They were impressed by the rapid industrialisation of the country, completed with the fulfilment of the first Five Year Plan in 1934, and by the great social achievements in the provision of, for example, education and medical care. Admiration of soviet achievement extended far beyond the confines of the communist movement. The American liberal Lincoln Steffens visited the USSR and said on his return, 'I have seen the future, and it works.' In Britain the trend is well

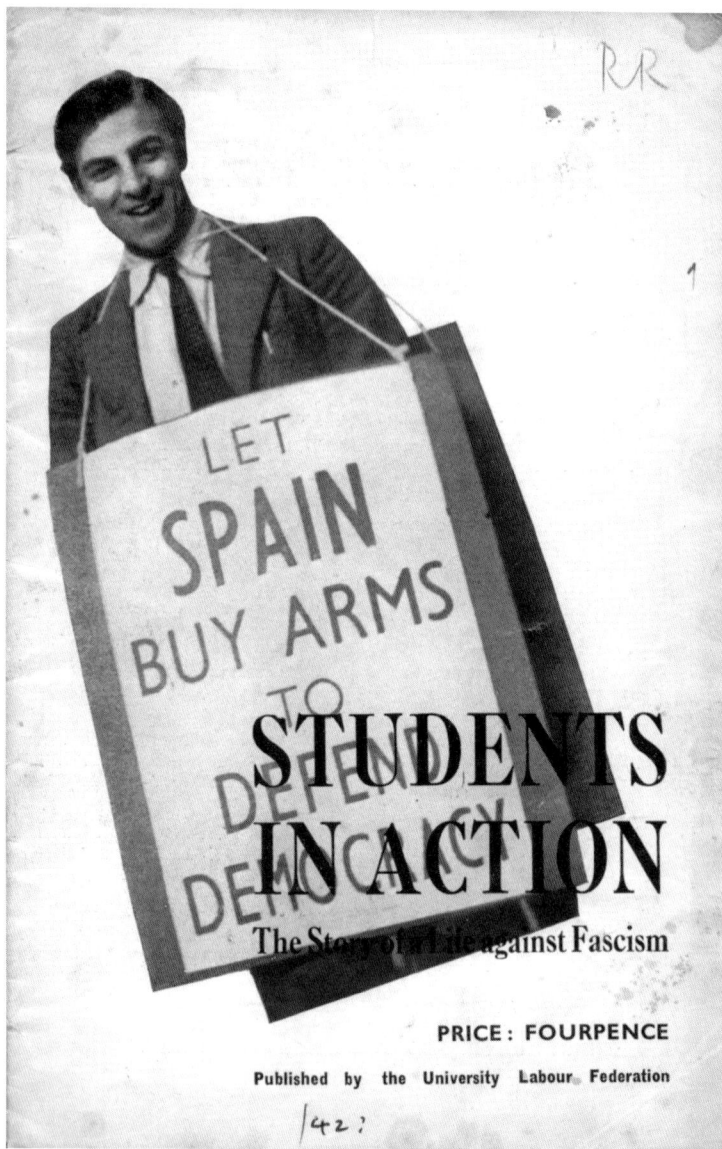

Ram Nahum; cover of a pamphlet published after his early death

described by Andrew Sanders in his *Short Oxford History of English Literature*:

> The beleaguered Bolshevik state, first assaulted by armed Western intervention, then wracked by civil war and the destructive manoeuvres of international capital, emerged for many postwar intellectuals as the model progressive society.★

He points out that Sidney and Beatrice Webb, whose theory of socialism (though Sanders does not say this) was about as far removed as it could be from that of the communists, published in 1935 their massive study of soviet society and entitled it *Soviet Communism: a New Civilisation?* and in later editions dropped the question mark.

The mood of the time was reflected in many aspects of life. These were the days when Unity Theatre flourished, its productions reflecting a militant anti-fascism and a broad acceptance of socialist ideals. Unity made a real mark in the world of theatre. Some actors who later became famous began their acting careers there; its active supporters included people like Michael Redgrave and Paul Robeson. I remember it best for its satirical reviews. Many of their songs expressed the growing indignation at government policies, both at home and internationally –

Love-on-the-dole- oh that's a luxury we can't afford, for they don't believe in

Love-on-the-dole on the Unemployed Assistance Board

There was a song to the tune of 'Let him go, let him tarry.' The man sings –

My girl she said "I'm willing for to raise a family

But if you won't get wed you'll find no happiness with me."

I told her she was crazy with conditions what they are,

For I care too much for children for to want to be a pa.

123

She rebukes him

My girl she said 'Defeatist! You're a traitor to the cause,
Our children won't be fighting in imperialistic wars
Our children won't be cannon fodder waiting to be killed
They'll be workers in the Britain that the working class will build.'

One of the Unity Theatre actors whose name I don't remember was a marvellous mimic, and Chamberlain's idiosyncracies made him an easy target for mimicry. At the time of the disastrous appeasement policy the actor would appear on stage in Chamberlain's old fashioned style of dress, with his ever-present umbrella, and would start to speak in a hesitant, monotonous, uninspiring voice. 'When I was a little boy' – pause – 'my mother told me' – pause – 'If at first you don't succeed' – pause – 'try, try, try again.' – pause – 'That's what I am doing now.'

What his government was actually doing was the subject of several Unity songs, like this one set to a well-known popular tune

Who starves workers on the UAB? Who put tuppence on the workers' tea?

Who wants war because he'd like to see swollen profits sweated out of you & me?

Who's laid plans upon conscription bent? No-one but the National Government [1]

That is why the ranks of labour all united shout, "Cut your stick & beat it

Neville! – Clear out!"

For people who have had their formative adult years in much later times when the political lines were less starkly drawn, it is probably impossible to imagine what those days were like. This is not in the least surprising, because even those who experienced them sometimes find it difficult to recreate for themselves the full picture. I recently read what Dorothy Parker, no doubt with all this in mind, wrote years later. 'The 1930s were progressive days. We thought we were going to make the world better. I forget why we thought it, but we did.' Though I haven't forgotten as much as she had (or said she had) I too have needed to think quite hard about this, both to reassess my own views, and also to try to explain it to people who did not live through that time.

This is not easy, because people today, including progressive people, already have a picture of those days, which they have been given by a long and still continuing process of 'suppression of the truth and suggestion of the false' *(suppressio veri; suggestio falsi)*. That picture is an exceedingly inadequate one. It represents Britain's rulers as doing all they could to avert war by making concession after concession to Hitler, until at last they realised that there was nothing for it but to make a stand. There is, of course, truth in that picture, but another vital element of the truth is completely missing, one which has been discreetly 'forgotten' by history – that is, the active sympathy for Hitler which dominant sections of the British and French ruling classes felt. Albert Axell's recent book, *Stalin's War* ★ gives examples of this:

> The desire to improve relations with Adolf Hitler was at that time strong among some British diplomats. It is recorded by the German Ambassador Herbert von Dirksen that Lord Halifax [who was Foreign Secretary at the time] told him it would be 'the finest moment in my life' to see the Führer drive along the Mall in front of Buckingham Palace together with the British royal family.

If many of Halifax's friends were less explicit than he was, that was more because of their distaste for Hitler's style than for the substance of the Nazi outlook. They saw fascism as a 'bulwark against Bolshevism' and the containment and if possible destruction of Bolshevism had been their dominant aim since 1917.

Their active sympathy for fascism became completely evident with the outbreak of the Spanish civil war. Almost the entire British press – with the honourable exception of the now defunct *News Chronicle* – from the first reported Franco's forces in the most favourable light, giving them the ludicrously inappropriate name of 'Nationalists' – 'nationalists' who saw themselves as fighting for the interests of their nation by bringing in colonial troops and massive aid from Italy and Germany to overthrow its democratically elected government. These British and French 'democrats' thought democracy was fine so long as it did not threaten their dominance; when it started to do that, fascism was much to be preferred.

The war in Spain had become an international issue. Mussolini sent 50,000 men to Franco's aid, and Hitler sent 16,000 men and the Condor Legion of the German airforce.★ The British and French contribution was to adopt a policy of so-called 'non-intervention' on the absurd plea they if they denied the legitimate Spanish republic the opportunity of importing arms, the Germans and Italians would refrain from arming Franco.

If the traditional accounts are at pains to conceal the very active sympathy of the British and French dominant classes for Hitler, they conceal also the fact that these governments had an alternative to their appeasement policies. They could have concluded an alliance with the Soviet Union to stand firm against Hitler and to come to each other's aid if any of them was attacked. That such an alliance was a practical possibility had already been shown. In February 1935 France had led the way by signing a mutual assistance pact with the Soviet Union. It did not go through without opposition – there were many who were hostile to any alliance with the Soviet Union, even to save themselves from aggression by Hitler.★ But the pact *was* signed, and the Soviet Union, communists everywhere, and many non-communists everywhere, urged Britain to follow France's suit so that a British-French-Soviet mutual assistance pact could be concluded, and form what we called a 'peace front'.

If nowadays people aren't even aware that this was ever a serious possibility, that is not surprising, because for the past sixty years and more they have never been told. They are still not being told. I recently read a history booklet for schools, *International Relations, 1919-39*, first published in 1987 and frequently reprinted since.★ In it Franco's forces are still called 'the Nationalists' and the French-Soviet pact is not even mentioned.

Axell reminds us this policy predates Chamberlain:

Some months before he was replaced by Neville Chamberlain in 1937, the British Prime Minister, Stanley Baldwin, discussing with colleagues Hitler's desire for living space, said 'And if he should move east, I should not break my heart.'★

With Chamberlain as Prime Minister this trend was even more pronounced. He once said that 'any agreement with Russia would become a yoke around Britain's neck.'★ His aim was not in fact to stop fascism nor to prevent a disastrous war in Europe, but simply to save *Britain* from being involved if a war should happen. Behind the appeasement policy was the hope that Hitler would attack the Soviet Union, and that Germany and the Soviet Union would weaken each other, to the considerable advantage of Britain and France.

The British government was fully aware that a Soviet-French-British pact was a realistic option. An item in *The Guardian* published on 1 January 1970 says

The Cabinet papers for 1939, published this morning, show that the

126

Second World War would not have started in that year if the Chamberlain Government had accepted or understood Russian advice that an alliance between Britain, France and the Soviet Union would prevent war, because Hitler could not then risk a conflict against major powers on two fronts.★

Churchill, who until 1937 had himself been an advocate of 'appeasement', later declared that 'there never was a war more easy to stop.'★

The fact is that the British and French governments had the chance both to halt the spread of fascism in Europe, and to prevent war – yet for six years together they pursued policies which actually *strengthened* the forces they eventually had to go to war against in 1939. That was a lot clearer to people at the time than it has been since, and it was one of the factors that moved many intellectuals in a left wing direction. They saw that it was the left which consistently pushed for policies which could have created an effective counter-pressure to Nazism, and could have saved us all from the disasters which in the end engulfed Europe and much of the world.

The understanding of international issues which people on the left had at the time took into account these vital aspects of the situation which the traditional accounts omit. It is of course the case that our own understanding proved later to have been limited in important respects, and I shall say more about all this later. But in our understanding of the international situation we were better informed, and had a better estimate of the real dangers, than our adversaries. A Franco-British-Soviet pact of mutual assistance was the outstanding need at the time, to prevent war, and to halt Hitler's advance.

The picture as we communists in the Cambridge branch saw it in 1937 and early 1938 was this. Alongside the threat of fascism, there were signs that progressive forces were gaining ground. Already in 1935 the united capitalist front against the Soviet Union had been breached, and that too by France, a major capitalist power. Within a year of the 7th World Congress of the Comintern announcing a popular front strategy, people's front governments had been formed, first in France and then in Spain. The armies of the Spanish Republic were fighting against the rebel forces of Franco and his generals and seemed as likely as not to prevail. There were national liberation movements against colonial domination in India and elsewhere. All this could lead to the world-wide victory of socialism, and we expected it to happen in the near future. Pieck, one of the leaders of the Comintern, had said in 1935:

Not quite fifty years were required from the first real bourgeois revolution, the Great French Revolution of 1789, to the time when a wave of bourgeois revolutions swept over Europe, destroying the power of feudalism ... A considerably shorter period of time will be required from the victory of the first socialist revolution, the great October Revolution of 1917, to the victory of socialism throughout the entire world.*

We were optimistic, and we, with thousands of non-communists had every right to be so. The fact that subsequent events showed how grossly *over*-optimistic we were does not invalidate that judgement.

The atmosphere among students at Cambridge reflected the prevailing mood in the country. Of a student population of about 5000 about 1000 were members of a Socialist Club, a united socialist-communist organisation that was under our predominant influence. In the year before I arrived several student communists had been among those who went to join the International Bridgade, and one, John Cornford, had been killed in action in Spain. None of those in my years did – by this time the Party was not encouraging its members to do so, arguing that we could serve the Spanish republic better by doing all we could to build up mass pressure to compel the British government to change its disastrous policy. And this was what we tried to do. I remember one satisfying confrontation with the forces of reaction when some members of the International Brigade, now returned from Spain, were invited to address a meeting at Trinity College. A group of rowdies turned up but took one look at the line of International Brigaders sitting in the back row and decided that discretion was the better part of valour.

As a branch we were active and well organised. In every college where we had members, these constituted a group; larger groups, in which two or three of these college groups came together, met for political education and joint discussion of our work in the university. Aggregate meetings of the whole branch were held at regular intervals. The branch elected a branch committee of about twelve, of which I became a member, and the committee elected a secretariat of three to five members. The secretariat met regularly three times a week at midday, and meetings could be called in emergency even between these times, so that we could react almost immediately to all new developments as they occurred.

We stressed friendly joint discussions of differing viewpoints between all those who were genuinely concerned with the growing menace of war and with the fascist threat to democratic liberties. We urged 'people's front' policies, taking proper account of the diverse levels of consciousness to which we had to appeal, and seeking to mobilise, at each level, the maximum unity around the demands appropriate to that level. We also tried to prepare for the formation of genuinely representative democratic organisations of all students, then non-existent in Cambridge, like the students' unions in the universities other than Oxbridge, and to develop ways of linking Cambridge students with the National Union of Students. At one stage we had formal joint 'popular front' activities with the liberals. Unity with the socialists on a common programme we already had, for the Labour Party leadership in that period tolerated the existence of a single socialist student organisation, and did not operate the proscription against communists which was in force, for instance, in the Labour Party League of Youth.

There was a strong sense of internationalism, of solidarity with people in many countries who were trying to create a better society. There was an International Brigade songbook, produced in Spain, with songs from all of the countries from which volunteers had come; and a book of Soviet songs with words in English. A member of our branch, Harry Hancock, could play the piano and I got him to play me the tunes of the ones I didn't know. Another we used was a new book of left wing songs that appeared about this time, which in the spirit of the popular front included songs about nationalist struggles that weren't particularly communist. Some of the ones I liked best were settings of new words to traditional songs, like the beautiful old Welsh tune, 'Cum Rhondda'

Land of Wales, so long subjected, when will you awake from sleep? From your hills a voice of thunder bid you your own harvest reap?

Another moving tune was the pre-revolutionary Russian funeral march used in the film of Gorki's *Mother*, to which a left wing poet had set words (the last line of which I regrettably can't remember)

Our banners are lowered, they droop on the street And the pulse of our sorrow is marked by our feet We bring to a rest that their lives never knew

Our comrades who fought & died to save the many from the few.

But we will not mourn them as lost to the fight

Nor death shall defeat them, whom none could defeat

Their spirit lives on in the fight we maintain ...

As internationalists we were concerned to support movements for colonial liberation, and of these the most prominent in our minds was the movement for independence in India. Nehru's *Autobiography* had been published in Britain in 1936, and many had been influenced by it and by his outspoken anti-fascist views. Gandhi had visited Britain and made a different kind of impact, with his identification with the poor, and his commitment to pacifism. Ever since I had joined the party I had taken a keen interest in Indian affairs. I had had some slight contact with Krishna Menon and his India League, and regularly took its publications. Now for the first time I had the chance to meet Indian fellow students and I became close to a couple of them – Indrajit Gupta ('Sonny', as he was called) and Mohan Kumaramangalam. We all knew that they must be at any rate communist sympathisers, but the Communist Party of India was illegal so they could not openly avow that they were communists.

∞

The university vacations – Christmas, Easter and summer – were long, and I spent them in Holme upon Spalding Moor, cycling there and back. Bob too used to cycle to and from his home, and we would laugh a lot at things we saw on the way. To this day you can still see painted on the sides of houses advertisements for products which no longer exist, and in those days there were more than there are now. One which amused us advertised

Moore's Meridian Breast Reliever
Red rubber bulb and glass receiver

130

I had a habit (and still have) of setting words to any bit of music that they fit, and fitted this one to the tune to which someone had set Edward Lear's nonsense poem about the chair and table.

The village looked much the same, and material conditions had changed little over the twelve years since we had moved away. There was still an outside lavatory where you sat on a wooden seat and emptied your bowels into a capacious bucket, the contents of which had to be buried from time to time in a pit dug for that purpose. It was good to escape the pretentious atmosphere of Cambridge and be back among ordinary people, and surrounded again by Yorkshire speech – not just the accent, but the way people said things. On the Hasholme farm with Uncle John's son Arthur, I noticed that a hole had been made in the brick wall of an enclosure where pigs had been kept. When I asked how this had happened he said the pigs had done it. I expressed my surprise, and he said, 'Yes, they're wonderful strong in the snout, is a pig.'

During my first vacation I crossed swords, or, more accurately, attempted to cross swords, with my father. Before I went up to Cambridge my headmaster had got me a grant of another £40 from somewhere, but this sum was paid not to me, but to my father, who, of course, spent it. When I had learnt of this I had written him an indignant letter, to which he had not replied. Now, in my first vacation, before I could say anything to him he said, 'I didn't much like the tone of the letter you wrote to me' – and that was that. My mother knew of this and told me, quite mildly, 'It's no good saying anything to Daddy. He can never see that he's ever done anything wrong.' I was impressed by her frankness, and said no more.

People in the village took some pride in the fact that someone who could almost be said to be from Holme was now at Cambridge. I subsequently discovered that the vicar was a Cambridge man and that St John's had been his own college.* When he learnt that I too was now at St John's he presented me with an India paper volume of the complete works of Homer.

I had intended to get paid work during the vacations so that I could pay my parents for my keep. But the only work available in Holme was farm work and that of course was seasonal, with little to do in the fields in winter. So I spent most of my time reading. I remember being absorbed, all day and every day, in Fielding's *Tom Jones*, inspired to read it by Doouss's judgement that it was 'the greatest novel in the English language.' I loved it, and went on to read all his other novels – and lots else besides. I remember also the great impression which Catherine Carswell's wonderful *Life of Burns* made on me. I went on to enjoy his poet-

131

Returning to Holme-on-Spalding Moor

ry. The fact that his love poetry is about ordinary country lasses appealed to me a lot, and I was not in the least put off by the need to discover the meaning of a lot of the Scottish words.

In the summer there was more chance of field work. I had none of the experience and none of the skills of the male agricultural labourers, but in busy seasons farmers took on women to do the less skilled tasks, a woman 'ganger' being called on to find the necessary hands, and I had (to say the least of it) no objection to working with women. Both Wilfred and I were taken on by a ganger whom everyone called Ma Pearson – I still don't know what her first name was. Ma's husband Jim was a pigman to a farmer named Thornton Ibbetson, and it was always, if I remember rightly, Thornton for whom we worked. The rate of pay was sixpence an hour, so for a forty-hour-week we earned £1. Most of the work that I remember was picking up potatoes. A horse-drawn plough would move along the potato rows turning up the roots with the potatoes clinging to them, and we would move along behind it, on our knees all day, with a large basket which we would fill and then take up to a point in the field where we would pour its contents into a sack.

The composition of the gang was a fairly stable one of half a dozen or so. There were two young women, Ma's strapping daughter Vera and Marie Livesey (née Sherwood), two years older than me; and a number of middle-aged women, including Rose Oretta Cox, Mary Cox (no relation), and less regularly, Mrs Emmeline Danby and Mrs Wiles, whose first name I never knew. I liked all the regulars. Ma was a big fat woman with a swarthy complexion, black hair and a handsome face marred only by a hare lip. She was a very jolly woman, in free and easy relationship with her gang, whom, I later learnt, she worked appreciably less hard than other gangers worked theirs. She was always singing the praises of her elder daughter Rosie. 'Oor Rosie, missis, she's beautiful! And there isn't a purer girl in Holme than oor Rosie.' And indeed Rosie was pretty in an insipid sort of way, though I always thought Vera more attractive. Their use of language was interesting. They always said 'redchestered' instead of 'registered' and would talk about 'liberating' their baskets instead of 'emptying' them. There was a lot of singing of lewd songs, enjoyed by one and all. Ma was quite foul-mouthed, but that suited me all right, because I was too, (and so was Wilfred). On one occasion she had emptied several baskets into a sack and hitched it up to make room for more only to find that the sack was rotten, so that the bottom fell out, whereupon she exclaimed with great fervour, 'damn and fuck and bugger and blast it.'

Ma liked to show me off to any of her acquaintance that appeared upon the scene – 'This is Ralph Russell, missis, from Cambridge College.' She also had a fund of anecdotes, many of which she would introduce with the words, 'And will you believe this, then?' One concerned 'a gypsy lad' who became 'a hofficer in the British Harmy, missis, with a leather case, and him a gypsy lad!'

It was quite hard work, and, naturally, harder for me than for the others, who had long been used to it. Later we worked behind a machine called a spinner. This was a tractor-drawn thing with – I don't quite know how to describe it – a row of spinning spokes which turned up the soil more rapidly and effectively than the plough. Following this I learnt for the first time what it meant to have to work at a speed set by a machine, like factory workers on a conveyor belt, and an unpleasant experience it was. The spinner would go up one row, turn and come down another some way distant from the first, and then turn again to go up the row next to the first. You had to have finished the first row before it came round again. I regularly fell behind, and Marie Livesey, who generally worked on the row next to mine, would leave her own row to help me out.

I had known Marie (and her sister Lena) as a child at school and had always thought her a very pretty child. Between my starting school at five and leaving Holme for Loughton at the age of seven, we must often have encountered each other. I now proceeded to fall in love with her. But she was married, and I had resolved after my sultry episode with Mrs Dyson that I would never again allow myself to get involved with a married woman. So I refrained from declaring my love for her, although I guess that she would soon have had a pretty good idea of what I felt. I didn't know her husband, who was called Sid Livesey, because he had long been in a TB sanatorium quite a long way from Holme. In those days advanced TB was fatal and we all knew that he was dying. I thought to myself that I would then propose marriage to her. I know that Ma Pearson and the others saw the closeness that had developed between me and Marie, and though they didn't say anything, and though Marie showed no signs of reciprocating, they showed fairly unmistakably their disapproval of her, a married woman 'encouraging' another man, and doubtless imagined us in situations far more colourful than the facts at that time warranted. I didn't take much notice of this, but it did bother her.

Wilfred, with his way of instinctively adapting to the people around him, had now become part of village society as once he had identified with the local children in Loughton. Though we worked alongside each other in the fields, for me this was a temporary part of life, while he was in Holme all year round. Like other local men – and unlike me – he

Village work: with Wilfred, digging a pit to empty the lavatory bucket

Ma Pearson

The women of Holme: The Women's Institute; my mother back L, laughing

used to spend evenings in the pub, and knew everyone. I don't think he bothered too much about what did or didn't lie ahead. I began to be dimly aware that he was in in some ways influenced by me. He had begun reading on political themes, and his sympathies had been particularly caught by colonial liberation struggles. After years of being on the edges of the things Rex and I were interested in, he now seemed to be developing in a somewhat similar direction.

He occasionally talked to me about personal things. There was a woman in the village called Dot Livesey (married to the brother of Marie's husband) who somehow exuded sexual attraction. I felt it myself, and was slightly puzzled by it because she wasn't particularly beautiful. But Wilfred felt it more powerfully and was I think was confused as to what to do with these feelings. Another time when we were talking I was mocking the then current idea that a woman wouldn't become pregnant unless she and her partner came simultaneously. Wilfred's face fell – he didn't say anything, but it was obvious that he too had assumed he could rely on this as a safety device.

It was through Wilfred that Marie and I first found opportunities of spending some time together. Her (unmarried) sister Lena took a fancy to Wilfred, and it was considered OK for her and Marie to visit Wilfred and me together at my parents' house, where the four of us would then retire to my bedroom. Soon after these visits had started Marie said to me, 'Do you and Wilfred like me and Lena?' I said, 'Yes,' and she then said 'We more than *like* you.' I then felt it OK to tell her openly of my love for her.

I think my parents suspected that mild but illicit activity was taking place in the bedroom, as indeed it was. I don't remember much of what Wilfred and Lena did, but I remember for the first time feeling Marie's breasts and her saying 'I can bear *that!*' But things didn't go any further than that.

Despite Ma Pearson and Co's disapproving imaginings about what was going on between Marie and me, their merry banter about sex in general was still maintained. Their attitude was a mixed one. I remember a song which (I think) Ma Pearson sang to simple repeated tune of 'One man went a-mow' – one of those where the indecent rhyming or near-rhyming word is dropped and the song goes on to the next line –

Come & sit down, drinks all round, bread & cheese for supper

If one man sleeps with another man's wife he's a fool if he doesn't →

Send his kids to school, to teach them with the stick
Before they've learned their ABC they're playing with their
Tommy Perkins had two rabbits; one of them was a buck
He put them in a rabbit hutch to see if they would

It ended

'P' stands for pudding and 'R' stands for rice
'F' stands for something else: it's naughty but it's nice.

There were absurd and mildly indecent bits of doggerel, like

Is your hair all right?
Are your trousers tight?
Is your pompom bigger than mine?

And allusions to oral lore with which I was unfamiliar – for example laughing references to 'possible.' I could gather that 'possible' meant 'penis' but didn't know why until a good deal later, when I was told that it was an allusion to a story of two maiden ladies who had to wash their bed-ridden brother and in reply to a question about how they managed, replied, 'Well, we wash down as far as possible and up as far as possible, but we don't wash possible.' No doubt general laughter at 'Never mind your hair; hold your hat on,' was a similar allusion, but I never discovered what the allusion was to.

Things were enlivened too by anecdotes, apocryphal or otherwise, about women in the village. One was about Ma Pearson. Some chap who was courting a woman some distance from Holme had said that he used to call in upon Ma, whose house was on his way, to have a bit with her so that he didn't get out of control when he got to the woman he was courting. Another was about a girl who worked with us for a while. It was said that when she had barely reached puberty a lad took her behind a hedge and when asked what she was like had said that she was 'just sprouting.' Another story was told by Marie, who at one time had worked in the house of the village headmaster. His wife suffered from constipation, and on being asked at the breakfast table, with Marie in attendance, how she had fared when she went to the lavatory had said, 'Oh, only two tiny blobs.'

There were also parodies of songs like 'Cock of the North', in which, predictably, 'cock' was used in the sense of penis.

Cock a doodle, Cock a doodle, I'm the cock of the north

And if any young lady wants a baby I'm the cock of the north.

I'm the cock of the north, the cock of the south, the cock of the east & west

And of all the cocks I've ever seen Ralph Russell's is the best.

'It's naughty, but it's nice,' the women sang. But although the naughtiness added spice to the niceness, they thought that it *was* naughtiness all the same. Not that furtive sexual activity was regarded as very sinful provided it did not lead to pre-marital pregnancy. And there were standard sentences allegedly spoken by a girl to her boyfriend after first sexual intercourse – 'Do it again. I like it!' and recommending it to her friend, 'It's luvely, tell ya muther.' But furtive was the operative word. No nice girl was expected to be curious about contraception, which was dirty, and regarded by the older women as something which could only lead to unbridled sexual licentiousness. The women all knew that Ralph Russell (from Cambridge College) was undesirably broad-minded about sex and would talk about it to them. I remember being surprised on one occasion when I said to Marie that in intercourse it was common for the man to 'come' first, and leave the woman unsatisfied. She said, 'Well, that's where you're wrong then' – but didn't elaborate. On one occasion Ma's daughter Vera, who was engaged or semi-engaged to a railwayman named Roland, asked me to lend her a Left Book Club book I had, entitled *Modern Marriage and Birth Control*. She, of course, concealed it from Ma, but Ma found it, and played wars (as Yorkshire people say). A typical attitude was in evidence when a girl got married. Only if she was a virgin was she entitled to wear white, but if she was someone people didn't much like, she was in a no-win situation. If she wore white people exclaimed at her effrontery in doing so, when 'everyone knew' that she wasn't entitled to. And if she didn't, that was an admission of sex before marriage.

7

In September 1938, in the weeks before I returned to Cambridge to begin my second year, Chamberlain made three journeys to Germany to negotiate with Hitler. Already earlier in 1938 there had been ominous signs of change in the international situation, and now Britain's shameful (and ultimately disastrous) surrender to Hitler's demands was bringing these to a head.

Back in Cambridge, I remember Ram Nahum saying after Munich that war was now inevitable, and that Dimitrov in his article *After Munich* had implied this. I was shocked, because at that time I accepted the pseudo-communist argument that even to consider the possibility of failure of our plans was to show a lack of faith. I didn't want to sink deeper into sin by asking him why he thought that, and what in that event the line of the communist movement would be.

Once again I applied myself energetically to work in the Party branch. In addition to being on the committee I was now elected as a member of the secretariat. Bob had left Cambridge but we wrote to each other occasionally – he once wrote that he was learning to play the flute, 'which makes a melancholy and cathartic noise', and also that he had met a nice Esthonian woman called Aira. And I was able to tell him that among the branch members the 'proletarian' norms which he and I and others had pushed for were increasingly accepted, and gradually the more glaringly upper-class features of our members' style of thinking was disappearing – though not perhaps as thoroughly as I thought at the time. I now think that our progress in this area was more due to Ram Nahum than to us. It was he who, admitting the limitations of his own and the others' class background as we never admitted the limitations of ours, urged on us the need to show understanding and patience, and work in closer unity with the other members. Which I think we then did.

In both the committee and the secretariat we functioned as communists should, in a free, frank, friendly atmosphere in which mutual criticism was normal and was not resented, and decisions really were collectively reached and collectively acted upon. Of course not everyone behaved consistently as good communists should. I remember one meeting of the branch committee where Arnold Kettle showed a

George-Miles-like attitude which I had thought we had long ago got rid of. It was early in 1939, and we were discussing a government proposal to introduce conscription, which we on the left opposed. Arnold suggested that we put out a leaflet expressing an attitude which would appeal to the student population but was in fact not our real attitude at all. A fellow member of the committee, Eric Barbour-Mercer, who had a bad stammer, expressed the general reaction by an explosive 'F, f, f, f, fuck me!' and Arnold's suggestion was decisively rejected.*

Such lapses aside, we worked well and with a considerable measure of success. We were of course helped by the fact that we were living in a period in which it was not difficult to raise people's political awareness, and we also had a lot of practical things on our side. We were students, with much time at our disposal, and considerable freedom of choice of times for meeting. We were in a university where all of us were spending the greater part of the day within the boundaries of a quite small area. No other party except the Communist Party as yet gave any serious attention to the universities or attempted to establish a party organisation there, so we faced no organised opposition. But none of that would have amounted to much if we had not been strongly committed, and that we were.

My comrades in our branch were in general a jolly lot, not at all the severe, humourless people which people who had never met a real, live communist conceived them to be – and which, indeed, in some cases they were. Not us – and nor were we 'narrowly political' in our interests. It was the time of the Marx Brothers films (no connection with Karl), which to me and many of my generation were infinitely funnier than anything else on film.* One of my favourites is the song Groucho sings in *Horse Feathers*

I don't know what they have to say, it makes no difference anyway –
Whatever it is, I'm against it!

There was a distinct shortage of women in Cambridge, there being only two women's colleges, but our group probably had a higher proportion than in Cambridge as a whole, and there were several I found attractive. But our circle widened considerably each summer, when the Party organised summer schools for its student branches at a place near Guildford – where one of my memories is of a young woman from Oxford who impressed me (and doubtless others) by swimming, naked and uninhibited, in the swimming pool.

Another of our Oxford comrades produced wonderful parodies of the cliché-ridden speeches of Soviet communists – phrases like 'life itself has shown,' 'tested in the crucible of practice', 'it could not be otherwise', used in the most mundane of contexts. We had a healthy irreverence towards the often ludicrous words of revolutionary songs. One, the United Front Song, was a bad translation from German –

A man is only human, he must eat before he can think

Kind words are only empty air & not his food & drink

So left right left, so left right left, there's a place comrade for you

Join with us in the workers' united front, for you are a worker too.

One verse began

And since a worker's a worker, he'd rather not have boots in his face

Rather not, indeed! Another had a quotation from Marx

The emancipation of the working class is the task of the workers alone.

Someone produced a take-off that ran

The workers sit in their hovels cleaning their heads of lice
The socially necessary labour time determines the commodity's price!

(It should have been 'value', not 'price', but never mind.)

We sang French songs too. One called *La Jeune Garde* had words written by Louis Aragon, then one of the French Communist Party's leading intellectuals –

Demain si l'peuple bouge nous descendrons sur les boulevards

La nouvelle Garde Rouge fera trembler tous les richards

which means

Tomorrow if the people move, we shall come on to the streets.
The new red guard will make all the rich tremble.

Not exactly poetry, but its meaning was unexceptionable. But the song
continued

Nous sommes les enfants de Lenin(e), par la faucille et le marteau

Which means, if you please

We are the children of Lenin by the sickle and hammer.

I thought, 'If Lenin conceived us on the sickle and hammer it must have
been a painful experience.' But I think most people sang all this without
paying much attention to what the words actually said.

One song, not a parody, was a home-made humorous one about
Harry Pollitt. It began

Harry was a Bolshie, one of Lenin's lads

but he was foully murdered by counter-revolutionary cads

It went on to describe his imaginary communist activities, first in
heaven, then in hell. Another song, whose words I don't remember, was
a skit on the proceedings of the Moscow trials, to the tune of 'The man
who broke the bank at Monte Carlo.'

We made up words to fit to the tunes of well-known songs, humorous expressions of what were to all of us serious issues. One went to the
tune of 'There is a tavern in the town'

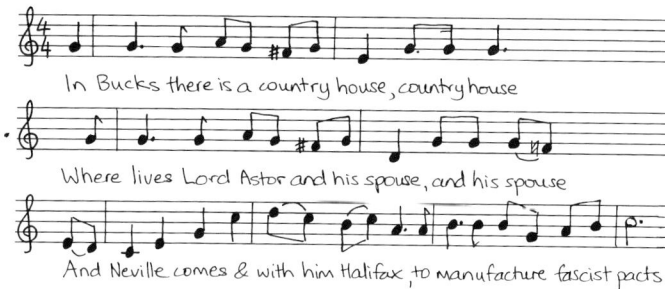

In Bucks there is a country house, country house

Where lives Lord Astor and his spouse, and his spouse

And Neville comes & with him Halifax, to manufacture fascist pacts

(Lord Halifax was foreign secretary at the time.)
The chorus went

143

Fare thee well the League of Nations,
Welcome peaceful penetrations
No more nonsense about international law, Oh Lor!
Adieu democracy, adieu, adieu, adieu
We have no further use for you, use for you
We'll pin our hopes on fascism and war
What is the British Empire for?

To the tune of 'Daisy, Daisy' we had

Hitler, Hitler, implacable Aryan lord
A right-wing deviation we cannot at present afford

The 'right wing deviation' was particularly absurd, since it was supposed to be Chamberlain or one of his cronies speaking, and no non-communist ever used such ridiculous phrases – communists, regrettably, did. The verse continues

There's always those dirty Bolsheviks
Who're always up to their Bolshie tricks
So let's agree, and we shall see the sickle cut short by the sword.

In another verse the Japanese speak

Honourable gents, honourable gents, listen to honourable plan
Let's condone aggression whenever and where we can
For could there be anything finer than defensive war in China…

It was not only political songs that we sang. One of the Oxford comrades could sing to the guitar. I learnt from him Wann I komm, and another song to a simple but beautiful tune, one I still sing

Long years ago, when I was young, the flowers they bloomed & the birds they sung
A sailor lad and his lovely bride stood weeping by the ocean side.

It tells how he was drowned at sea, and ends with his widow singing

And would that I were sleeping too
Beneath the waves of the ocean blue

My soul to God and my body to the sea
And the dark blue waves a-rolling over me.

The whole experience of working in the branch was a very important one for me. I had thrown myself energetically into all its activities. I had spoken at meetings on current issues, and on the political theory that we communists believed was the essential tool for analysing how to move things forward. I realise in retrospect that this was my first experience of a sort of teaching, and I both enjoyed it and discovered that I could do it well. This has remained a central feature of my life ever since, but at the time I thought of it simply as something every communist needed to be able to do, and I was glad I could.

My understanding of how to work politically increased, and so I think did the genuine liking and esteem which most of the members felt for me. Years later when I met people who had been in the Cambridge branch in those years I realised that they thought I had what in later years came to be called charisma. Of course those who don't feel this generally have no occasion to show that they don't, and I expect there were many such in our branch. I remember two members, academically senior to me I think, called Ford and Winkler whom even the old mandarins had felt were awkward customers, who made no secret of their superior amusement at my zeal.★ But there were many more who genuinely and wholeheartedly felt the same commitment to communism as I did. My frequently expressed admiration for Dimitrov earned me the nickname of Georgi – this was at a time when the mandarins in the Cambridge branch seemed to think that nobody except Lenin mattered much. Since Dimitrov symbolised for me the qualities of an ideal communist, I was very happy to be called by his name.★

For readers who did not live through the thirties, a great barrier to understanding the widespread sympathy for communist ideas at that time arises because they know that communists themselves failed to understand much of what was happening in the Soviet Union. But it is important to realise that if communists and others on the left were blind to the atrocities that were being committed, this was because the great majority of them didn't *know* what was happening. Neither, with a few exceptions, did anyone else. It was not easy for anyone to see it except the soviet citizens who were on the receiving end of it, and at that time they had no means of letting the world know of their experiences.

In later years when the horrors of the Soviet regime became known it became common to mock the, as people thought, pathetic gullibility of western communists who couldn't see what was going on. But we communists were by no means the only ones, and anyway we had no way of estimating what we were not being told, and the soviet communist leaders had an amazing capacity for presenting in the most convincing detail a picture of what *should* have been happening as though it *was* happening. So we were blind to the horrors which those whose great achievements we and others rightly admired were at the same time inflicting on their people.

It is true that we saw *some* things (if only very few) which made us uneasy, but we regarded these as blemishes on an otherwise lovely complexion. We were, as Claud Cockburn puts it, 'sheathed' by 'two suits of protective clothing.' His account could well, if space allowed, be quoted in full, but I must be content to quote only a short passage from it.*

The first [suit of protective clothing] was the fact that during a great part of my life I had listened to anti-Communists telling the wildest lies about Communism and Communists, and on occasion had even seen the lies being manufactured. The result was that even when they told the truth one almost instinctively rejected it.

The other protective suit was of a different material and texture. It was woven principally of two beliefs. One was the belief that after all, on balance, the Soviet régime was, so to speak, on the side of the angels – that is to say that despite many deviations and shortcomings its mere existence was an asset to the oppressed of the earth, a challenge and a threat to the oppressors.

But out of that belief grew a second article of faith which was more dangerous – the conviction that, in such circumstances, actions which would be violently condemned if performed by any other régime must be quite differently assessed when performed by the Government of the U.S.S.R.

Anyone can see and say that that is a dangerous attitude. But to recognize it as such does not solve the dilemma of – in particular – the Western intellectual looking for peace, progress and the fall of the Bastille. For the moment he accuses the Russian Communists of some hideous malpractice, he finds himself to his horror in the approving company of half the leading ruffians of the Western world, people of whom he feels certain that, given half a chance, they would behave in the same way themselves. It is like advocating the abolition of capital punishment and being patted enthusiastically on the back by the bloody hand of a man who has just murdered a child.

146

One of the main issues of this kind was the series of trials of leading members of the Soviet Party, which were reported in the west and which many people in the Party, and we ourselves in the Cambridge branch, were disturbed by. The trials began on a small scale in 1935 with one in which Zinoviev and Kamenev were charged, and ended in what the Stalinist historian Andrew Rothstein calls 'the last and biggest' of them in March 1939. We were presented with the situation Cockburn so well describes, a question of whom one believes when one is receiving from different sources incompatible descriptions of what was going on. We witnessed the ludicrous spectacle of the capitalist press, that had hated the revolution and all it stood for, suddenly applauding the revolutionary heroes who had fought in that noble cause and were now being shot at Stalin's command. Their obvious vested interest in giving the Soviet Union a bad name made one instinctively discount anything they reported, and look for other sources to find out what was going on. And we believed those sources because we had not yet had any experience which had led us to question their honesty and dedication to the cause of true communism.

To us in the Cambridge branch, imbued with so strong a sense of positive purpose in what we were doing, although these trials were disturbing there seemed to be no reason to doubt that the accused were guilty. On behalf of the branch secretariat I wrote and circulated to all our members a letter in which I said (to the amusement of some of them) that if you had to decide whether it was Stalin or Zinoviev and Kamenev, whom Lenin called 'strikebreakers' on the eve of the revolution, were traitors to the revolutionary cause, then obviously the answer was Zinoviev and Kamenev. It was only many years later in talking with Chris Freeman that he and I reached the conclusion that the correct answer to the question 'Who was the traitor?' was probably 'Both.'

Communists were far from alone in believing the official version of the trials. We were, for instance, in the company of the American ambassador to Moscow, Joseph E. Davies. He reported to the US government on February 17th, 1937, that he and nearly all the foreign diplomats in Moscow who had attended the trial of the previous month were convinced that the defendants were guilty. He says the same thing in *Mission to Moscow* (1941), recording on March 11, 1937, the opinion of an unnamed diplomat who

said that the defendants were undoubtedly guilty; that all of us who attended the trial had practically agreed upon that; that the outside world, from the press reports, however, seemed to think that the trial was a put-up job (facade, as he called it); that while he knew it was not, it was probably just as well that the outside world should think so.

The Webbs too, in a book on the trials published in 1940, reached the same conclusion. Most striking of all was the judgement of an American engineer John Littlepage, reported in Axell's book. Littlepage had spent ten years in Russia and had written about it for various US publications. He was asked by friends whether the accused were guilty and said without equivocation that most of them were; and what surprised him was that it had taken the Soviet leaders to long to realise the 'other communists are the most dangerous enemies they have.'★

That all of us, from communists to the American ambassador, were wrong to believe official Soviet sources is now obvious. But this is only obvious in retrospect, with the knowledge none of us could have had then. What we *did* know about was the extraordinary transformation of Soviet society which was being achieved at the same time, and under the same leadership, and which immeasurably improved the conditions of life for so many people. This has been largely obscured in the minds of many in subsequent generations, for whom the horror at Stalin's crimes blocks out any possibility of seeing the good that was achieved.★

The crimes against his own people which Stalin was responsible for were not only a human disaster, they distorted the nature of the Soviet experiment and eventually undermined the whole world communist movement. Our conviction that senior communist leaders necessarily exemplified the highest communist principles led us to serious misunderstandings of our own task. No one can regret that more than true communists. But the knowledge of it only came at a later period. It simply was not part of our consciousness at the time.

What was very much to the fore of our consciousness was the increasingly uncertain international outlook. Early in 1939 the Spanish People's Front government was defeated, after nearly three years of civil war – a real blow to those who opposed fascism. Yet still it seemed possible to hope that Britain might come to its senses, follow France's lead, and make an alliance with the Soviet Union. That the Soviet Union was in earnest about keeping to its side of the bargain in such an alliance was demonstrated by its attitude towards Czechoslovakia in 1938. Both France and the Soviet Union had pledged themselves to come to Czechoslovakia's aid if Germany attacked. By 1938 it was beginning to be clear that France was unlikely to honour this, but the Soviet Union promised that it would do this even if France failed to. At one point it seemed as though Czechoslovakia would be ready to take up this offer, although aware that it would incur Britain and France's disapproval. But in the event its courage failed it.★

In the student party branch, and in the Socialist Club through which we worked, we put our efforts into raising public pressure on the government to enter into a pact of mutual assistance against Hitler. Across Britain there was widespread support for an Anglo-Soviet alliance – a public opinion poll in April 1939 showed 87 per cent in favour. And Hobsbawm's book *The Age of Extremes* tells us that even in the fanatically anti-socialist USA 'when asked in January 1939 who Americans wanted to win, if a war broke out between the Soviet Union and Germany, 83 per cent favoured a Soviet victory.'★

∞

It had by now become obvious to my teachers that I was not giving my academic work much attention. The Cambridge degree –for which, of course, Cambridge had its own term, the Tripos – was taken in two parts, with Part I at the end of the second year and Part II at the end of the third. By early 1939, as the Part I examination approached, my tutor intervened and suggested that for the Easter vacation I should go on a study holiday in the Lake District. My costs would be paid, and hopefully this would be a setting in which I could concentrate. I was even provided with a lift to get there, by no less a person than the Master of St John's, a man called Charlesworth who was himself a classicist. All this made me revise the judgement I had made earlier when I had been offered a holiday in Greece – the college really was prepared to put itself out for its students' benefit, provided that help was of the kind that fell within the patterns they were used to.

I regret that the holiday didn't achieve quite the results they hoped. In the Part I exam I got an upper second – my tutor told me that I had 'just missed a first' – but this owed almost everything to what I had already acquired at school and very little to any work I had done at Cambridge.

By the time I returned to Holme for the summer vacation of 1939, it seemed that the British government was finally beginning to toy with the idea of a pact with the Soviet Union – but it soon became clear that 'toy with' were, as they say, the operative words. On 15 August 1939 they sent a mission to Moscow to negotiate. A vivid picture of this mission is given in Axell's book.★ To negotiate with Hitler a year earlier, Chamberlain himself had rushed to Germany by air, three times in one month. To negotiate with the Soviet Union a delegation was sent headed not by Chamberlain, not even by the Chief of the General Staff, but

149

by an obscure Admiral, Sir Reginald Drax, and it went by sea, 'in the ageing 13-knot cargo-passenger steamer *The City of Exeter*' which 'took five days to get to Leningrad.' Moreover, Drax had no plenipotentiary powers.

After a week of British evasions the Soviet Union realised the British were not serious, and at once signed a non-aggression pact with Germany. Everyone in Britain at once began shouting about the Soviet 'betrayal.' But it was not the Soviet Union but Britain and France who had betrayed all those who were struggling to prevent a war. What had happened was the logical outcome of appeasement. The British and French had been angling to get a commitment from the Soviet Union to come to their help if they were attacked, without themselves giving an equally clear commitment to come to the Soviet Union's help if Hitler turned east instead of west. Stalin, in a speech to the Congress of the Communist Party of the Soviet Union in March 1939 had warned, '[We] must be cautious and not allow our country to be drawn into a conflict by warmongers who are accustomed to have others pull their chestnuts out of the fire for them.' In other words, We are not going to be manoeuvred into a situation where we alone stand up to Germany while Britain and France opt out. To have done so would have been suicidal – as good as an invitation to Hitler to attack. Had he done so, nothing would have pleased the British and French better. Now they were hoist with their own petard.

That British and French policies had this outcome ought to have surprised no one. But in Britain even people on the left, including us communists, had, I am sure, felt that the Soviet Union *would* pull our chestnuts out of the fire, and we were considerably shaken that it was now clear that it wouldn't. Now if war broke out we would have to go and fight, and perhaps get killed, and we didn't like the prospect.

I soon recovered from the shock this news gave me. I concluded that the Soviet Union had been right to do what it did and that if this entailed unpleasant consequences for us, well, too bad. But it was now becoming increasingly obvious that war could no longer be prevented, and I and other communists needed to work out how we should face such a situation. In retrospect it seems remarkable that the world communist movement had not had much to say about this. For four years we had been following the 'peace front' strategy laid down by the 7th World Congress of the Comintern, but the Congress had not discussed what the communist position should be in the event of this strategy failing. We all ought to have foreseen that the 'peace front' might well not come into being, at any rate not in time to prevent the outbreak of war.

To me, as to many others, the logic of the communist position was clear. If fascist aggression led to war, we should fight on the side of the democratic powers, whether the Soviet Union joined them or not.

On 3rd September Britain declared war on Germany. The first response of the communist parties of Western Europe was what I would have expected – they declared it a just war against fascism, and called upon communists to be in the forefront. Thorez, the Secretary of the CP of France, set the example by presenting himself for military service. I was now of an age to be conscripted but was saved from having to face up to this because the British government deferred call-up for students completing the final year of a degree course. I ought to have offered myself anyway – as several better communists than I did. But I didn't, without any explicit attempt to justify my decision either to myself or to anyone else.

In October 1939 I returned to Cambridge for my final year, with my thoughts very much on the international situation, and very little on my studies. I was now the leading member of the student Party branch – Ram Nahum had taken his degree, and though he stayed on in Cambridge to do research in nuclear physics, his political energies had shifted elsewhere. With the declaration of war, the London School of Economics (LSE) was evacuated to Cambridge. This brought us the reinforcement of the LSE communists, but also brought a group of right-wing Labour Party supporters, including the same Nat Whine who, speaking from a portable platform at the side of the road in Woodford, had convinced me that the cause of war was capitalism. From this group we now faced an organised, and quite skilfully led, anti-communist campaign.

I knew a lot of the responsibility for how we handled this was going to fall to me, and I decided to make my minimal attention to academic studies even more minimal than it had been hitherto and to devote all my efforts to political work. I was in any case unenthusiastic about what I was expected to study, having discovered to my annoyance that Part II of the Classics Tripos offered essentially more of what we had done in Part I. There were new things I would have been interested to read – particularly the history and literature of the Hellenic period after the conquests of Alexander the Great – but Part II made no provision for this. Luckily I found out that it was possible to change subjects after Part I of the Tripos. I decided to switch to historical, political and economic geography, calculating that no one in that department knew me and I could hope to spend almost all my time on Communist Party activity without my academic supervisors noticing. That was in fact the case. For a long time I cut lectures and tutorials without anyone even realising that I should have been there. In any case, whatever little I might be obliged to learn in my new subject would be more politically useful than more Greek and Latin.

The addition of the LSE comrades changed the character of our branch, in a direction I welcomed. They were from a much broader social spectrum, and included some people with whom I developed my closest relationships. One was Alan Brooks, the son of a Yorkshire miner, who became a member of our branch committee. I found his accent very attractive. It had a feature common to several Yorkshire dialects which made his quite often repeated statement, 'I agree with Georgi', sound like 'I akree with Cheorchi.' Another was Leslie Lickerish, also a proletarian, with a personal style that caused a sensation among our upper and upper-middle class party membership. He had been in the YCL – Young Communist League – before coming up to Cambridge, and like many YCLers wore a sheath knife hanging from his belt. Quaint, and rather shocking, they thought. His arrival caused a real problem to the university authorities, because he was married – something unheard of in undergraduates of those days – and they had to agree to his finding his own accommodation without requiring their approval.

There was also a greater proportion of women in the LSE contingent than in Cambridge itself, and we now had three women in our branch committee. The one I was closest to was 'Freddie' (i.e. Winifred) Lambert. She had sandy hair and (a feature which I have always found attractive) a gap between her two front teeth. She was also a great hockey-player, and her walk somehow seemed to express this, which, for me, was another attraction. I never felt any desire to do anything much about this attraction because she already had a steady boyfriend (John Vickers, another communist comrade) and I was committed to Marie. I considered both of these commitments binding but I saw no harm in giving suitably limited expression to my feelings. At committee meetings I would sit on the floor beside the chair she was sitting in and keep feeling her ankles. She found this unobjectionable, and quite amusing.

The most important of my new LSE friends was Chris Freeman. He quickly became my closest communist comrade and my closest friend, and has now been that for so long that I find it difficult to recall what first made us close. Part of it was that as a person he is warm, open and unpretentious, and we were from the start completely relaxed in each other's company. But I suppose what really drew us together was that it very soon became clear that we had the same concept of what being a communist meant. He too had become a communist very young. At

152

Wilfred visiting me in Cambridge

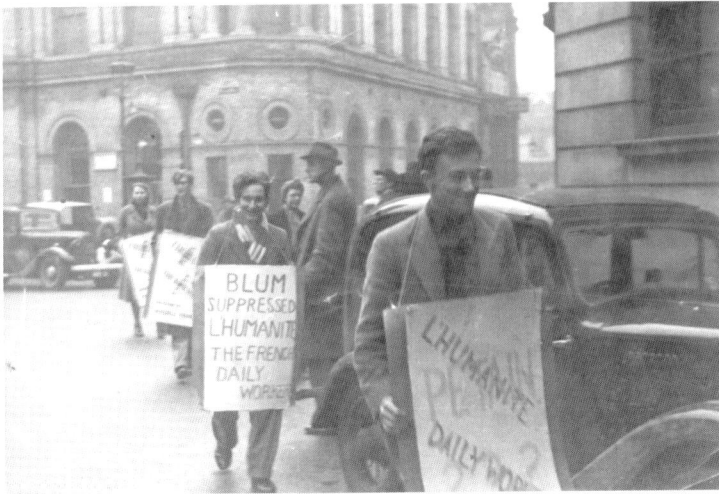

Chris Freeman (at front) taking part in a demonstration

fourteen he had read Trotsky's *The Revolution Betrayed* and decided he was a Trotskyist, then after discussions with a communist friend he was persuaded that Trotsky had been wrong, and that the only way forward was to work within the main communist movement. He then helped to set up a branch of the Young Communist League at his school – a quite effective branch, with about fifteen active members. Like so many others he felt a sense of urgency to do something to stop fascism. But most of all what I liked and trusted in him was that he was constantly thinking things out, and calm and honest in his judgements.

Our appreciation of each other was mutual. We took our friendship for granted as a natural thing and didn't discuss it much. Once years later he wrote 'I have always liked and admired you more than anyone else I know' – something I valued the more since it came from someone not given to fulsome personal statements. On another occasion he surprised me by saying that one of the things he admired about me was my political integrity, that I would never go along with something unless I believed it; and that once I was clear what ought to be done, I was 'never afraid'. I would never have thought of describing myself that way; and it had not occurred to me that there was anything to be afraid of.

That year Chris and I shared a house in Round Church Street with Alan and a young chap called Jack Peters, whom we used to call 'Horse' because of the clumping great boots he wore. He didn't resent this and laughed about it. We all slept in a row on the floor, and Chris and I would often run our fingers through each other's hair – an action Alan regarded as evidence of undesirable homosexual tendencies. But Alan's disapproval didn't bother us.

Together in the Party branch we began working out how to deal with the new challenges posed us by the outbreak of war. The big stick that Nat Whine and his group were using to beat us with was the Soviet-German pact, joining the chorus of Britain having been 'betrayed' by the Soviet Union. I regarded this view as intellectually contemptible – if the people who held it had put themselves for a moment in the position of the Soviet Union they would have seen that its action was justifiable, but British people right across the political spectrum are accustomed to assuming that British interests override all others, and on that assumption the Soviet action was of course outrageous.* But it was clear that many who had been sympathetic to our views were now confused, and we knew there was a lot we needed to do if we were not to lose the gains of previous years.

But more important than reacting to the Soviet-German pact was the issue of how Britain was going to conduct the war, given the situation we were landed in. At this stage the British Communist Party's policy was one I wholeheartedly agreed with – the task was to support the war while continuing to try to change the government to one which could be relied upon to pursue it energetically. This was a message that had a widespread resonance. Throughout the thirties people had been hoping to avoid war. Now they were in it, and many people felt, 'Oh God, Chamberlain's got us into this mess, and God knows how we're going to get out of it. Certainly *he's* not fit to cope with the situation.' It was clear that his government hadn't wanted to go to war, and many people thought, and had good reason to think, that even now he was probably hoping to do some sort of deal with Hitler.

Then suddenly, within weeks of the start of term, we were faced with a situation very much more complex, for the British Party changed its line to one of opposition to the war. Though not openly admitted, it was obvious that this must have been in response to a Comintern directive. The argument was that, like the 1914-18 war, this was an imperialist war. Dimitrov, general secretary of the Comintern, concluded one of his statements with the declaration that, 'the working people of the world must put an end to this war after their own fashion, in their own interests, in the interests of all labouring mankind.'

This about-turn caused a temporary crisis for us in the branch, and for British communists everywhere. For years communists in Britain had been inspired by the urgency of the need to fight fascism. However half-heartedly Britain had been drawn into war against Hitler, it was obvious that war was now the only way to oppose fascism. This was therefore a just war that must be supported, whether the Soviet Union took part in it or not. How could we now accept the Comintern line and start thinking about it as 'an imperialist war' – as if both sides were equally to be opposed?

To you who are reading this more than sixty years later it may well seem incomprehensible, not to say unprincipled, that – however reluctantly – we eventually did persuade ourselves to think about it in the way we had been told to. 'Unprincipled' is certainly not the right way to describe it; it would be more accurate to say that we were faced with a conflict between two sets of principles, and we chose the one that seemed the more fundamental. We saw ourselves as disciplined soldiers in a world-wide revolutionary army, fighting in a period when in the near future victory would be ours. Victory would eventually bring the transformation of society for the benefit of all humankind. In this fight we were led by the Comintern leaders who constituted its general staff; as disciplined soldiers it was our duty to obey. There are always situations where a general staff issues orders which are felt to be wrong but which disciplined soldiers obey, because it is the general staff's job to take the bigger decisions and the soldiers' job to carry out its commands unhesitatingly whatever their doubts about them. This represents an adherence to principle too.

Of course we could do what was required of us more easily if we could convince ourselves that the general staff was right, and most of us proceeded to do just that. For me, the task was made easier by the fact that the Comintern's General Secretary was Dimitrov, and it was he who transmitted its orders to us. Claud Cockburn's autobiography expresses very well what I and many others felt.

> I had profound admiration for Dimitrov. He was one of those true heroes who really had been out in the wind and the rain, facing day after day the probability of torture and murder by Goering's young men ... Nobody under the age of fifty or so today can possibly have any notion of what Dimitrov was to us in the way of a symbol, a flame in darkness, a proof that, however bad things seem to be, the courageous, even the apparently foolhardy backers of a sixty-six to one chance may still win ...
>
> There was at work in the minds of many people on the extreme Left a general feeling that if, for example, Neville Chamberlain was on one side of a question and Georgi Dimitrov, hero of the Leipzig trial, was on the other, then the probability was that Dimitrov was right and Mr Chamberlain was leading one up the garden.*

So we began to try to get our minds round the idea that the war was an imperialist war. What did this mean for us? The first task was to get our own thinking clearer. In the branch committee we started trying to see what the parallels there might be with the 1914-18 war. Communists then had tried to 'turn the imperialist war into a civil war', that is, they took advantage of the fact that the imperialists were weakening themselves in mutual conflict in order to overthrow them. This had had demonstrable success in Russia and not inconsiderable success elsewhere. But there was no suggestion from the Comintern that we should react in this way now. We decided to write to the *Daily Worker* asking for clarification. We didn't get any – instead we received a lecture on how good communists didn't need to raise questions of this kind.

We ignored this put-down and decided to educate ourselves and our members further on the question of communists' attitude to wars. The most comprehensive statements were from the 1928 World Congress of the Communist International. When I first joined the Party these 'theses', as such statements were called in the communist jargon of the

156

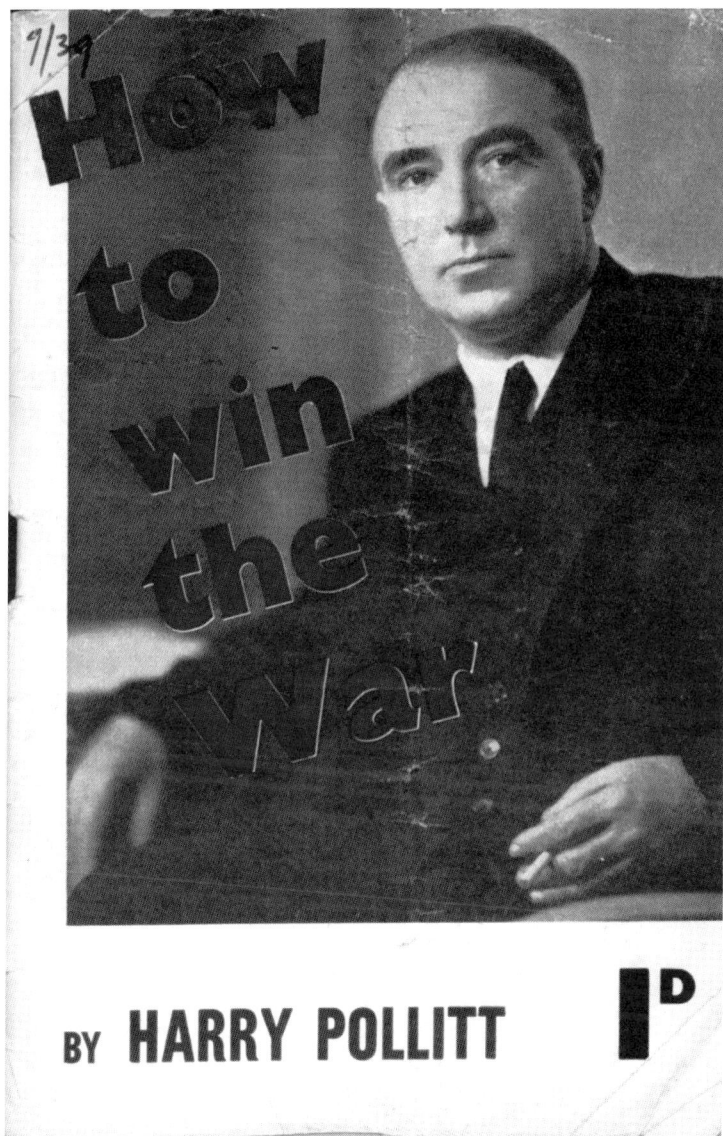

The Party's first reaction, September 1939: the title of the pamphlet reads: 'How to win the War'.

time, were still available, along with a couple of short articles by Lenin in a pamphlet entitled *The Attitude of the Proletariat to War*. This pamphlet was now out of print, but we reproduced it in cyclostyled typescript – a considerable labour! Our attempts to seriously study this question were promptly rewarded by an angry command from the East Anglia District Party Committee, under whose authority our branch came, to withdraw this pamphlet from circulation at once. This command was conveyed to us by the District Committee's full-time secretary Maurice Cornforth, without any explanation.*

We were cross, and didn't understand the response of higher Party authorities. But as disciplined communists we did as we were told, dropped the matter and 'got on with the job.' This was the phrase generally used, then and for years afterwards, by rank and file communists when they felt that the understanding of things like this was beyond their intellectual powers and that they had better assume that their leaders knew best and leave it at that. I also believed in 'getting on with the job' though I did not cease to think about the issues we had raised.

'Getting on with the job' now meant undertaking the difficult task of trying to persuade people, against the opposition of most of them and against our own personal doubts, that the Party was right to oppose the war. In fact, hostility to this anti-war message was, at any rate in student circles, less strong than those who were not around at the time may now find easy to credit. People nowadays may have a vague picture of the British population in 1939 burning with zeal to be 'up and at 'em.' Well, it wasn't like that at all. There could not have been a greater contrast between the mood of 1914 and the mood of 1939. In 1914 there was universal patriotic frenzy, and those who opposed the war had a very rough time of it. In 1939 there was nothing of this, partly because so little seemed to be happening. A few British troops had been despatched to France, but beyond that nothing. People felt, 'We're at war, so why doesn't the government *do* something instead of making us sit on our arses waiting for something to happen?' It was difficult for anyone to get a sense that they were caught up in defending anything.

So our view was not so much at variance with the mood of people at the time, and our support among the students from previous years gave us a strong base to build on. An indication of the extent of continuing good will towards us was that we planned a big and spectacular public meeting and booked a large venue, the Guildhall, confident that we could expect enough people to fill it. In the branch meetings I urged that we should make clear that it was organised by the Communist Party rather than the broader Socialist Club within which we usually worked.

Ram had always tried to present as broad a front as possible, but it was we who had taken the lead and done most of the work, and now in this more complex situation I felt people needed to know that, and have a clearer idea of the political choices they faced. This time the others agreed with me.

We prepared very thoroughly. The main speaker was to be John Gollan, a national leader of the Party who later succeeded Harry Pollitt as General Secretary. And a very good speaker from the LSE contingent of our branch was to be a second speaker. We prepared large posters carrying suitable quotations to adorn the walls. I insisted on including the one from Manuilsky which I quoted earlier:

> Our strength and our achievements belong not only to the peoples of the USSR, not only to the communist vanguard, but to the working class of all countries ... to the toilers of the whole world, irrespective of nation and race, language and colour.

The meeting was indeed spectacular, but in a very different way from what we had anticipated, for only a matter of hours before the meeting was due to start came the news that the Soviet army had attacked Finland. This was a complication we certainly had not needed! The hall was invaded by large numbers of people who proceeded to break up the meeting. Some of them attempted to rush the platform, but to their intense astonishment one of our members, Mary Rose, punched one of them on the nose and was clearly prepared to do the same for any of the others, and they withdrew. Gollan, sweating with fear, as well he might be, attempted to speak but soon gave up. Our LSE comrade had already decided that he couldn't risk speaking. I got up to speak, but no one was interested any more and everyone was streaming out of the hall.

For almost all of my last year at Cambridge, right up to May 1940, nothing seemed to be happening in the war. In Britain this period came to be called 'the phoney war', and the French had a similar phrase, *la drôle de guerre*. The fact that we were officially at war was of course beginning to affect people's lives but the call-up was slow to take effect, and the regular army was still gearing up to deal with thousands of new conscripts. It was an uneasy time, knowing something cataclysmic could happen at any time, but meanwhile this strange and unreliable pause. No one could make plans with any certainty.

I spent a great deal of time reading. The war had a great deal to do with what I chose to read, for I felt the need to prepare myself to understand the situation we might be approaching. As early as 1933 the Comintern had declared that a second 'round of wars and revolutions' was

159

'closely approaching' and the 7th World Congress had re-affirmed that forecast. The forecast had proved correct, at any rate where the 'wars' were concerned, and as a good communist I assumed that the 'revolutions' bit would be fulfilled too. So I began a closer study of the relevant theory. If people might become ready to turn towards revolutionary solutions of their problems, it was important to show them how revolutions could be made, and how they could establish a really just society, in which the needs and aspirations of the mass of the people were recognised as paramount and were increasingly fulfilled in practice. The Soviet Union was the one country where a socialist revolution had triumphed, and where – as I thought at the time – such a society had been created. So it seemed vital to study the experience of the Soviet Union, and draw lessons from it for our own period.

My main reading was in works either written by Stalin or produced under his watchful eye, and in particular, *The Short History of the Communist Party of the Soviet Union*, published in March 1939. I remember the great éclat with which it was launched. It was to be *the* text book for the education of the communist movement throughout the world, and issue after issue of *Inprecorr* carried articles telling us with what immense benefit it was being studied in this, that, and the other country. Ram Nahum viewed it with a scepticism derived as much, I think, from his upper-class background as from his Marxist convictions; when the veteran intellectual of the British Party, R Page Arnot, was invited to speak at Cambridge, Ram asked whether the *Short History* really *was* such a great work of Marxism as it was being made out to be. Arnot replied that yes, it really was – 'comparable with *The 18th Brumaire'* – Marx's great analysis of mid-19th century France. I never shared Ram's slightly cynical scepticism – indeed it always rather shocked me. I studied the book with considerable eagerness.

I was also increasingly interested in following what was happening in India. In our lone struggle against what we then characterised as the imperialist war, it was important to understand the role that might be played by India and the other countries still subject to imperial control. With impressive secrecy Ram put me in charge of the Party's liaison with an Indian communist student, Arun Bose, who with even more impressive secrecy from his rooms in Trinity guided his fellow Indian communists. The need for secrecy was in fact real – the Indian communist party was illegal and it would have been naive to think that the security services were not monitoring the doings of the few highly visible Indian students during their time in Britain. One of our group of Cambridge Indian students, Mohan, was a year ahead of me and had by now finished his degree but I saw him briefly in London before he returned to India. A few months later we learnt that he had been imprisoned.

A number of copies of the *National Front*, the de facto organ of the Communist Party of India, had been reaching England. From them we knew that Britain's declaration of war had led to a crisis in Indian political affairs, making a mockery of the very limited amount of representation Britain had been forced to concede. Two years earlier when Britain had agreed to elections in India's eleven provinces, the Indian National Congress had – to Britain's dismay – won in seven of them. Yet when Britain declared war it at once did so on India's behalf too, without any consultation with Congress. The provincial governments resigned in protest, and Congress passed an excellent resolution refusing to 'offer any co-operation in a war which is conducted on imperialist lines and which is meant to consolidate imperialism in India and elsewhere.'

We hoped to hear that Congress was following this up with mass action, but by now copies of *National Front* had creased to arrive, and we were cut off from all real news from India. The last we heard was of the great strike of the Bombay workers against the war; after that, almost complete silence.

In Britain too we were beginning to have to adjust to the need for caution. Since the Party had declared itself opposed to the war the *Daily Worker* had been banned, and – although we as ordinary Party members didn't know it at the time – the Party leadership was making serious preparations for continuing to work illegally if it too was banned. It seemed likely that any active communist might begin to attract the attention of the police. I reckoned that the police would certainly know that I was a party member, but not perhaps that I occupied any sort of leading position, so I thought it sensible to take some precautions against this fact becoming immediately obvious. Before setting off for the vacation in Holme I handed over my volumes of Lenin and Stalin to Chris Freeman, to lodge with someone less likely to be the object of police investigations. And I took with me reports that I had written as secretary to the branch, reporting on our activities to the aggregate meetings of the student branch of the Party. When I got to Holme I buried them in a box in the back yard of the house where my parents were living. The house itself has since been demolished but I guess the papers are still there.

The war had begun to have its effect even in Holme. Rex and Froude had now also moved there, for Rex had lost his job in London when paper rationing was imposed and advertising firms laid off staff. He had not yet been called up and meanwhile they had to do something to earn a living. In Holme he, and I think Froude too, got agricultural work, and later Rex worked at timber felling. They rented a cottage on the outskirts of the village – Alberries Cottages – and increasingly in my vacations it was their home rather than my parents' where I spent my free time.

They had brought with them from London a diminutive refugee from Austria named Karl. In common with many other people on the left they had volunteered their homes to refugees from the Hitler terror, communists, trade unionists, Jews and others. One device was to marry such people, because in those days marriage to a British citizen automatically gave British citizenship to one's spouse. I remember that George Miles had married a German woman, and I in my innocence had wondered why he had married someone in whom he showed no romantic interest. Rex had contacts with several refugees of this kind, the closest being a German communist and his wife and their little boy.

Karl had no pronounced left sympathies but had had to flee because he was a Jew. In Holme he too got field labourers' work, and found lodgings with a Holme couple. He was in Ma Pearson's gang, and the women all liked him and found him very amusing. He used to take the mickey out of Ma. Whenever she introduced one of her anecdotes with her standard, 'And will you believe this then?' before she could get any further Karl used to call out, 'No, Ma, I believe this not.' I don't think Ma was ever disconcerted by this.

When I wasn't working in the fields I used to sit for hours listening to Rex and Froude's gramophone records. I made my first acquaintance with a lot of Irish songs, all of which I still love, and still sing, like the Easter Week version of 'The Foggy Dew', one called 'The Spinning Wheel', and a comic one about the finding of Moses. Most of all I liked songs like 'Jackets Green', in which a woman sings of her love for a fighter for Irish freedom, and it is clear that he wouldn't *be* her beloved unless he were committed to the freedom struggle:

No hoarded wealth did my love own, save the good sword that he bore

But I loved him for himself alone & the colour bright he wore

For had he come in England's red to make me England's queen,

Ma Pearson's gang: front, from L, Marie, Karl

Marie

I'd have roved the high green hills instead for the sake of the Irish green

She accepts without question his need to fight and if need be die for the cause, to which she too is completely dedicated –

> *When William stormed with shot and shell*
> *at the walls of Garryowen*
> *In the breach of death my Donal fell*
> *and he sleeps near the Treaty Stone.*
> *That breach the foeman never crossed*
> *while he swung his broadsword keen;*
> *But I do not weep my darling lost*
> *for he fell in his jacket green.*

The feeling in such songs seemed to me a striking contrast with that of English girls who often had no interest in their communist lovers' commitment, and resented their giving time to such activities instead of to them. The songs kindled my interest in the Irish struggle – for instance in 'the men of 98' (that is, 1798) –

> *They rose in dark and evil days to free their native land*
> *And kindled there a living blaze that nothing can withstand –*

a struggle in which something like 30,000 lives were lost. I felt a boundless admiration for such people. As communists we were fighting the British ruling class; here was a people who had been doing so for centuries, suffering defeat after defeat but still fighting.

In the years that followed I learnt more and more Irish songs. At a rough estimate I must know thirty or forty of them, and most have a poetic quality which is not there in most of the revolutionary songs I had learnt earlier. 'Jackets Green' is a good example –

> *Oh Ireland, sad is thy lonely soul and loud beats the winter sea.*
> *But sadder and higher the wild waves roll o'er the hearts that*
> *break for thee.*

Rex and Froude's presence in the village made possible a new development in my relationship with Marie. They were a respectable married couple, and in the eyes of the village it was therefore quite acceptable for Marie to come and visit me at their cottage. They were entirely supportive of our love for each other, and it was only Marie's slowness to become ready to express this sexually, and my respect for her inhibitions, which made progress as slow as it was. In due course Rex and

Froude encouraged us to go upstairs and lie together. We did that, but lay together fully dressed until, on perhaps the second or third occasion she said she was afraid her dress would get creased. I said 'Take it off, then,' and she did. But she wasn't prepared to take all her clothes off and we didn't make love. I had no inhibitions about stripping off, and would on occasion bath in the tin bath on the rug in front of the living room fire, to Marie's mingled surprise and admiration at my brazenness.

Then Marie's husband died. I thought we should get married at once but she wouldn't agree. She said that for us to marry so soon after Sid's death would scandalise the village. I was perfectly ready to do that and felt that she too should be, blithely oblivious of the consideration that she had to live there all year round and I did not. Experience soon showed that she was right in her estimate of village attitudes. One Saturday we decided to go to York to spend the weekend with her sister Ada and her husband George. We were on the York-bound bus, sitting together on the back seat, when Rose Oretta Cox got on. The glare she gave us was more than enough to show her strong disapproval. Then, in my innocence I had assumed that we would sleep together at Ada's, but Marie now informed me that she didn't think Ada would allow this, and indeed she didn't. The result was that although, as Marie reminisced later, 'We *were* in love that weekend', I slept very uncomfortably in a single bed with George, and Marie slept with Ada.

The end of my Cambridge course was approaching and I had given very little thought to what I might do next. There seemed little point, since I knew I would be called up. But after that? All I thought was that whatever I did, it must be something in which I could give all my strength to working for communism. I had read, and been very moved by Nikolai Ostrovsky's autobiographical novel first published in an English translation by a British publisher under the title *The Making of a Hero*. (A later Soviet-issued translation was entitled *How the Steel was Tempered*.) In it Ostrovsky describes how the hero of the novel is standing by the graves of revolutionaries who had been shot by the Whites (counter-revolutionaries). He thinks

Man's dearest possession is life. It is given to him but once, and he must live it so as to feel no torturing regrets for wasted years, never know the burning shame of a mean and petty past; so live that, dying, he might say: all my life, all my strength were given to the finest cause in all the world – the fight for the liberation of mankind.

I assumed that, like most other people, I would eventually have to get a job of some kind to keep me alive while I fought for the communist cause, but the nature of the job was unimportant to me. I assumed that I should take from the income it brought me only enough to meet the necessities of life, and that the rest, little or much, would go to the communist cause, which I thought of as synonymous with the Communist Party. Marriage wouldn't make any difference to this – I had been clear for a long time that I wouldn't marry any woman who did not accept that this was how my life should be lived. My plan to marry Marie fitted into this context. I didn't think she would want to live anywhere except in Holme, and I was quite content with the prospect of becoming an agricultural labourer so that we could go on living together.

Beyond that, my strongest aspiration was to become a full-time worker for the Party. I thought that men and women who were chosen by the Party to work for it were the most fortunate people in the world – and if the movement really had been a communist movement, and had chosen its best people to be full-time party workers, that would have been so. I once talked of this ambition to Jack Cohen, the full-time student organiser for the Party, and was both disappointed and puzzled when he responded with, to say the least of it, a marked lack of enthusiasm. I assumed there must be some good reason why he discouraged me, and left it at that.

In May 1940, as we prepared to write our final exams, the news came that Germany had invaded the Netherlands and Belgium. The phoney war had ended. For months Britain might have had the chance to take the initiative but had not been ready to use it. Now that chance was gone.

With great suddenness, the mood in Britain changed radically. Chamberlain was replaced by Churchill. British troops were evacuated from Dunkirk, and by mid-June France had fallen to the Germans with almost no resistance. With all of Western Europe now in German hands, everyone knew that the next step might well be an invasion of Britain, but there was now really little to do except wait and see. It was striking that though people did that quite calmly, no one seemed willing to give any thought to the prospect that an invasion might be successful, and what they would do it it were. Churchill's famous speech – 'We shall fight them on the beaches, we shall fight them on the landing grounds ... We shall never surrender' – doubtless struck a chord in people's hearts, but the mood was not so much one of heroic defiance as the rather matter of fact feeling that we were British, and the British don't get conquered; they conquer. People just seemed to assume that somehow or other we would survive, whatever the Germans could throw at us.

I made no assumptions, either that the Germans would successfully invade or that they would not. All I knew was that no matter what happened I would continue to try and live as a communist. I might have to face a Nazi conquest and the imposition of the same terror which the German and French communists were already facing; or possibly something else one couldn't yet imagine. I had entered a period in which neither I nor anyone else could plan our future course in life. For the years ahead the guiding principle had to be, Take things as they come.

With all this in the air, we wrote our final exams. My neglect of my academic work produced its inevitable result, and I didn't achieve even a Third. The degree which Cambridge awards is usually described as a BA Hons. The piece of paper I received from the university certified that I was now a BA, but I had no idea whether this was a BA Hons or not. But by now such trivia didn't matter. The moment exams were over I was called up for military service – no time even to go through the formal degree-awarding ceremonies, but that was a matter of satisfaction as I have always hated ceremonies of this kind.

My Cambridge comrades and I would henceforth be leading separate lives. I knew there would be little possibility of following what was happening to them, and I accepted that. Like them, I was now on my own.

8

I was introduced to army life in the Northampton regimental depot, presumably because Northampton was near Cambridge where I had registered for call up. The depot covered quite a lot of ground. Near the entrance was a huge parade ground with one or two brick buildings to one side of it. From there, on land that sloped downhill, was a collection of green single-storey huts, each large enough to hold about forty men. Ours was towards the bottom of the slope. The whole place was dead boring, with no greenery of any kind, but we were worked hard and didn't have time to contemplate our surroundings, except when we went out on route marches. I liked the countryside around, as I like all kinds of countryside. Of Northampton itself my recollection is practically zero. We passed through bits of it on marches, but it made little impression.

Despite the hard physical work, the first weeks in the army seemed to me an enjoyable long holiday. For the past year political work had been a strenuous business, and now I found myself positively enjoying the lack of all freedom – and hence the lack of all responsibility – a life in which you even awoke to the command of reveille and from then until the command of lights out, never for a single moment had the responsibility of deciding what you should do, because you were all the time ordered what to do and the orders had to be obeyed. I learnt, to my own surprise, to understand the 'fear of freedom', as Erich Fromm has called it, the mass sentiment which, among others, enabled the fascist powers to make such a strong appeal to the people of their countries. Actually it would be more accurately described as a strong desire not to be free. I think there are millions of people who want nothing better than to feel as I did, and every revolutionary needs to be aware of that.

The evenings and weekends really *were* a holiday. I was often alone in the barrack room, immersed in reading – to the astonishment of my fellow soldiers and the rather uncertain disapproval of the corporals and sergeants. The men were only too eager to use their precious free time to go out on the town, but I had no desire to – I wouldn't have known what to do there. For the regular army sergeants it was an unwritten rule that a soldier off duty must be 'in bed or out of barracks' but I think they couldn't quite see how they could do anything about my odd behaviour and so let it pass.

It was now that I first really discovered Dickens. My only previous acquaintance with him had been at Chigwell, where we had had to read *Barnaby Rudge* – prescribed because in the early part the setting is Chigwell. I had hated the long descriptions, and felt impatient to get on with the story. Now I started on *Pickwick Papers*, loved it, and have loved ever since nearly all of Dickens that I have read. I remember, years later, reading *Martin Chuzzlewit* and finding it unputdownable. Even *Barnaby Rudge* I read again only a year or two ago and found it OK, though I don't think it is one of his best books.

I also read a lot more that I had not had time to read before, including all the remaining novels of Fielding, and I used from time to time to write about what I was reading to Margaret Horton, the friend from my Loughton party days with whom I had enjoyed discussing literature. I remember her being taken aback by the ferocity with which I assailed her for her poor opinion of Fielding's novel *Amelia*. She didn't feel any sympathy at all for the novel's heroine – and I told her that *I* thought of the heroine as having all the best qualities of her (Margaret) and Marie. Despite the differences between a country lass and a sophisticated intellectual, they had much in common – a complete unpretentiousness, a love of the countryside and all the pleasures of everyday life, and a strong loyalty to those they loved.

Politics, even in its most general form, rarely entered into our barrack-room conversation. Almost everything else did. In a barrack-room of thirty plus men which for the time being – a long time being – is your home, there is no privacy, and you soon cease to feel any need for it. I remember one morning at reveille the orderly corporal came round to see that everyone was out of bed, and found one man still lying under a blanket. He whipped the blanket off to reveal a proudly erect penis. Everyone laughed – not maliciously – and the owner of the penis seemed to feel no particular embarrassment. A regular cry of this orderly corporal was, 'Come on! Out of your wanking chariots.' Lewd songs, jokes and remarks were common currency.* So were 'sexually explicit' accounts, as the current phrase goes, of real or fictitious sexual conquests. Men home for a weekend with their wives were asked on their return if they'd spent the whole time 'on the nest' and commiserated with if they'd found that 'the robin was on the nest' – i.e. that their wife was having a period. Men back from leave would talk about their lovemaking with their wives. One said how surprised he'd been to find how tight his wife's vagina had become in his absence. Another told me his favourite time for intercourse with his wife was when she'd just come

169

back from hospital after having a baby and her pubic hair was still prick-ly. It was he who acquainted me with the ruder (and probably original) version of the 'Home late last night' song that we had innocently sung in the Boy Scouts. In this the wife's replies to her husband's questions were not in the unexceptionable language which we had been taught. Her every response began with

> *You're drunk, you're drunk*
> *You're drunk, you cunt*
> *You're drunk as drunk can be.*

These are the things I remember best about life in the Northampton depot, but I should also say something about what we were there for. The idea was to teach us the basic soldierly skills, and, of course, the norms of discipline we must learn to accept if we were to exercise these skills properly. It was generally the sergeants whose job it was to teach us both, while the officers, in most cases newly commissioned, swanned around, supposedly to check that everything was being done properly. My first experience of disciplinary norms came on the first morning. The sergeant lined us up ('Get fell in!') and inspected us. When he came to me he said, 'You've not shaved, Russell.' I said, 'No, sergeant, I only shave every other day.' 'In the army you shave every day,' he said. Most other disciplinary rules were quite easily assimilated and not par-ticularly irksome.

A lot of time was allotted to weapon training – teaching us to use the tools of the trade. How to fire a rifle, a light machine gun (Bren gun), and an anti-tank rifle, and how to use a bayonet. Also, for some reason, a pistol, though only officers carried pistols. And before we used any of them we were taught the naming of parts. Henry Reed's brilliant poem of that name is a wonderfully accurate description of how this was done, and reproduces almost word for word what our sergeants said – not sur-prising, I suppose, since most things in the army were done by the book, and word for word.

> *Today we have the naming of parts*

the poem begins, and when it comes to the piling swivel of the rifle,

> *Which in your case you have not got.*

Well, in our case too we had not got it.

The standard rifle was the Lee-Enfield 303, but there was a shortage of these, so we used an obsolete rifle called, if I remember rightly, a P14, indicating that it was of 1914 vintage. Another was the Bren gun, so called, we were told, because it had been produced in Brno (the correct pronunciation of which in our case we had not got.)⋆ Equally obsolete was the anti-tank rifle, although everybody knew (and those who didn't were told by the men back from Dunkirk) that it was quite useless against tanks. One thing I liked about it was that the foresight was enclosed in a circular housing, and if you aligned the backsight with this circle you got a 100% correct aim. I could never understand why the foresights on other weapons weren't similarly enclosed. On these you had to align the foresight with the shoulders (so to speak) of the backsight. Learning to use the pistol showed me how absurd were the scenes portrayed in film Westerns. It is a most inaccurate weapon except at very close quarters. It's not much of an exaggeration to say that if you can hit a barn door at a range of fifty yards you are doing well. There was a shortage of ammunition, so we didn't get much practice in actually firing these things on the range and on the few occasions we did I didn't do very well.

Weapon training was full of sexual and smutty innuendo. To fire a rifle from a lying position you were supposed to lie at a slight angle from it with your legs splayed, and if you didn't the sergeant would bawl at you, 'Open your legs, you won't get fucked here!' On the other hand, to fire the light machine gun you lay in line with the gun with your legs together, and if you didn't you would be told, 'Close your legs, your breath smells!' A particular piece of the light machine gun was called the body-locking pin – 'the body-locking pin or ladies' delight', as the sergeants called it. Underneath the gun was a shutter which you were supposed to close after firing and you had to feel underneath it and find a little knob which you put your finger on to pull the shutter closed. If you had difficulty in finding it the sergeant would say, 'You'd soon find it if we put some hairs round it!' – and despite the fact that I now had sexual experience I hadn't much idea of what he was on about. So too when the men referred to the clitoris as 'the boy in the boat.' I think I probably had no idea that there was such a thing as the clitoris, let alone why it was important.

I hated the bayonet fighting drill, not only for the obvious reason that I had absolutely no desire to thrust a bayonet into anyone, but for other reasons too. Our bayonets, like our rifles, were obsolete – World War I pattern – and much longer and heavier than the current ones. Soldiers used to regard the old kind as a handy substitute for a toasting fork and I remember a cartoon of a soldier using the new one and cursing because he had to lean right back and hold his arm fully extended because of the heat. Bayonet practice was totally absurd. The enemy was represented by a straw-filled sack, and the main thing that was impressed

In the Nottinghamshire Regiment: Ralph centre front

upon us was that as we thrust our bayonets into it we had to let out a blood-curdling yell. It was quite obvious to me that if you did get that far you would need all your breath for what you were doing. This went with a lot of other World War I crap – 'Remember that the Hun hates the bayonet' etc. However, I remember the attractive simplicity of an action called 'Parry, butt-stroke and kill.' This was designed to turn the tables on your attacker. You put your bayonet to the right of his, pushed it vigorously to the left and followed through by raising your rifle and hitting him such a violent blow on the head with the butt that he would be felled to the ground, after which you would jump on him and finish him off. These movements seemed to me to have a simple, economical grace about them. Practicalities were another matter. I, and I suspect most others, wouldn't have had anything like the physical strength needed for the parry and butt-stroke. But we learnt this like everything else.

The sergeants would occasionally take the piss out of the young officers who circulated among us. One was teaching us how to clean a rifle barrel after firing. This involved inserting a piece of cloth called a four by two into the loop of a pull-through cord. In the presence of an officer who was observing the proceedings the sergeant said, 'You will on no account pack the four by two with a matchstick', and when the officer had gone said, 'Personally I always pack the four by two with a matchstick.' Sometimes we ourselves got the opportunity of taking the piss. A little bloke called Albert Simpson – shorter than me, perhaps about five foot two – who had an amazingly resonant bass voice, used to take a great delight in this. Once on a route march we were marching in threes behind a young second lieutenant who was given to making supposedly morale-building remarks. He ordered us to lengthen our stride, with the cheery remark that this would get us home all the sooner. Whereat Albert boomed out, 'If we stride like this, Russell'll soon have a cunt.' On another occasion we were all assembled to hear a namby-pamby looking army padre warning us of the risk of getting VD (as sexually transmitted diseases were then called) from our 'lady friends.' At least, that was the object of the exercise, but the padre handled it so delicately that you might well not have understood what he was on about. Coming out of the hall Albert, in the presence of the officers, expressed his appreciation of the padre. 'Wasn't the padre lovely! I could fuck her!'

By and large we got on well with the sergeants, who knew very well that a heavy-handed insistence on 'good order and military discipline,' as the Army Act calls it, would not work with us conscripts. One used to butter us up by saying, 'Of course, you *have* to be in the army. I was a bloody fool, I volunteered.' One was a hopeless teacher and had to

173

resort to reading out of the military manual what he was supposed to be teaching us, absurd stilted language which he himself probably didn't fully understand. I remember him reading out, 'A proportion of the personnel will be retained at the rendezvous' which came out as 'A proportion of the personal will be retained at the rendyvuss.' Another, Sergeant Webb, used to like letting us know what a hardened old campaigner he was, and how he'd served at Razmak, on the Indian North-West Frontier. 'Sometimes you want to shit,' he said, 'and you can't. You just have to bake it.' If you needed sex, he said, it was better to use boys than to go to prostitutes, because 'a foreskin full of shit is better than a dose of pox.' But most of the sergeants were ordinary pleasant blokes doing their not very interesting job with the minimum of agro. One of them was called Dyson, and looked so much like the husband of my Mrs Dyson that I was tempted to ask him if he was related to him – a temptation to which I quickly realised it might be dangerous to yield.

Army food was pretty bad. It was common knowledge throughout the army that the NCOs (non-commissioned officers) in charge of the cookhouse sold some of the rations on the black market, and I guess ours did this too. On one day our pudding consisted of two pineapple cubes and a spoonful of juice. Officers on orderly officer duty would stop at each table and ask 'Any complaints?' and their standard response to any complaint about the food was 'It's the same as we get in the officers' mess', which I am sure was not true. There were jokes about entries in the army ordnance catalogue, which listed all the things that the army supplied to its personnel. One ended 'scale per 50 ORs, [other ranks] one'. Another – probably but by no means certainly fictitious – was 'Pots, chamber, rubber, without handle, officers, lunatic for the use of.'

We learnt from the old sweats the traditional words set to the army bugle calls. The words to the reveille call were

Get out of bed! Get out of bed! You lazy buggers!

The call to come for food,

Come to the cookhouse door, boys, come to the cookhouse door,

Dinner's ready, fill your belly, come to the cookhouse door

The officers mess call was

Officers' wives get puddings & pies & sergeants' wives get jelly

But privates' wives get nothing at all but a big prick up their belly

The arrival of mail.

Letter from lousy Lizzie, letter from lousy Lou

The general salute call was

Stand to attention you raw recruit! Don't make a fuck-up of the general salute.

And, to the same tune, the changing of the guard

Fall out the old guard, fall in the new,
We don't care a bugger what the old guard do.

Because my call-up had happened in the wake of the fall of France, I had expected when I arrived in the army that at any moment we might be facing an invading German army. As a first step the German airforce was attempting to destroy Britain's air defence. Once, in early September, if I remember rightly, there was something that I took to be an invasion scare, though no one told us that this was the case. We were ordered out at night to a hillside to man trenches. We were told that attacks were usually launched just before dawn, and that we must be fully awake and absolutely still and silent. I didn't feel afraid but I have never felt so desperate in my whole life. To stay awake when you have to be still and silent and there is nothing you can do to distract yourself needs an almost superhuman effort. However somehow I managed it.

By the 16th September the Battle of Britain had ended the danger of a German invasion, for the time being at least. But by now the bombing of British cities had got underway on quite a wide scale. In November from our barracks in Northampton we heard the waves of bombers overhead, on their way to bomb Coventry.

All this time I was naturally giving thought to what I, as a communist, could and should do now I was in the army. Dimitrov at the 7th World Congress had said something dear to my heart. Speaking of the qualities which every true communist should try to develop he had said 'The man who is afraid of taking responsibility is no leader,' adding that the party does not value 'the man who cannot act on his own initiative and so always does only what other people tell him.'* I had always thought along these lines, and was surprised when in later years I discovered that there are plenty of communists to whom this idea seems quite alien, and who think that unless there are several other communists around then the question of systematic communist work simply doesn't arise. I had also taken to heart Lenin's words, that a communist must 'work wherever the masses are to be found'.* It was in line with this principle that the communists in the first world war had gone into the imperialist armies and not 'conscientiously objected' to military service – because you can't turn imperialist soldiers into revolutionaries if you deny yourself the opportunity to be with them, share their experience, and help them draw the proper conclusions from it.

To apply this principle fully is, in normal times, one of the most difficult things a communist has to do, but here this difficulty was solved for me. For twenty-four hours a day I was 'where the masses are to be found.' From reveille to lights out they saw everything I did. All of me was open to inspection, whether I liked it or not (and as a good communist I did like it) and I knew that all of me should command liking and respect, even in areas where my views might evoke incomprehension or hostility. I knew that if I was really a good communist they couldn't fail to be drawn towards me, because a good communist must necessarily be in many ways what the ordinary person aspires to be, and all that is best in people responds to that.

Many years later I heard Sam Aaronovitch, the only party organiser for whom I have felt a great respect, say to a meeting of communist university teachers that we needed to guide our work by the principle, 'They who are not for us are partly for us.' That is true, and it doesn't contradict the better-known principle of 'They who are not for us are against us'. Both things are true, and remembering the one shouldn't mean forgetting the other. In other words, you should stand by, and fight for, your convictions and not pretend to common ground where there isn't any; but where there *is* common ground, no matter how little, you need to find it and build upon it. To do this successfully I needed to be a communist person, not just a communist political animal, and I was that.

Of course I don't mean that I proclaimed the full range of my communist beliefs. In the British army in 1940, with the Communist Party opposing the war, to tell people outright that you were a communist or to propagate views which only a communist could hold, would have been to run the serious risk of being thrown out of the army or put in jail, where opportunities of contact with 'the masses' would have been somewhat limited. So if anyone had asked if I were a communist I would have had to say No. But they didn't; and all that I did say, all that it was safe to say, was the true expression of what I believed, and not in contradiction with the things I couldn't yet say.

It was not in fact too difficult to spread what was essentially an anti-war message, for it was without enthusiasm that most of the men accepted that this was a war that must be fought – a significant difference from the raving jingoism which greeted the outbreak of war in 1914. C Day Lewis's words, that we were fighting to 'defend the bad against the worse' describe very well what people felt. They felt no enthusiasm at all for those who were in command of them, and with good reason. One of the units in Northampton depot, known as the depot company, comprised fully trained men who had already seen service in France and had come out in the Dunkirk evacuation and for one reason or another were not yet posted to further active service. Their experiences had made them a pretty mutinous lot, and their tales of the bloody-minded stupidity of some of the officers who had commanded them were hair-raising. The British army's anti-tank rifle – more powerful than an ordinary rifle, firing a larger calibre bullet – ought already to have been obsolete, because it was totally ineffective against modern German tanks, and the men knew this. What it *could* do was get a bullet through a brick wall behind which enemy troops were taking cover, which an ordinary rifle could not. One of the returnees told me that he had been forbidden by an officer to use it in this way because it was an *anti-tank* rifle.

Not long after I had been called up I got a letter from Marie, written in rather cryptic terms which I didn't have the wit to interpret. But in September all of us recent recruits were granted leave, and once back in Holme I found out what she had been trying to tell me. Rex had been visited by the police, who had taken away various papers and books and carted him off to the police station at Market Weighton, where they held him for, I think, a day and a night and questioned him before letting him go. To his amusement he learnt that they had got on to him not because of anything he had done, but because of something my mother had done – her letter condemning Britain's policy towards Spain, sent to the MP for Holme, Major Carver. He was outraged that one of his serfs could be so impertinent, and had put her down as a men-

The family in Hohne, 1940: L-R: father, mother, Ralph, Rex, Froude, Wilfred

ace to the British state. It was on his say so that Rex had been taken in for questioning. Perhaps it would have embarrassed them to take my mother in.

I spent most of my leave at Rex's house, and it was there that Marie and I at last went upstairs, stripped naked, and made love. I remember it all vividly. She said, 'Be gentle; it's been a long time since.' And I was. She said afterwards she would never forget the tender love that my face expressed. She has also told me that at one point in the proceedings I called her 'lovely lubricating Marie,' and this sounds so completely authentic that I'm sure I must have done, though I don't remember it. I'm sorry to say I ejaculated prematurely – outside her, because I had risked 'contraception' by withdrawal – and she said, 'Oh, hell, I thought it would last longer than that!' Still, we were both very happy. She had never taken all her clothes off for me before, and now said, 'Now that you've seen me, do you like me?' – a remark which she doesn't remember! I later reported it to Froude, who disapproved of my telling her, and told me so. She said that such intimate things shouldn't be told to anyone else.

I was afraid that I might have made Marie pregnant, but my fears proved to be unfounded. A letter from her after her next period told me, 'OK about everything done on last leave.'

Only in the months that followed did I come to realise that Rex's encounter with the police had had quite an effect on Marie. She had more than once said to me, 'If we got married you would always put the Party first, wouldn't you,' and I, proudly and unhesitatingly, always answered, 'Yes.' I don't think she ever thought of what, in normal circumstances, 'putting the Party first' was likely to mean in practical terms, and I was too proud of my communist purity to think that I needed to think about this. Otherwise I would have realised that in normal circumstances it would not have involved anything disruptive of our married life. But circumstances in 1940 weren't normal, and since Rex's experience she had visions of my being arrested and having to spend long periods in jail. I don't remember whether she said this to me direct or to Rex and Froude who passed it on to me, but she once said 'I've had one husband who couldn't be with me and I don't want another.'

I think her misgivings might eventually have been overcome, but meanwhile she became friendly with one Ronnie King, who had come from Crakehall in North Yorkshire to work in Holme on the construction of the aerodrome. She wrote and told me this, saying that it was 'just friendship, and nothing more than that.' I didn't believe that it would remain 'just friendship and nothing more than that' and wrote and told her that if she was going to knock about with another bloke while I was away in the army it was high time she learnt something about birth control. Froude told me when I next came on leave that this had been much too harsh a letter, and perhaps she was right. In any case I felt we were at a turning point. It was now up to her to decide whether she was going to have an exclusive relationship with me or call it all off.

My friend Chris Freeman, too, was facing decisions in his personal life. He was younger than me and still at university, but was likely to be called up as soon as he finished. While I was in Northampton he came to visit me, together with Peggotty, the girl friend he had acquired after I had left Cambridge. In the course of conversation they asked me if I thought they should get married. They felt that a marriage ceremony was perhaps a violation of some important principle. To me this was a non-problem. If a marriage ceremony is of no significance, then it is of no significance whether you have it performed or not. There was a strong practical advantage in their being married before Chris was called up, for then Peggotty would get an allowance from the government. They saw the point and acted accordingly.

Because I had been to Cambridge I was regarded by everyone as potential officer material, a ridiculous conclusion but one universally drawn. So I was put forward for promotion to the dizzy rank of Lance-Corporal. To qualify we had to show our proficiency in various martial activities, including throwing a hand-grenade. I knew how to do this but I couldn't, because it had to be thrown overarm and I've never been able to do this. As a result I could not throw it far enough, and if it had been a real one and had exploded, I and not the enemy would have been the casualty. But I was promoted nevertheless (acting, unpaid), together with, among the others, David Willcocks, who had also been at Cambridge.*

Now we were taught other skills deemed by the army to be necessary for holders of that rank. One was the ability to drill a platoon (about thirty men) and have them fulfil such commands as 'Attention!' 'Stand at ease!' and (not the same thing) 'Stand easy!' Or the commands of army drill, 'Slope arms!' 'Present arms!' 'Order arms!' None of these required the men to move from where they were standing. To get them on the move you would command them to 'Quick march!' – sometimes 'Double march!' (i.e. at twice as quick a pace as usual) or 'Right wheel!' You could hold up their advance by 'Mark time!' and finally tell them to 'Halt!'

Then there were the more complicated commands such as 'At the halt, on the left, form platoon', the details of which I no longer remember, except that it began with the left-hand man taking three paces forward. The mnemonic for this was a verse to the tune of 'Three Cheers for the Red, White and Blue', and ran

At the halt on the left, form platoon, at the halt on the left, form platoon

If the left-hand man don't take 3 paces forward

How the hell can the rest form platoon?

The fixing of bayonets was another complicated drill. 'On the command Fix! you don't fix. The righthand man takes three short, sharp, shit-hot paces forward' – and does something I can't now remember. 'On the command Bayonets! you whips 'em out and whops 'em on.'

I used to like drill, both being drilled and drilling others. Whether it has any real military use I doubt, but the experience of moving in unison with others I always found very satisfying. I also liked marching in the big, formal parades to the music of the military band. One regimental march began with one tune and passed straight on to 'The Lincolnshire Poacher'–

When I was bound apprentice in famous Lincolnshire

Full well I served my master for more than 7 year

Till I took up to poaching as you shall shortly hear

Oh, 'tis my delight on a shiny night in the season of the year.

God knows why – as far as I know the Northamptonshire regiment had nothing to do with Lincolnshire. There was also a very nice tune to accompany the slow march which I have never been able to identify

181

There was another tune we marched to that I particularly liked but had not heard before. It has a lively, light sense of forward movement ideally designed to keep you moving in time –

Many years later I told my brother Noel and began to hum it, and he at once said, 'That's the Rising of the Lark' and proceeded to sing –

> *Rise, rise, thou merry lark,*
> *Whose upward flight I love to mark at early dawn of day*

I later discovered that it is the regimental march of the Welsh Guards and that it had been in my school songbook, *British Songs for British Boys*, but we had never sung it at school. I may have seen it in the book but couldn't recognise it for what it was because I couldn't read music, either in the regular musical notation or in the tonic sol fa notation, both of which the book provided. I still can't – the tunes given here have been written down for me by a musical friend.

I have two other clear memories from my time as lance-corporal. One is being put on a charge under the catch-all section 40 of the Army Act, 'conduct to the prejudice of good order and military discipline.' (Before my time there had been a charge of 'dumb insolence.' You could be charged with it if, without saying a word, you looked at an NCO or an officer in a way he didn't like. But this had now been abolished.) This incident was a good illustration of the absurdities of army life. At reveille the orderly sergeant came round shouting 'Feet on the floor!' which meant we had to be out of bed and getting dressed. On one occasion I was getting dressed all right, but because the floor was cold was standing on the bed to do so, and the orderly sergeant put me on a charge for disobeying his order, 'Feet on the floor.' The trial to which, having been charged, you were subjected was as ludicrous as most other things in army disciplinary procedures. You were in due course summoned to the orderly room, where you awaited your turn to have your case tried by your commanding officer. When your turn came you were commanded to Stand to attention and then Quick march, Right wheel, Left wheel, until you got to the desk behind which the commanding officer was sitting, when you were commanded to Mark Time! and then Halt! The orderly sergeant or whoever was charging you was then called upon to make his statement. He would salute and then make it in standard form. In my case it would have gone like this. 'Sir! On the 25th of the tenth 1940 I was orderly sergeant. Reveille had sounded and I had given the command, 'Feet on the floor!' The accused stood on his bed. Sir!' Another salute. The accused would then be asked if he had anything to say, and sentence would then be passed. In my case I chose not to 'have anything to say.' I knew perfectly well that the maintenance of 'good order and military discipline' would compel the commanding officer to support a sergeant against the lower ranks, no matter how ridiculous his charge might be. So I received my sentence, which was 'reprimand.' It could have been 'severe reprimand.'

The other memory is of a fellow lance-corporal, recently promoted like me, to whom I lent Ostrovsky's autobiographical novel, *The Making of a Hero*. He was much impressed by its fervent communist message. His response is indicative of the friendly feelings towards the Soviet Union that until 1939 had been quite common, and that still survived here and there. At some level there was in the army a sort of awareness of what the Russian revolution had been about. I learnt that every now and then 'soviets' – called that by the men and their commanders alike – would be held, at which everyone was at liberty, with immunity from punishment, to speak his mind freely and voice any complaint he wanted to. To which I must add that I don't remember one happening in my time.

By February 1941 I had spent nine months in the ranks – 'other ranks', as the military designation has it, to distinguish them from King's, or Queen's, commissioned officers. I had enjoyed the experience very much. I was with 'the masses', not with toffee-nosed Cambridge types, and I would have liked to stay in the ranks and continue to enjoy that atmosphere. But in due course I reluctantly went forward for selection for officer's training. It was only my communist conscience that drove me to do so, reinforced by the arguments of James Klugmann. I had first met James when he came to visit our branch in Cambridge just after the outbreak of the war and had taken an immediate liking to him. He was a leader in the international organisation of communist students and one of the few foreign communists who met Mao in China years before the Chinese communists came to power. No doubt I was impressed by his status (which he never showed off about) as an international communist leader. Anyway I acted upon his advice, though I can't remember when it was that we could have talked about it, for he wasn't anywhere near me when I eventually submitted my application. I was duly selected, and sent to Bulford on Salisbury Plain to an officer cadets' training unit in March 1941.

The training took three months, and was totally inadequate. We were not made to acquire most of the skills that an officer should have. (Later in the war training was more adequate and much more tough, as I know from friends who underwent it.) I remember one amusing incident associated with an exercise called TEWT – Tactical Exercise Without Troops – designed to see how well we would cope with a critical situation. All of us gathered around a large board presenting a miniature picture of such a situation. The officer in charge said to me 'You're here, and the enemy are here' – on opposite sides of the board. 'You have to attack across open ground. How will you go about it?' Somehow I knew the answer to that one. A direct attack on the enemy's position would mean that they could get our men in their sights one by one and pick them off. The drill therefore was to have different men stand up at different times, run forward quickly, and then drop down before the enemy could get them in their sights. You didn't do this in regular order, left to right or right to left. You had to prepare the men beforehand, e.g. that number three was to get up and run first, then number seven, then number two, and so on. When I had said my piece the officer in charge asked the other cadets what they thought of it. Not knowing whether he expected them to approve or disapprove, they said something vague. The officer said very sharply, 'Russell has given an excellent, clear appraisal'!

In June 1941, while I was still at Bulford, we heard that the Germans had invaded the Soviet Union. This was headline news for everyone, but to communists it changed the whole character of the war, for the only socialist state in the world was now threatened by Nazi forces. The opinion of my fellow cadets was that the Germans 'would go through the Russians like a hot knife through butter' – a phrase also used by Sir John Dill, Chief of Britain's Imperial General Staff. The US Secretary of the Navy Frank Knox said that Hitler would knock Russia out of the war in six weeks, and Secretary of War Henry Stimson said that Hitler would 'be busy' with Russia for four weeks, at the most twelve. German estimates were that it would take them between six and seventeen weeks. There was a general feeling of contempt for the Russians during the summer, when the Germans were rapidly advancing – not very appropriate in people whose own armies had performed so lamentably in 1939-40.*

To the considerable astonishment of my fellow cadets, I confidently prophesied that the Russians would defeat the Germans. My estimate was based on a book by Max Werner published in 1938 as a Left Book Club choice, *The Military Strength of the Powers*, which had forecast a rapid and successful offensive if the Soviet Union was forced to go to war. Before the substantial build-up of German military strength made possible by British and French appeasement, this could possibly have happened; but not now. But though my estimate of Soviet martial prowess was certainly an overestimate, it was still much less wide of the mark than the prevailing opinion. Within a short time it became clear to all observers that the Soviet Union was putting up an extremely spirited defence, contrasting sharply with what had happened in France, and British public opinion towards the Soviet Union now began to change from hostility to admiration.

To me, as to all communists at the time, the war was now clearly a just war that we must wage with all our strength. So the Party's opposition to the war must at once change to full support of it. But I was much taken aback by a statement made by William Rust, editor of the still banned *Daily Worker,* that the ban should be lifted because the Communist Party would now support the war and the government. *And the government!* The British government included people like Moore Brabazon, who had openly said that Germany and Russia should be left to exhaust each other while we sat back and reaped the benefits. True, these weren't in the majority, and the majority, led by Churchill, at once declared for a British-Soviet alliance; but such an alliance could provide a respectable cloak for a policy different only in degree from the 'let them exhaust each other' line. I saw no case for the Party to declare its support for the goverment – we should have supported them only in those measures which clearly corresponded to the demands of the situation as we saw it.

Of the few communists I was able to meet over the next months, all supported the Party's new line. I thought their arguments absolutely puerile. They asked me, 'How can you support the war and yet not support the government that's waging it?' as though this involved so self-evident a contradiction as to make any further argument superfluous. To me it was clear that we should have supported the war, but at the same time continued vigorously to oppose the government and press for a new one fully committed to genuine, concrete help to the Soviet Union, and to a policy at home which advanced the interests of ordinary people against those of the rich. And this, incidentally, was what we had proposed to do in September 1939 before the Comintern's intervention had made us change our line.

At the end of June 1941 I was commissioned, becoming a Second Lieutenant. I was posted, at my own request, to the East Yorkshire Regiment, whose depot was in Beverley. Beverley is not all that far from Holme, and I knew also that Marie's elder sister Gertie lived there.

When I was off duty I used to visit Gertie, and was soon going to her house almost every evening. By now things had gone wrong between me and Marie. What I wanted from her was a clear decision either that she was going to marry me or that she wasn't, and when I didn't get it, I decided that it was time to make or break. I probably had no right to expect her at that time to be capable of such conclusive thinking, but I did expect it and reacted accordingly when it didn't come. I did not feel, either then or later, that I had ceased to love her. If she had at any time chosen to commit herself I would have been overjoyed. Gertie was, so to speak, on my side and hoped that Marie would repent and be saved. So too was Lena, her younger sister, though in her case I think this was mainly because she thought an army officer a good catch for a simple village girl. I liked Gertie a lot, and also her twelve-year-old daughter Barbara and her seven or eight year old son Stephen. Barbara was illegitimate, the child of one of the Sherwoods' neighbours, but Gertie had not followed the general pattern of 'having to get married' to the father of the child. I was pleased with what I assumed had been her independence of mind, and it wasn't until much later that it occurred to me that it may not have been her decision, but that *he* had refused to marry *her*. Gertie's husband too had made her pregnant before they were married. Their relationship was not particularly harmonious, but not particularly stormy either. He and I quite liked each other, but he was quite a selfish man, while Gertie was anything but that. She liked me a lot, among other things because to her amazed admiration I saw no reason why I shouldn't do 'women's work' like washing up. She fairly openly favoured Barbara over Stephen, and Stephen often protested about this. 'Oh, me muther, you are mean!' he would say, 'You're always hitting me, and you never hit oor Barbara' – a perfectly legitimate complaint. I would greet Stephen with, 'And how are you, cock?' and he would respond, 'They doan't call me cock, they call me 'tephen.' His speech was pure East Yorkshire. He would say, 'I'm not off to' meaning 'I'm not going to,' and I loved to hear him talk.

I went back to Holme occasionally. Rex had been called up and was going into the Navy. Noel was in the air force and had been sent to Canada for training. Wilfred was getting married to a barmaid in the

Blacksmith's Arms in Holme, a girl from a family of farmworkers. In the wedding photo I am in my lieutenant's uniform; Wilfred is still in civilian clothes, so his call up must have happened a little later.

The German assault on the Soviet Union continued. People in Britain were increasingly aware that the Soviet Union was the only one of the allies actually fighting the Germans, and admiration for the Soviet troops' tenacious defence grew steadily. In late August British troops occupied southern Iran and Soviet troops the north, to pre-empt any move by Germany to break through in that direction; apart from that there seemed little for British infantry troops to do. After the fall of France the army had cried aloud for more officers, shortened the officers' training courses to three months and pushed through any old Tom Dick and Harry. Now they had so many junior officers that they didn't know what the hell to do with us.

As a result we had plenty of time on our hands. When on duty (if you can call it that) I used sometimes to get a regular army corporal that I liked to take me out on Beverley Westwood and teach me how to use a range-finder. He had many interesting things to tell me. One of them was that during the 'troubles' in Ireland after the first world war discontented British soldiers used to express their discontent by singing the Irish nationalist song about Kevin Barry ('Ireland's boy hero') who was hung by the British at that time

In Mountjoy Jail one Monday morning, high upon the gallows tree

Kevin Barry gave his young life for the cause of liberty.

The last verse begins

Another martyr for old Ireland, another murder for the Crown
Brutal laws to crush the Irish cannot keep their spirits down.

Singing it was a punishable offence.

After only a couple of months in Beverley I was sent to Brecon (for less than twenty four hours, if I remember rightly) and then to Huyton, near Liverpool. Liverpool had been for some time subject to bombing with incendiary bombs, and our duty was fire-watching at night. We went to our various posts for the night, but nothing happened – it seemed the raids had stopped by the time we got there. (In looking back

187

At Wilfred's wedding

With Rex in his naval uniform

I regarded this as my second experience of something that continued throughout the war – I was posted to places of danger, but just before I actually got there the danger had passed. The first experience was being called up immediately after the fall of France, expecting to face an invading German army which never came.)

Because we were on duty all night we were given the daylight hours to rest in. I used some of my abundant leisure time to write a long letter to the Party's Central Committee, expressing my fundamental disagreement with their policy that support for the war required us to support the government. Bearing in mind the character of the audience I was addressing, I supported my argument by reference to the latest addition to holy writ, the *Short History of the CPSU*, pointing out how the Bolsheviks had handled a similar situation in 1917. During the days when the government was headed by Kerensky, and the Bolsheviks were working against it, General Kornilov marched on Petrograd aiming to crush both of them. Kerensky appealed to the Bolsheviks for help. But they refused. They called on the workers and soldiers 'to put up active armed resistance to the counter-revolution … But while mobilising the masses to crush the Kornilov revolt, the Bolsheviks did not discontinue their struggle against the Kerensky government.'

I took a weekend leave to go to Cambridge to hand my letter over to Freddie Lambert, who was still there, asking her to get it to the Party Headquarters. I felt she didn't welcome my visit and behaved as if it was an interruption to more important things. I don't know whether she ever delivered it – I never received either response or acknowledgement to the letter, and I had got the impression, perhaps unfairly, that she didn't think it mattered much whether she got it there or not. But simply writing that letter constituted a landmark in my development because it was the first time since I had become a communist that I had disagreed, and maintained my disagreement, with the 'Party line.'

Eventually I landed up at Richmond, Yorks, which was henceforth to be the combined depot of two regiments, the East Yorkshire regiment and the Green Howards. There I became very friendly with a fellow-officer who came from Beverley – and for whom, I learnt later, Gertie had worked as a cleaner. Like many others, now that the Soviet Union was our ally, he was interested in what had happened there and very willing to listen sympathetically to what I could tell him. Once when I was in full flow I said that my complete loyalty was to communism and to the Soviet Union, where communists ruled; and if ever in the future Britain turned against the Soviet Union and made war on it, I would fight actively for a Soviet victory. This proved a bit too much for him and he went and reported this to a regular army major in the depot.

The major summoned me, told me that he knew what I had said, that he didn't want me here any more and that he would post me elsewhere as soon as he could arrange this. He did, and I was sent to a battalion assigned to coastal defence at Hartlepool.

Here for the first time I was given command of a platoon. A platoon is a unit of about thirty men, commanded by a junior officer, assisted by a sergeant (who usually knew what he was about much better than the officer did) and divided into three sections of ten men, each headed by a corporal or lance corporal. This so-called coastal defence was a farce. The Germans were fully committed on the eastern front and the danger of invasion was nil. The battalion, officers and men alike, knew this and very sensibly behaved accordingly. Not so Second Lieutenant Russell. He was a responsible officer, and was much concerned that the bit of coast which his platoon was to defend should be in a fit state to do that. He found that our main weapon was a machine gun of World War I vintage and that only one man in the unit (a corporal) knew how to operate it. In any case it was all clogged up with sand, and so too were the communication trenches connecting the sections with platoon HQ. I gave orders, to the silent amusement of the men, that these should be cleared.

Our battalion was then moved to Middlesborough. What exactly we were supposed to do there I can't remember, but what we did can be adequately described in the words 'nothing much.' For some equally unremembered reason I had a lot of contact with an officer in the Intelligence Corps, of whom I have two main memories, one of a visit with him to a wonderful performance of Handel's Messiah by a local chapel choir, and the other of a joke he told me, which went as follows. Two soldiers were going to a dance. One said, 'But what shall we do for partners?' The other said, 'That's OK. Leave that to me.' They arrived at the dance hall, went in, and surveyed the scene. Then the 'leave that to me' soldier said, 'You wait here. I'll be right back.' The other watched him go up to the prettiest woman on the floor and saw how a moment later she slapped his face. When he came back his friend asked him, 'What on earth did you say?' He said, 'What I always say – do you fuck?' 'Good God,' said the other, 'you must get an awful lot of rebuffs,' 'Yes,' he said, 'but I get a lot of fucks too.' I have always accepted the moral of this story, which is, 'If you want something, go ahead and ask for it. You won't always get a refusal.'

I used my plentiful free time to read. From when I had first joined the army I had felt that now I had the chance to fill in the still substantial gaps in my education, in both literature and history. In a bookshop I found a bargain, limp-cloth Moscow edition of the historical works of

Marx and Engels – sold 'under the counter' because (I believe) it infringed Allen and Unwin's copyright where some works were concerned – and I started out on a serious study of its nearly 700 pages. I have a habit of marking the dates when I read things, and see that I'd already read about 200 of them by November 1941.

∞

In December things suddenly began to move. On the 4th news came that Soviet troops had held up the Germans at Moscow. For everyone in Britain this had a powerful morale effect, for it was the first real setback for the Germans. But then came news of an opposite kind. The Japanese bombed Pearl Harbour. On 8th December the US declared war on Japan, and the Germans and Italians declared war on the US. A week after Pearl Harbour Japanese forces crossed the southern border into Burma and advanced northwards with amazing rapidity towards the capital, Rangoon. On December 23rd Japanese planes began to bomb Rangoon. The shock to British official consciousness was immense. Not since British colonial power had been established in these areas had it been challenged by a rival power, and the Allies were completely taken by surprise by the extent of threat they now posed. And if Britain lost Burma to the Japanese, then India too would be at risk.

For this possibility the British authorities in India were totally unprepared. Their understanding had been (and school geography text-books had said) that India had never been invaded except from the north-west, and could never be invaded except from that direction. The eastern frontier was believed to be naturally impregnable. Now here were the Japanese advancing rapidly towards this 'impregnable' frontier. The British in India responded by a sudden expansion in the size of the Indian Army, and a call went out for officers from the British Army to be transferred to work on attachment to the Indian Army.

These distant events soon made their impact on me personally – my company commander came into the officers' mess and informed me that I was one of those who was being posted to India. The news was not welcome. Of course I was interested in India – ever since I had become a communist I had felt a strong identification with the struggle of Indians to free themselves from colonial domination, and my involvement with Indian students in Cambridge had strengthened this. But it had never even remotely occurred to me that I might be sent to India, and I knew quite well that as a communist I would have little prospect of doing anything in India other than keeping my eyes open and learning what I could. Since the Communist Party of India was illegal I thought it unlikely that I should even be able to contact it, especially as I knew that my commanding officer was well aware of my political views and might possibly pass on his information to the military authorities in India. On the other hand, if I stayed in England I should be able to continue to keep in touch with political developments, get the Party's publications, perhaps develop contact with party branches wherever I might be stationed and – most important of all – influence the men under my command, most of whom were young conscripts who had been called up in the summer of 1939.

But it quickly became clear that there was absolutely no prospect of getting my posting cancelled. I accepted what was going to happen, and soon began to look forward to the positive aspects of the situation.

I know from letters – though I have absolutely no memory of it – that while I was awaiting transfer I was posted to Leeds – presumably I and other officers posted to India were assembling there until arrangements could be made for a troopship to take us. I spent Christmas at home, where I packed as many of my books as weight restrictions on baggage allowed, and then went back to Leeds, where I discovered an excellent public library, and used the time of waiting to read Benn's Sixpenny Library *History of Ireland*, Dimitrov's *Letters from Prison*, and Harry Gannes' *When China Unites*. Then in early January we left for Greenock near Glasgow, from where our ship would depart. I thought regretfully of all the books I had been about to read but had not had the foresight to buy while I was in a place where books could be got. My last act before the ship sailed was to post a letter to Froude, with a cheque and a list of books for her to send on to me in India – wherever, and whenever, that might be.

9

We set sail early on the morning of 4th January 1942. It was dark when
we set out, and by the time it was light we were out on the open sea.
We were in convoy, and our ship, the *Strathmore*, was the leading ship.
Out on the flanks were warships – a destroyer and a much larger ship,
perhaps a battle cruiser. We were to sail via the Cape because of enemy
control, or near-control, of the Mediterranean, which made it impossible to go via Suez; and we headed more or less down the middle of the
Atlantic, to diminish as far as possible the danger from U-boats.

I had never been on the sea before, and I loved it. For the first few
days there were terrific winds blowing, the ship pitching and rolling all
over the place, but no matter how rough the sea I did not feel seasick. I
would stand near the prow of the ship and watch it rearing up until I
could see nothing but sky, and then plunging down again into the
troughs of the huge waves. Out on the left the destroyer – light, built for
speed – would be tossing about like a cork and the battle cruiser would
keep a level course simply ploughing through the waves. On calm
sunny days I would watch the rainbows in the spray and the sea changing colour as the light changed.

After some days we put into Freetown. I was up on deck watching
as we came in. It was a brilliant sunny morning and the sea was almost
motionless. The contrast between this and the cold, dull of Glasgow in
January was extreme. I remember vividly the brightness of the colours –
the red sand, the palm trees growing right down to the edge of the
shore, the white or pale yellow buildings, then a little way up the hill
dark timber houses with bright red tiles, and finally behind them closely wooded slopes climbing steeply to the horizon. We weren't allowed
ashore and had to be content to hang over the rails watching naval officers coming and going in smart white motor launches, usually with a
fine looking tall African standing on the front holding the boat hook.
We had hardly anchored before scores of small boats began converging
in from all sides – 'bumboats' – long narrow shell-like dug-outs that the
bumboatmen paddled with their hands at amazing speed. They
swarmed around the ship all day long, singing and diving for money.

After that we didn't see land again until for about six weeks.

My travelling companions on the ship didn't constitute an army unit. We were a miscellaneous collection of infantry officers gathered from different companies. We were all, to put it mildly, surplus to requirements in Britain, and being sent off to staff the now greatly expanded Indian Army. So far as I know the 'other ranks' in the bowels of the ship were a similarly miscellaneous bunch, but we had nothing to do with them. I only once had occasion to go below decks where they were quartered. I was appalled at the squalor I saw there, and shocked by the extreme contrast in the conditions in which we and they lived. James Klugman, the man who had persuaded me that I should accept the opportunity of becoming an officer, later said to me, 'A troopship is an illustration of the most crude and exaggerated communist picture of capitalist society' and he was right.

For an officer, life on board ship was very comfortable. We had no duties of any kind. Food was excellent and there was plenty of fruit. The only 'hardship' was being five to a cabin designed for one or two, but that was really no hardship at all. In my cabin was a small Scotsman who rapidly became a friend, a large and jovial machine-gunner from Cardiff, and a man named Rufus (no doubt from his red hair) who had a degree in music. He heard me singing a song he didn't know – the Red Cavalry Song, 'When the White guards invaded' – and aroused my unbounded envy by writing it down in about two minutes in musical notation –

When the White Guards invaded & the Donbas was raided, in those grim unforgettable years, swift our columns assembled, how the earth heaved & trembled, as we galloped with song & with cheers

He was organising a choir to sing at concerts for the officers and troops, and asked me to teach him other Soviet songs. He then worked all the hours that came at arranging them, parts for sopranos, 1st tenors, 2nd tenors, 1st basses and 2nd basses, while I helped by copying the words onto each part and making suggestions based on the records I had heard of them. We did 'Song of the Plains', 'The Partisans' and 'Death of Chapayev' –

The steppes lie uneasy, the night foul & grey. The foe like a fox

through the gloom makes his way. Chapayev hears nothing –

his men are asleep. The whites towards the drowsy red sentinels creep

U-ral, Ural, so silent flows, no murmur, no glimmer shows.

The choir shared his enthusiasm to learn these songs – a sign of the lively interest in the Soviet Union since it had become our ally, and especially since Soviet armies had halted the Germans' advance on Moscow.

My other musical experience was listening to a group of pipers playing bagpipes on the deck one night, an experience I really enjoyed – though I didn't feel quite up to joining the group of officers being taught highland dances.

The Army meanwhile was providing us with its brand of orientation to the life we were heading for. The first part was the arrangement of classes in which a British colonel taught us some elementary Urdu. Urdu was the official language of the Indian Army and any Indian who enlisted had to learn it, so even though it wasn't in the event the mother tongue of most of the Indian soldiers I was to command, it would be our only vehicle for communication. I was really keen to learn it well but within a couple of weeks I had reluctantly given up because the officer instructing us didn't seem to know the language – especially the pronunciation – well, and I knew that I should find it very difficult to unlearn incorrect pronunciation. The rest was something of a shock. We were called together in the lounge for a lecture on India by Brigadier Battersby. He began very well – said how much we should like the country and how pleasant an officer's life out there was. Then to my amazement he went on to say that one never worked more than a couple of hours in the morning, and took the afternoons and evenings off. There was plenty of polo and pleasant social life at the clubs. One employed one's own civilian bearer (personal servant) at a very cheap wage which made a negligible difference to one's income. He represented life in the Indian Army as a pleasant and leisurely round of social activity, interlarded with a few hours nominal 'work' every morning. At least, he said, that was how it used to be; war-time might have brought a few changes. I was astounded. Only days ago we had heard on the radio news of what Churchill called the 'greatest disaster to British arms in history' – the surrender of Singapore, the major British naval base in Asia. Control of the Indian Ocean had now passed to the Japanese, who might soon be threatening India – and here was this stupid bastard, a high ranking officer, commander of a brigade of 3000 men, bound for India, nattering away about polo and drinking in the club.

But there was worse still was to come. He went on to 'say a little about India itself.' We would like the cities. Bombay and Calcutta looked quite like home, with buses and trams running in the streets ('though of course you don't use them – you take a taxi or a rickshaw'). Things had changed greatly from what they were. You could no longer legally prevent an Indian who had a first-class ticket from travelling in the same compartment with you. It was no longer legal to beat or hit an Indian, so it was important to make sure that there were no witnesses when you did. Remember also that it was sometimes dangerous to hit them – most of them were physically weak, had enlarged spleens or something of the kind, and could easily be killed by the shock alone. It was safer to use a stick than actually to lay hands on them …

I looked around the room and was dismayed at the apparent placidity with which the audience was listening to his words. At last he finished speaking, and asked for questions. A young Irish officer stood up and said, 'You spoke in your talk, sir, of how you could not legally prevent Indians travelling with you in the same railway carriage. Don't you think that as we and India are fighting the same war we should rather be glad to travel with them?' He stood up, smirked, and replied, 'Oh, I don't know. You see, they smell.'

I later heard something of the previous history of this particular gentleman. Many months later I heard an officer telling a story about an important infantry exercise in which he had to act as an umpire, and how he was approached by a Brigadier who had lost contact with the whole of his brigade. He didn't know where his brigade HQ was, or what position any of his three battalions had taken up. He asked the umpire to help him. As he was describing this Brigadier and the secret glee with which he pointed out that, as an umpire, he was forbidden to give information about the position of any troops, the impression was growing on me that I had come across him somewhere before. I asked the name of this Brigadier; it was Battersby. I asked him to describe him, and his description left no doubt that this was the same man who had lectured us on the ship. The last the officer had heard of him was that he had been deprived of his command and posted elsewhere. And so it emerged that this incompetent ass, retaining his Brigadier's rank, was being sent out to a country threatened with invasion to take command of the lives of several thousand men.

With nothing else required of me, I settled in to the satisfying prospect of two months of almost uninterrupted reading. Within a few weeks I had finished my study of the 700 plus pages of the historical works of Marx and Engels, and went on to read R Palme Dutt's *India Today*. Rajini Palme Dutt was the son of an Indian father and a Swedish mother. He had been a brilliant student at Oxford during the 1914-18 war. He was already a convinced communist and quickly became a leading member of the British Party – one of the few with any claim to intellectual brilliance – and dedicated his whole life to it. His *India Today* impressed me as a very fine book. I was particularly impressed by its analysis of the different stages of the national movement, and my own understanding of India is permanently indebted to it. I still admire the book today, despite the fact that I see many defects in it now which I could not see then.

Most of my fellow officers reacted with puzzlement and mild disapproval to the spectacle of one who spent most of his time just reading. (*Reading!* – I ask you!) I don't remember any of them showing any curiosity about what I was reading. For my part, I was completely absorbed, and reading Marx and Engels' lucid analysis of historical events was an experience as enjoyable as it was instructive. Woven through it was a wealth of fascinating historical detail – on the Great French Revolution, the Civil War in England, the social structure of the USA, ancient Rome, military strategy, and techniques of street-fighting, just to mention a few. I decided to make a subject index to the entire book – which (the index, not the book) I am sorry to say I have since lost. I particularly enjoyed the fact that they wrote freely and vigorously, saying what they thought without worrying whether their every sentence could be justified by argument from Marxist theory – an independence of mind in keeping with Marx's statement, 'I am not a Marxist.' The writing was full of striking phrases that I remembered long afterwards – 'A set of sentimentalists who, too cowardly to act, had made up their minds that in doing nothing they were doing exactly what was to be done' or 'That courage which is a result of a clear insight into the state of things' or 'That peculiar industrialism proper to the Jewish race' or 'One of those low creatures who do the basest actions from an innate inclination to infamy.' One passage was about 'the petty trading class', but honest people, regardless of class, may recognise in it a description of how they might react in testing situations:

It was lavish in its promises to sacrifice its blood and its existence in the struggle for freedom; but … on the day of danger it was nowhere, and it never felt more comfortable than on the day after a decisive defeat, when, everything being lost, it had at least the consolation to know that somehow or other the matter *was* settled.

Equally striking were things that were clearly *wrong*, including prejudices that which no rational person could react to with anything but contempt. In *Germany, Revolution and Counter-Revolution* the most arrogant German chauvinism is expressed with the same verve and lack of inhibition as everything else. In discussing the resurgence of Slav nationalism, they make absurd generalisations about the 'civilising' mission of the German nation:

> These dying nationalities…had tried to profit by the universal confusion of 1848 in order to restore their political status quo of A.D. 800. The history of a thousand years ought to have shown them that such a retrogression was impossible; that if all the territory east of the Elbe and Saale had at one time been occupied by kindred Slavonians, this merely proved … the physical and intellectual power of the German nation to subdue, absorb, and assimilate its ancient eastern neighbours; that this tendency of absorption on the part of the Germans had always been, and still was, one of the mightiest means by which the civilisation of Western Europe had been spread in the east of that continent;…and that, therefore, the natural and inevitable fate of these dying nations was to allow this progress of dissolution and absorption by their stronger neighbours to complete itself.

The effect of this passage upon me was no doubt the more pronounced because I was reading it at a time when German fascism, with German chauvinism as one of its most powerful ideological weapons, was everywhere on the offensive. Another passage had a similar contemporary resonance, particularly since I was on a voyage to India:

> The several Slavonic languages differ quite as much as the English, the German and the Swedish, and when the [conference] proceedings opened, there was no common Slavonic tongue by which the speakers could make themselves understood. French was tried, but was equally unintelligible to the majority, and the poor Slavonic enthusiasts, whose only common feeling was a common hatred against the Germans, were at last obliged to express themselves in the hated German language, as the only one that was generally understood!

This was on a par with the British imperialists' mockery of the Indian independence movement on the same puerile ground that the only common language of its leaders was English.

My strong objection to these passages signalled a change in my approach to the Marxist classics. In my early years as a communist I was, like most of my fellow communists, affected by the 'kosher' principle – I would no more have read the writings of Trotsky or of other 'renegades' than I would have torn up my Party membership card. And I felt uneasy about disagreeing with anything that *was* kosher. When I had doubts about what one of the Marxist classics said, I used to ask myself, 'Who are *you* to think you know better than Lenin (or Stalin, or Marx)?' But by now I had developed the confidence to answer such doubts differently. I was a fellow-communist, inspired by the same desire to understand reality in order to change it, and examining reality in the light of the same fundamental principles. It was my job to apply a critical mind to what they were saying, and judge for myself if I agreed. Until I was truly convinced, I should have been ashamed to call myself a communist if I hadn't continued to maintain the view that I believed to be correct .

I think I have always been free of what can be justifiably described as the religious and superstitious sentiments which so many enthusiastic adherents of Marxism have been a prey to. They approach these classics as the Muslim approaches the Quran, or at one time many Christians approached the Bible, feeling that if only they studied them with sufficient care and reverence, they would provide the answers to all problems. To me such attitudes cannot be reconciled with Marxism – they run counter to its whole spirit. Marxism is a scientific approach to questions of how society is and can be organised; it requires you to be both critical and self-critical. This remains the case even if Marx himself was guilty of lapses from these standards. The quasi-religious style of thinking has been brought into the revolutionary movement by those numerous men and women who can't live without some element of fervent, irrational devotion to sustain them amid the problems of life. Its dangers are obvious: a Stalin, a Mao, a Castro or any other revolutionary leader who encourages or allows his followers to idolise him – as no true Marxist could possibly do – finds in these attitudes a powerful support, and behaves accordingly.

We had by now rounded the Cape and about the end of February we docked in Durban, where we spent about a week. We were met by the intense heat, which I afterwards found out was hot even by their standards. There was bright burning sunlight all day long. The heat of the pavements made your feet burning hot just walking slowly along the streets. Yet to my surprise I didn't find the heat at all oppressive although I've never sweated so much in my life. I had to change my shirt every time I came back to the ship – it was always soaked.

Officers were granted shore leave every day from eleven a.m. to two a.m., and as the local English population had a reputation for being very hospitable to the troops, it was a welcome experience. A wide street ran along the seafront bordered with lawns, tropical flowers and fountains, and all the way down the centre a stretch of grass with tall cocoanut palms. There were plenty of canteens, free for the troops, and – what interested me more – several large bookshops. But along with these pleasant impressions was the all-pervasive colour bar – separate bus-stops, separate seats in the parks and at the side of the roads, separate cafes, cinemas, in fact separate everything for Europeans and non-Europeans. One of the officers on our ship overheard two soldiers from the convoy being rebuked in the street by a South African white woman, because they were conversing with a black African. They said, 'Why not? He is flesh and blood, isn't he?' She replied, 'That's a ridiculous argument: so are monkeys.'

Almost as soon as I got off the ship I saw a paper called the *Guardian*, and a moment's reading of it was enough to show that it was a communist or at any rate near-communist paper. I turned to the page that gave the address it was published from and went straight there. I was welcomed as I assumed any communist from any country would be welcomed, warmly and without reserve. I spent all my leave time with my South African fellow-communists. One I spent a lot of time with and liked a lot was H A Naidoo, a man of South Indian stock. I visited his house where for the first time I saw dozens of cockroaches scurrying about the place. Another was an Afrikaner whose name I have forgotten but whose lucid expositions of South African issues much impressed me. He had also lived and worked in Portugal's African colonies, spoke Portuguese, and was well acquainted with conditions there. I greatly admired all of them for the courage and constancy with which they fought their difficult fight. But I was puzzled by what seemed to be their poor grasp of communist principles of internationalism. At a meeting of the Party I was surprised to find communists arguing that the war against fascism might be a just war for other countries but not for them. They were under the rule of a colonialist, semi-fascist government and therefore they could not support it. I couldn't see how, after the Nazis invaded the Soviet Union in June 1941, any serious communist could come to such a conclusion. The struggle for communism was a world-wide struggle, and while tactics might differ considerably from country to

A troopship, The Stratheden, sister ship to ours, which looked identical

Trade unionists march in the streets of Durban

country, there was always a single united aim. If the fight to defeat Hitler's fascism was a just fight, it was so for *all* the people of the world, regardless of the character of the governments they lived under.★

We resumed our voyage, and I settled in to read the fresh supplies of communist literature I had picked up in Durban. One was the Soviet writer Leontiev's *Political Economy*, a lucid account of Marxist theory on the subject. I read, understood and digested it all, but found it not fully convincing. While it explains a good many things it leaves a good many others unexplained. After that I was at a loss until I found, to my great joy, that another officer in the cabin had a copy of the Sri Lankan Marxist Shelvankar's Penguin book, *The Problem of India*.

By now we had been at sea two months, and I would have been perfectly happy for the voyage to last another two. In this, I discovered, I was almost alone. I had been amazed to realise that many of my fellow officers, left to their own resources to interest themselves and keep themselves happy, found that they hadn't *got* any resources worth speaking of. By the time we reached Bombay most of them were practically crawling up the wall.

∞

We docked on the 7th of March and were marched straight from the ship to the train which was to take us to our destination – though, typically, no one had told us where that would be. My memories of that brief encounter with Bombay is of a series of surprises – seeing red stains on the pavements and thinking, 'Good God, everyone here seems to have TB.' It was only much later that I discovered that these stains were made by the red spittle people spit out when they've been chewing *paan* – a cone of betel leaves enclosing various ingredients, which people use in much the same way as Americans use chewing gum. Another was finding Soviet novels on display in the station bookstalls. With the Communist Party of India being illegal, I had assumed that anything that could be thought of as Soviet propaganda would be illegal too. I had thought of the British regime in India as not too dissimilar from the Nazi regime in Germany and was surprised to find how velvet the glove was that clothed the iron hand.

I have vivid memories too of that long train journey. The carriages the officers travelled in were roomy and comfortable – what arrangements there were for the men was another matter. We were five to a compartment, with bunks on each side and a little bathroom to ourselves. There were no corridors, and at meal times the train stopped and we all clambered out and made a mad rush for the refreshment room. It was already dark when we left Bombay, and when we awoke the next morning we were passing through the countryside of Gujerat going north. I remember to this day the constant pleasurable thrill of excitement with which I took in the scenes through which we passed. I saw for the first time the picture which I had so many times had described to me – the unbelievably small fields being ploughed in the burning heat by bare-footed peasants dressed only in loin-cloth and turban, following a fragile-looking wooden plough drawn by two white bullocks.

Our first halt was at a small wayside station. The hot morning sun beat down on the whitewashed buildings. In the brilliant sunlight the colours stood out with an extraordinary distinctness – the platform the colour of red powdered brick, the dark green foliage of the trees, the clear blue cloudless sky and the grey parched-looking earth. The still, sunny atmosphere, undisturbed by even a breath of wind, emphasised the peacefulness of the whole scene.

At each station the train seemed in no hurry to move on, and we had plenty of time to get out and around. There were people selling papers and books, cups of tea for which we had to provide our own cups, sweets, toys, fruit, people wanting to sweep out our carriage, barbers wanting to cut our hair. At one small station one of the officers in our carriage went out into the village and came back with a couple of little earthernware pots which he had bought off an old man who was making them. For some reason these always caused great merriment amongst Indians of all ages who gathered round whenever he produced it for them to put his tea in.

On the second evening we reached Delhi. The train was stopping there several hours so we were told we could go off into the city if we wanted to. I went out with an officer called O'Neil, wandering right round the bazaar, past little shops on the sidewalk all lit up like sideshows at a fair, smelling all kinds of pleasant and unpleasant smells, seeing all kinds of sweatmeats and food being prepared, watching a camel train coming in. All the way back to the station we were pursued by a boy about seven or eight years old who kept running along beside us, stopping to touch our feet and saying *bakshish*. It was now dark and growing chilly and he wore nothing except a small piece of dirty cloth round his loins. God knows where he came from and where he was going to sleep and how he lived. We gave him two small coins and he went off. *Bakshish* – the word regularly used by Indian beggars when asking you to give them something – was the first Urdu word I learnt to recognise and understand from context. (I later learnt that its literal meaning is something like 'largesse'.)

Out of Delhi we headed north and west. As we got further north the scenery changed considerably, and by the evening of the third day we were getting into the hill country. At one of the stations a small boy asked me for bakshish and I gave him a great pile of English and South African halfpennies. I tried to explain that they wouldn't be any good to him, but either the little Urdu I had learnt on the ship wasn't up to it or else his delight prevented him paying much attention to what I was saying. He was as pleased as Punch.

By seven the next morning we got to a place called Havelian, to find that this was where the railway line ended and the nearest point to our destination. We would do the rest of the journey by army truck. This was for me the most enjoyable part of the journey. The journey took about an hour, the road climbing steadily to 4,300 feet above sea level. It zigzagged on up the hillsides, often with a sheer drop down to a broad and stony water-course on the left, while on the right it rose up just as steeply to the horizon, with great out-jutting slabs of bare rock shoving through the grass. I got my first sight of a camel train, which we passed on the way up, and we passed through very lovely country. Everywhere where cultivation was possible were groups of mud huts with terraced fields – even right up on the hilltops far above the road. It was early spring, with some of the fruit trees beginning to blossom, the young fresh green leaves coming out and the crops on the hillside showing up in pale green and bright yellow patches in the morning sunlight.

At the end of the road was Kakul, our destination. We arrived at about nine o'clock at the army camp, still dressed in the tropical kit we had been wearing for the last two months – to find, to our surprise, men in standard army battle-dress. And it was certainly quite cold enough for it up here.

Kakul is about two miles north of Abbotabad, in Hazara District of North-West Frontier Province. It lies in a plain surrounded on all sides by great rocky hills – not mountains by Indian standards, but not far off by mine. Some of the higher ones were still snow-clad when we arrived, and people told me that at least one within one day's walking distance was permanently so. A dazzling gleam appeared all along the crests of the hills in the morning long before I could actually see the sun, and bathed all the hills on the opposite side of the valley in a beautiful warm light. The crops were bright green or else the bright yellow of rape grown for oil-seed, little fields with clusters of peasants' flat-roofed mud huts.

Life in Kakul was quite pleasant. We were there to be trained as officers in the Royal Indian Army Service Corps, and we worked about

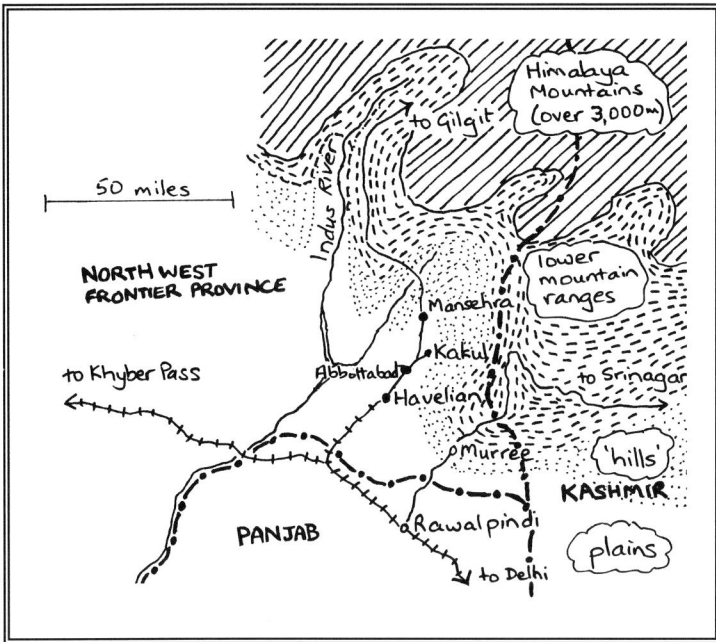

Kakul and around

eight hours a day, with weekends off. The Service Corps has two wings, departments – call them what you will – one motor transport and one supplies. Training in one is totally irrelevant to training in the other, but the army being the army, we were all supposed to be trained in both. The training was given by inexperienced and on the whole mediocre instructors, and I remember little about it except that we were first treated to a series of lectures explaining how lorries worked – engines, sparking plugs, transmission, gears and all that – and then put in a lorry and expected to be able to drive it. No one had the wit to see that it was the second, practical part that should have come first. Of the supplies training I have not the least recollection and I think I may have missed out on it altogether.

More enjoyable were the Urdu classes. We had regular classes taught by *munshis* – 'munshi' really means a rather superior grade of clerk, but it was the term used in the Indian Army for civilian employees who had the thankless task of teaching Urdu to unenthusiastic British officers, most of whom didn't see why they should waste time and effort on this inferior language. I seemed to be almost the only one who took learning Urdu seriously. From the moment I had known I was going to India I had realised I would need to become fluent in an Indian language, for there would be no other way to communicate with ordinary people around me – which, both as a human being and as a communist, I naturally wanted to do. So I wanted to learn it as quickly and as thoroughly as possible. I was soon getting reasonably fluent in a number of limited, everyday situations. One of my treasured memories is of the munshi who surveyed our class and said, 'All of you gentlemen are good,' which was far from being the case, 'but *this* gentleman [indicating me] is *appreciable*.'

We lived in tents – two to a tent. They were more like small marquees than anything else and properly furnished, with concrete floors, two beds, bedside tables, two other tables, two armchairs, two large cupboards and a proper fire-place. The one thing I found difficult to get used to was having a bearer – a personal servant. In the army in Britain every officer was served by a soldier called a batman, so I suppose I too must have had one though I don't remember a thing about it. Here in India the system was that until we were posted to an active service area we would have a civilian bearer, trained in Raj styles of subservience that made me extremely uncomfortable. My bearer was a little Kashmiri called Sabaz Ali Khan. I am not tall – the army recorded my height as five feet four and three quarter inches – but Sabaz Ali came only up to my shoulder. He had a grave and rather shy air about him. He had long moustaches and dressed in a turban, a shirt worn outside his big baggy trousers – the standard *qamis* and *shalvar* of the people in that area – a long brightly coloured jacket and sandals. I soon learned the way an English officer sahib was expected to behave. I could never do anything for myself. He would lay out my clothes, choosing the appropriate ones himself, send my things to the laundry whenever he thought fit (i.e. after about two hours' wearing), hold my mirror up for me to do my hair, go down on the floor to take off my shoes, even hold my trouser legs off the floor while I was putting them on. I couldn't even peel an orange without him standing at my right hand ready to take the peel from me and carry it across to the waste-paper basket. I began to make him let me do a few things for myself, like insisting on taking my own shoes off. It took him a while to get over his initial astonishment and reconcile himself to the fact that sahibs were now not the pukka sahibs they used to be.

I was now getting to know my other fellow officers. Though we had all been on the same ship, I had been so absorbed in reading that I had hardly bothered about anyone beyond my own cabin mates. Now that we all worked and ate together every day I began to realise that a lot of them were worth bothering with – they were, in fact, the best lot of officers I had yet been with since leaving the ranks. My Scots friend regrettably stayed with us for only three weeks and was then taken into hospital to be treated for some obscure form of VD, and remained there for months. But I had become equally close to Rufus the musician, and soon became so with three Irishmen, two Ulstermen and one from the South. Sullivan, the southerner, interested me most. He was the man who on the ship had questioned Brigadier Battersby's attitudes to Indians. Before joining the Army he had worked as a land-worker, bricklayer, ganger, dishwasher, and finally, policeman in London. He was an Irish speaker – he had spoken it from before he knew English – and taught me many Irish songs that I hadn't heard before. He also used to recite to me an over-rhetorical Irish poem that he thought was marvellous. It was addressed to 'My dark Rosaleen, my own Rosaleen', and had lines like

O the Erne shall run red with redundance of blood
The earth shall rock beneath our tread.

I only learnt years later that 'Rosaleen' actually meant 'Ireland' – an apparently quite common device to disguise as love poems what were really rebel songs.★

I also began to realise that there was a pattern behind how we had all been selected for duty in India. When the call for transfer of officers had come, our commanding officers – being what they were and not what one might have hoped commanders of 1000 men would be – had hastened to select those who for one reason or another intruded upon their peace of mind. There were some with double-barrelled names who were so useless to man or beast that even their COs couldn't have helped seeing it, but they were the exception – the others were basically there for being independent minded. Fred John, the large Welshman who had been in our cabin on the ship, had incurred disfavour because he was a far better machine-gunner than his company commander. Another man had had trouble with his CO because he pointed out that the officers' mess was filching rations which should have gone to the men. Of course, I only know what my fellow officers told me, but I have no reason to think that it wasn't true. The reason *my* CO had decided he would be better off without me wasn't hard to deduce.

There were a couple of other communists in our group, and others who had known people on the Left. One was John Carswell, who I discovered was the son of Catherine Carswell, whose biography of Robert Burns I greatly admired. John was a historian and I learnt a lot from him. I lent him the volume of Marx's historical writings which I had read on the ship and he was very impressed by them. Another who became a frequent companion whenever I was free was Peter Rick, who had worked for the Party in the then relatively new industrial area of Slough.

It was a companionable time. A group of us often used to foregather round the fire – it was still cold at night – and talk and drink tea together, often until well into the morning. We valued the friendship, knowing that before long we would be sent off in different directions, and to an uncertain future.

Up here in the hills, far from where the war was happening, we listened to the fragments of news that came through about what was happening on India's eastern borders. The British had been forced to evacuate Rangoon, the capital and only significant port in Burma. The Burmese civil administration collapsed in a matter of weeks. The two divisions of the army on whom the defence of Burma depended had already suffered terrible losses, were tired, demoralised, short of equipment and ammunition; having lost Rangoon there was no prospect of reinforcements getting in. Air cover was inadequate and they were constantly subject to Japanese bombing. It was only much later that anyone outside Burma learnt just how unprepared the senior British military administration had been for the task of trying to hold on to Burma. British troops were untrained in jungle warfare. They were dependent on vehicles that could only move on roads, of which there were very few, which made them an easy target for the more mobile Japanese. In the whole British army Corps there was only one officer who could speak and read Japanese, so the British armies had virtually no intelligence about Japanese movements, and were constantly subject to surprise attacks.*

Though the details only became public knowledge much later, there was no hiding the fact that things were going badly. It was also clear that if Britain was to stage any kind of come-back, and mount a proper defence of the Burma/India border, it was going to need to recruit large numbers of fresh troops in India. But with Congress still opposing the war, the British were not at all sure how far they could rely on the loyalty of Indian troops.

All of my close friends among the officers, and quite a number of the others, felt a lot of sympathy with the Indian freedom movement, and more especially with the trend in it of which Nehru was the main spokesman, so they understood the issues from the Indian side, but they much regretted that Nehru and other Congress leaders' had refused to join the war. At the end of March a delegation was sent from Britain to negotiate with Congress leaders, headed by Stafford Cripps, a man who, unlike most other members of Churchill's government, had always shared Nehru's anti-fascist views. My fellow officers hoped the Cripps mission would achieve something, but it was a complete failure, as it was bound to be. The British were prepared to make only the most absurdly insignificant concessions until after the war was over. Gandhi was said to have described the British offer as 'a post-dated cheque on a failing bank' and though I have since learned that these were not his precise words they were a very apt description.

In the conditions in which we were living we encountered very few Indians. The one I saw daily was my bearer, Sabaz Ali. We got to the point where he stopped pestering me on what I ought to and ought not to do, but we didn't ever get onto a relaxed footing personally. He had been a bearer more than twenty years, too long for him to be able to change, or feel comfortable with the idea of a relationship other than subservientce. He also had a habit that I found extremely trying, of charging me for imaginary items of expenditure. It didn't take long to realise that this was a long-established system, tacitly sanctioned by both bearer and officer; but though I sympathised with his reasons, I thought it a detestable system which would never have arisen if bearers had been paid a decent wage. I tried to get him to understand that I would will-ingly pay ten rupees a month extra for the pleasure of his not cheating me of five; but I completely failed.

Finally his petty swindling got me down to the point where I con-fronted him forcefully. I realised belatedly that I had caused him a quite unintended level of distress. He was under the impression that I was in a towering rage and subsided into a state of mind where the whole thing preyed on him dreadfully. I only realised the extent of his upset when he resorted to bringing his uncle to intercede on his behalf. The uncle was very old and august and had been a bearer for forty years. Sabaz Ali treated him with profound respect, drawing up a chair for him and standing silent during the whole ceremonial interview while the older man did all the talking. The whole event had the air of a sort of state visit, and the uncle's role was to help me understand the proper role of a sahib. In that he didn't succeed, but at least we cleared the air, and after that Sabaz Ali considered my wrath was appeased.

On one point Sabaz Ali and I did understand each other. When he saw that I really wanted to learn to speak Urdu, he willingly agreed to only use Urdu when speaking to me, and from then on he took a benevolent interest in my progress. He would sometimes talk with me quite a long time into the evening, about the war, about the ways of British officers, about various people in the camp – which were 'rogues' and which 'good men'. I gradually learnt a little about his family – he had a wife and I think two children in Kashmir, whom he saw only on a brief annual leave. All the rest of the year he was working in the plains. I now know that this life-pattern was almost certainly typical of most servants of his kind.

Apart from the bearers and other camp servants, almost the only Indians we saw were hawkers of various commodities who used to come round our tents. Most of them combined a fawning servility with a duplicity and roguery that had to be experienced to be believed. The reason was both obvious and understandable, but that did not make it any easier to get past that to a more natural way of interacting with them. Then one day a young hawker – a lad of about sixteen wearing the standard *qamis shalvar* and a red fez with a black tassel – came to my tent selling books. It was almost immediately obvious that he was different from the others. He had a self-confidence, cheerfulness, and independence almost unique amongst Indians of that class who had any dealings with the British. We started talking – my Urdu was still very limited but enough to find out that his name was Qabul Shah, that he worked for a bookshop in Abbottabad and lived in one of the nearby villages. We took to each other from the start. He often used to stay for up to two hours, talking to me and Rufus (the red-haired musician) which was both pleasant and very good for our Urdu. His own language was Panjabi, or maybe Hindko, but his Urdu was good, and like many others around Abbottabad he could read and write it.

Less than a month after our arrival in Kakul I got dysentery and was taken into hospital in Abbotabad. To my pleasure, Qabul Shah used to call in to see me on his way back from work three or four times a week.

My stay in hospital was not without compensations. In those days dysentery was either amoebic or something else which I can't now remember; one was more serious than the other and I had the less serious one. The treatment was mainly to starve the patient, which didn't cause me much distress. Far more troublesome was an abcess that developed under an old filling in one of my teeth. For two nights the pain defeated all sleeping draughts, until finally they took the thing out. After that I settled into enjoying the unexpected chance to read a lot – mainly Tolstoy and a lot of Soviet novels – and getting time to do some more detailed study of Urdu. I was learning to read and write the script – 35 different letters, I explained in a letter home, each with a different initial, medial, final and detached form, and most of the vowels not shown.

I emerged from hospital at the end of three weeks feeling weak but otherwise OK. I had missed out on being trained in supplies, but no-one seemed to think that mattered much. We were now learning to drive, across open country where I would never have believed motor transport could go. Handling a three ton lorry over terrifying mountain roads was quite a challenge. If the truck was OK, so was I. But if the steering was loose or the accelerator jerky or anything else wrong, I hadn't any idea what to do about it.

Qabul Shah was still coming almost every day to chat to Rufus and me. Rufus tried to persuade him to be his bearer, but he would not agree. He told us that his father had died when he was about three or four, and he lived at home with his mother. She would never allow him to go away as she would always be worrying if he was OK. So we dropped the subject.

Sometimes Qabul Shah brought with him a friend, Muhammad Akbar, and every now and then on a Saturday night we would all four go to the cinema in Abbotabad. Rufus and I had heard that the language of popular films was actually very good Urdu, and thought it would be good for our own progress to listen to this kind of everyday colloquial speech. The whole event was very entertaining. We sat upstairs in a sort of balcony for first class ticket holders (one rupee four annas) – in armchairs, far more comfortable than cinema seats in England. The balcony was split in two by a great board partition, and on the other side sat the first class ladies. Down below was a sort of bear-pit where the second and third class sat. A lofty wooden fence of stout palings across this space ensured that no third class person could sneak into a second class seat, and I wondered how people could see through it to the screen. Down there the sexes didn't seem to be segregated. It was a vocal and appreciative audience. The first time we went the film was showing a woman calling the roll at a women's adult education class, and the spectators were calling out all kinds of names of their own in addition, amidst great peals of laughter. When the sound track failed for thirty seconds or so you'd have thought all hell had been let loose – a great whistling and chanting – altogether creating a very enjoyable atmosphere.

Some of the films were very good, and had some good songs and music – unlike most of the English I have never found Indian film music at all unpleasant. I remember one called *Doctor* which had a song sadly recalling the days when his wife was still alive:

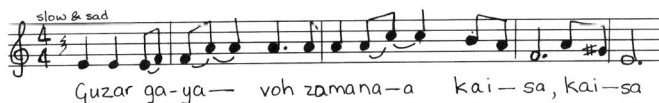

Guzar ga-ya— voh zamana—a kai—sa, kai—sa

(That time has long past. How long ago, how long ago.)

211

The film I enjoyed most was called *Bombay-Wali* (Bombay Girl) in which the heroine was an English actress. It had plenty of villains and crooks, plenty of fisticuffs, and a dog like Rin-Tin-Tin (dog-hero of films I had seen in childhood.) The chief villain was a large landlord who was ultimately prevented from swindling all his poor tenants and neighbours by the astuteness of the Bombay-Wali, ably assisted by her dog. The enthusiasm of the audience was terrific. I had a marvellous time, and as for Qabul Shah, I'd never seen him so engrossed. He always slipped off his sandals and put his feet up on the seat, and so sat squatting with one knee level with each ear throughout the performance.

The only educated Indians we met were the munshis. On a couple of weekends I and a fellow communist went with the chief munshi, a Hindu, up the lower slopes of the hills behind the camp. We took our lunches with us and climbed quite a long way up the hills. There was a marvellous view from the top. The rocks jutted through the thin soil and the grass was coarser than any I had ever come across in England. High up on the mountainsides there were isolated peasant huts each with its little terraced fields, goats and cattle feeding on the grass. and people mowing it for hay. We were never alone however far we climbed, and the children especially swarmed around us and seized our haversacks, hoping to act as our guides and make themselves useful in other ways and so earn a little bakshish. We shared our lunches with them, and while the others were talking, I tried (without a great deal of success!) to converse with them, took my turn in throwing stones at things and seeing who would be first to hit the mark, running races and so on. Even if they couldn't understand much of what I said, they seemed to take to me all right. After dinner, by my special request, they sang songs to us in Panjabi – I think that many or perhaps most of the people of Hazara are Panjabi – and the munshi translated them to us. They were traditional folk songs, love songs chiefly, and very good too, though very different from ours. Then they demanded that I should sing in return, so I sang them the Irish song 'Kevin Barry'. Though they didn't understand a word of it – as I had understood none of theirs – they seemed very pleased. After that we were firm friends. They were very nice looking children with strong white teeth, jet black hair, and gleaming brown eyes. All but two of them – there were five altogether – were barefoot. The rocks are very sharp in many places, and the soles of their feet must have been like leather, because they ran and leapt about along the mountain paths without turning a hair. I ultimately returned down the mountainside with one small child on either side firmly clasping my hand and chattering away in great spirits. All this much to the astonishment of the villagers, who according to the munshi were not likely to have ever seen an English sahib doing such things before.

The one upper-class Indian that I got to know quite well was Aurangzeb Khan. He was one of the munshis, and about my own age. I should think that in many ways he was a typical Muslim intellectual of the Frontier Province. He had taken his degree at Panjab University and spoke fluent but atrocious English. He had read all of Shakespeare and would quote reams from him, and he knew a great deal of English literature that I didn't. He was a fervent supporter of Jinnah and Pakistan and an equally bitter (and stupidly ignorant) opponent of anything Hindu. He took a poor view of my taste for popular Indian films and of my association with such low company as Qabul Shah. Needless to say I never paid much attention to his sour looks on these subjects.

Aurangzeb Khan's father was a big landlord at Manshera – not many miles from Abbottabad – where he owned about 3000 acres. Aurangzeb Khan explained to us, with a beaming smile, that it was 'just like the feudal system'. The poorest tenants, who had practically nothing of their own, were provided with seed and the loan of oxen and plough, and in return paid the old man seventy-five percent of their crop in rent. There were extra dues to pay when the landlord's eldest son was married and on all sorts of other occasions. We once got the opportunity to glimpse this lifestyle for ourselves when Aurangzeb Khan invited Rufus, me and two others to his home. Manshera was an interesting little town, showing no trace of European influence – no European inhabitants, no Europeanised shops. Like most of the North-West Frontier Province, its population was almost entirely Muslim, but Aurangzeb Khan pointed out to us a narrow smelly alley which he said was the Hindu quarter. In his father's home we were given a colossal meal of Indian food – a novel experience for us, for the officers' mess was conventionally British. We ate with our fingers and washed our hands before and after in a stream of running water poured from a jug by one small boy into a basin held by another. Some of the sweets were covered in a film of silver paper, which we were told one eats. It was all delicious, but I couldn't help wondering what the tenants were eating.

Aurangzeb Khan was amusingly meek and mild in the presence of the august old man. He waited on all the guests, remained standing the whole time, and ate his own meal only after everyone else had finished. A great contrast to his normal arrogance. After lunch we all sat under a sort of verandah while two more small boys got a hookah going and then carried it round for the guests to puff at in turn. The most interesting was an old man who was an Afridi, from a region not administered by the British. He talked about the social organisation of the tribe, and also about various types of small arms – I remember him saying that he liked the Mauser better than any other rifle for a quick shot, because the trajectory is flat up to 400 yards and therefore you don't have to bother about sight-setting.

The men in the Khan family – we saw no women – I found rather trying, and pigheaded in the extreme. The family had served the British for over fifty years. They had organised the hottest possible reception for Congress leaders visiting the district, and now felt injured because they had not got what they regarded as their just reward in the way of government contracts and something more than a lieutenancy in the Army for Aurangzeb Khan, who had no military experience of any kind.

Everything was new – the places, the people, the countryside, the routine of life in an army camp in India. It was tantalising to be surrounded by, and yet so little in contact with, the people among whom I was going to be living. I had read and thought about issues facing people in other societies; now for the first time I had the chance to piece together my own fragmentary bits of personal experience, against the background of my broader political understanding.

From the early days on the ship I had been writing long letters home, wanting to share everything I was experiencing. I wrote to people from all the parts of my life – to Chris and Peggotty, now married and presumably awaiting Chris's call up; to Rex and Froude in Holme; to Gertie, Marie's sister in Beverley; to Margaret Horton from the Loughton communist party days. Also to my parents, though these were shorter letters, written mainly from a sense of duty. Some of these letters were saved and returned to me. Reading them six decades later, it is striking how many of the incidents are described in almost exactly the words and phrases I have used here. So perhaps it was the act of writing them down at the time that fixed them in my memory. Other details, like who I shared my tent with for the two months in Kakul, are simply gone – and perhaps those are ones I didn't ever happen to write about.

Writing any letter was sending messages into the blue without any assurance that they would arrive. When we heard of ships being sunk we knew that along with the lost lives would be our lost mail. Even when all went well we were told it was taking at least three months for a letter to get to England, and letters back were taking even longer. The number of British troops and officers in India had expanded so rapidly that the army sorting office was struggling to deal with mail for this vast number of men, all constantly being moved around. For five months

Glimpses of another lifestyle

the only mail I received was one letter from Rex and Froude and a couple from my mother, all written while I was still on the ship. I still did not know whether any of my letters had reached people back home. The more I was cut off from the people I felt close to, the more I felt the need to record what was happening to me. My letters to Rex and Froude began to take on the character of a diary. I began numbering the pages consecutively from one letter to the next so they could check they had received everything I had sent. By the end of May I finally received confirmation that at least one of my letters home must have arrived safely, for a cable arrived for my birthday, correctly addressed to Kakul. To my amazement and delight, it was from Ma Pearson of the potato-picking gang.

In my occasional moments of homesickness, one of the things I missed most was being able to follow what was happening in Britain politically. My letters to Rex and Froude were full of questions – which I don't know if they ever got the chance to answer – about the changes in the political atmosphere back in Britain. From the fragments of news that reached us it was clear that the mood of people in Britain had been changing, and quite rapidly. The vacillation of the late thirties had given place to an atmosphere in which anti-nazism was the norm. There was growing interest in and admiration for the Soviet Union, stirred by the heroic defence the Soviet armies were putting up against the German invasion. And in the wake of that came a much greater openness to left wing ideas.

Though I could rejoice in these changes, there was nothing I could do to participate in responding to them. The task for me and other British communists who had been sent to India was to work out what we could do to further the cause here; but until each of us knew where we were to be posted, and in what sort of situation we would be working, it wasn't at all obvious what that might be. The one thing that was clearly going to be critical was getting myself fluent in Urdu. Here, just as in the army in Britain, to live and work as a communist I would need to be able to communicate as fully as possible with the ordinary people around me, those that the communist movement exists to serve. In that sense learning Urdu well was not just a matter of personal choice, but a necessity for a communist who took his responsibility seriously.

I once got talking about this with my communist fellow officer, Peter Rick, and was amazed to discover that he saw no particular point in trying to get fluent in Urdu. He seemed to assume that the only meaningful contacts with Indians he could expect to have would be with those who spoke English – which would mean people like

Aurangzeb Khan or Indian army officers, people from backgrounds of extreme privilege, who were hardly likely to be interested in communist ideas.

Our sojourn in Kakul ended on the 2nd of June 1942. Despite my non-existent training in supplies and my very inadequate training in motor transport, I was to be sent off along with all the rest. Rufus, Sullivan and I were to go to Allahabad in the north Indian plains, a city that was much in the news at the time for it was experiencing the most severe heat for twenty years. A number of people, including even Indians, had died of heat exhaustion. I had found hot summers even in England very trying and trembled to think what Allahabad would be like.

Just a few days before we left, the exhausted remnants of the allied armies in Burma had straggled across the border and into India. The Japanese conquest of Burma was complete. The whole thing had clearly been a major military disaster. It was a standing joke in the army that a retreat would be announced as 'Our troops have withdrawn to previously prepared positions' and sure enough even in this case British officialdom in its usual asinine way declared that this had not really been a defeat at all. Within two days of each other the British and American generals came out with directly contradictory statements. On 26th May 1942 the American General Stilwell, who had himself been with the troops struggling out of Burma, said, 'Burma was taken by only 50,000 Japs; we got a hell of a beating.' Two days later the British commander, General Wavell, announced from the safety of Delhi, 'General Alexander's army was not beaten; the withdrawal is not the result of defeat.' The contemporary writer of satirical verse, Sagittarius, quoted both in his poem, *Burma Story* –

> *Through the hell of Burma's jungle allied forces hacked their way*
> *Stilwell's troops and Alexander's on the road from Mandalay;*
> *Stilwell's beaten force retreating, mile by mile compelled to give,*
> *Alexander's marching northward on their own initiative.*

Whatever anyone back in Britain believed, to people stationed in India the consequences of the defeat in Burma were obvious. The Japanese were now preparing to launch an invasion of India.

10

We were to have ten days' leave in Murree before heading for Alla-habad. Murree was a 'hill station', a place in the foothills of the Himalayas to which British civil and military top brass would go on leave in the hottest weather to escape the heat of the plains – and with the prospect of the heatwave in Allahabad before us, we were happy to do the same.

Just before we left, Qabul Shah suddenly announced that he was willing to become a bearer after all, and would like to come with me. I jumped at the chance, and dismissed Sabaz Ali, probably quite unfairly. Rufus hired Qabul Shah's friend, Muhammad Akbar. So the four of us and Sullivan set off together for Murree. Murree was only about forty miles away but the journey took us two days. An army truck took us back down the steep road to Havelian, where we waited for a train. At the station a few of us got talking to some children and persuaded them to sing to us. I thought them extraordinarily pretty and found their Urdu clear and easy to understand, but maybe that was more to do with my own competence being now greater. The train took us to Rawalpindi – a place I remember for its discomfort – sweltering heat by day, and mosquitos swarming all night. The last stretch we did by taxi, rising dramatically up to about 7,000 feet, and into a complete change of climate, beautifully cool. We were surrounded by magnificent scenery – great pine clad hills, with little terraced fields, the earth a deep purple colour, and in the distance the snowy peaks of the Himalayas.

My most pleasant memory of those days is of Rufus and me taking Qabul Shah and Muhammad Akbar to see the Walt Disney cartoon film *Pinocchio*. In Abbotabad the cinema audience had been almost entirely Indian, but here the audience was almost entirely British, and *Pinocchio* was not dubbed and had no sub-titles. We had considerable difficulty in convincing the lackeys in the box office that we really meant what we said in asking for the same price tickets for our bearers as for ourselves, but we ultimately got inside. Qabul Shah, to my great amusement and joy, behaved quite normally, squatted on his seat and stared quite unconcernedly at the scores of majors and their ladies on all sides. I once saw him spit in the gangway, to my secret malicious delight, though I subsequently cured him of that habit. I don't think he understood much of what was happening, but Muhammad Akbar, who knew quite a lot of English, with a little help got the whole story and enjoyed it, though he was a little disappointed when Rufus confirmed his opinion, expressed with due gravity after the first ten minutes or so, that the actors were not real people, but only drawings!

I also gave Qabul Shah an intensive course in his new duties as a bearer. He'd never before cleaned a pair of shoes, polished a Sam Browne belt, made a bed, or had anything to do with European clothes. But he learnt these skills quite quickly. We got on very well together; he seemed to have lost his doubts about coming away from home. He said he was ready to come on active service with me – and wanted to visit England with me after the war.

The five of us left Murree together on the long train journey to Allahabad. Late one night after we had been halted at some station for a long time and were just moving off again, Sullivan came back into the compartment and told me with satisfaction that he had just been talking to a young English-speaking Indian who supported the war. Sullivan, characteristically, had asked him why he wasn't in the army (!) and the Indian had replied with a long explanation of his political position, from which I deduced (as Sullivan had not) that he must be a communist.

I took the next opportunity to go and seek out this man in his compartment. My guess had been right; he *was* a communist. His name was Amrit Rallia Ram, and he lived in Lahore. There seemed little chance I would ever be in Lahore – we were at that moment heading in the opposite direction – but he invited me to visit him if ever I was.

No one had told us what we would be doing in Allahabad. When we got there, it transpired that the answer was Nothing. We were in transit, to somewhere as yet unidentified. There was nothing to do except to wait for orders to proceed elsewhere.

The heat was less of a problem than I had feared. I sweated profusely and ceaselessly, and valued cold water to an extent I would never have believed possible, but I could not only survive but even maintain my normal energy. Anti-heat precautions were set out for us, and I had enough common sense to apply them. We were camping out, living under a thatched roof supported by a pole at each corner and open to the air on all four sides. One of the more pleasant aspects of life was the presence of small boys who worked the punkah all day and were very pleasant to talk to. The punkah – which is simply the Indian word for fan – is a rectangular piece of cloth nailed to a short length of wood. A rope attached to it runs to outside the shelter and is pulled by a small boy so that the fan moves back and forth and causes a draught.

Life in Indian cities: Delhi, Chandni Chowk market

A paan seller

We were living out in open ground well away from the city. At first I thought our distance from the city was to do with wartime needs, but I soon discovered that this was a normal, long established phenomenon. The standard layout of a big Indian city was determined by the exigencies of colonial rule. There were three largely separate areas: the cantonment (a word I'd never heard before) where the troops were stationed, civil lines (another term new to me) where British and higher grades of Indian civilian officials lived, and the city, where the mass of the Indian population lived. No British person ever went into the Indian city, and British officers didn't see much of anyone who wasn't also a British officer. Perhaps in peacetime they had mingled with British civilians, but now the realisation had dawned (except on Brigadier Battersby) that we were at war, and troops must be got ready to play a part in it.

Qabul Shah, who had never been far south of the Frontier province, suffered much more than I from the heat. He begged me for permission to go back until the hot season was over, and I agreed. But a day or two later he said the money I had given him for his fare home had been stolen; and by then he seemed to have adapted to the heat, so he stayed. I can't remember what led up to it, but one night while he and I were in my tent talking, we had a tentative sexual encounter. It seemed to come about quite naturally, without either of us feeling that it was any big deal. I just remember sitting with him on the edge of a charpoy (string bed) holding his rock-hard penis. He said, 'Have you ever seen a Muslim's?' – Muslims are circumcised, while the great majority of Indians are not. I said 'No, but some British people are circumcised like you, and I am myself.' I think that was all that happened; we neither of us did anything to achieve orgasm.

After five days in Allahabad Sullivan and I were posted to Lucknow. Rufus was posted elsewhere and passed out of my life. Lucknow, to my surprise, was appreciably cooler than Allahabad. I hoped that here I might at last be able to settle to some useful work, but we were once again merely awaiting the next posting. For twelve days we hung about with nothing to do. I read. I wrote letters. Once Sullivan and I went to a film in the town. And I was very glad of Qabul Shah's company. Though the things we could talk about were inevitably limited – both by the limits of my Urdu vocabulary, and by his youth and lack of experience of life – he was a cheerful and high spirited youngster to have about the place, and he helped me a lot with my Urdu. In many ways he was as responsible for my education as I for his, though it was a while before I realised the extent of this. I remember one incident when I was playing with my swagger stick – a two-foot long cane that officers used to have to carry. I discovered that if I dropped it on its end it would bounce up again. The cement floor of our quarters was crawling with little black ants and I started amusing myself bombing them by dropping my swagger stick on them. Qabul Shah sharply rebuked me, and of course I stopped, since it obviously upset him. I think I already knew that Jains and many Hindus would on principle not take the life of any living thing, but I didn't know that Muslims would have something of the same feeling. I still don't know how many of them do.

When he first came to work for me he was talking about getting married and mentioned the modest sum of Rs 200 (about £15) as a suitable wedding present from me. I discovered that his mother had already made provisional arrangements for his marriage; he was very pleased with himself because he thought he had worked out who it was had been chosen as his wife. It had never occurred to him that he might choose his own. I explained this system to him. He didn't seem very interested at the time but he later informed me that he would see to his own marriage and choose his own wife. I don't suppose he ever did. All of this now seems very naive of me. Only years later when my contacts with Indians was much broader than the conditions of army life allowed, did I begin to understand that the issue of arranged versus free choice marriage is a much more complex one than I had thought.

Two incidents stand out in my memory from those days waiting around in Lucknow with nothing to do. It was here that for the first time I spoke to ordinary Indians on explicitly political issues. It was a hot afternoon, just before the rains. I was talking to Qabul Shah and another bearer, a man of about 30 whose name I cannot now remember. Somehow we got talking about the United Nations. I drew the flags of Britain, USA, the USSR and China in the dust and explained the significance of each. I spent a lot of time explaining the red flag and the sickle and hammer, and also used the Kuomintang flag (the exact meaning of which I did not – and still do not – know) as a peg upon which to hang a short account of China's national revolution since 1911. All this led on to Indian political questions, the nature of the present war and what I thought was the right policy for the Indian people to pursue in it.

Qabul Shah took very little part in this, but the other bearer became very interested and talked quite a lot. He told me that he had once met a British CQMS (company quartermaster sergeant) who spoke Urdu well and had similar views to mine. I was surprised to hear that such people were to be found in Britain's peace-time army of occupation.

At the time I had not paid much attention to Qabul Shah's unwonted silence – he was normally anything but taciturn. Only later did I fully take in that so far as he was concerned I was talking in riddles. I didn't at that stage realise that his unawareness of, and lack of interest in, even the most generally known international events was far more typical than the interest which the other bearer had shown.

The other incident happened one evening when Qabul Shah and I were alone. He told me that anal intercourse could be done without discomfort. The way he said it suggested that he had personal experience of this, and he proceeded to enable me to verify the truth of his statement. Just as before, all this happened in a relaxed way, with no particular strong feeling on either side. The only mildly awkward moment was when he said that he had obliged me and now it was my turn to oblige him. This seemed a very reasonable request but I couldn't bring myself to meet it. He accepted this quite calmly.

On our last days in Lucknow the weather began to change, signalling the arrival of the long awaited monsoon rains. Beautiful sunsets after very hot and sultry days; then one day at midday a long and heavy shower of rain, welcomed with tremendous pleasure and relief after the burning weather we had all endured. But it was a one-off, and soon the heat built up again. Now there were scores of little glossy green dung beetles about, busily rolling out big balls of dung from the cow-packs and rolling them off somewhere or other. Their legs had a very wide straddle, one pushing in the direction they were going, while the other walked backwards , turning the ball with its legs. There were all sorts of other insects I had never seen, one most unpleasant looking but apparently harmless, about four inches long, oblong and brown and flying around in a clumsy way. And lizards of all sizes, ranging from about two inches to eighteen.

On the lst July I was posted to a unit in Delhi. Sullivan was sent elsewhere, so of the group of British officers I had been close to over the past months none now remained. Around the fire in Kakul we had promised to keep in touch by letter, and occasionally we did. But it was a poor substitute, and we gradually lost contact as each of us was moved again and again in different directions.

To my disappointment the Delhi posting was yet another temporary one, with little chance of building up a new set of friends. But at least this time I was given some work to do. The army unit was a new one, one of many that was being raised in response to the need to reinforce the Burma/India border. The sepoys, as soldiers were called in the Indian army, were all new recruits, and the officers' time was spent looking after practical arrangements for this sudden new intake – their food, clothing, etc – working long hours, from 6.30 a.m. to 6.30 p.m., right through the fiercest heat of the day. Then to everyone's relief the rains really settled in, but still it was a long day and there was little time left in the evenings for reading or letter writing. Some of the officers went off to the late session at the cinema in the town, but I valued my sleep too much.

The recruits seemed a fine, sturdy young lot, and I looked forward to getting to know some of them. I watched with amusement the way the NCO went about instructing them in weapons and elementary tactics. He would hold up his rifle and say, 'Yeh kya hai? Rifle; yeh kya hai? Rifle.' (What is this? A rifle. What is this? A rifle) until the sepoys could themselves shout in unison 'Rifle' when he asked the question. All the sepoys came from the areas around us and to the east – UP and Bihar as far as the Bengal border – where some variety of Hindi or Urdu was the mother tongue. To the Muslims it was Urdu and to the Hindus Hindi, but at the everyday spoken level these are practically identical languages. They use a different script but the sepoys were almost all illiterate, and here in the army they would be taught to write their language for the the first time, using the Roman script. I knew I could help them with this, and looked forward to improving my own spoken Urdu by talking to them. I was less sure about the next stages, when they would move on to learning about vehicle driving and maintenance – my own training in these being decidely sketchy.

But before I could get to know any of the recruits I was withdrawn from contact with them and put onto office work. I was extremely fed up by this. Instead of being allowed to get on with tasks that would have used what I had been trained for, I was stuck inside all day like a glorified office boy, dealing with papers and forms. I could barely understand what I had to do, much to the amazement of my commanding officer; after all, I was a Cambridge graduate. I was filling in meaningless figures, supplies in, supplies out, on absurdly cumbersome forms. There was also something called an imprest account, but I have no idea what it was for. Twice I had what amounted to a stand-up fight with my commanding officer and I think he was beginning to see it might make sense to take me off work I hated –

And at that point I came down with an unidentified fever and was admitted to hospital.

I spent twelve days in hospital. I felt, as I described it in a letter to Rex, shagged out. The fever receded but then recurred. The original diagnosis, sandfly fever, was abandoned. All the blood tests were negative but still the fever was there. What was wrong God alone knew, and as Ma Pearson used to say, he won't tell. But it got me out of that office, and for that I was extremely grateful.

An Indian Army
Urdu coursebook

THE

JADID HINDUSTANI TEACHER
(HINDUSTANI BY A NEW METHOD)

BY

MUNSHI SIDDIQ-UL-HASAN KHAN,
(Certificated Teacher of the Board of Examiners)

Translator, Fauji Akhbar, Army Headquarters, Simla
&
Author of the Jadid English Teacher

Manuscript revised

BY

Major F. R. GIFFORD, O. B. E., M. A., (Oxon.)

فصل تہرے ے نہیں دور خدایا کچھ ہوی • بار آور ہو یہ ناچیز سی کوشش مہری

(359)

6. Prisoners are not permitted to converse with any one during their exercise or hard labour.

   Exercise *ya mushaqqat ke waqt qaidion ko kisi se bát chít karne ki ijázat nahín hai.*

7. Prisoners will hand over their cash etc. to the Guard Commander on being confined.

   Line *qaid ki saza milne par qaidi apni naqdi wagaira Guard Commander ke hawále kar dénge.*

8. Prisoners sentenced to Simple Imprisonment will carry out two hours' punishment drill daily.

   Jin qaidion ko qaid bina mushaqqat mili ho woh har roz do ghante saza ki drill kia karénge.

9. No other rank will leave the lines, except on duty, without notifying his Section Commander.

   Koi other rank siwáe us waqt ke jab keh woh duty par ho apne Section Commander ko batáe bagair lines se báhar nahín ja sakta.

10. Except when on duty no bachelor other rank will enter the married lines.

    Siwáe us waqt ke jab keh woh duty par ho koi other rank jis ki shádi na hui ho un lines mén nahín jáega jin mén bál bachchon wále ranks rahte hon.

11. Roll Call will normally be 2 hours after Retreat.

    Háziri ám taur par retreat ke do ghante bád hua karégi.

12. The time of Roll Call will be published in Routine Orders.

    Háziri ka waqt Routine Orders mén chhapa karéga.

13. All other ranks, except those absent on leave or duty, will attend Roll Call.

    Tamám other ranks siwáe un ke jo chhutti ya duty par báhar gae hon háziri ke waqt maujúd honge.

14. On the bugle or other Signal sounding, all ranks will fall in by platoons.

    Bugle *ya aur koi Signal bajne par tamám ranks platoon-on mén fall in ho jáenge.*

FIRST EDITION

rved]

1933

Price Rs5/-
or 7sh. 6d.

rn Printing Works, Allahabad and obtainable from "Qamar Brothers, Simla" or from Principal Booksellers.

The kind of language officers were thought to need

225

I remember several pleasant things about that time in hospital. One is my amusement when a fellow-communist was admitted and caused a major administrative crisis when he was asked by the form-fillers what his religion was. He said 'None.' They simply couldn't understand that this could be a correct reply. Eventually, I think, without consulting him further, they classified him as Church of England. The other is the welcome break it gave me to catch up on letter-writing, reading, and doing some more intensive Urdu study. I was preparing to enter the army's Lower Certificate in Urdu at the end of July, and as the fever receded I got stuck into studying military textbooks in Urdu.

As for my more general reading, over the past year this had more and more taken on the character of a programme of study I had set myself. In my letters to Rex and Froude I attempted to list everything I had been reading since I came to India and others that I intended to read – books on the history, society and politics of India, South Africa, China, Russia, Japan, Mexico, Ireland; literature that for years I had wanted to read, and never before got round to – Homer, Dante, Carlyle, Shelley, Jane Austen, Oscar Wilde, Yeats, Gorki, Sholokov. I wrote in detail about what I was reading, using the letters as a substitute for the lively discussions that had always been a big part of my friendships – my reactions to Forster's *Passage to India*, Maude's monumental *Life of Tolstoy*, Graves' *I Claudius*, Haldane's *Science and Everyday life*, Wavell's *Generals and Generalship*. One such passage ends, 'I often kick myself for not having brought out more books from England. Many officers had twice as much luggage as I, in spite of weight restrictions.' The issues the books raised, the characters in the novels, their life experiences, the values they exemplified, all this nourished an inner life that went on developing in the long pause while I waited to be given some useful work to contribute to the war effort.

Meanwhile it seemed that no one in authority had any plan for deploying me. I came to the conclusion that this was a re-run of what had happened in England at the time I was commissioned. Hundreds of infantry officers had been pushed through a hasty and inadequate Service Corps training (the three months' course we had done in Kakul would have taken two years in peace time) and now they had a glut on their hands. After two years in the army I was clearly still surplus. 'Hardly encouraging,' I wrote to Rex and Froude, 'but one must do one's best' – at what was not quite clear, except perhaps at accepting that there was nothing to be done.

Out of hospital and back to work – though fortunately not this time in the office. I began to have some contact with the recruits, and took what chances I could to talk to them; but these were limited and anyway I knew I would soon be moved on. I was increasingly impatient to be given a posting to a unit of my own, where I would be able to work alongside the same men day by day and get to know them, to enter into their concerns, to find what we had in common.

We were stationed in a place called Kingsway Camp, a good distance from the city. But occasionally in my time off I got out into Delhi, to explore the city and its bookshops. Once I cycled out to see the nearby Jumna River, which in the rains had broken its banks. Whole villages were underwater, the villagers were coming into relief camps, and some of our men were put onto rescue work.

I was beginning to discover that Qabul Shah, with all his good qualities, was also sometimes a bit of a handful – rather lazy, and very quick-tempered, though he wouldn't sulk for long. These qualities caused some amusing scenes from time to time. I usually let him take my hired bike to go down to the bazar for his morning meal. When I needed it myself one morning for various duties he demanded to know all the whys and wherefores and went off in a huff when I refused to let him have it. He never cheated me – which given the income disparity was not to be taken for granted – but he did have the characteristic of combining a genuinely-felt friendship for me with an equally genuinely-felt right to whatever he felt he needed financially. If he thought he would like a new suit of clothes he would just come and ask me for it and would see nothing indelicate in such conduct, however often repeated.

It might be thought that our sexual encounters in Allahabad and Lucknow would lead him to take liberties, but he never did. They had been one-off events, with no sequel, and he seemed to be quite content, as I was, to regard them as such. He behaved with me as freely as he liked, but he had always done that from the very beginning. I did begin to notice that some of the Indian veterans, Viceroy's Commissioned Officers, holding a rank between the sepoys and the King's Commissioned Officers, had a knowing grin on their faces when they mentioned Qabul Shah to me. Perhaps he was giving his sexual services to them from time to time, and they assumed that I too was availing myself of them. This kind of sexual episode must have been a common experience for British soldiers posted to India. I remembered Sergeant Webb back in Northampton exhorting us to act on the principle that 'a foreskin full of shit is better than a dose of pox.'

His firm personal attachment to me meant that he responded to my influence to some extent. I tried to persuade him not to spit all over the place. He stopped doing it in my room, but I would still catch him at it

227

in his own quarters, and found it difficult to persuade him that the fact that the sweeper would sooner or later come to sweep the floor was no reason for spitting as and where he pleased. In this, as in many other ways, he was my starting point in learning how ordinary Indians viewed the world, and how that fitted – or didn't – with things that *I* felt strongly about.

He was only just beginning to see beyond the horizons of life in his native village – and if village horizons were narrow in England, I was beginning to get some idea of how infinitely narrower they were in India. News of events outside rarely reached them and most of what did wasn't anything in which they were very interested. One night he happened to hear me talk of France and it occurred to me to ask if he knew where it was. He unhesitatingly replied that it was somewhere near Calcutta. The war meant practically nothing to him; he didn't know what it was all about. But he *was* interested in my peculiarities. He used to be frankly and amusingly curious to find out why I was always disposed to talk to everyone without assuming the dignity of my lofty rank (second lieutenant!). I used to tell him that society depended for its life on the people who worked and produced – mainly the workers and peasants – and that rich people owed everything to them and could do nothing without them: that people like myself who realised this respected working people – including sweepers, cooks, and other menials alike – more than any others, and that the day would come when that attitude would be adopted by everyone, and the rich people, now so universally respected, would be despised for their idleness and their uselessness to society, and would either be made to work or else sent packing. This gave him plenty of food for thought. He accepted it so far as it affected relationships between the rich and himself; but to swallow it in so far as it affected his own attitude to sweepers and others whom he had from childhood regarded as his inferiors was a bit difficult. After all, a sweeper was a sweeper. How could you regard him as someone who had the same basic rights as you did?

I was finally beginning to get letters from many of the friends I had been writing to. I drank in thirstily every bit of news, even developing a lively appreciation of letters from my mother and Auntie Tats. A particularly welcome one from Rex, one from Margaret Horton, from Roper, still chaplain at Chigwell. The most surprising one came from my Uncle Will – the Little Old Man Cut Down. I can't think what possessed me but I had written to him while I was in Kakul, and I now received a postcard reply addressed to me not at Kakul but Kabul. Will, in characteristically pompous style, explained, 'You gave your address as Kakul, but remembering Lord Roberts' famous march from Kandahar, I assumed you must have meant Kabul.' I was amazed that it reached me, since Kabul is in Afghanistan

Froude's letters in particular made me homesick, describing spring in the fields and the woods around Holme, and the small doings of people we both knew. Noel was in the RAF and had been sent to Canada for training. Wilfred too was headed for the RAF but I didn't know whether he had yet started. Rex, I worked out, would by now have finished his training as a naval officer but I had no idea what kind of work he had been allocated to, or where. The same applied to Chris in the army, and to all my other friends in the forces. I heard of one friend who had been taken prisoner in the war in north Africa, and yet another had been lost and was presumed dead. Various others were said to have been posted to India, but the people who mentioned this in their letters gave me no addresses for them. In any case, the chances of us meeting up were remote.

From India we could now send aerograms that took weeks rather than months – my handwriting was getting smaller to fit everything into the space allowed – but the system didn't yet operate in the other direction so the news was all at least three months out of date. I was by now addressing most of my letters to Froude, asking her to pass on to others whatever bits she thought appropriate. She in turn became the channel for letters and news going between me and Rex, sent me books I asked for – which arrived, if at all, many months later but caused great joy when they did – and was also my most steady source of news of others in Holme, including occasionally of Marie. Though Marie's and my relationship as lovers was officially over, I had not stopped thinking about her and couldn't imagine any other woman taking her place in my feelings – not that I was likely to encounter any other women for a good long time. And perhaps that too accounted for the fact that my love for her seemed to be suspended in a timeless state, in which nothing could move forward but equally nothing happened to supplant her. Froude gave me the impression that, for the moment at least, Marie had decided not to marry Ronnie King until the war was over. That left a chance – a very slim one – that if I got back alive she might still be available and might be willing to reconsider returning to me. I wondered if I should write to her; but knowing that Froude's comment was already three months out of date made me hesitate. Maybe Marie had already changed her mind – or would have by the time she got my letter – so hearing from me might cause difficulties for her. I didn't drop the idea of writing to her, but didn't do anything about it either.

Another comment I seized on as being potentially significant was

Froude's opinion that Marie had been more influenced than I had realised by the political ideas she had first encountered from me, and that she now continued to be exposed to through her friendship with Froude. To me that was *really* important news, whether or not we ever got together again as lovers. Froude talked about a group that 'shared our views' being formed in nearby Beverley, and seemed to suggest there might later be one in Holme itself. She was supplying them with newspapers and other reading material. Wilfred was helping her – he seemed now definitely headed in our direction. I expressed to Froude my pleasure that he was at last 'doing something useful' – and then added, 'though you needn't tell him I put it so cuttingly!' I wanted to help from a distance in any way I could, and was sending her money, but I was disappointed at how little I had been able to save. Before coming I had heard that officers in India were better paid than those back home, and I had assumed I would be able to donate a lot of money to the communist cause. But though I was getting double what I had got in England, the Indian Army top brass still operated on the peace time assumption that an officer was a member of the upper classes, probably with his own means, who just happened to be attached to the army, so out of our salary we were expected to meet far more of our own expenses than an officer in Britain. Until we were on active service area we got no rations and had to buy our own food. In Britain there had been an allowance to cover costs of furniture; in India we had to hire, quite expensively, anything we needed. We had to employ and pay the wages of our own civilian bearers, whereas in Britain an officer was provided with a soldier-batman. And the cost of the only things I'd been accustomed to buying for myself – like books – could be twice as much as in Britain.

I felt keenly the frustration of not being able to write freely about some of the things I and my friends most wanted to discuss. I knew that in Britain attitudes towards the Soviet Union were changing, but had no way of estimating what official attitudes might be to communist activity of the kind Froude was referring to, so any references to such things were elliptically expressed. From my side, all troop movements had to be kept secret so I hadn't even been able to name the ports we had stopped at on our voyage, which seemed absurd, given that there was only one way to get to India. Nor could I share half of what I was learning about Indian politics without the censors getting their scissors into it – and a number of my letters arrived with bits cut out, though often oddly inconsequential bits.

The censors aside, there was a constant refrain running through the letters of how many things I still hadn't found time to write about. An urgency to communicate runs through them, but I was gradually having to come to terms with the fact that the people I wanted to share things with were out of reach, and would remain so for as far into the future as anyone could see. Letters were a lifeline, but they couldn't substitute for an active present.

It has probably always been part of my nature to be self-sufficient, interested in other people but content with my own company. The experience of these months was, I guess, strengthening that quality in me.

While we sat in army camps waiting to be given a job of work to do, the political situation around us was becoming ever more tense. The Indian Communist Party, which a month or two earlier had decided the war must be supported, had in consequence been legalised. But there was very little support for its stand. Congress, the party with by far the widest popular support, remained adamant in its opposition to the war. In senior army circles it was said that Congress activitists were campaigning against recruiting, and attempting to suborn sepoys from their allegiance.★

On August 9th an event of the utmost political significance happened – Congress launched a 'Quit India' movement. This was a civil protest designed to pressure the British into conceding independence. The government at once jailed all the Congress leaders, and the result was a spontaneous upsurge of mass violence, much worse than anything that would have happened if the Congress leaders had been there to direct and control it. The 'disturbances', as British officialdom described them, occurred all over India, and were most extensive in U.P. and Bihar, where railway stations were attacked, signalling instruments destroyed, railway lines torn up over considerable distances, and for days at a time supplies could not be got through. In all the major cities troops were being called out to crush the movement. Stuck out in Kingsway Camp we saw nothing of the rioting in Delhi, but I might easily have been one of those sent to quell them, and I felt very fortunate that I was not.

After a while things appeared to quieten down, but I wrote of what was going on in a letter home – a letter I'm surprised that the censor passed – 'I don't know what the English press is saying, but you may take it from me that a widespread mass anti-British struggle is going on all over India, that unless there is a radical change in the policy of the British government, it will certainly not cease, but in all probability increase, and that after the war, if not before, anything that has happened in the past will be child's play compared with what will happen then. I am not exaggerating in any way.'

In late August I was finally given a permanent posting – as far as anything in the army is permanent – to a unit due to be sent on active service. I was delighted – the only drawback being that Qabul Shah and I now had to part company. We had both known this would happen, for civilians were not permitted to accompany units on active service. We had known each other for nearly seven months and been daily in each other's company for four. He had always retained the quality I had first liked about him – his independence and the fact that he was never servile.

My new posting was to 317 Motor Transport Company, currently stationed outside Delhi. It was a unit of fully trained men – but a transport unit that as yet had no transport. In this we were not unusual. Since the retreat from Burma, the priority task of the British forces in India was to build up capacity on India's north-east border, from which to attempt to retake Burma. But there were no viable roads in the area, and the terrain presented immense difficulties. Even to get troops into the area, let alone to keep them supplied, was going to be a major logistical feat. General Slim, subsequently the commanding officer of the allied forces in Burma, said 'I knew that the campaign would above all be a supply and transport problem.'* It required not just the raising of thousands of new Indian recruits to man new transport companies like ours, but the import of vast numbers of additional heavy duty vehicles to get them operational. Until our trucks arrived on ships from the USA, we had no function.

It was mid-September before we finally got the order to proceed. Our trucks had come in at the port of Karachi, hundreds of miles to the west, so we set off by train to collect them. We camped in a place called Drigh Road, then some miles from Karachi, and were duly supplied with our lorries. Now the rumour was that we were about to be sent overseas, perhaps to Iraq or Persia, the nearest active service front to Karachi. A year earlier Persia had been occupied by Soviet troops in the north and British in the south, to oust a regime sympathetic to the Germans. A sense of expectation rose – but within a few days the orders were changed. We were to prepare to take our new lorries back to Delhi.

By now I had been in the army too long to be disappointed. I took a quick chance to get into a bookshop in Karachi, posted a couple of letters, and then got involved in the feverish activity as for the first time

Police in action against demonstrators

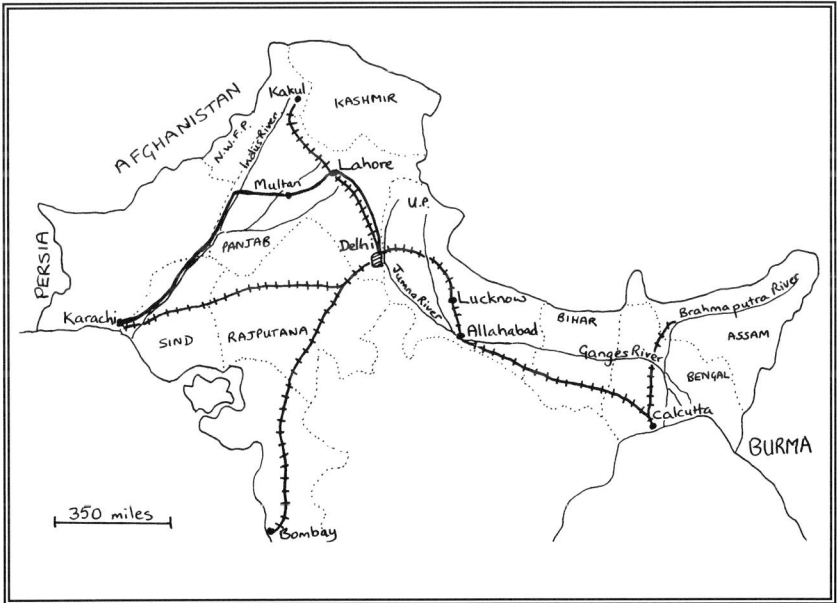

Journeys in North India, 1942

233

our company of four hundred men, finally equipped with transport and arms, prepared to take the road.

'Road' is a misnomer. A single-lane-width metalled road took us some way out of Drigh Road; then it became two concrete strips for the vehicles' wheels, with nothing between them; and then for miles and miles and days and days there was nothing but a dirt track. Every day by evening we were all covered with a layer of compounded dust and sweat. We drove right up the Indus valley, skirting the Sind Desert, through territory where operations against rebellious Sindhis were going on and martial law was still in force, on as far as Multan (the hottest military station, though not quite the hottest place, in India) where we rested two days, and then to Lahore.

I remembered that the communist I had encountered on the train journey from Murree to Allahabad – Amrit Rallia Ram – lived in Lahore and had invited me to visit him if ever I was there. So now I did that. He invited me to dinner, and I found myself, for the only time in my experience in India, made unmistakably unwelcome by my hosts. Many have testified that even in these extreme times the behaviour of Indians towards individual Britishers was almost universally courteous and hospitable, but this was certainly not the case with Amrit's parents. I discovered that I had walked into the middle of a major political battle in the family. Amrit, as a communist, supported the war. Amrit's parents were Christian, and unusually for Indian Christians, staunch Congress-men. They were justifiably extremely bitter against the fierce British repression then in full swing and as far as they were concerned, to support the war was a betrayal of the independence struggle. All the time I was in the house Amrit was being verbally attacked with a bitter hostility of which, obviously, I too was indirectly the target. In an effort to bring about a less uncomfortable atmosphere Amrit suggested that the subject be dropped, pointing out that they were hardly being polite to their guest, whose views on the present situation were similar to his own. His mother replied, 'It doesn't matter. He is simply hearing what all right-minded Indians think', and continued as before. I was very glad to escape after dinner and return to the Company.

With our arrival in Lahore we had joined the Grand Trunk Road, built centuries ago and running the whole length of the great Indian Plain from Peshawar to Calcutta. We drove along this to Delhi, where we arrived at midday on Sunday 18 October, fourteen days after leaving Karachi. I had found the whole journey very interesting, and had very much enjoyed it.

Back in Delhi, we were stationed on waste land outside the city while we awaited posting to somewhere nearer the front line.

I was now gradually beginning to get to know the people in my company. There were four sections, each with about 100 men and 30 vehicles. The whole company was commanded by a major, and once we had the full complement of officers there would be a second in command, a captain in charge of the care and maintenance of the vehicles, and four lieutenants, two British and two Indian. I was now a lieutenant (after six months as a second lieutenant one was given automatic promotion) and to my great pleasure I was at last going to be in charge of a section of my own. I could at last rely on the fact that I would be with the same people for a long time, and would be able to form continuous relationships with them. 'Life,' I wrote to Froude, quoting Stalin without naming him, 'has become more joyous.'

Before I was in de facto command of my section, something happened which I realise now must have been very unusual. I made a cryptic note of it at the time – 'A meeting of the men in my section. Its suppression.' It is probable I didn't know about the meeting until after it had happened, but it must have been held to discuss something which official channels didn't allow for. Much to my regret I now can't remember any more about it. I never heard of such a meeting all the rest of the time I was in India.

While we waited for our posting I took whatever chance I got to talk to begin getting to know the men in my section, the sepoys and the NCOs. NCOs in the Indian army had ranks named lance naiks, naiks and havildars, corresponding in function to what in the British army were called lance-corporals, corporals and sergeants. They and the sepoys were all essentially people like Qabul Shah, simply villagers in uniform. They were nearly all very young, in their late teens or early twenties, mostly from peasant families, and almost all from South India – 'Madrassis', as they were called, since they came from the Madras Presidency, an area which included all or most of the teritory of the present day states of Andhra, Karnataka, Tamilnadu and Kerala. The recruitment of Madrassis to the Indian army was a relatively new phenomenon. Earlier the policy had been to recruit from what the British classified as 'martial races', with a preponderance of Panjabis. But now with the need to rapidly expand the army, the old restrictions were loosened and Indians who had hitherto been denied the honour of being classified as martial races were being admitted.★

Looking back I can see that in those early days in 317 Company there were three strands in my attitude towards the men. Basically I saw them as fellow human beings in all essentials the same as me, no better and no worse, and that of course was quite right. Secondly, as a communist I saw myself as having much that I could teach them; and this too was right. Thirdly, I thought that as the product of conditions which deprived them of the opportunity of learning things that I had been able to learn, they had nothing much to teach me. And that was quite wrong. It took me a long time to learn this and to appreciate how much I could learn from them. My last major lesson in this field was not learnt until a few months before I left India to return to Britain.

I remember vividly one conversation during our time in Delhi, in which all of these strands were present; and perhaps the reason I remember it so clearly is because of what it reflected about my own lack of awareness at the time. I was talking to a naik named Bhimanna. He was about twenty-one, an Andhra from one of the coastal districts of what was then Madras Presidency. In civilian life he had been a tailor, and in his childhood had, like many Andhras of his home district, been in Burma. I therefore assumed that he might have a greater knowledge of world affairs than most, and certainly than Qabul Shah had had, and I started asking him a lot of questions to try to find out exactly what he did and didn't know, to understand how he saw the world.

I asked if he knew which nations were fighting against us in this war. He said, 'The Italians.' After being pressed for more he added, 'The Japanese.' Who else? I asked. But he didn't know. I then asked how he knew about the Italians. He said it was because there was a large prison camp full of them near their training centre at Bangalore. And he knew about the Japanese because we were about to go up to the front and he had heard the Japanese were there. I told him that the Germans were also fighting against us, and were a much more formidable enemy than the Italians, and possibly than the Japanese too. I then asked him who was fighting on our side. He thought a bit, and looking rather embarrassed, said he didn't know. Eventually after thinking a while he said, Yes, he'd got one, the Americans. (They were just beginning to arrive in Delhi at this time.) 'Who else?' I asked. 'I don't know,' he said. I prompted: 'Chinese?' 'I don't know.' 'Russians?' 'I think they are fighting against us, but I don't know.'

Of course I told him, and hoped he would remember; but at the time I was pretty shaken. It was not until much later that I came to see that I had no reason to expect that he would know these things. Why should he? Like most of the great numbers of war-time recruits he had joined the army 'to fill his belly', and wasn't in the least concerned with whatever it was the army had recruited him to do.

This experience set me thinking seriously. If I was to exercise any influence upon any of the numerous people like Bhimanna whom I was

MRS R. C. RUSSELL,
ALLBERRIES COTTAGES,
HOLME ON SPALDING MOOR,
YORK, ENGLAND

41 8232

Write the message very clearly below this line.   Please see instructions on reverse.

23 Oct. 1942   Sender's Address   2/Lt. R. Russell, E. Yorks. R. att. RIASC,
(21)   c/o Lloyds Bank, Hornby Road,
                                  BOMBAY.

Got yr. airgraph dated 3 Sep. today. Thanks v. much.
It has taken a long time to get here, but has been forward-
-ed by Lloyds to Karachi + then readdressed to me from
there. I haven't really got much to say just now. Glad
the two airmail letters and also the 11-page airgraph
have arrived. I will shortly write you another airmail
letter, including the long-promised political survey,
incomplete tho' it will have to be. I am starting on it
tonight, in fact. The difficulty is going to be that before
long the company will be living under something more
resembling active service conditions, and that being
so — especially now that I have a section of my own —
work will occupy daylight hours pretty fully + artific-
-ial light after dark will be a luxury difficult to
come by — let alone tables + chairs, etc. So if the volume
of my correspondence falls off a bit you will, I hope,
understand why. As soon as I can — if ever — I shall
tell you where we are going. Meanwhile you must guess,
and if you have noticed that both generals + politic...

A wartime airgraph (actual size)
the last one to Froude before being sent near the front

going to be with, I must start with things nearer home. Whatever they did or didn't know about what went on elsewhere, they certainly knew that they lived under British rule. They would surely have heard the names of leaders like Gandhi, Nehru and Abul Kalam Azad, and of course knew that Congress was currently in violent conflict with the British. I must find ways to let them see that I was opposed to the fierce repression which the government was practising, and that I sympathised with Congress aspirations.

Opportunities were not easy to find, but I took advantage of such as offered and learnt a good deal that was new to me – and once again, disconcerting. I had naively thought that once we had established common ground on support for Congress I could move their political awareness on to the next stage by explaining to them that this was a war against fascism, and that people like Nehru had a much better record of opposition to fascism than the British government did. The British, rather than imprisoning them, ought to be working out an agreement with them and granting the concessions they asked for in return for their support for the war effort. I soon discovered that I might as well have saved my breath. None of them liked British rule but they didn't see that there was anything they could do about it and so they took little interest in current developments. If Gandhi, who had the education and the spiritual strength, chose to do something, *he* perhaps could achieve something. Reverence for Gandhi was general, but names like Nehru and Azad meant nothing to them. And fascism? Anti-fascism? What were they? And whatever they were, what had they got to do with India?

In November 1942 we finally got confirmation that we were heading for the Burma border. Our destination was Dimapur, in Assam. Though it was some 200 miles behind the border, it was the rail-head – that is, the nearest point on the railway for supplies to the main concentration of front-line troops. On either side of the border British troops and the Japanese confronted each other in an indefinite stalemate. The Japanese divisions that had been pursuing the retreating British armies had halted the other side of the border, for they had lacked the resources they would have needed to advance further. The British forces too could do no more than stay where they were and hold on. Meanwhile they had to be supplied, and our company was to be part of this process.

Amidst the general preparation for departure I made my own arrangements. With all the moving around I had asked my friends to use the address of my bank, which then forwarded letters to each new posting. Now there was no knowing when we would be settled in one place or what the mail arrangements would be, so I instructed the bank to hold on to anything that came. I wrote to Froude warning her and others that I had no idea what conditions would be like, but I didn't expect to find it easy to write. We would be working in all the hours of daylight, and who knew if there would be provision for lighting after dark. I could not, of course, tell her where we were going; but I didn't think it would take a genius to guess. About Marie I said, 'I think I will certainly write to her sometime, though I shall probably find it hard to write anything which she will want to read. To tell the truth I always found that hard before; I could always talk to her, but letter-writing is a very different matter. Still, we shall see. It is idle to speculate, and I never do, expect to the extent of thinking that, unless several thoussnd miles is a less powerful deadener of influence than I think it is, she will be already married by the time I return.'

And having posted off my letters I mentally settled in for the next stage of life, one step further out of contact. I was more than ready for it. With a hundred men in my unit to get to know, my focus was already on the new relationships, not the old ones.

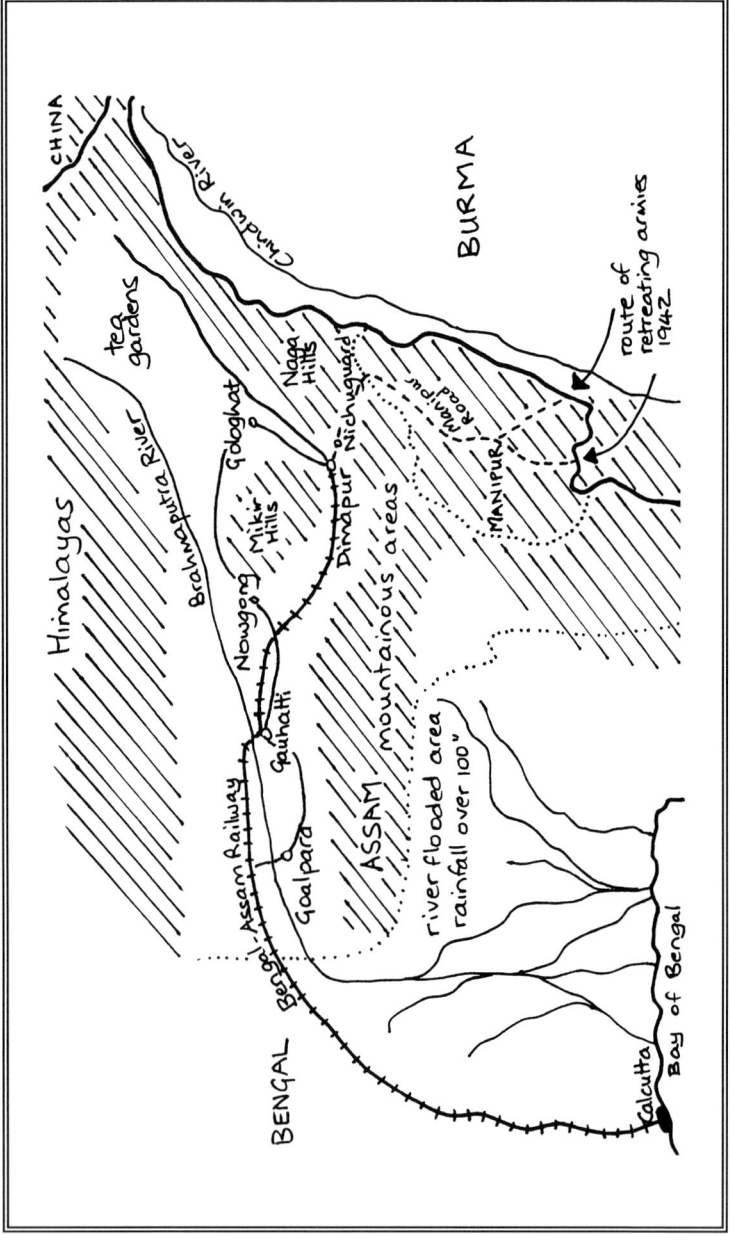

The route to Dimapur

11

Half of 317 Company was to proceed first, led by the Major, who would then return to Delhi to bring up the rest. My section was in the first lot. We travelled most of the way to Dimapur by train, with our lorries loaded on railway wagons, and us, so to speak, loaded on our lorries. It was a long journey with plenty of time to read – I got stuck into Leo Huberman's radical history of the United States, *We the People*. The railway ran east down the Ganges plain until it reached the Brahmaputra River, which in the south gives way to a vast area of inlets and floodland. Here the railway line turned north and ran up the west bank of the river. We left the train at a place called Goalpara, just beyond the great right-angle bend which the river takes as it flows out of Assam into Bengal, for here it was possible to get our vehicles across. It took us a day – a short run in the early morning down to the Brahmaputra, and then a whole day ferrying the vehicles to the other bank. We had to eat on the ferry, and a dark-skinned Indian officer from another company that was crossing at the same time raised hell because we had to eat Indian food. I wondered why on earth an Indian should object so vociferously to Indian food until I learnt that he was a Christian. Very many Christians paraded their loyalty to their fellow-Christian British rulers, and were often more British in their tastes than the British, and more royalist than the king.

Once on the other bank we stayed overnight and then went on by road, a three-day journey. We were driving roughly parallel to the Brahmaputra though we couldn't actually see it at all from the road, which ran partly through jungle and partly along a narrow embankment with paddy fields on either side. There were no towns of any size on our route. The first day took us to Gauhatti, the capital of Assam but even so quite a small town. For a few days we broke journey there, and during our brief stay there I made an accidental but fruitful discovery. One of my sepoys had had an accident, and had to be sent to hospital there. In the evening, on my way to visit him, I noticed a thatched, whitewashed mud-brick building bearing a long signboard on which was painted, in resplendent gold lettering on a white background 'Communist Party of India – Section of the Communist International.' I took the first opportunity to slip off there for a few minutes, but found nobody there but a tailor squatting in the verandah working at his sewing machine. He seemed to have no connection with the sign above his head, and didn't seem to know what it said. But a later visit brought me face to face with Gaurisankar Bhattacharya – then, and for many years later, the leading communist in his area. Before we moved on I was able to have long conversations with him and with other communists there, including a student party member who I discovered lived near where my section's lorries had parked.

These discussions gave me a much clearer understanding of the issues Indian communists had been facing. After the Germans had invaded the Soviet Union there had been long discussions within the Party, similar to those I had observed among South African communists in Durban, as to whether this was a war that Indians should regard as theirs. They eventually concluded that it was. While continuing to oppose the British government, the Party was explaining to its followers the need to make common cause with the Soviet Union and others in the fight against fascism. (This was what I had always thought the British Communist party should have done.) The change was reflected in the title of the Party's weekly paper, *People's War.* Declaring support for the war effort had had an immediate practical result for the Party. After years of having to operate underground, it was now legal again, and the activists who had been in jail were being gradually released. But in the fervour of the Quit India movement their stand was unpopular, and party members were still being cautious as to how far they could trust the supposed new government tolerance towards them.

At one point I was asked about the political awareness of my men. I said that I could find no trace of any. But I felt very pleased at last to have a connecting point with the party, and Gaurisankar and I agreed that we would try to keep in touch. Whether that would be possible – and if so how – remained to be seen.

The second day of our journey brought us to Nowgong and the third to a point near Gologhat. On the morning of the fourth day we left the Brahmaputra and swung south, along a very rough and bumpy unmetalled road running through stretches of jungle, waste grassland, and an occasional village in the paddy fields. And finally into Dimapur. It was only seventy miles south of Gologhat, but it had taken us most of the day to reach it.

Dimapur lies mid-way between two geographic extremes. About two hundred miles to the north, just across the Brahmaputra River, rise the Himalayas; about two hundred miles to the south are the steamy, jungle-covered, malarial infested hills and river valleys of north Burma.

Dimapur lies between the two, quite lowlying but far enough north to be free of the worst tropical diseases. It was mid-winter when we arrived, chilly at night and first thing in the morning, but by nine-thirty I could go around in a cotton shirt and shorts and feel quite warm.

Dimapur itself was something of a surprise. I don't quite know what I had expected. Not the large, distinct areas of cantonment, civil lines and Indian city, but perhaps something of the same kind on a much smaller scale. But if there were any civilian administrators there I never saw them, and there were certainly no 'civil lines.' The native 'city' was something a bit larger than a village and much smaller than a town. I can't remember even going to see it more than a couple of times. So, for all practical purposes the population of Dimapur was us – 317 Motor Transport Company. I presume there must have been other companies working in the area before we arrived, but we never set eyes on them.

Until the fall of Burma, Dimapur was nothing more than a sleepy station along the railway line that had been built to service the tea estates of north Assam, which lay in the hills below the eastern sweep of the Himalayas that border on China. When the line had been built there was no thought of using it to reach the Burma border, and it was most inconveniently placed for doing so, for it ran roughly parallel to the border but always two hundred miles to its west. But it was all there was, so everything that the troops on the border needed to keep them going – all the food, tents, hospital equipment, vehicles, arms – now had to be transported the 600 miles up from Calcutta by rail, off-loaded at Dimapur, and somehow taken across those 200 miles by motor transport companies such as ours. To do so, they had to cross a series of mountain ranges. They were sparsely inhabited, and mostly by the Naga people who in Indian terminology are known as 'tribal' – i.e. indigenous groups, ethnically and socially quite distinct from the majority of Indians. Only a few tracks ran through this area, used by people on foot or with animals. The largest of these rose out of the Dimapur valley, crossed a range of mountains and then dropped down into the plain of Imphal in the small princely state of Manipur – and so was usually described as 'the Manipur Road'. It hardly deserved the name of road – a geography book I had, published in 1937, described it more accurately as a cart track. This track had now to be converted into a road worthy of the name, capable of carrying traffic that could supply the needs not just of the troops but also of the thousands of men at work on the road itself.

By the time we arrived, work on the road had progressed quite significantly, but communications between various points on the line of supply were still primitive. For five months the men had been working through the monsoon, that washed away half of what they built. Nine miles up the road, at Nichuguard, a big supply depot had been established. The task of our lorries was to carry supplies that arrived by rail up to this depot. I and one other officer were left to be jointly responsible for this work while Major Perry went back to Delhi to bring up the rest of the company.

We were allotted a site near Nichugard and began to dig latrines. To our horror, we kept digging up decomposing bodies – hastily buried refugees from the retreat from Burma. And now, from a British officer who had been on the Indian side of the border at the time of the retreat, I began to learn more about what had happened. The remnants of the British armies had reached India in the early summer in a condition unbelievably bad. Retreating across one river after another they had finally made their way through hundreds of miles of uncharted jungle – with minimal food, often without water for days. The area they were walking through was sparsely inhabited, and for good reason – it is one of the most unhealthy in the world. Malaria was rampant, a far more potent killer than warfare.* The death toll was overwhelming, and those who got over the border were in a dreadful state, hardly more than skin and bones and most of them suffering from dysentry or jungle typhus. For the last stretches of the route they were overtaken by the monsoon and had to drag themselves through the beating rain, while all semblance of tracks disappeared in mud. In a sense the monsoon also saved them, for the Japanese were no more able than the British to fight through the torrential downpour.

Some of the behaviour he and others had seen was disgraceful. Many senior officers crossing into India had no idea where their troops were, and their only concern was to grab a north-bound lorry and get out as quickly as possible. Apart from the soldiers there were many thousands of civilians fleeing across the border, arriving in the Imphal plain. There was not enough transport, nor hospitals to attend the sick, nor anything like adequate supplies of food. Most people had no choice but to attempt to walk those last two hundred miles to the railhead, climbing yet another set of mountains out of the Imphal plain. The decomposing corpses we had unearthed were of people who had made it all the way to Dimapur, and not had the strength to do those last few miles.

It was while we were having latrines dug that I noticed with delight that there was a large and beautiful lake nearby. As soon as I was free I walked across to it, intending to walk along the shore, and found to my great disappointment that there was hardly a square inch not covered in shit. I had of course known that Indians clean themselves with water and consider the European practice of using toilet paper a disgusting one, but I hadn't realised as I now do that every stretch of water is bound to have piles of shit along the bank. Alas, alas, but there it is.

For some reason I can't now remember we were ordered to move from that site, and given one nearer Dimapur. Our accommodation was of the most rudimentary. The number of tents we had was quite inadequate for even half of the men of the unit, and had to be supplemented by two rickety bamboo and thatch shelters – open at the ends and walled to half their height along the sides. But even that wasn't enough, and there were always some men who had to sleep stretched out across the driving seats of their lorries.

The other officer with me was one of the two Indian lieutenants, Muhammad Nawaz Khan. In Delhi I had seen very little of him – he had only just joined the company and had not as yet been allotted any definite job. He had not long been married and his wife was in Delhi, so he spent all his spare time with her. Now that we were left alone in charge, I was gradually getting to know him, though it took a while for he was rather proud and reserved. He was a man about my own age, a Pathan from the North West Frontier Province. He held himself aloof from the men. He often professed that he couldn't understand them and said he did not like them as much as Northern Indians. But he always treated them reasonably and fairly, and though he was not popular, they respected him

The work of the base hinged upon the clearing of the railhead and keeping it clear, and when trains were coming in fast work continued uninterruptedly, day and night. The men were working an average of fourteen or fifteen hours a day, seven days a week. Khan and I, as the only two officers, each took twelve hours duty, midnight to midday and then midday to midnight by turns. The sidings were crowded with lorries going in and out, and often stuck, for the depot roads were simply one-way tracks of large stones laid straight down on the damp, soft jungle earth. At night work went on by the light of big arc lamps. No one took any notice of blackout precautions. We never had any air attack, for which we were very thankful.

The drivers had the hardest time of it. On more than one occasion they were out thirty-six hours at a stretch. The road to Nichuguard was being widened but still consisted of a central tarred one-way strip and stamped earth on either side. We had Studebakers, big heavy all-metal six-wheelers, with all three driving axles, five gears and reverse, and a low ratio lever which would reduce all gears, giving a total of ten different speeds. They were fine lorries, and their performance over difficult country had to be seen to be believed, but it was no uncommon thing to see them stuck in the mud on the main road where they had had to pull off the centre strip to let another lorry pass.

I should not have liked to be the drivers out on those winter nights. Though it was warm enough during the day, the nights were cold. When a bulb was broken replacements were very rarely obtainable, but work had to continue just the same, so much of the time they were driving without lights on dark, moonless nights, on unlit, half-made roads. Driving must have been pure guesswork. It was if anything worse inside the depots where the trees closed over the road and shut out a lot of the light even in daytime. The drivers got along somehow – God alone knows how – but of course there were accidents.

Once there was an accident of a completely unexpected kind. A river flowed past Nichuguard, and my men would sometimes take their lorries there and drive them a little way into the water to wash them. One day I was there watching them doing this. The river was low and there had been nothing but clear skies for days on end. Suddenly the water began to rise. It was an eerie experience, for there was still no sight of rain. I subsequently learnt that if there is heavy rain in the hills, the water comes swirling down and rises extremely rapidly. The men evidently knew more about this phenomenon than I did, and immediately started their lorries to drive them out of the river bed. Those who couldn't get them started in time left them where they were and made a dash for the shore. In the middle of the night someone brought me the news that one man and his lorry were missing. I at once set out to see what could be done – but there was absolutely nothing that I or anyone else could do. The driver was standing on top of the cab of his lorry and water was swirling all around him. It was impossible to do anything to help and he was eventually swept off and and borne – luckily – to the shore. As he reached it a root of a tree extending into the stream made a bad gash in his leg. He was sent to hospital but I don't remember what became of him after that.

In the base area around Nichuguard we occasionally met officers from other companies that were passing along the road. Some were headed for the point nearer the border where troop strength was gradually being built up, while others who had been at the front some time were being sent back to the army base near Calcutta where new units were being formed and troops trained in the style of warfare that would be needed once an attempt was made to retake Burma.

I remember talking to one officer who I think had been with the army as it came out of Burma and who certainly knew quite a lot about it. But thing that I remember most clearly is his description of how amused he was at watching naked fellow officers going into the stream, and how their balls rose rapidly as soon as their scrotum hit the water. I was of course familiar with this phenomenon – there was in fact a rhyme about it well known in the army, sung to the tune of the sailors' hornpipe.

When your balls hang low you can swing them to & fro

You can tie them in a knot & you can tie them in a bow.

When you get that randy feeling you can bash them on the ceiling

O isn't it a bugger when your balls hang low?

For myself, I was glad at last to be involved with some real work. I knew that what we were doing was vital, and I was glad to feel that I could finally contribute to the war effort. My own work was not difficult – what I mostly had to do was walk about supervising men who were well able to do the job without much supervision, and I would have welcomed something a bit more challenging. But at least we were outside much of the time, and the weather at this time of year was pleasant by day. I liked the fact that Khan and I were alone in charge and could do things our way. Khan never ate English food, and since the major had in any case taken the officers' mess cook with him, we decided to have our meals with the junior Indian officers, the VCOs, in their mess.

By far the most important aspect of the absence of the other officers was the freedom it gave me to get to know the men in my unit without being observed.★ I was already on the way to establishing easy, warm relationships with most of the men. The work I had done practising Urdu was paying off – I could now speak with reasonable fluency, and have natural conversations. It wasn't difficult to find common ground. For a start, I liked Indian food, and two fortuitous things helped me gain their good opinion. Most Indians don't drink alcohol, and people who do are not so well regarded as those who don't. I rarely drank and I was certainly never drunk, which was more than could be said of the other British officers, who displayed their drunkenness on more than one occasion to their men. Secondly, I didn't smoke – I never have. And though most Indian soldiers smoke they regard it as a weakness, and a

Dangers of transport driving in the Naga Hills

man who does not smoke is admired. Then, I enjoyed the more popular type of Indian music, like film songs and folk songs – a taste very few British people in India shared. One song I learnt at this time was *zindagi hai pyar se.*

zindagi hai pyar se, pyar men milae ja

husan ke huzur men apna sar jhukae ja, apna dil uthae ja

The first verse translates

> *Life comes from love, immerse yourself in love*
> *In the presence of beauty bow your head, lift up your heart.*

Simple words, but the way 'lift up' was expressed involved an Urdu construction which at that stage I did not know, so I asked one of my naiks to explain it to me. He was a man called Chandra Reddy who came from Hyderabad where Urdu was the state language, so he knew it quite well. But this, I found out later, was a common construction – and for that very reason he couldn't see, and hence couldn't solve, my difficulty.

The song came from a still popular film of some years earlier called *Sikander* (Sikander being the Persian and Urdu version of Alexander the Great.) The film portrays the invasion of India. I never saw it, but I was told that the cavalry are portrayed riding into battle singing this song – which is quite striking, giving its meaning. Only years later I came to understand that the sentiment of the song is central to most Urdu poetry, and there is almost no context in which it would seem out of place to Indian listeners.

The men would say things to me that they would never have said to other British officers. I remember an early conversation with another of my naiks, Sardar Muhammed. He was a Panjabi – odd man out in a company of South Indians – and he knew Urdu better than many of the others, for it is a north Indian language like Panjabi while the south Indian lanuages are completely unrelated to those of the north. I often used to talk to him and found that he could also read and write Urdu. One day he said 'I know how to swear in English.' I said 'Go on then.' He said 'Bloody fuckan bloody fuckan bloody fuckan.' I asked 'Do you know what 'fuckan' means?' He said 'No', and I thereupon wrote with my finger on the dusty side of a railway wagon its Urdu equivalent, *chodna*. He was highly delighted with this newly acquired knowledge.

The main thing that made communication easy between us was that they sensed my real interest in them as people. I talked to them about my experience of village life in Yorkshire, and they knew I was interested in their experience of life in Indian villages. I knew that these men, young as they were, had experienced more than their share of the hardships of life. They had lived by their labour and never exploited others. I thought I could help them to begin to understand, and eventually to claim, the rights to which they and all working people were entitled; to find the confidence that they could and should claim these rights, and as an aspect of this, should support in whatever way they could the struggle for Indian independence. I regarded them not only as friends but if you like as potential recruits to the communist cause – not in the sense that I envisaged that they would become communists, but in the sense that I could help them start on the road of which I saw communism as the ultimate end.

I knew that if I was to do that, I would need to win their confidence and convince them that I was, so to speak, on their side. This would not be a simple matter. If I expressed 'pro-Indian' sentiments to them they

249

might well suspect that this was a ploy to draw them out and then haul them up before the authorities, and only time and patience would serve to create the trust I wanted. So I worked with them and talked with them about everything that interested them, and gradually they got to know me and like me as a person, and one who they felt could be trusted not to say or do anything that would make their life difficult. Every now and then I was able to move cautiously towards political themes, and occasionally I had the impression that I might have evoked a response, however passive.

Major Perry now returned with the rest of the company, and the normal patterns of company life began to form. The officers' mess was set up and Khan and I were expected to join the others there for our meals. Officers were expected to socialise only with other officers. My period of being unobserved had come to an end. My growing closeness to the men had to be discreetly kept out of view.

I gradually got to know the other officers, and though our world views had little in common, at the superficial level our relations were quite amicable. Major Perry was a professional, career soldier who before the war had been in the Army Education Corps, and this implied that he was not quite as thick as most officers. He had also taken the trouble to learn enough Urdu to communicate with his sepoys − or rather, to try to. It was not so much a deficiency of Urdu that impaired his ability as the fact that he spoke it with a pronounced Wessex accent, mispronouncing and misunderstanding some of the most useful words. For instance the word *malum?* has two long vowels (the *a* being pronounced like the *ar* in 'car' and and the *u* to rhyme with the *oo* in 'boot') but he would pronounce both of them short and clipped − *mall'em*, rhyming with 'Hallam' − which made it completely unrecognisable; and he used it hoping that it meant 'do you understand?' whereas in fact it means 'do you know?' When he saw sepoys doing anything he disapproved of he would shout, '*Eeei! Eeei! Eeisa kubby mut kuro! Yeei boat kerab bundebust hay, mall'em!*' − by which he meant, 'Hey you, don't you ever do that! That's a very bad arrangement, you understand?'

Sometimes the British officers all spent an evening together in the officers' mess, quite jolly occasions, enlivened by Rosa rum which (in moderation) I drank too. The jollification being of a specifically British male type, this tended to happen when our two Indian lieutenants were either on duty elsewhere or made their excuses to leave early. Major Perry was very fond of a comic radio programme in which an amiable idiot in the artillery called Gunner Golightly figured, and he would repeat with great gusto bits of programmes that had especially appealed

250

to him. Bilton, the workshop officer in charge of vehicle maintenance, had a dog, Buster, of which he was very fond, and he seemed almost equally fond of the company's big breakdown vehicle, a Scammell, which he always called the Old Lady. He had worked for some years before the war in the USA and was an absurdly fanatical banner-bearer for Chevrolet, for whom he'd worked, and an absurdly virulent hater of Ford. I think at one time he'd been a racing driver, and he certainly knew how to drive very skilfully at great speed. I remember also that he used to sing a jingle

No wonder dad was angry, no wonder he was wild

She never had no mother, poor little orphan child

I can't think of any context in which it could have been meaningful, but who cared?

Mike Hill, second in command to Major Perry, had a nice dry sense of humour. We had a gramophone with records of American and English popular songs. One of the records was Noel Coward's 'London Pride'; when it came to the verse beginning

Cockney feet mark the beat of history

he would grin and say 'That'll be Russell's favourite line.' I once asked him if he was related to Christopher Hill, the Marxist historian. He said, 'Yes, remotely,' making it clear that the remoteness was desirable.

The other officer was de Jong, who had been an actor. He was a useless officer but an excellent mimic, especially of Cockney women's speech, and would regale us with lewd stories of an over-amorous husband who would appeal to his distinctly unamorous wife with the words, 'Mrs Jones, your place if you please.' Mrs Jones would relate such incidents to her women friends and tell them, 'No, I says, and claps me 'and over it.' After which Mr Jones would turn over and masturbate and she would have to listen to 'the drip drip drip of his nasty nature on the linoleum.'

Among the records we all enjoyed listening there was a deliberately suggestive song in which the first chorus was

But she had to go & lose it at the Astor, she couldn't take her mother's good advice

Now there aren't so many girls today that have one,

And she wouldn't let it go at any price

Throughout the song you are left to think that 'it' is her virginity until the final lines

They could only stand & gape, there was Minnie's sable cape

And they thought that she had lost it at the Astor

Two songs celebrated the attractions of Latin American women:

He was a handsome young Irish lad & she was a Mexican beauty

It was fiesta &, I might add, romantically he was on duty.

A boy & a girl 'neath the stars, I can tell it in twenty four bars

His Irish heart went bingo when he saw the rose of Tropez—

Conchita Marquita Lolita Pepita Rosita Juanita Lopez.

They dance, kiss, fall in love and marry, and the next day ride away on a mule to his home town, where you may see

Conchita Marquita Lolita Pepita
Rosita Juanita O'Toole

252

presiding over a family of fourteen children of pre-school age and a number of others who now to go school.

Another was 'There's a place in Rio de Janeiro'…

Where they sing an American love song
in a South American way –

Its jaunty chorus begins

I, I, I, I, I, I want to hold you tight

You, you, you are too too too divine

If you want to be in someone's arms tonight

Just make sure the arms you're in are mine.

But beneath the superficial ease of my relations with my fellow officers, there were serious issues to be considered. I knew it was necessary that they should not be aware of the kind of relationship I was developing with my men. To explain why this was, I will need to say something of how communists in the army were viewed by their non-communist fellows.

This was on the whole a period of exceptional tolerance towards communists, caused almost entirely by the great admiration which Soviet armies inspired in the Allies for their heroic fight against the Germans; and the longer this went on, the greater did this admiration grow. Elsewhere too there were developments that were good for morale; in October 1942 the British offensive against the Germans in north Africa had begun, and by early November the Germans were in full retreat. But British achievements were modest compared with the great Soviet victory at Stalingrad. The Red Army and the civilian population had defended the city with incredible tenacity, and now in January 1943, not long after we got to Dimapur, we heard that a Soviet offensive had trapped the entire German 6th Army and compelled its commander to surrender, with the Russians taking 92,000 prisoners, including twenty four generals. Communists in the British forces generally enjoyed a sort of reflected glory from these Soviet victories. The general tolerance extended to senior levels – communist officers like James Klugman were entrusted with quite sensitive positions in the war in Europe. They could express their views openly, both to their fellow officers and their men, because they were all united in the conviction that they were fighting a just war.

In India the situation was completely different, because the history of colonial oppression made a sense of shared humanity between British and Indians an impossibility. And because of this, to be a communist and an officer in the Indian army raised problems that communists did not encounter anywhere else in the British armed forces. Today, fifty-plus years after independence, it is hardly possible for people who were not in India at the time to have any idea of how revolting British attitudes were. There is an eloquent illustration of them in Hilary Spurling's life of Paul Scott, the novelist whose Raj Quartet is set in the last days of British India. In a letter in 1945 Scott described how, travelling on a troopship towards Singapore he 'had caused a first-class row … by insisting, as the commander of the only Indians aboard, that British soldiers be prevented from spitting in his men's drinking water.' His superiors' anger was directed not at the British soldiers who did this, but at Paul Scott for insisting that they be prevented from doing it.★ Such contemptible attitudes were the norm. This is, of course, not the picture of British-Indian relationships which one gets from British administrators and the professional, regular full time British officers who commanded Indian troops. These professed to believe, and in most cases probably really did believe, that the mass of the Indian people were happy under British rule and that the 'trouble-makers' who supported the Indian National Congress were disgruntled intellectuals linked via Gandhi with numerous innocents who had been deluded into following their lead. Those British officers who were professional soldiers and had commanded Panjabi troops in the peace-time Indian Army did have some grounds for taking this view. Panjabi troops constituted, as the old buffers used to say, 'the sword arm of India.' After the uprising of 1857 ('the Mutiny') the British did a great deal to secure the loyalty of the Panjab. Irrigation brought vast areas of land into cultivation, and grants of land to soldiers and their families consolidated widespread support for their British benefactors. To the very end of British rule there was neglible support for Congress in the Panjab countryside. This gave rise to what someone has called a sort of 'symbiosis' between these British officers and their men, and these officers assumed, understandably but quite wrongly, that what was true of the Panjab was true of India as a whole. And it is their voice that has most generally been heard.

There were of course large numbers of British in pre-war India who were neither administrators nor professional army officers, and their perception of indians was very different. Nirad Chaudhuri in his book *The Continent of Circe*, has decribed it very well. After the 1857 uprising, he says, 'The life of the British community in India was haunted by a great fear, which never left their imagination. It was the fear of a sudden uprising of the disarmed masses of the country, followed by massacre.' It followed that 'the whole of the British community in India was to make common cause against the whole of the Indian community, without reference to the merits of the case. Anyone who did not follow that code was a traitor.'

It was a universally understood principle that no British person would publicly admit that any other British person had been at fault in his or her dealings with Indians. This extended even to the most blatant crimes. Chaudhuri describes what happened when someone as powerful as Curzon, the Viceroy, tried to challenge this. A native cook in a British cavalry regiment in Simla was beaten to death by some of the troopers, and no-one in the regiment would give any evidence as to who had done it. Curzon punished the entire regiment by transerring it to a distant station. Later in Delhi the regiment took part in a parade, with Curzon present, and the whole of the British community present rose and cheered the regiment as it marched past.★

The 'great fear' of which Chaudhuri wrote took on new dimensions in the conditions of war. With the Japanese threat on India's borders, the British had no choice but to rely on Indians to fight their war for them – and they did not know if they could trust them. Government propaganda that Congress was pro-Japanese was almost universally believed. The slim basis for this accusation arose from the activities of Subhas Chandra Bose, the most radical of the Congress leaders. At the outbreak of the war he had seen Britain's difficulty as India's opportunity and had made an agreement with the Germans to raise an army under his leadership to fight alongside them. This didn't materialise, but later he made a similar agreement with the Japanese, and formed an 'Indian National Army' from Indian troops taken prisoner by the Japanese at the surrender of Singapore. Bose's line and activities had been condemned by Gandhi and other Congress leaders, but this fact was completely overlooked.

Most British officers were in fact pig ignorant where serious politics were concerned, and knew nothing of what the real stand of Congress had been. Their outlook was in any case that which, a generation later, astonished intelligent people when it again found an eloquent exponent in Margaret Thatcher. 'We're British and proud of it,' the line went. 'Our interests are paramount, regardless of what other people's interests may be. Our rule in India is a glorious thing, and any means that may be needed to uphold it are fully justified. Indians should do as they are told and not concern themselves with matters which they are not capable of understanding.' In this atmosphere any Indians who showed signs of being able to think were automatically regarded as being subversive, and it was certainly not the job of any Briton to encourage them to do so.

From August 1942 the Quit India movement and its ruthless suppression had intensified this long-standing racial arrogance and fear of a backlash, and what the average British person in India felt, British wartime soldiers had additional reason to feel even more strongly. They had never wanted to come to India and didn't like either India or the Indians. Moreover they were here fighting in a war which they thought it obvious that all right-thinking people must support, but which they saw that Indians didn't see as being in their interest. Spontaneous mass demonstrations all over the country were making this abundantly clear. In this situation, any sympathy that a minority of liberal officers might previously have felt for Indian aspirations was now in most cases swept away, and those who still felt such sympathy were almost completely isolated.

One such, Jim Fyrth, in his account of his years as a serviceman in India in 1944-1946, describes how the officer commanding a unit to which he had just been posted told the newcomers, 'Now, I've seen some of you chaps talking to the Indians around the place. Now I don't want to see any of you talking to Indians. You must remembr that you are here as an army of occupation and that any one of you is better than anyone in this country.' A sergeant in the same unit saw Jim talking to the tea-seller and called him aside to tell him, 'If I see you talking to that man again I will put you on a court-martial charge.' A corporal in the same unit told the newcomers how he had knocked down an old woman while driving his truck. 'I didn't want her reporting me,' he said, 'so I backed the truck over her to finish her off.' When they expressed their horror he shrugged, 'When you've been here as long as I have you get to hate these people.'

Fyrth reports ruefully how an Indian friend had asked him to give a talk to some sixteen to seventeen year old schoolboys. At question time after the talk 'There was some shuffling and giggling and looking at one boy, who rose and asked: "Are there any good Englishmen?" After my fumbling affirmation that of course there were he asked, "Then why do we never see them?'

My fellow British officers by now knew that in my student days I had had communist sympathies, and that in itself didn't bother them – everyone knew that this had happened to many Cambridge students in

256

General Slim with a Panjabi officer: the special relationship of long-time professionals

the thirties, even quite nice chaps; and I benefitted from the tolerance engendered by the Red Army's prowess. But their ignorant and intense anti-communism was never far beneath the surface. I knew that at the first sign that I constituted some sort of a threat to British control in India, their real attitudes would emerge. In particular, they would have been horrified at the idea of my discussing political issues with the men – or indeed of my talking to them seriously about anything at all except their military duties. For the more reactionary among them, to see an officer treating his sepoys with respect would in itself be considered inappropriate, for sepoys were nothing but stupid peasants. But if a British officer actually encouraged them to think, the only possible conclusion would be that he too was a subversive.

In this they would have been correct. I wholeheartedly agreed with the Indian communists who, while supporting the war, did *not*, like the communists in Britain, support the government. How *could* any communist, Indian or British, have supported the British government's complete denial of the rights of Indians in their own country? I was quite prepared when circumstances made this possible to encourage my sepoys not only to oppose current government policies but, when conditions were ripe, to put an end to British rule in India, if need be by force of arms. But to do this as a British person in India was of course treason, and could be punished as such. A communist – even if he were a British officer – was still a communist, and as they thought, a dangerous enemy of the social and political order that they were there to uphold. An enemy of the social order I of course was; 'dangerous' I certainly was not, though people like these were the sort who see a red under every bed.

Indian troops were thought, on the whole, not to be actively subversive, for the rigorous screening of potential recruits eliminated any with previous connections with political movements. In nearly three years I found only two with previous political experience, which the police had somehow failed to discover. Longer established British officers may also have believed the myth so proudly propagated by the army top brass, that the Indian Army was 'the largest volunteer army in the world' – with the totally false implication that it consisted of men loyal to the British and ready to uphold British rule. Sepoys were volunteers only because they were poor and had no other prospect of earning. So, as they themselves put it, they joined the army 'to fill their belly.' But for my own protection and that of the men I befriended it was essential to keep our developing relationships hidden from the officers. I felt confident that, provided I was cautious, they would never realise what was going on, for it would have not occurred to them that I would *want* to talk about such things to sepoys.

So I avoided letting them see me doing or saying anything that would arouse their latent hostilities, and cause them to make life difficult for me. I wanted them to think I was a nice chap, and if in the 1930s I had been red or pink, well, what of it? That was water under the bridge. So to them I *was* a nice chap.

I also felt it necessary to keep the two Indian officers in the dark. Indian officers were recruited exclusively from the Indian upper classes, and I did not expect to have anything in common with them politically: if they had not been pro-British, or at any rate not opposed to British rule, they would never have gone into the Army. Khan was from a feudal landowning family, and the other, Gopal Singh, was a Panjabi Sikh. He represented the third generation of his family in military service, and his eldest son was destined to follow in his footsteps. His family's connection with the army was typical. By the time I was in India there were hundreds of families in Panjab whose comparative economic security arose from the military service of their grandfathers, and was still completely tied up with service in the army. Gopal Singh's grandfather had, after many years of continuous army service, been granted land by the government in the then recently irrigated and settled district of Lyallpur (now re-named Faisalabad).

My personal relationship with both was friendly. They sensed that socially they were far from being accepted by their British brother officers, while I accepted them as my equals. Khan by now knew me well enough to express his amazement that – with the single exception of myself – none of the British officers after nine or ten months in India had so much as bothered to learn that easily acquired minimum of Urdu without which they could neither understand their NCOs and men nor be understood by them.

So much for the officers – or, to give them their full designation, King's Commissioned Officers. Next in rank came the Viceroy's Commissioned Officers – VCOs. This was a category peculiar to the Indian Army, but there was a near equivalent in the British Army in men whom Kipling in one of his verses called 'gentleman rankers.' They were men from the 'other ranks' who had been considered fit to be promoted to full officer rank because of their experience and capabilities, despite their lack of the otherwise essential qualification of being gentlemen. The 'gentlemen' always made it clear to the 'gentlemen rankers' that they weren't *real* gentlemen. In India it would have been unthinkable to promote an Indian from the ranks of the common soldiery to king's commissioned status, so the specially invented category of VCOs was devised. Those who were still serving during the second world war were veterans, or semi-veterans, from pre-war times. They had the attitudes you'd expect from long-serving professional soldiers; if they had not been loyal servants of the British, they wouldn't have been there, and part of their role traditionally was to be part of the unit CID – to watch out for and report any rebellious tendencies among the sepoys. If they had seen me talking too freely with the men, and reported that to the officers, both the men and I might have been in quite serious difficulties.

But there were a couple of factors that diminished the risk in our Company. All except one of the VCOs were northern Indians, who knew neither English nor any Southern Indian language and couldn't understand what the men were talking about. The army would normally have appointed Madrassi VCOs to a Madrassi unit – to use the word then commonly applied to all South Indians – but enough who were qualified for VCO status could not be produced in a hurry; so the already long-serving VCOs had to man the Madrassi companies. In our company there was a Sikh as Indian adjutant, a Garhwali as quartermaster – Garhwal is on the lower slopes of the Himalayas – and three Panjabis as section VCOs. In the fourth section there was a Madrassi VCO but he was on other duty and rarely came near railhead. There was generally speaking a cordial mutual dislike between Panjabis and Madrassis – and particularly between Panjabi regulars and Madrassi war-time soldiers – which usually ensured that the last thing in which a Panjabi VCO wished to interest himself was the way in which the Madrassi recruit thought and acted in his leisure time.

I realised more and more as time went on that the social, economic, communal, cultural, and political complexion of the South was different from that of the north. For example, in the north, Hindu-Muslim antagonism was strong and widely prevalent. To the 'Madrassis' this was hardly an issue. The vast majority of them were Hindus, and though there were relatively small numbers of Muslims and Christians in South India, the others felt no antagonism against them. A sort of national consciousness in each of the regions from which most of the men came – Kerala, Andhra and Tamilnadu – was far stronger than the religious-communal consciousness which prevailed in the north. Even the British, with their divide and rule policy, couldn't do much about applying it in the South. In the army units that recruited mainly from the North there were separate cookhouses for Hindu, Muslim and Sikh troops, and each would have been horrified at the thought of eating food cooked by others than their own co-religionists. Not so in South Indian units. There everyone shared the same food. So the idea of friendly relations between Hindus and Muslims was a commonly approved one. All this was strange to VCOs from the North, and increased the distance between them and the sepoys.

In any case, if I wanted to talk unobserved with one of the men there were plenty of ways of avoiding the attention of VCOs. Work went on from an hour before dawn until several hours after dark – usually until midnight at least – so there were frequent opportunities of being with the sepoys during hours of darkness, when we could discreetly withdraw to talk in some place from which one could see without being seen. Even in daylight hours there were possibilities. The sidings were always cluttered with goods trains and lorries and it was quite easy to disappear, though for shorter periods than at night time. And if we *were* seen, the common assumption would be not that I was talking politics but that I was pursuing a homosexual interest in the man I was with.

This was not in fact the case, though in those days I did begin to feel strongly the homosexual urges which most men do after long periods in the exclusive company of men, and many of them physically beautiful South Indians. I remember one day clowning with Khan's orderly, Subhan, in a way which he (rightly!) thought showed that I fancied him. He laughed and said, 'I'm not a woman, Sahib, I'm a man.' I don't think he was shocked; homosexual liaisons between the men were commonplace, and though formally disapproved were treated with amused tolerance.

The other officers, including the commanding officer, stayed in company lines, about a mile away. They very rarely came near railhead and were ignorant of practically all that occurred there. The major spent most of his time either in the company office or at sub-area headquarters, or running around base in his station wagon. He was not a bad bloke but he lacked the personality to make his lieutenants work, and so as long as Khan and I were getting things done, he didn't bother about what the others did. Even Khan and I saw relatively little of each other, for during my shift he either slept or went over to Company headquarters.

This meant I spent twelve hours every day with the sepoys and NCOs of my section, unobserved by any of the officers – and that suited me fine. They were in any case the people who interested me most. I liked them best as people, and it was unusually easy to win a full response to the affection I felt for them. When months later I met my Cambridge friend Indrajit Gupta, and he asked me if I was popular with my men, I replied that it was out of the question that any normal decent English officer, who treated his men in the same way as he would treat

261

British troops under his command, should *not* be popular. Even those British officers who did not actively ill-treat their sepoys, usually showed such lack of understanding of – or even interest in – their needs and desires that anyone who showed even the minimum of consideration was bound to be popular. All the officers except Khan had been in the company several months by this time but they did not know the names of more than half a dozen of their men, whereas by now I knew the names of all the hundred men in my section, and a fair number in the rest of the company too.

A pleasant and unexpected surprise during these months was the discovery that Khan was a much better man than I could have expected any Indian officer to be. He and I shared a small 180lb tent. He was a devout Muslim, and before I got to know his regular prayer-times I often used to fling into our tent in the evening to find him standing there barefooted, dressed in white baggy trousers and shirt and red fez, with his hands clasped and eyes closed in prayer. He would never take any notice of my interruption, and I would retire until his orderly – always a Muslim sepoy at that time – told me he had finished his prayers. I never ventured to ask much about his private affairs but came to know that he was a graduate – had studied constitutional law, English, and Persian at Panjab and Aligarh universities – was the son of a landlord, and came of a family which had long been in British government service in the North-West Frontier Province. He had joined the army as an officer cadet in, I think, mid-1941, and was commissioned early in 1942 to a supply depot at Karachi; he had been there only a short time when he was posted to 317 company.

He was not a demonstrative man and for quite a long time we used not to talk much, but he gradually developed a liking for me, and I sensed this. Long afterwards he told me that the main reason was that I was the only British officer in the company who treated him without showing any trace of racial prejudice. He told me that before he had been commissioned he had never had the slightest idea that such discrimination existed in the Army, whereas actually he had come to see that it was universal. His first reaction was naturally a feeling of frustration and bitterness at the petty humiliations which his position constantly brought upon him, turning gradually to a secret contempt, rarely expressed even to me. He saw more and more that none of the officers except us two was doing a hand's turn of work in the company. Perhaps Gopal Singh was; but he was not with us at railhead, and I don't remember what he was doing. The other officers at that time openly expressed the opinion that their men were worthless and contemptible riff-raff, and justified their own idleness by telling one another that it was hopeless to attempt to make anything of such material as the men under their command. Finally Khan objected to the somewhat uproarious drunkenness which from time to time occurred in the officers' mess. He used to say that it was beyond his comprehension that any sane and intelligent man could sit down for the evening with the object of getting drunk.

Even so, I didn't venture to talk politics with him. I remember only one reference to politics at this time. We were both lying in bed, talking before we went to sleep, and he said something about the speed of demobilisation after the war, post-war grants of land, and so on. I said he couldn't argue anything on the assumption that the British government, which had never shown any concern for the interests of the peasants, would do so now. We were lying in the dark, so I could not see his face, but he made no reply.

I was by now writing to the friends in India whom I had acquired in the earlier months of moving about, like Amrit Rallia Ram in Lahore, and Gaurisankar in Gauhatti. Gaurisankar was regularly sending me *People's War* and other pamphlets, and writing quite frequently. I was a little surprised at his complete openness. He wrote of Party matters without concealment and asked me to send money to him for the Party by money order, made out in his name and addressed to him at the Communist Party bookshop in Gauhatti. I concluded that if Gaurisankar considered such openness to be OK it must be – at least in correspondence with civilians – and replied equally openly, and sent him all the money I could spare. But I still didn't write about my conversations with the men in my unit.

Politically these conversations were still very tentative, for I assumed that to talk about communism or the Communist Party of India would be beyond their comprehension. Influenced by Gaurisankar's tone, I now began to think that perhaps there was scope for more openly expressing my communist views, at least to those of the men who were educated enough to have some idea of what communism was. Perhaps the reason why I had previously evoked so little response when I had ventured near political topics was that I had not been making my own stand unequivocally clear.

So, still taking care not to let the officers be aware of what was happening, I began to switch my main attention from the ordinary sepoys to the much smaller number of men who knew English. There were several at railhead, as other army units had depot representatives there and this work required English. These men were by definition more educated, and I assumed would probably have a broader view of the

Lorries on the Manipur Road

world than ordinary sepoys. I now began to say quite openly in conversation with them that I was a communist. One or two used to listen with interest to my views, and, more rarely, question me and argue with me about them. One was Kuttappan Nair, a naik in our company, though not in my section. He did duty at our vehicle check-point checking the lorries' timings in and out of rail-head. He was quite well educated and spoke excellent English and I often used to talk to him at nights, sitting with him at the check-point until all lorries had returned for the night. He was from Kerala, and lived in Trivandrum, Travancore State. At first he kept off all Indian affairs, but asked me a lot about Russia, China and other countries, and about communist theory and the working class movement in Britain. About this time I lent him Minoo Masani's book *Our India*. This was a book written very simply for children telling them of India's potential wealth and actual backwardness and instilling into them the determination that their country should overtake the rest of the world, banish its backwardness and take its place among the great nations of the world. At the same time there was nothing explicitly political in it. Kuttappan liked it very much and asked me if I had any more like it. From that time on we began to discuss Indian affairs also. I subsequently lent the book to most of the supply depot clerks of the railhead detachment, always with good results.

It was a while after arriving in Dimapur before my mail started reaching me, but then a fair batch came. One from my mother enclosed a letter she had had from Noel, now in Canada on RAF training, which only reinforced my poor opinion of his social attitudes. I wrote to Froude, 'He is becoming a perfect specimen of his type and writes more and more like the boys in the Sunday papers. What a waste of paper and postage.' And then added, 'You'd better not let the old folks see these harsh words.' From Gertie, Marie's sister, I heard that Marie was getting married to Ronnie King, and that 'a little prince or princess' was on the way. I had an idea that she had 'had to get married' (as the idiom of the time had it) because Ronnie had made her pregnant, and this proved to be the case. I decided that I shouldn't contact her again, but leave her to be as happy as she could be in her marriage. From Chris's wife Peggotty I heard news of the first of my friends to be killed. Ram Nahum, who was a brilliant physicist, had not been called up but had stayed on in Cambridge doing research related to the war effort. A rare bombing raid on Cambridge hit the building in which he was living, and he was killed instantly. When I next managed to arrange a transfer of money home, I asked Rex to send some of it to the memorial fund Chris and Peggotty were raising in his name.

But all of this seemed increasingly far away. I wrote to Rex, 'I find it difficult to imagine the state of affairs in England now, and difficult to remember what I am told even about personal matters like what various people have been doing and where they have been since I left.' And now that I was in an active service area there was even less of significance I could write to them about my own life. I couldn't say which part of the country we were in, not describe the base, nor even write about the type of work we were doing, since all of these were military secrets. Still it felt important to try to share with them how I was changing through the experience of living in India. In a long letter home written on Christmas day 1942, I described my pleasure at the warm and relaxed relationship that was developing with the men in my unit; how I had changed over to eating Indian food. Tea and a chapatti first thing, a meal mid morning, and another early evening. Rice, vegetables, dhal, hardly any meat, and everything laced with chillies. The perpetual stomach troubles of the British in India, I decided, were probably caused by eating too often and too much …

Letter writing, I wrote to Froude, is like keeping a diary. You write down the things that strike you at the time and then find after a few weeks that you have missed out all the more important things because they have all developed imperceptibly.

I began to wonder what would happen after the war. I would be shipped back to England, and of course I would want that. I would look for a job in a factory. I didn't go along with the communist orthodoxy that intellectuals should mainly work among intellectuals – I knew, both from working in the fields in Yorkshire and now alongside these Indian peasants, that I could establish easy relationships with ordinary working people, and was sure I could do useful political work with them.* Then after a while I would perhaps be able to do what I had always hoped to, and get a job as a full-time party worker.

I hoped I could maintain contact with India after the war. I had put so much effort into learning to speak to ordinary people and trying to understand how they saw things, it would seem a pity not to use that experience longer term. Perhaps when the war ended I might stay on for a while? There would certainly be political work to be done here too.

12

In January 1943 we heard that there had been an appeal for officers on the Burma front to volunteer for transfer to the Navy. Since the disastrous retreat the Allied armed forces were being gradually reformed. The lessons from the defeat made it clear that Burma could only be regained by a greatly increased strength of allied forces, in a combined air, land and sea operation. The naval force had to be built up more or less from scratch, and the appeal for volunteers was an urgent one. I knew that my height, or rather absence of it, would count against me (the Navy being more particular in these matters than the Army) but I decided to apply. I was still feeling decidedly under-used – my only contribution to the war effort so far had consisted of supervising men who scarcely needed supervision. Staying in Dimapur was undoubtedly the safer option – being part of a possible naval invasion of Burma would be a far riskier business than being behind the lines in a transport company. I had no special desire to be killed but I was restless to do something more useful to contribute to the defeat of fascism. If I had been able to make more headway with my sepoys politically, *that* would have made it worth staying, but progress in that direction was so slow as to be almost imperceptible. So I sent off my application, and waited to hear.

Then one day in February 1943 something happened which signalled the beginning of a change in my feelings about my potential usefulness where I was. A havildar-clerks named L B Swamy, from Kerala, came into my tent at railhead, bringing a message from headquarters. While he was talking to me he noticed a pile of copies of *People's War* on the floor. The top copy had a photo of P C Joshi, general secretary of the Communist Party of India, on the front page. After delivering his message he said, 'Excuse me, sir, what is that paper?' I picked it up and showed it to him, explaining that it was the weekly organ of the Communist Party of India. He said 'This is a photo of P C Joshi.' 'Yes,' I said: 'Why? Do you know him?' To my surprise he replied 'Yes, I know him personally. I was with him in Bombay before the war.' He said that up to 1940, when he had joined the army, he had worked in the Girgaon district of Bombay amongst the Malayali workers there. (Kerala is the name of the region (now a state); its people are called Malayalis and their language Malayalam.) He had once been secretary of the Hotel Workers Union, which was led by communists. I felt a little uneasy about him. I wondered how it was that he had not noticed what I was trying to do. He said that I had at first attracted his attention, but he had concluded I could not be worth anything when the old head clerk (who was a Christian) told him that I used to read his Bible when I was on night duty in the Company office! This was a fact: I had often read the Bible when I was on duty there; it was the only good literature available in the Company office. The head clerk had drawn from this the quite erroneous conclusion that I was a devout Christian, and had told Swamy so: and Swamy, who soon revealed himself as an exceedingly intolerant atheist, had forthwith abandoned all hope of me! I couldn't help being amused at his explanation, but it annoyed me that he had not troubled to meet me and form his own estimate. If he had, we could have been working together.

I also had doubts about his political position. I doubted whether a genuine Party sympathiser, in India of all places, could have joined the army during what we then characterised as the imperialist phase of the war. He said that he had spoken to his communist colleagues about his decision to enlist, and they had raised no objections.

I soon found that many of Swamy's political opinions were highly dubious. He took an out and out anti-Congress line and had an equally rigid attitude towards religion. He said that when the Party conquered power it should forcibly suppress religion and begin a sort of anti-religious reign of terror! Then in February 1943 we heard that Gandhi had gone on hunger strike in jail, in protest at what he called the 'leonine violence' of the British authorities. Swamy said he hoped that Gandhi would die of it, and that this would constitute a great advance in that it would remove his influence, which operated against the revolutionising of the Indian masses. On this point I was ready to agree with him, for I myself had many reservations about Gandhi's political role. R. Palme Dutt's *India Today* showed clearly that Gandhi had always called off mass action against the British at times when it began to threaten the interests of the Indian landlords and capitalists, whom he regarded as trustees for the welfare of their tenants and employees – trustees who needed only to be persuaded to realise their responsibility and act accordingly. The strength of reaction to this wish for Gandhi's death taught me an important lesson. Earlier in Delhi I had discovered that Gandhi was the only national leader that most of the sepoys knew of, and that he was greatly revered, but I had not realised the depth of that reverence. To criticise him, let alone wish for his death, was regarded as a sort of sacrilege.

Swamy had apparently made no effort to keep any contact with the Party since his enlistment and had still less any idea that he should attempt to carry on any communist work amongst the sepoys. I suggested that we should try to get together some time and decide how we should do this, despite the fact that, as I told him, the vast majority of the men knew little or nothing about politics. He at once ridiculed my assessment of them. He pointed out – what I had not till then known – that in parts of Malabar (the northern region of Kerala) the Party enjoyed undisputed leadership of the peasants, and assured me that there would be hardly one Malayali sepoy in the Company who did not know the names of our Party leaders in Kerala – men like K P R Gopalan Nambiar. I was to get immediate and striking proof of this. We were speaking in English, but when he mentioned K P R's name a Malayali sepoy who was sitting nearby looked up quickly and asked Swamy some question in Malayalam. Swamy told me he was asking what was the latest news of K P R, who had then been some two and a half years in jail. I was naturally elated at this sudden brightening of political prospects in the unit. I now realised, with Swamy's help, that it was only political wariness which had caused the lack of any widespread response to my efforts, and now envisaged that, with Swamy to vouch for my reliability, we should make good progress. I began to read all I could in *People's War* about Malabar and to talk about what I had read to any Malayali who would listen to me. This created a great stir; my newfound ability to talk of the political affairs of their own part of India convinced many of them that I really did know something of Indian politics. I don't think that they were inclined to be any the less wary about me or any more satisfied about my sincerity and integrity; but I am sure that whereas they had previously noted my utterances with only a casual interest, and determined in any case not to risk giving themselves away, they now began to watch me more closely in an effort to determine whether I could be trusted or not. This shift in attitude was to have its effect later on.

In spite of my reservations about him, I was extremely glad that I had met Swamy. I started to learn all I could from him. He knew the war-time history of the movement in Kerala very well and I learned a great deal about it from him. He had also travelled all over Southern India and could tell me quite a lot about the home districts of many of my men. Most of all I hoped that he would be able to convince people of my trustworthiness and so remove the greatest barrier standing in the way of exercising effective political influence upon them. It was clear that I would have to persuade him that this could and should be done, because when I had first suggested that we should get together to do this he had made some quite non-committal response. But I hoped I would be able to do this.

One day a letter from Gaurisankar arrived to give me rather a rude shock. He wrote that he had shown some of my letters to comrades from Bengal, and that they had asked him to warn me not to speak so frankly in corresponding with him. ('After all,' he wrote, 'this is a colonial country.') In view of the fact that in doing so I had only followed his example, I was rather annoyed and quite shaken by this reproof, for I had not written anything that I regarded as politically sensitive. It didn't occur to me at the time to ask myself why Party leaders higher up the hierarchy than Gaurisankar didn't feel, as Gaurisankar evidently had done, that now that the Party was legal such caution was unnecessary. Perhaps they were concerned to protect me, for as a British officer I was vulnerable to a possible charge of treason. But I think it more likely that they were so used to working illegally that this sort of caution had become a habit.

Shortly after receiving this letter I read an account in *People's War* of the activities of the Assam Police. I was appalled, and now understood why the leadership was stressing the need for caution. The Assam Police were concentrating all their attention on harassing and persecuting the Communist Party, even though it was now legal and the *only* party with a mass following that was struggling to persuade the Indian people to support a policy of active national defence. It was the greatest good luck that none of my letters or money orders to Gaurisankar appeared to have been intercepted by the police.

I drew in my horns quite considerably after that. I left off corresponding with Gaurisankar except on the most non-political lines, and then not more often than necessary. I destroyed his previous letters, and kept the party publications which I had received under lock and key. I left off talking politics to all and sundry and concentrated on Kuttappan and others whom I had picked out as likely to be both sympathetic and discreet.

By March 1943, when I had been in Dimapur almost four months, I was due for leave. I planned to use it to get in touch with the Indian Party leadership. I wanted to break my isolation, to be able to discuss with others the work I was trying to do in my unit, and to get their advice. The Indian communists I had known as students in Cambridge were my starting point. I knew that Indrajit Gupta was in Calcutta, and Mohan Kumaramangalam in Madras. I had heard that Mohan had been jailed on his return to India but was now out of jail and secretary of the Party in Tamilnadu. It so happened that Kuttappan too was going on leave a few days before me and would pass through Madras, so I entrusted him with a letter to deliver to Mohan, telling him where I was and what I was doing. The third of my Cambridge comrades was Arun Bose. In Cambridge he had guided the work of his Indian fellow-communists, and I had heard that since his return to India he had become the leading light in the All-India Students' Federation, AISF. Though this was a broad movement, it was communist-led, and Arun was then working on its monthly paper, *The Student*. Their offices were in Bombay – which was also where the Party headquarters were.

So that was where I would go for my leave. I hoped that through Arun I could get introductions to people in the Party leadership, with whom I could talk about my work.

I spent my first week of leave in Gauhatti, staying with the student party member I had met when we had bivouacked near the his house on our way to Dimapur. This time I met and talked with most of the Gauhatti comrades, and especially with Gaurisankar. I was still a bit apprehensive about security. I suggested that we should not walk about the streets together, for a British officer in conversation with an Indian civilian was so unusual a sight that it immediately attracted attention and curiosity. When we wanted to talk either he could come to the house where I was staying or I would come to meet him at some pre-arranged rendezvous.

One morning Gaurisankar took me to the Party office. As we sat down to talk I said that I didn't feel too happy about meeting him alone in broad daylight in such a place, but he said it would be OK, and I acquiesced. After about ten minutes a police inspector appeared at the window and calling Gaurisankar outside began to speak to him in Assamese. Of course I could understand nothing, but I saw him nod in my direction once or twice as he spoke. After a while he said to me in imperfect English, 'I am going away for twenty minutes, and must ask you as an army officer to make yourself responsible that your friend does not leave this place until I return.' Feeling somewhat shaken, I assented.

When he had gone I asked Gaurisankar what it was all about. He said that everything would be OK: the police were enquiring into the activities of a group calling themselves the Progressive Youth League who were then pursuing an 'objectively fifth-column line of activity' in Assam i.e. activity which would help the Japanese. The police had assumed that this group was the Communist Party because during the years the Party had been illegal its members had met in the guise of a study circle calling itself the Progressive Union. Gaurisankar said he had given the inspector information proving that there was no connection

271

between the two, and the inspector had now gone to verify this. I asked what the inspector had said about me. Gaurisankar said he had asked who I was and he had said I was a personal friend whom he had met when he was a student in Calcutta. I felt very annoyed at this. Had the police cared to check up they could find out without the slightest trouble that I had been in India less than a year, i.e. after Gaurisankar had finished his studies at Calcutta, and that in actual fact I had never been near Calcutta. He could easily have stuck close to the truth and said that he met me through the student party member when my unit moved up to Manipur Road the previous November. Gaurisankar agreed but said that the inspector was not particularly interested in me and that everything would be OK. And actually when he did return he professed himself quite satisfied. Still for my remaining days in Gauhatti we did exercise rather more care.

On my way to Bombay I stopped off at Calcutta, where I was to be interviewed about my application to join the navy. Since there now seemed a prospect of making some political headway among my sepoys, I had decided I didn't want to go ahead with the application, and I went to the interview in some trepidation. To start with I was a day or two late, though I can't remember why; more important, I feared that withdrawing my application would evoke an indignant and probably cutting response, and I could scarcely explain my reasons. But I was not rebuked, and while the officer who interviewed me made it fairly clear by his attitude that he didn't feel that the navy would suffer unduly by my not joining its ranks, he was not unpleasant about it, and all was over in a matter of minutes.

On my arrival in Bombay I went straight to the office of *The Student* and was warmly welcomed by my Cambridge friend Arun Bose. I stayed there throughout my stay in Bombay – about twelve days – sleeping on the floor with the other student comrades and getting to know several of them well. One, Nargis, was the wife of a prominent Party worker called Batliwala who had until recently been in jail with the veteran trade union organiser Dange.

Most of my time I spent in the Party headquarters in Khetwadi Main Road, reading and making notes on back numbers of *People's War* and other Party documents. I had my meals with the leading Party comrades who lived in the building. There must have been about fifty of them, each with their own room (or share of a room), and with separate apartments for the married couples. One of the married women was the sister of my Cambridge friend Mohan Kumaramangalam. She and one other were expecting babies, and there were a few couples with chil-

Bhagat Singh
and his
Comrades

by one of their colleagues
AJOY GHOSH

CHITTAGONG ARMOURY RAIDERS
REMINISCENCES
KALPANA DUTT

هل اور هنسیا

قومی دارالاشاعت بمبئی

With The
Ploughshare

And The
Sickle

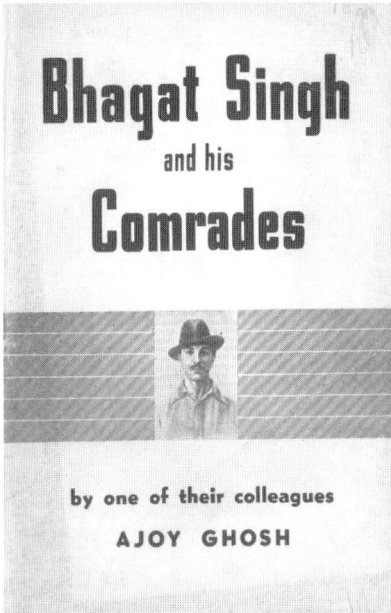

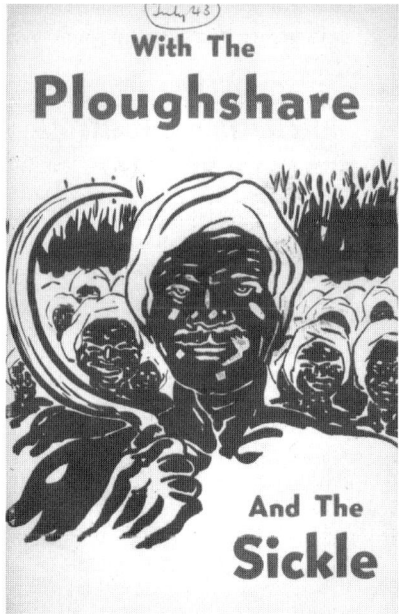

Indian Communist Party publications

dren. Another Cambridge friend, a Ceylonese comrade, Pieter Keune-mann,★ was visiting at the time, and told us that on his way to Bombay he had met Mohan, who had told him of the work I was doing in my unit. If Mohan knew that, it meant he must have got the letter that I had entrusted Kuttappan to deliver. I also found someone who knew Swamy, and so could could verify what he had said about having worked under the guidance of the Party. I learnt that he had never been a Party member but had worked actively in the trade unions under Communist Party leadership. He was considered personally reliable – that is, loyal to the Party – but politically somewhat erratic.

It was an optimistic time for Party workers. Since the Party's legali-sation in July 1942 they had been able to work everywhere openly, and without having to compete with the Congress, most of whose active workers were now in jail. Organisations led by the Party, like the very popular Indian People's Theatre Association, were getting a response from mass audiences in different parts of India, and they were having similar successes among students, peasants, and industrial workers.

After being isolated for so long from people who shared my political outlook it was highly stimulating to be surrounded by such comrades, and I naturally enjoyed being received as one of them. I was introduced to Adhikari, who was regarded as the Party's leading theoretician, and to Dange, the veteran who many years earlier had organised the first effec-tive militant textile workers' union in Bombay, and was then just out of jail. I met Keraleeyan, the Malabar peasant leader, N K Krishnan, and many other lesser-known comrades from all over India. A comrade called Lila, who I think was the Party treasurer, showed me round the main industrial areas of Bombay one afternoon. Several times I sat next to P C Joshi, then General Secretary to the Communist Party, who said I ate 'like a pukka Madrassi', mixing up each handful of rice and veget-ables into a homogeneous mass before putting it in my mouth. (Joshi came from UP: northern Indians don't usually mix all their food together.)

The person I saw most of was E M S Namboodripad, with his wife and child, a young boy of about three. E M S talked to me a lot about Kerala and the history of the Communist Party of India since 1939. During the years 1940-2, when the Party was still illegal, he had worked underground from a hiding place in a room of a peasant house, without ever being discovered by the police. Like most Communist Party lead-ers in Malabar and Andhra, he was ex-Congress Socialist Party, and I also learnt from him about the recent history of the Congress Socialist Party, the women's movement, youth in India, and so on. His *Short His-tory of the Peasant Movement in Kerala* published at the time (1942) was by far the most interesting of the publications I acquired in Bombay.

My acceptance by all these leading Party comrades pleased me, but I didn't reflect much at the time on what it signified. The assumption that we were all comrades, and the apparent lack of hierarchy, was what I would have expected of communists the world over. I was naively unaware that my being British had something to do with it. To suggest this at the time would have seemed outrageous to British and Indian communists, but there is no escaping the fact that Indian communists respected their British counterparts not just as comrades, but because they were British. Even here the long-standing imperialist relationship had had its effect.

Another reflection of this was Arun Bose's position. The son of a wealthy Calcutta family, he had, I think, become a communist in England, so his experience of revolutionary work in India before that had been nil. Yet on the strength of having been in the Party in Britain he had been promoted rapidly to a leading post on his return to India. I was introduced to the others there, in his presence, as the comrade who had *trained* their leader Arun Bose. Arun said nothing to correct this picture, which was totally false – and I regret to say that as far as I remember, neither did I, though, obviously, it was even more incumbent upon me to do so than it was on him.

It was not as easy as I had hoped to interest people in my work in my unit. But I did spend one evening talking about it to Batliwala and made many suggestions about Party work in the armed forces. I also expressed my views – based on my reading of *People's War* – about the limitations of the propaganda material the Party was producing. (The word in those days carried the neutral sense, 'to propogate ideas', without the pejorative connotation which it generally carries now.) Too little space was given to Indian issues, and too much to past and present Soviet achievements. These did need to be publicised, but an Indian communist party should devote its *main* attention to reporting on, and assessing, what was going on in India. Batliwala suggested that I should elaborate on both subjects in writing and send them in to Party Headquarters, and I promised to do so. I also asked to be linked in to Party structures, and it was arranged that one of the Bengal Provincial leaders, Biswenath Mukherjee, should look after me in the work I was doing.

I saw P C Joshi alone only once – for about ten minutes on my way to catch the train leaving Bombay. My reputation based upon the letters I had written to Gaurisankar had obviously preceded me. He said I had been rather rash, but that I had now corrected this mistake and as far as possible guarded against the dangers it might yet produce. He said I should carry on as I was doing, keep contact with the Party as far as possible, but not with rank and file party members – only responsible provincial leaders.

I arrived back in Gauhatti to find that word from Party headquarters had preceded me. Gaurisankar had had orders that I was now to stay not with the party member with whom I had previously stayed, but with a party sympathiser nearby. I was not to come into town in the company of any member or sympathiser, and was to discuss my visit and my work there with no one but Gaurisankar, who would either come to see me or arrange a suitable rendezvous where I could come to see him at night after dark. I was not to visit the Party Office or the bookshop in Gauhatti. Naturally I was far from objecting to these precautions.

On my first day with my host family, the children were naturally curious to see this Englishman who had come to stay in their house, and appeared as I was starting on my midday meal. They no sooner set eyes on me than they started giggling. I asked my host why and he explained in some embarrassment that it was because I was using both hands in eating, and that Indians never touch food with their left hand because this is the hand they use to clean themselves after going to the loo. I hadn't known this, and my sepoys hadn't told me, though they must often have seen that I ate with both hands. Thereafter, of course, I conformed to Indian custom.

I spent most of my time inside the house writing the two documents that Batliwala had suggested. The first was a letter containing my suggestions for the improvement of party publications. The second was a thesis (as such pieces were called in the communist jargon of the time) on Party work in the Indian armed forces. I expended much thought and care on this. I felt much concerned at the Party's virtual ignoring of the Indian armed forces. Already in my early days in the Party it had been impressed upon me that systematic communist work in the armed forces was part of the duty of every communist party. Of course, at different times and in different circumstances the amount of energy allotted to this would vary. In wartime Britain the issue was straightforward, because the communists, along with the great majority of the population of military age, were conscripted. In India, of course, this was not the case; at the time of its maximum size the Indian Army was about two million, that is, one soldier for every 200 civilians. Obviously the overwhelming part of the Party's work lay among the civilian population; all the same it should have sent *some* of its workers into the army and given guidance on the lines on which they should work. Indian communists had good reason to believe the Comintern's forecast that 'a new round of wars and revolutions was closely approaching.' It was already clear that once the war was over mass pressure would put an end to British rule, and this, as we all believed, would be the first step towards a social revolution in India. When that stage came, the role of the two million men who had been in the army could be critical.★

I left the two pieces I had written with the Gauhatti comrades, to forward to the Central Committee of the Party. I presume that they must have reached Party Headquarters, but I never received any acknowledgement or reply. I don't now think that anyone in leading circles would have thought it important to pay the slightest attention to them.

Before I left Gauhatti we discussed how contact with me was to be maintained. This presented a very difficult problem. Dimapur was seventy miles away from the nearest Party member, Jadu Saikia, the Assam Valley secretary, who lived at Gologhat. But in any case it seemed that he had become somewhat unreliable, and there was some doubt as to whether he should know anything about me and my work. From Gauhatti to Dimapur was a journey of twelve to fifteen hours by train, or, alternatively, nearly 250 miles over pretty bad roads; and since Dimapur was now a military area, any civilian entering it required a pass. But any civilian reliable enough to be an intermediary between the Party and me was very unlikely to be able to obtain a pass, and even if he could it would be impossible for him to meet me except by roundabout means, involving contacting me through someone whose presence in or near my unit lines would not attract attention and arranging to meet in circumstances which would not cause my absence from unit lines to be noticed.

We were forced back upon the expedient of my visiting them in the unlikely event of my passing through Gauhatti on duty, or when I could get leave. But leave was granted only once a year (for twenty-eight days) and casual leave in between times was very difficult to obtain. Moreover, on proceeding on leave you had to give the address where you were staying. No one would class Gauhatti as a 'leave station' and any address I gave there would provoke curiosity, if not worse. The solution might be to stay in Shillong (fifty miles from Gauhatti and a recognised leave centre) or else go to Calcutta or some other big centre and risk breaking journey in Gauhatti for a few days en route. Then again, as I could not write beforehand telling them of my impending arrival, I might easily turn up at a time when all leading comrades were touring in other parts of Assam, as they frequently did. The only other chance of contact would be through some reliable sepoy in my unit going on

SOUTH INDIA

STATES, before 1947
- ▨ ruled by Indian princes
- ○ British ruled provinces

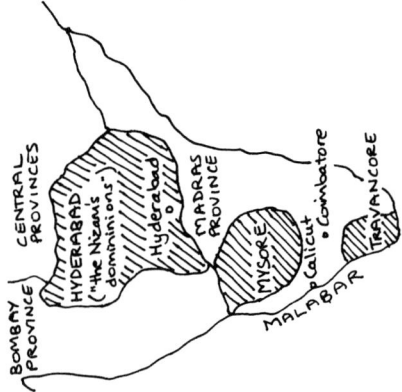

BOMBAY PROVINCE | CENTRAL PROVINCES

HYDERABAD ("the Nizam's dominions")

Hyderabad ○

MADRAS PROVINCE

MYSORE

Calicut ● Coimbatore

MALABAR

TRAVANCORE

LANGUAGES
- ····· post 1947 state boundaries reflecting main language areas
- ▭→ state name

South Indian languages spoken south of this line

TELEGU

KANNADA

TAMIL

MALAYALAM

Andhra Pradesh

Karnataka

Tamilnadu

Kerala

Languages and states of South India

leave: but for sepoys it was even more difficult to get leave than it was for me, and it would be very difficult for them to break journey; besides, reliable sepoys didn't come along every day.

The second difficulty arose over my receiving Party literature by post. What I needed for my sepoys would be publications in the South Indian languages Malayalam, Tamil, Telegu or Kannada, and I had made a start by bringing back from Bombay a few papers and pamphlets in Malayalam, the language of both Kuttappan and Swamy. But these needed to be kept from official eyes, because clearly the only reason for having papers in a language I couldn't read was to exercise communist influence over my men. So getting them through the post was not on. Publications for my own use were less of an issue – Joshi had seen no objection to my subscribing to *People's War* and its Urdu equivalent, *Qaumi Jang*, for I could read and write Urdu script, though not without some difficulty. But the Assam comrades, who after their former laxity on security matters had now swung to the other extreme, thought even this unwise, and I acquiesced in their advice not to take any of these papers by post.

So I returned to my unit with the prospect of being out of touch with the Party and its publications for perhaps another twelve months, and of carrying on as best I could on my own. Not a very encouraging prospect; but it had been a very enjoyable and profitable leave, and I was feeling positive and full of energy. With the helpers I already had in Kuttappan and Swamy, I hoped that when I next returned to Gauhatti I should have substantial progress to report.

I got out of the train at Dimapur and walked across to the goods sidings, which at this time of day were usually crowded with our lorries. Immediately I realised that something odd was going on – the lorries were not ours. I asked one of the naiks of the Railhead Supply Detachment. He explained that our company had been taken off railhead duties shortly after my departure and allotted to different work elsewhere.

This was a great blow. If railhead work was now finished, our section would now be rejoining the rest of the Company, and opportunities for conversation with the men would be much more limited. This was depressing enough, but it was not the only surprise in store for me. My own section, though no longer working on railhead, were still living just opposite together with some from B section, and I went across to ask one of their naiks whether Kuttappan was back from leave. He said that he wasn't, and added, grinning broadly, 'And he *won't* return, either.' I was completely taken aback. 'Why do you say that?' I asked. He said, 'Everyone knew that when he got leave he would desert.'

I felt more than somewhat mortified. I had never dreamed of this possibility, but in retrospect I could now see it clearly. Kuttappan had once been a havildar and had been reduced to naik on a trumped-up charge framed by the Indian Adjutant. He had applied for permission to transfer to the Navy or Indian Air Force, where his educational qualifications would have got him a much more highly paid job than he could ever get in the army – or at any rate in his present company. His application had been rejected outright by the bloody-minded commanding officer, who had refused to forward it. If he deserted he would probably be able to re-enlist in the Navy or Air Force without his previous army service being traced, and he had no doubt decided to try this out.

I went over to my quarters. Khan and I had been moved from the tent to a disused thatched building of the mud-plastered whitewashed type so common in Assam. It was divided into three rooms, a large one at one end, a rather smaller one at the other, and a narrow one in between where our orderlies worked and slept. Khan had taken the smaller one for himself and given me the large room. On my bed I found a sealed envelope. It contained a letter from Swamy, telling me that for 'personal reasons' he had asked to be posted to Jhansi.

That evening I received a visit from my commanding officer, Major Perry. Clearly something was wrong, for he very rarely visited his officers in their rooms. Without wasting time he said he had received a letter from General Headquarters enclosing an intercepted letter of mine and had to give an account of what he knew of my political leanings. I asked to whom the letter was addressed – hoping it would not be one to Gaurisankar. It was to Amrit Rallia Ram, of Masson Road, Lahore. I told him how I had met Amrit on the train, and that he had invited me to come and see him any time I was in Lahore. The major broke in to say that according to General Headquarters, the Rallia Rams were prominent Congressmen in the Panjab, and this was what he particularly had to report on – my ideas about Congress and my connection with it. I said yes, they were active Congress supporters, but Amrit was a communist. But of course the major was unlikely to know anything about the differences between the policies of the two parties, so I explained: Congress called for political struggle against the British irrespective of the damage to the war effort which would inevitably result, but the Communist Party put support for the war in the forefront of its programme and exerted its influence against the Congress 'struggle' policy. This was why the Government had legalised the Communist Party whilst banning Congress. My corresponding with Amrit, far from implying sympathy with Congress policy and friendship with his father, in present circumstances indicated the opposite; and I described to him

280

the hostility I had encountered from Amrit's parents.

The major seemed to accept that, but it was not the end of the questions. Where had I stayed during my leave at Gauhatti and Bombay? Things were now getting closer to the bone. The major already knew in a vague way that I had left wing ideas, and since GHQ were now interested in me I saw no point in trying to conceal this. But I definitely didn't want them knowing the extent of my involvement with the Party, or to have any suspicion that I was talking to my sepoys about such things. I said, in Gauhatti I had stayed with a student I had met when our convoy passed through, and in Bombay with a friend who had been with me at Cambridge and was now a journalist on a left wing student paper. I said my own inclinations had always been toward communism, though I tried to create the impression that since leaving Cambridge and joining the army my interest in politics had become purely academic. I hoped to God he would not be able to disprove this last point! (Had any of my correspondence with Gaurisankar been intercepted?)

The major said, OK, but there was a distinctly curious passage in my intercepted letter which he would like me to explain. At the end of my letter I had said there was a lot of other news which I would like to tell him but couldn't. What did this mean? I said it meant simply that the most interesting items of news – anything to do with where we were or what we were doing – could not be discussed, though it was exactly these things which one most wanted to describe.

He seemed satisfied, and I ventured to ask what reply he had given to their enquiries. He said that he had replied quite shortly to the effect that in the few months he had known me he had found me quite a good officer and that as far as he knew I had no sympathies or contacts with Congress. He then departed and left me alone.

All this time Khan had been in his room next door. After the major had gone he came in and asked me what it was all about. I hesitated a moment, and then decided I could do no harm by telling him as much as I had told the major. I was a little apprehensive as to how he would react – it was the first time I had said in so many words that I sympathised with the communist viewpoint. All he said was that he did not see that I had done anything discreditable and that every man was entitled to his own views; but I knew that if he had felt any hostility he would have remained silent.

Once I was finally alone I tried to survey my new situation. I felt overwhelmed. I would have to start all over again, and in conditions much

281

more unfavourable than those which, less than twelve hours before, I had been so fondly and optimistically envisaging. I was angry with Swamy, who with all his faults was an old political worker, who might have been expected to stay as long as he could in a unit where he knew that a basis for political work had been laid. Yet maybe the 'personal reasons' had been strong enough to justify his decision. About Kuttappan I couldn't at first make up my mind. He had every reason to wish to get out of his unit and find a better job by enlisting elsewhere, and having made up his mind to do this it would have been madness to give me any hint of his intention. I still felt sure he was essentially trustworthy. True, he had gone off with my money, about 50 or 60 rupees that I had given him to buy Party publications. But how could he have refused to take it without being able to give any reason? And he could hardly return it to me now, because that would afford a means of tracing his whereabouts. Perhaps he had concluded that I would never miss it – an understandable thing for a man drawing twenty seven rupees a month to conclude about an officer drawing five hundred. And he *had* taken the trouble to break his journey at Madras to deliver the letter to Mohan – for how else would Mohan have known what I was doing?

Perhaps Kuttappan might still return? But the weeks passed, and he didn't. And now I sensed something curious in the attitude of the VCOs when I spoke of him. They were well aware that my sympathies had been on his side in his troubles in the unit; perhaps they thought I had encouraged him to desert and helped him with money.

The really serious change to my situation was signalled by the letter from General Headquarters. Whilst I thought that the Major was satisfied with my explanation and valued me as an officer sufficiently to wish to keep me in the unit, I nevertheless realised that General Headquarters might have given him instructions about me of which he had deliberately told me nothing, and that I had better be careful, and keep myself 'clean' in case unexpected trouble should crop up. I destroyed the diary that I had been keeping and left off keeping one from then on. I memorised necessary addresses and burned the notes of them which I had made. I decided to stop writing to more people than was necessary, even though my letters might be harmless. General Headquarters might start questioning the people to whom I wrote, either to find out more about me, or, to check up on whether my friends too sympathised with the national movement. I decided there was no need to get rid of Party publications in English and Urdu, but what to do about the Malayalam publications I had brought back from Bombay? I now had no reliable Malayali to give them to, and everyone knew I couldn't read Malayalam; but I was loath to abandon them. I decided to risk keeping them until, hopefully, I found a Malayali to replace Swami and Kuttappan, but to be prepared to destroy them at short notice.

The one good thing was that no one in authority had raised any queries about the nature of my conversations with my sepoys. That at least meant that the precautions I had been taking so far had been adequate. Now, deprived of the information and (to some extent) guidance I'd had from Swamy and Kuttappan, I would have to work out myself the best way to approach people.

∞

Having been taken off work at railhead, 317 Company had now been to put to work for the Engineers, at a place called Milestone Four, about half-way between railhead and the big supply base at Nichuguard, five miles further on at the foot of the hills. We had to haul shingle from the river-beds and bamboo from the jungles, along mud roads just cut straight into the jungle to a distance of ten to twelve miles, and at the same time prepare new company lines in the jungle. Sections were being moved in as and when accommodation for them was ready, and our section was the last to move. We had to do a lot of the work of getting our accommodation ready ourselves. The Engineers were building the main roads and the bashas (long bamboo and thatch structures with floors of stamped earth) but nothing else. Trees and creepers in the section area had to be cut down, a road made so that the water lorry could drive right up to the cookhouse, and beds and shelves constructed in the bashas. I shall always remember the sheer beauty of this new location. It was hard work, but very enjoyable, because once the undergrowth was cleared we were in the shade of great tall trees, taller than any I have ever seen in England, and it was a joy to be there.

To get this work done I was sending the lorries out with only one driver and keeping the others in lines, with a few NCOs to supervise them. I would sometimes go out with the lorries for a quite unnecessary 'supervision' of what was being quite adequately supervised without me; but more often I stayed behind with the men who were working in the lines. Running around in my fifteen hundred weight truck to the various places where my men were working I often encountered gangs of civilian labourers. I soon learnt that they were Malayalis, and a sort of ritual developed. I would shout 'Malayalam!' and they would all laugh and chorus back, 'Malayalam! Malayalam!' I had a great regard for Malayalis, beginning with those in my own unit, and they have been my favourite Indian nationality ever since. Cheerful, relaxed, self-confident,

Roads cut through the jungle

and not in the least put off by others' disapproval of some of their ways. Alone among my sepoys, some of them would bath in the streams completely naked and not care a toss about what anyone else thought of their shocking immodesty.

Perhaps Khan had missed me during my absence on leave; or perhaps my openness about my views prompted him to open up to me in response. Anyway he now behaved with less restraint. He would come into my room after his evening prayer and talk about his religion, explaining its doctrine and ritual. He also spoke a lot about his personal affairs, especially about his wife, of whom he was very fond. He told me in reply to my question, that his marriage had taken place in the usual way, and he had not known his wife until after the marriage ceremony was over, though he had seen her once or twice before. He thought himself very fortunate in that, in spite of this, (as he told me with great emphasis), he 'liked her in every way' and became daily more fond of her. I asked him about purdah, and he said that he was opposed to it, but that in his own home area it was quite impracticable to act upon his convictions. His wife kept strict purdah there. But when she was with him in Karachi, and later in Delhi, she did not. During this time he never referred to my political views; he would sometimes talk a bit about England, asking me about my village and about student life at English universities. I came to like him more and more: his sincerity and the quiet but confident way in which he followed his own convictions without regard to others' opinion of him appealed to me; and in his work he was quite capable without being fussy.

My main concern now was to take up again the work that I had tentatively begun with Kuttappan and Swamy, and the first step was to find others to replace them. In conversation with Namboodripad and others in Bombay I had learnt of the popularity of communists in some areas of the South, like North Malabar and certain districts in Andhra, so I thought the most likely possibilities were men from these areas. One such was P V Damodaran Nair, a boy of about 18-19 who lived near Calicut, in South Malabar. I had been struck by his quite unusual knowledge of current affairs and of political geography. He was at that time in Company HQ, and drove the water lorry which distributed the daily water ration to sections. He usually asked me what was the news from the various fighting fronts whenever he came round, and I used to tell him.

Once he ventured to to ask me if it was true that Mahatma Gandhi was fasting. I said that it was quite true and explained why, quoting

Gandhi's own statements, and adding some of my own. I asked him what he thought about all that. He laughed, and at first would say nothing. Ultimately he said that in his schooldays he had been a Gandhi-ite himself. I asked why, if he was a Gandhi-ite, had he joined the Army? He again laughed and said that he had always been quarrelling with his elder brother, who was a communist and disagreed with right-wing Congress policy in Malabar. One day they had quarrelled violently and he had run away and joined the army – and he added, with a broad grin, something to the effect that it was a case of 'out of the frying pan into the fire'. I asked him whether he still held the same views, but he would not be drawn, and said that nowadays he had no political views. I did not press him, but the opening was too good to miss. I told him that in my opinion the communists were right, and then gave him what amounted to a lecture on what was happening in the world arena. When I think of it now, the tenour of what I said makes me smile, but I felt it was really important that he and others understand these things; otherwise how would they be able to see that support for the war - for such war effort as the British were making - was *not* a betrayal of their struggle for independence? I said that communists had been second to none in working for India's freedom and they now saw that her people's way forward lay in throwing their full strength into the anti-fascist struggle. The leadership of this struggle was already being taken by the Soviet Union and the Chinese republic, the friends and allies of the Indian people. The British and American imperialists were already being forced to concede more and more to the will of the people and if India strove to take her place in the struggle, showing at the same time that the British were denying her the opportunity to make her full contribution, nothing could prevent her from winning her rightful place on the battlefront of the free United Nations, and victory over British imperialism would be assured. (This was the line of argument that P C Joshi had advanced and which the Communist Party of India had ultimately accepted.)

'People say,' I said, 'that when the communists oppose the Quit India struggle, they are betraying their people. But Gandhiji himself has now said that the 'struggle' is *not* what he or Congress called for. He has declared concern about the increasingly acute food shortage. Congress just says that because of British policy nothing can be done about this, but the Communist Party calls for active work to solve the people's problems – *they* are the ones who are ready to do something about it.'

Damodaran listened to all this but made no comment. I asked him before he went not to tell anyone else what I had said. He smiled and promised not to. After that he would come into my room and talk practically every time he brought water to my section cookhouse – provided no other officer was about – but he rarely spoke of Indian politics. I came to the conclusion that he really had abandoned all active interest in these issues.

The next one I tried was a lance-naik named P Ramunni Nair. He too was a Calicut man, and I knew from the VCO's gossip that he had once been a Congressman. He could speak a little English. One evening I called him over and found some way to start talking politics, beginning with the war news, then via Gandhi's fast to the political situation in India generally. In obvious terror he protested his ignorance of all such matters and then raised his voice in what he conceived to be 'God Save the King'. It was both ludicrous and pathetic, and I was genuinely sorry I had given him such a scare. I did my best to reassure him – said he needn't speak of such things if he didn't want to, and that I would be the last person to hold his political past against him. As far as I was concerned all that mattered was his present military duties under me, and I found his performance of these perfectly satisfactory. I told him also not to let the VCOs frighten him by threats connected with this; I would see that he was OK. I don't know whether he believed me or not, but he mumbled his thanks, saluted, and went off.

Clearly I was not doing too well, but I didn't give up. No one else I tried to draw into conversation panicked as Ramunni had done, but whilst they listened to me with obvious interest they themselves would profess complete ignorance of such issues. In part this may have been true – the fact that men from Kerala knew and loved their communist peasant leaders by no means implied any interest in what these leaders had to say about wider national and international issues. I had thought they might know something about Congress policies because there had been a Congress government of Madras Presidency after the elections of 1937. But these young men had been children at the time, and all most of them knew about it was the name of the Congress chief minister, Rajagopalachariar. But whatever the topic, they would refuse politely but firmly to give any opinion of their own. They did not know enough, they said.

It was soon obvious that I was up against something more fundamental than lack of general knowledge or political caution. Why, for instance, did I continually find it so difficult to get a straightforward answer to even the most ordinary question? They would either give the answer they thought I wanted or if they couldn't guess what that might be they would say 'I don't know, Sahib,' or 'How can I say, Sahib?' or 'Just as *you* wish, Sahib.' Even if asked to express a preference for one of two things they would give the same reply, and the educated ones were little better than the rest in these things.

I began only gradually to understand that this derived from the kind of society they had grown up in. They had no historical or personal experience of the ideas and practices of democracy which I, like many English people, took for granted. The idea that everyone has the right to hold their own opinion, and at any rate in everyday affairs to express it, was unknown. To disagree with higher authority by expressing a different opinion was unthinkable, even on quite minor matters. If I asked any of my men why they had joined the army they would say, 'To help the British government' – though it was obvious to us both that this could not be true.

Eventually a stage was reached where most of them would speak honestly enough to tell me the real reason – and in almost every case it was as the result of some family quarrel or economic necessity. I only ever met two who had joined with their parents' knowledge, and not one who didn't regret having joined and wanted more than anything else his discharge from service.

You cannot work sixteen hours a day with a comparatively small group of men without getting to know them well, and I liked them more and more. Despite my slow progress so far, I was optimistic. I was learning from them all the time, and I was going to be with them for a long time. I began to notice who among them had strong personal qualities – those who, in the difficult conditions in which they lived still managed to keep themselves clean and tidy and their kit in good order, who looked after their lorries and were good drivers; and above all, who were intelligent and self-reliant, able to act on their own without needing to be directed in every little thing. With men like this, I was sure I could encourage a more adequate political consciousness, once I learnt the best way to approach them. And because they commanded the respect of the others, they would in turn be a valuable asset in approaching others.

∞

One afternoon early in May 1943 I was talking to one of my lance-naiks, a Tamil named Kannayan. My section was working as usual on the construction of the new lines, and everyone else was some distance away, out of earshot. I knew that in civilian life Kannayan had been a textile worker in Coimbatore, the great textile centre of South India, and I began asking him about working conditions in the mills. How long did he have to work? What time did he start in the morning? When did he finish at night? What wages? Any paid holidays? and so on. He told me all this, and I began to contrast the conditions he had outlined with those of the British working class, including what I knew of conditions in the Lancashire textile industry. I said that at one time – a hundred years ago – conditions in English mills had been much as they were in India today, but that now they were much better, and the main reason for this was trade union organisation. Were there any trade unions in Coimbatore? He replied that he had heard that there were but he had no first hand experience of them and did not understand such matters very well. I told him the basis for trade unionism, quoted a saying of a leader of the Russian workers named Lenin – (had he heard of Lenin? Yes, he had heard the name, but didn't know who he was) – that in their struggle the workers had only one weapon – organisation. I told him something of the sacrifices which the British workers had made to form their own unions and outlined the history of their advance to the powerful position they occupied today. He listened with great interest and then said that he had often heard of trade unionism, socialism and communism, but knew very little about it. Could I tell him about it? I said, Yes, but there was no time now. After the evening meal he could come to my room if there was no one else about, and we could discuss it all. He said he would do so.

Sitting in the back of the lorry on our way back to our old lines I noticed that he was unusually quiet. When we climbed out I went off to my quarters and had started to get undressed to have my evening bath when I saw him come up and stand by the doorway. I called out to him to come in and asked what he wanted. He said I had told him to come and see me in my room. I pointed out that I had said come after the evening meal. He said, All right, he would do so; then hesitated, turned his eyes away, and smiling awkwardly said 'I came to tell you that when we were talking this afternoon I wasn't telling you the whole truth. Nowadays one has to be careful, but I have heard enough to judge that you are OK. Actually I know something of what you were speaking about. Before I joined the army I was for some years active in the trade union movement in Coimbatore'. He paused, and then added 'I am ready to give my life for the cause of the working-class.' He was very agitated, and quivering with suppressed excitement. I shook hands with him, said I was in the British Communist Party, and that I was very glad we had got in touch with each other. We should have to get together more often and see what work we could do.

We had been speaking for some time now. He said, 'Should I come again tonight?' I said, 'By all means come.' He then went off to bath and

Kannayan with supply base clerks: Kannayan R, standing

get his meal, and I did likewise, wondering what prospects this new discovery opened up.

By the time I had bathed, changed my clothes, and had my evening meal it was dark, hot and clammy. The place where I was living had been unoccupied for several weeks before we moved in, and mosquitoes began to emerge in swarms from all the dark corners of the walls and roof as soon as the sun went down. The room was bare except for my camp-bed in the middle, with my mosquito net rigged up over it, two tin trunks and a suitcase containing my clothes, a five-foot plank on two empty wooden boxes, along which I had arranged my books, and a camp chair and small square wooden table (the latter made and presented to me by one of my naiks who had been a carpenter in civilian life) where I used to sit to have my meals or to write. For light I had a small hurricane lamp.

I could see Kannayan hovering about the doorway, and I walked across to tell him to come in. When I got there I was surprised to see that another sepoy, Dasappa, was standing there with him. I called Kannayan inside and asked him what Dasappa was doing there. He said that Dasappa wanted to come with him and hear what I was going to say. I felt a bit dubious about this, and I suppose I must have looked it, for Kannayan grinned and said 'He is all right: he won't tell anybody.' 'All right,' I said, 'If you're sure, then let him come.' Kannayan went and called him inside, and both of them sat down on the floor next to the open doorway with their backs against the wall facing me. I told them to tell me if they heard anyone coming and we would start talking about their home affairs or some other harmless subject. In the meanwhile what should be talk about? Kannayan said, 'Explain to us how it was that the English, who are such a small nation, could conquer our people and hold them in subjection so long.' I hesitated, and then said it would take a long time. He grinned and said they could stay till midnight if that was OK by me.

So I told them. If you are interested you can look up the sources I used – Marx's articles written for the *New York Tribune* in 1853, particularly the first, on British Rule in India, and the last, 'The Future Results of British Rule in India'; that section of R Palme Dutt's *India Today* which brings the story up to date from 1853, Stalin's speech to the University of Toilers of the East, and that part of his speech on the Chinese question which outlines the three main stages of revolution in the colonial countries. You might think that this was tough meat to offer to a semi-literate sepoy. At one time I would have thought so myself, but if I had any idea when I started speaking that this might be so I soon abandoned it. They were deeply interested in all I said and fully understood

291

it – the destruction which British rule had wrought, the way that it had at the same time unwittingly laid the basis for the transformation of India into a modern, developing society, the different reactions of different classes to British rule, the eventual emergence of the demand for complete independence, the need at the present time for the working class to try and establish itself as the leader of the independence struggle and to organise the village poor and ally with them and so after independence to lay the basis for the advance to a socialist society. Literacy and level of education are not relevant issues here. Villagers may be totally illiterate, but simply by asking the right questions and by leading them to draw conclusions from their own and their parents' experiences you can demonstrate to them that they can readily understand all these things. And you can also inspire them with the confidence that they and people like them have the power to bring about fundamental social change. Dange, the veteran communist leader, and one of the first to involve himself in the building of militant Indian trade unions, once said to me that when Indian workers become politically conscious they come direct to communist politics. I am sure that at any rate in those pre-independence days there was no reason why the landless labourers and poor peasants who came into the army could not also come direct to communist politics. They only needed our people to be there to tell them.

Kannayan and Dasappa found no difficulty in grasping these fundamental ideas. In fact they understood them far more easily than they understood current issues. Until now I had been making the common assumption that people can be drawn in to an interest in political theory only though their compelling day to day concerns. The reverse is often truer – they will often become interested in an immediate programme of action only after they have thought about how to attain long term objectives. By the time we broke up that night, after nearly five hours discussion, I was for the first time beginning to see this clearly. I had spoken for about an hour – and when I reflect on it now I feel quite impressed by the realisation that I had been able to do all this in Urdu.

Life in my unit entered a new phase after that night. From now on Kannayan and I met regularly, and he became my mainstay for a good many months. We began to develop a shared idea of what we might do together in the unit. He both saw the point of consistent work to create political consciousness among the sepoys and knew how to go about it. Now at last I had a comrade, and one who time proved to be steadfast and reliable.

13

The new company lines at Milestone Four were now ready and my section moved into them. I have vivid but disconnected memories of life in our new lines. The rains came soon after we moved in. I had already experienced this in Delhi the previous year but this was much more vivid. There was the same excitement as their coming always brings – the delighted relief after the scorching heat, with everyone dashing out to soak in the torrential downpour. But here in the jungle the whole effect was heightened by the din of the croaking of thousands of frogs, the innumerable lizards dashing about on the walls, gobbling up insects, and above all the sudden lushness of the rapidly growing vegetation. My bamboo and thatch hut had a veranda whose roof was supported by pillars made from tree trunks, recently cut from the jungle, and one of these suddenly produced a shoot which seemed to grow before my eyes, longer and stouter every time I looked at it.

Another memory is that a culvert had to be dug, and I decided I would dig this myself. In all my time in the army the activity I probably enjoyed more than any other was wielding a pick, digging slit trenches, and so on. So I set to work – to the mingled surprise, admiration, and mild disapproval of my sepoys, who thought that this was not the sort of thing a lieutenant should be doing.

Now that we had our quarters with the rest of the Company there were fewer opportunities for unnoticed conversation, but Kannayan and I took what chances we got. Through him I learned of others in the section whom we could hope to win. The first and the best of these was a naik called Chandra Reddy – so good, in fact, that I ultimately came to estimate him more highly than Kannayan himself. He came from Hyderabad, capital of the old Nizam's Dominions, and was generally said to have had Congress sympathies before he joined the Army. I had once asked him if this was true, and though at that stage he had no reason to trust me he replied unhesitatingly that it was. Perhaps this was because he thought the fact too widely-known to be concealed, but his bearing nevertheless impressed me, and I felt an admiration for his dignity and self-respect; and I never had cause to revise my estimate of him where these qualities were concerned. At the time he wouldn't be drawn further, taking the line that he had left politics behind him when he joined the army; but later he responded to my own expressions of contempt and hostility to the Nizam and to the princely states in general and began to talk a little more freely. Still, it was Kannayan's influence that contributed most to his further development.

Chandra Reddy was a very important accession of strength to us, for he was extremely highly regarded by the men of the section. He had great personal integrity, intelligence and mature understanding. But he hadn't the common touch that Kannayan had, and there was a certain reserve and aloofness from the sepoys.

The three of us now began to meet regularly as an organised group. We managed this fairly unobtrusively on the nights when I was orderly officer. Chandra Reddy, Kannayan and I spoke to each other in Urdu, and all the men knew some Urdu. But political work could be done much more effectively in the men's different mother tongues, and this made it important to win a Kerala man. The three major languages of the unit were Tamil (the language of Kannayan's native Tamilnadu), Telegu (the language of Andhra, Chandra Reddy's area) and Malayalam (the language of Kerala). So our first aim now was to pick some promising sepoy from Kerala and try to develop him politically. We discussed the problem and chose a young lance-naik named A V John, and decided how we would approach him.

With Dasappa – the man who had been with Kannayan that first night in my tent – there were problems. As we talked more it became clear that he had pro-Japanese inclinations. I made what I thought were successful attempts to counter these, but I now doubt whether I was in fact successful at all. Just as widespread sympathy for the Nazis developed in Latin America because Germany was the enemy of *their* great imperialist enemy, the USA, so in India sympathy for the Japanese was extremely widespread. Dasappa also had a tendency to assume that now that we were on friendly terms he didn't have to work so hard, and I had some difficulty in remedying this situation. The more I came to know him the more I felt that he was a cynic, able to keep himself to himself and to do what was best for Dasappa without bothering too much about any sort of principles which would have inconvenienced him. At the same time I don't doubt that such opinions as he saw fit to acquaint me with were quite sincerely held, and though he pursued his own interests I don't think that he ever attempted to betray us.

Through my friendship with Chandra Reddy and Kannayan I began to understand more about the ways of life and thought of ordinary Indians. Chandra Reddy was learning English and had made good progress, so once when I got a letter from Rex – a rare event – I read out part of it to him, thinking it would encourage him to realise that he could now understand the English written by one Englishman to another. I discovered, to my great surprise, that he couldn't understand the way in which Rex and I addressed each other. I had written about what I thought might do once the war was over, and Rex had replied, 'I quite agree with you about your post-war plans.' Chandra Reddy didn't understand this section of the letter at all. He stopped me. I read it again. He still looked puzzled and said 'I thought he was your elder brother, Sahib.' 'Yes,' I said, 'he is.' He paused and then smiled and said 'In our country no man will speak to his younger brother like that.'

Everything I subsequently learnt showed this to be true. Even in the most trivial matters the younger brother would not venture an opinion until the elder had spoken, and when the latter did, it was in a tone of authority. The younger might then disagree, but he would never *say* that he disagreed. Khan too always used to express surprise at the way in which Rex and I wrote to each other. He told me for example that he would never call his elder brother by name, any more than we would call our mothers and fathers by their first names, and for the same reasons.

All this time Khan's interest in, and sympathy with, my politics was growing quite rapidly. His interest in constitutional law led us into discussions of the 1935 Government of India Act and thence to the Soviet Union's new constitution, adopted in 1936.* I lent him Pat Sloan's book *How the Soviet State is Run* and he was favourably impressed. He was interested in the communist attitude towards religion, and said that communism would make a great appeal to Pathans (the people of his own part of the country) were it not for its irreligiousness. He was interested also in social questions, especially as they affected the peasantry. He asked me once whether if he became a communist that would oblige him to give all his lands to his tenants. I said I didn't think so, but that he ought to encourage them to speak up for themselves and that he should reduce their rents and obligations to what in present circumstances they thought, and the All-India Kisan Sabha (Peasant League) thought, were fair. He was clearly serious about trying to work out a principled way of living, but I knew that he would have to be willing to encounter immense opposition from his family if he ever tried to put them into practice.

When he next went home on leave, he told me on his return that he had acted on the principles he had come to accept during our conversations. Against the opposition of his family he had reduced the rents and obligations of the peasants on his land.

NAGALAND

Dimapur Nichuguard Kohima

Mao

BURMA BORDER

Ukhrul

Milestone 108

Imphal

Barak River

Imphal Plain

Palel

Manipur River

MANIPUR

Tamu

Kabaw Valley

Chindwin River

BURMA

Kalewa

Tiddim

Kalemyo

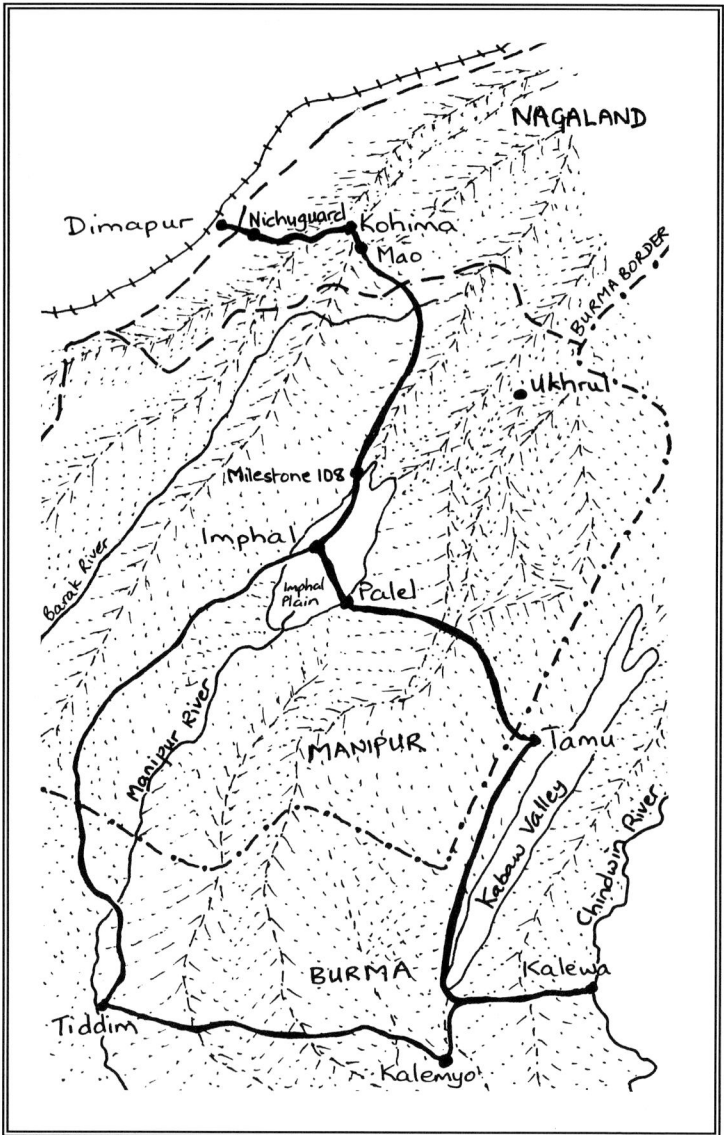

The central Burma front, and the Manipur Road

We met almost no one outside the men of our own company. But there was one exception, a little boy called Hadis Muhammad. I had first seen him soon after we got to Dimapur, at the time when our section was alone working on railhead. He appeared one morning in our cook-house, a small boy with an even smaller boy in tow. 'What are you doing here?' I asked. He cheerfully replied that he was begging for food. I was struck by the complete absence of that heart-breaking servility which in India one finds even in the smallest children, and I took to him at once. He told me his name and that he came from Bhagalpur, Bihar, about three days' train journey from Dimapur. He was about eight years old, as far as he could remember – most Indian villagers I met didn't know their exact age – and his young brother Hafiz about five. Their father was dead, and their big brother could not earn enough to support both his mother and them, so had told them they must fend for themselves.

I arranged for the boys to stay and help the cooks, and said that I would feed and clothe them in return. I often used to sit talking with them – it was excellent practice in colloquial Urdu. They were remark-able children, clean, cheerful, and above all perfectly self-possessed. I came to like them very much. Khan was an amused but sympathetic observer of how fond we were of each other. Sometimes he would say to Hadis, 'Give the sahib a kiss' and we would all laugh.

When my section moved to join the rest of the Company at Mile-stone Four, the Major told me I must get rid of the boys. I was very sorry to have to do so, and I tried to explain to them as best I could, fearing they would be upset. But they accepted it without a murmur and went off quite cheerfully. I think they were almost as familiar with the hundreds of miles of Eastern India's rail and river lines as they were with their own home town.

I never expected to see them again. But I did encounter Hadis again, months later and some three hundred and fifty miles from Dimapur. I had been away on some duty or other, and was due to stay at an army rest camp on my way back. I got off the train at the nearest station, but from the station to the rest camp was a good two miles, and as the train pulled out I looked about hopefully for waiting transport. There was none. I set off to walk down the dusty road, carrying my kit and sweat-ing uncomfortably in the hot sunshine. One or two trucks passed me, but none of them heeded my appealing signals and I was still walking when a convoy of three-tonners began to pass. 'No good expecting any of these to stop,' I thought, and walked on. Even as I was think-ing so I heard one slow down, and turned to see the driver, a broad

Madrassi grin on his black face, beckoning me to get in. 'He shouldn't have stopped,' I thought. 'He's supposed to be driving in convoy' – and for a moment I wondered whether I should not, in the interests of convoy discipline, tell him so. But his friendly manner and my own gratitude combined to dismiss so pedantic an idea. I got in and sat down beside him in the front seat. 'Can you catch up with the convoy again?' I asked. 'Doesn't matter,' he replied. 'I know where I have to go.' I grinned and relapsed into silence.

A little way ahead a small boy was walking along the road. There seemed to be something familiar about his carefree gait, and as we drew nearer I saw that it was Hadis Muhommad. 'Hadis!' I shouted. He turned round, and recognising me at once, laughed and waved, obviously as happy and unperturbed as ever. We had passed him now. I leaned out of the cab. 'Where's Hafiz?' I shouted. He shouted something back, but I could not hear him. The driver began to pull up. 'I can't stop him again,' I thought, and told him to drive on. And that was the last I saw of Hadis.

For five months, from May to September, it rained; and while the monsoons continued, there was no question of the Allies launching a major offensive on the Burma border. There were small actions at the furthest ends of the Manipur Road, around Tiddim and Tamu; British and Indian troops made forays across the border, into the Kabaw Valley and across the Chindwin River. But with the constant downpour it was hard enough just to keep the roads operational. Everything turned to mud; whole sections of the road were washed away and had to be constantly repaired. Malaria and other diseases were rampant. I was lucky, and got through the rainy season without any illness, but that was unusual.

The psychological effects of the disastrous defeat of a year earlier still continued. There was a widespread belief of the invincibility of the Japanese in jungle conditions, and an acceptance that it would be madness to challenge them again until the Allies could build up greatly superior strength. But while the main issues of the war were still to be fought elsewhere, no proper air or sea resources were available to the Burma front. As for land forces, even if the resources had been made available, both the road and the railway were still too overstretched to allow an adequate build-up of troops and equipment.

By August 1943 a South East Asia Allied Command (commonly called SEAC) was set up, with Mountbatten leading a unified command over all air, land and sea forces. A few months later the land forces along the Burma front, from the Chinese border in the north east to the

Arakan coast in the south west, were combined into the Fourteenth Army, headed by General Slim. Slim, who had had the unenviable task of leading the retreat from Burma, was now responsible for developing plans for an offensive to reconquer it. He knew that first the psychological state of the troops would have to be reversed. Along with the more obvious tasks of trying to improve lines of communication and doggedly arguing for additional supplies, he took vigorous action to improve their living and health conditions, insisted on more regular leave for those near the front, and on better communication to break their isolation.

The focus was, understandably, on the combat units of the army. For us in a transport company things continued much as they had always been, and it was only fifteen years later when I read Slim's autobiography that I understood the overall context of which we had been a part. I am not even sure that I knew at the time that we were part of the Fourteenth Army, and certainly had little concept of what its other sections were up to. But some of Slim's practical reforms did make an impact even on us. One was the campaign to control malaria. Everyone had to take a daily dose of mepacrine, and failure to do so was considered a serious breach of military discipline. Since mepacrine had the effect of turning you a jaundiced yellow, it soon became obvious if you were being lax!★

The radio linked us to the world beyond our jungle lines, and on the map in the officers' mess we now began to mark up a series of Allied successes. In July 1943, Soviet troops at Kursk defeated the Germans after the biggest tank battle in history – after Stalingrad, their second major defeat. At about the same time the Allies finally succeeded in driving the Germans out of North Africa. By mid August they had secured Sicily, and in early September began the invasion of Italy.

This move provoked widespread, and quite open, criticism. What Churchill called 'the soft underbelly' of Europe was anything but that, and fighting in mountainous country, the loss of life was terrible. People asked themselves why Churchill had chosen to send the troops into Italy, miles from the main German forces? The obvious thing was to open a front in western Europe that would directly engage the main German forces not already engaged on the eastern front, and so force them to fight on two fronts. To me and others on the left, the invasion of Italy seemed a delaying tactic, designed to ensure that the Germans and the Russians would go on killing each other and so be unable to pose any threat to the western powers once the war was over. Churchill's private comments, which only later became public knowledge, confirm this.★

In September 1943, as the rains were drawing to an end, I was told that I was to be detached from the Company to take a convoy of drivers drawn from a number of different companies to a place near Asansol in Bengal, near the border with Bihar. Here we were to draw new vehicles and bring them back to the forward area.

Before I left, Kannayan, Chandra Reddy and discussed how they would continue to work together in my absence. Army policy was now to replace non-Madrassi VCOs by Madrassis. Accordingly our old Panjabi Bhagwan Singh was posted away and replaced by a Malayali named B K Nayar. The newcomer would obviously be in a much better position to find out what went on in the section than Bhagwan Singh had been, and we had to take note of this and act with greater circumspection than hitherto. I felt confident that Kannayan and Chandra Reddy now had the necessary understanding and experience to cope with this situation. We agreed that they would take care not to let any special connection between them appear, and would not make any reference to politics in their letters home. They would keep looking for chances to talk to people when it seemed safe to do so and wouldn't keep silent on important issues simply from lack of confidence that what they said would be 100% correct. The biggest risk lay in having communist literature on them, so they would not send or receive any through the post and the only literature they would keep would be in their own language, and even that they would be ready to destroy at short notice. We discussed what would happen if they were caught – they would tell only what they were quite sure was already known, and where they had to lie, would keep the lying as near to the truth as they safely could. If they didn't know what to say, they would say nothing.

The convoy to Asansol was an interesting experience. On the way out we passed through Calcutta, where I was able to meet my ex-Cambridge friend, Indrajit Gupta and, briefly, P C Joshi, who was there at the time. Indrajit, knowing me as he did, gave serious attention to my reports of developments in my unit. It was only later that I came to feel that he was the only leading communist who ever did, and that was probably more out of personal regard for me, and some curiosity (and scepticism?) about what I thought I was achieving, than from any assessment that what I was doing might be politically important. I think he knew that the Communist Party leaders didn't think it so, but he didn't want to discourage me.

It was while I was in Calcutta that I read Tolstoy's *Childhood, Boyhood and Youth*, which made a very great impact upon me, and taught me, amongst other things, that if I had felt during the great spiritual crisis of my schooldays that I was a very peculiar sort of person, I had at any rate not been uniquely so, and that the great Tolstoy had experienced something very much like it.

The convoy operation dragged out to the best part of two months, and was characterised by the most incredible inefficiency from start to finish. On the way back we stayed a day or two in Gauhatti, and I was able to meet Gaurisankar three or four times. I remember he was horrified at the poor quality of the food we had as rations, and I felt pleased that I had shared this food with the sepoys (I was the only officer, and the only Britisher, on the convoy) without any sense of insuperable hardship. I learnt with satisfaction during these years that I could live quite happily in very hard conditions and with inadequate food, provided that I was with people that I liked. Though I hope I still have this ability, I have never since then had any occasion to test it for any prolonged period and so prove that I still have it.

But what I remember best about those months of journeying was the inescapable signs of the great famine then raging in Bengal. It still fills me with horror to think how the sight of people dying of starvation ceased to have any great impact after one had seen it repeatedly. I remember also being camped for the night in the Bengal countryside, watching people standing silently and hopelessly watching our evening meal being cooked in the hope that there might be leavings that they could have. I was awakened by some noise during the night, but, reassured by my batman, went to sleep again; and discovered in the morning that some of the sepoys had been elated to find that they could buy a night with a starving woman for a handful of rice.

I got back to my section to find a depressed Chandra Reddy and Kannayan awaiting me. The new VCO, B K Nayar, had organised a sort of CId in the section, and his main helper in this was A V John, the man we had hoped to develop as our most promising Malayali contact. Along with this had gone a consistent policy of favouring the Malayalis at the expense of the rest, a systematic persecution of all the best NCOs and men, and an alienation of them from the rest of the section which was playing havoc with its work. Kannayan thought that B K Nayar probably knew of our political work. Chandra Reddy did not think so; he said he thought B K Nayar sensed that there was some sort of special relationship between the three of us, but that it did not occur to him that this could be a political one. We decided to lie low for a while, and in the meantime I took steps to bring B K Nayar to heel – something which it was urgently necessary to do on military grounds alone. I knew my commanding officer would support me, for he had learned to value me as an officer who could actually communicate with his men and was not afraid of hard work under difficult conditions; and the case against B K Nayar was damaging and irrefutable. So he was brought under some measure of control, and things improved.

I had by now almost entirely given up writing to my parents. For almost the whole of the year 1943 all they received was a brief aerogram in September saying I was sorry I hadn't written for five months, but there was really nothing to report. I would try to be more dutiful in future, I promised – and then did nothing about it. Once my father cabled telling me to write, but I don't remember whether I responded. I justified my negligence on the grounds that ties of kinship meant little compared to the those of communist comradeship – that I wrote to Rex was not because he was my brother but because we were fellow communists. It was an attitude I felt no qualms about at the time, but one I now regret.

Life on the Manipur Road had for so long been our only reality that it had become difficult to react even to the most significant events in the lives of those back home. In November I received a cable from Rex. It read simply, 'Father died – make mother allowance'. So far as I remember, the cable was never followed by any longer communication; nor do I remember if I wrote to my mother even now. I think it quite possible that I did not.

In December 1943 my section was detached from the rest of the Company and sent to work on improving the seventy mile long stretch of road that ran to Dimapur from Gologhat, clearly as a part of the effort to improve communications and make possible a greater volume of supplies to the forward areas. Our lorries had to go into the jungle bordering the road and bring out stone from the hill streams. This was loaded and unloaded by civilian labour recruited and managed by the Indian Tea Planters' Association, and other labour, also recruited and managed by the ITPA, built the road, the army engineers providing the technical supervision.

We were there about four months. I much enjoyed my new situation. I was alone with my section, rarely visiting company headquarters, rarely visited by anyone from it, and I was running the whole work without interference from anyone else. The area in which we were working was very beautiful. Some of the roads ran up to about ten miles into the Mikir Hills, to the point where the lorries would stop to load stone from the bed of the hill streams, and the belt of woodland would end completely abruptly and give way to tall grass. The swift-running

Improving the road

streams were crystal clear and everything looked very beautiful in the clear winter sunshine. The Mikirs are, like the Nagas, a tribal people of Sino-Tibetan stock and speech, and I found them very likeable.

Work was hard, and opportunities to rest and talk were few and far between – though I do remember reading *Don Quixote* with great enjoyment during that time. The work of improving the road *ought* to have been regarded as extremely important, but I soon had to conclude that I was the only one of those supposedly responsible for the work who thought it so. I never expect to meet more utterly despicable men than two of the three planters (or, more accurately at that time, ex-planters) who were in charge of the civilian labour. Two were British and one Anglo-Indian, and they and I were very quickly at war. It began when Duncan, the chap stationed next door to my central detachment, where I myself usually stayed, approached me for free petrol to which he wasn't entitled. To his astonishment, I refused him. He then tried a sort of bribery. He invited me to dinner at his house – a quite spacious bamboo and thatch bungalow constructed for him free by

303

his labour force, from whom he had chosen a man to cook his meals and an attractive woman to share his bed. At dinner it transpired that this girl was now pregnant. He said that he would instruct the medical chap attached to his camp to give her an abortion, and if there were any complications he would declare that he knew nothing about it, and would suggest that it was the doctor that had got her pregnant. He said he would have a bungalow like his built for me, and hinted that he could arrange for the same comforts as he was enjoying. I told him that I had a tent, and that first priority in any case was accommodation for my men, who had none of any kind and were sleeping in their lorries. I think he thought I was mad, but there wasn't much he could do about it.

These fellows were not in the least concerned with the work they were supposed to be doing, and the army engineers weren't much better. There was no serious attempt either to build the road to strict specification or to meet target dates, and the result was that within weeks of having been constructed great stretches of road were breaking up under traffic amounting to little more than that of the lorries that were building it. In the early days there were repeated attempts at the regular Sunday morning conferences between transport (me), engineers (a British major) and labour (one or more of the three planters) to blame the alleged shortcomings of my men; but since I worked and they didn't I could prove with chapter and verse that my men were doing their job properly, and after a while they piped down.

In fairness to the third ex-planter I ought to add that I never heard complaints about him. I don't think he cared any more than the others about the work he was supposed to be doing, but his personal relations with his labour force and with my men seemed to be all right. He too had an Indian concubine, but all the indications were that he treated her as a wife. Both he and she were quite elderly at this time. In the evenings they could sometimes be seen taking a dignified stroll together, she walking respectfully a few paces behind him.

But with the other two ex-planters there were constant incidents between them and my sepoys; and they got the worst of it. Characters like these only knew enough Urdu to bawl filthy abuse. Duncan one day made the mistake of using it on one of my sepoys who had, very properly, given him a lift on the road and, equally properly, refused to take him on several miles out of his way. This boy, a young Maharashtrian called Raja Ram Kadam, had at once stopped his lorry, picked up the starting handle and told Duncan that he would hit him with it if he didn't get out at once. Duncan hastily did so, and Raja Ram Kadam then came straight to me at section headquarters to tell me what he had done. I congratulated him warmly and assured him of my full support if

Duncan should try to get any action taken against him. But I think Duncan by now knew what my attitude would be, and I never heard a cheep from him. The Anglo-Indian, Daly, went over my head to my commanding officer and complained to him that my sepoys did not address him as 'sahib'. My commanding officer asked for my comments. I told him that my men complained to me that this man frequently, and quite openly, molested the women working on the road under his supervision. I said that if he wanted to be called 'sahib' he should start behaving with common decency, and that in the meanwhile I was certainly not going to issue any orders about it. I heard no more of that either.

Politically my isolation from the rest of the company suited me very well, but the disadvantage was that the section was split up into three detachments, each separated from its neighbour by about twenty miles of bad road. This meant I could not keep all of the most politically developed men together in a single group; nor were they *so* politically developed that they always knew how to go ahead on their own when I was not there with them. Anyway, there was nothing to be done about that. I put B K Nayar in charge of one of the three detachments and saw very little of him, though I used to go there quite often to see that things were going reasonably smoothly. Chandra Reddy took charge at the other end of the road and I contrived to see him a little more often. I stayed in the middle, and Kannayan was with me as my truck driver. For some of the time a havildar-clerk called Srinivasan was sent on attachment to me. I had first met him at the time of the proceedings against B K Nayar. Now, as I got to know him better, I discovered that he was one of those rare men who had managed to get into the army despite having had contacts with, and sympathy for, the communists.

Chandra Reddy's political understanding and abilities to encourage others were developing steadily, and mainly due to his work numbers of men were now asking for Party literature in their own language to read. I felt, perhaps unfairly, that Gaurisankar wasn't particularly concerned to help us get hold of the literature we needed, but eventually we solved the problem ourselves by entrusting a man named Rajbahadur who was going on leave to bring back party literature in the South Indian languages. Once this arrived Chandra Reddy felt much relieved. There was now sufficient sympathy for our ideas among many of the sepoys that he and Kannayan were able to start collecting money for Party funds.

The rapidly increasing success we were now experiencing was in part an expression of what was going on outside the army. The Party had by this time rapidly extended its mass base, already strong in north

Kerala, throughout the south and more especially in Andhra and (though this didn't directly affect my unit) in Bengal. The sepoys almost certainly experienced something of this changing feeling, and that made them open to the ideas we were presenting. This strenghtened my conviction that if the Party would only give adequate attention to the army it could achieve a very important addition to its forces.

∞

Although we did not know this at the time, by March 1944 the allied forces around Burma were finally in a position to launch an offensive against the Japanese. The Fourteenth Army was deployed on a seven hundred mile front, from China to the Bay of Bengal, with a concentration in three areas, around Ledo in the north, Imphal in the centre, served by the Manipur Road, and Arakan in the south. The central front which we were supplying was the one Slim had months ago chosen for the start of the offensive. Intelligence reports received from fighting troops making brief incursions across the Chindwin River was that the Japanese too were building up to an offensive in the area. Slim's aim was to be in a position to choose the ground for the battle, and lure the Japanese into attacking there. Imphal provided the best option. It lies in a plain surrounded by mountains, and in almost two years of immense effort there was by now a substantial build up of supplies and troops. Advance notice of the arrival of the Japanese could be got by deploying forces on the mountains on the Burma side of the plain, and reinforcements would be flown in from both the other two fronts once the fighting began.

The timing was critical; both sides knew that if they did not administer a decisive defeat to the other before the monsoon arrived in May, the offensive might drag on in an unwinnable campaign, literally bogged down in mud. This was part of the reason why Slim was determined that the first significant encounter should be on Allied ground; the retreat from Burma had taught him that the worst position to be in was one with a very extended line of communication back to base.

In the event, the Japanese crossed the border slightly before the Allies expected them. To the south of Imphal, the Allies' advance units were pushed onto the defensive and had to fight their way back to Imphal, mile by mile. And to the north the Japanese by-passed Imphal altogether, swinging round over the mountains to attack at a point where no one had expected them – Kohima.*

The first we heard of these events was when an unexpected order recalled our section from the Gologhat road to our lines at Milestone Four near Dimapur. Here, stationed at company headquarters, we prepared to find ourselves confronted by the Japanese armies. The small garrison at Kohima was holding out against greatly superior numbers and it seemed only a matter of time, and a short time at that, before the Japanese would come down from Kohima to attack the vital railhead and supply depot at Dimapur. We also knew that fighting with the Japanese forces were units of the Indian National Army.★ What had been up to now a transport company might suddenly have to become a fighting unit, but without any training for it – and almost without weapons. To my surprise we were ordered to give up our firearms to supply the still continuing deficiencies of the fighting units. Only the officers had firearms at all. I had a tommy gun and a pistol. My men's only weapons were pick-handles!

One night we heard that an attack on Dimapur was anticipated. I knew very well that we had virtually no chance of withstanding it. I told the sepoys about the situation, and now suddenly began to realise how unconcerned they were about what, to me, was a very menacing situation. I had expected them to feel dejection and alarm but no one turned a hair, except, to my surprise and regret, Kannayan, whose morale I had expected to be the best of all.

The reason was made clear to me that evening when I spoke to my orderly about it. He had held that position of honour for some time and we got on very well, though he had never shown any political interest of any kind and I had therefore made no attempt to talk politics with him. I now said to him, 'You're all very calm. You know that the Japanese may attack tonight. What will you do if they *do* attack?' He said with a grin, 'What will *you* do?' I didn't understand, and must have shown it, because he went on, 'They aren't after us. They'll take us prisoner and ask us to join the Indian National Army – which we'll do. It's *you* they're after. What will *you* do?'

I was more shocked and disappointed at the time than I should have been. It now struck me forcefully that many ordinary Indians probably accepted the false logic of 'my enemy's enemy is my friend' and I could now see that the attitude my orderly was expressing must have seemed simple commonsense to most of my men. Even if they felt no great sympathy with the Japanese, there had certainly been nothing in their treatment at British hands which offered them any incentive to make common cause with us in so extreme a situation, and so put their lives at risk.

I said earlier that throughout my time in India I was continually being brought to realise how much I needed to learn from ordinary

307

Indians. This lesson from my orderly was indeed a major one! I had been living so closely with the men in my unit, thinking that I understood them, and yet I could still make so basic a miscalculation of how they would perceive things. Writing all these years later I can see how it happened that, with all my political awareness, I had been prevented from forming an accurate estimate of what Indian feeling was. Like everyone else, I was affected by the censorship of the press. Knowing you are not being told the whole truth only gets you so far – you still don't know the bits you haven't been told. I relied instead on what I learnt from the few politically conscious Indians I occasionally met, and they certainly should have been able to make me aware of things the press did not admit. But they had their own reasons for remaining discreetly silent on the question. As communists they were trying to rally mass support for the war, and did not like to admit – perhaps even to themselves – the strength of feelings that worked against this.*

In the event we were lucky – the Japanese attack on Dimapur did not materialise. It seemed astonishing that they should miss the chance, for it didn't take a military genius to see that the obvious thing for them to do was to cut the railway line and so starve the British troops further up the road. But apparently they considered it necessary to finish off Kohima first, and fortunately for us they never succeeded. Years later I found that General Slim, commander of the 14th Army which comprised our forces over this whole area, had been of the same opinion:

All the Japanese commander had to do was to leave a detachment to mask Kohima, and, with the rest of his division, thrust violently on Dimapur. He could hardly fail to take it. Luckily, Major-General Sato, commander of the Japanese 31st Division, was, without exception, the most unenterprising of all the Japanese generals I encountered. He had been ordered to take Kohima and dig in. His bullet head was filled with one idea only – to take Kohima. It never struck him that he could inflict terrible damage on us without taking Kohima at all. Leaving a small force to contain it, and moving by tracks to the east of Warren's brigade at Nichugard, he could, by the 5th April, have struck the railway with the bulk of his division. But he had no vision, so, as his troops came up, he flung them into attack after attack on the little town of Kohima.*

In retrospect it is possible to see what was not so clear at the time, that the failure of the Japanese to attack Dimapur was the turning point of the war on the Burma border.

For weeks still the battle continued to rage, one of the most bitterly

Kohima after the battle

contested conflicts of the war. Both sides fought with unusual courage
and tenacity – every foot of land around the small town was contested,
at the cost of tens of thousands of lives. It was early May before Allied
reinforcements could be got through. Already the first torrential rain
was slowing down troop movements and causing havoc with any
planned operation. By mid May the Japanese had finally been thrown
onto the defensive and the Allies began to regain control of the Kohi-
ma-Imphal road. Then the monsoon arrived in full force, closing off the
prospect of further Japanese advance. By late June they were retreating
from Kohima and being pushed back on the other routes leading to
Imphal. By mid July they were in general retreat back across the Kabaw
Valley and the Chindwin River, pursued by Allied armies.

A memorial in Kohima erected after the war commemorates those
who died defending it:

When you go home
Tell them of us and say,
For your tomorrow
We gave our today.

Through the remainder of the summer of 1944 Allied armies positioned
themselves for a new offensive to recapture Burma, to begin once the
monsoon was over. One East African division (chosen because of their

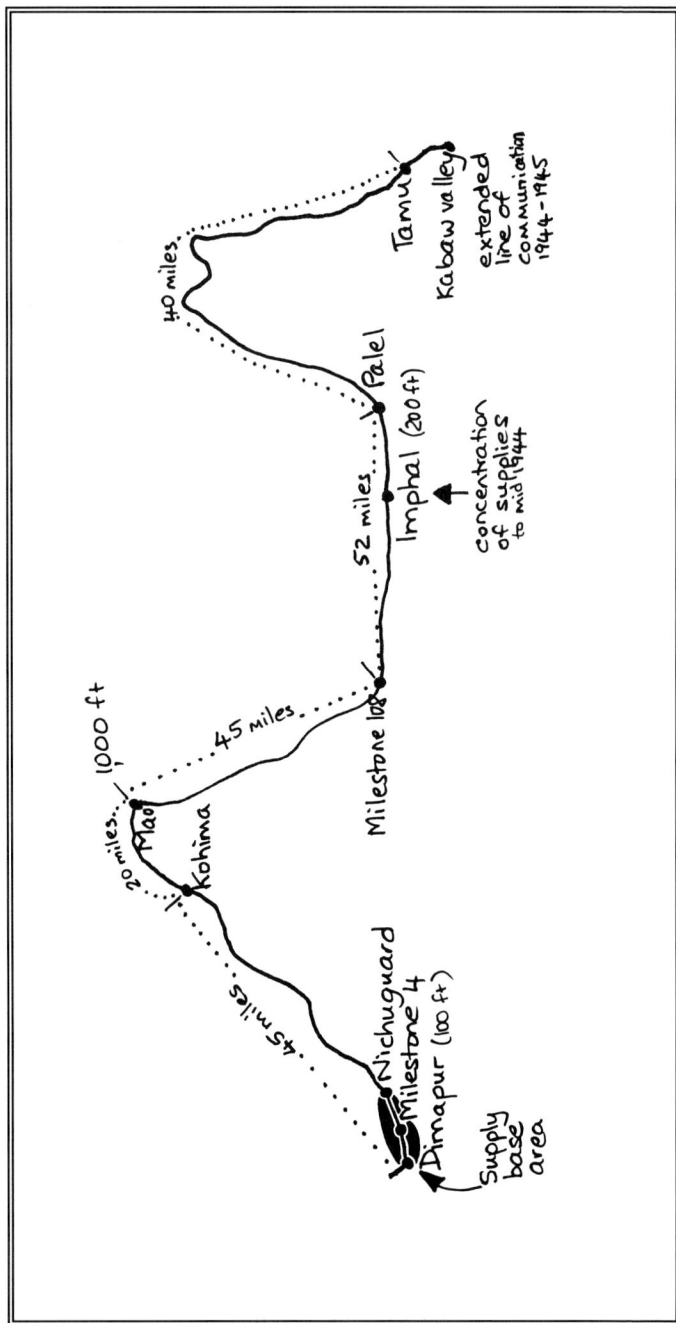

Manipur Road – cross section

supposed higher resistance to malaria) moved into the Kabaw Valley and across the Chindwin, to continue harrassing what Japanese troops were left in the area. Here 'conditions were so liquid,' says one historian, that they had to be supplied entirely by air, 'the pilots flying through tempest, turbulence and minimal visibility.'* Meanwhile the bulk of the Fourteenth Army would wait out the monsoon months in Imphal, where it would be possible to supply them by land.

With so many thousands of extra troops to maintain, the strain on the already overstrained supply routes intensified. New transport companies had to be brought in, and in October 1944 our company was moved further up the road, to a point just south of Kohima where we joined the fleets of lorries taking supplies forward from Nichuguard.

Kohima is only 45 miles from Dimapur by road, and by air must be very much less, but you climb steeply the whole way. Even in summer it is cold enough in Kohima for a fire in the evenings. We made our camp on the spur where the Japanese had made their last desperate stand. It was a badly scarred landscape, with the burnt remains of trees standing gaunt against the sky, and still plenty of signs of the battle – old Japanese rifles, barbed wire and sandbag positions. But the country around us was breath-taking in its beauty. Standing at the highest point and looking down the road descending towards Dimapur we saw mile upon mile of almond trees in flower. It is a sight I shall never forget.

In the other direction – the part we would now be working on – the road ran south through the Naga Hills to the plains around Imphal. Here it forked, one fork running on over two steep ridges to Tamu on the Burma border and the other through the hills all the way, to Tiddim. Almost two years earlier when we had first arrived in Dimapur, Tamu and Tiddim had been the most advanced posts held by our troops in any considerable force. For two solid years, twenty-four hours a day and 365 days in the year, work on the road had continued, and by now there was a double-width asphalt road all the way to Tamu. But it was still far from perfect, and was frequently blocked by landslides during the rains; and with the new offensive being planned, there was an urgent need to increase its carrying capacity.

Such transport as was available, and as the road could bear, had to work unceasingly to keep it clear. The men of 317 Company began to feel on their skins – what they may already have been vaguely aware of – that hard as their own work in the base had been, it had been holiday-making compared with the conditions under which the drivers on this section of the road had to work. On the steep hilly descents after a shower of rain you could only skid down and try to keep your lorry going straight. Scores of lorries went over the edge to fall hundreds of feet below. Every lorry carried two drivers; theoretically one could sleep, propped up in the front seat, while the other drove. But the road ran over ranges of hills, through appreciable changes of temperature as it climbed and fell, twisting and turning along the hillside with a drop of hundreds of feet falling sheer beyond the outside edge of the road for miles at a stretch. Trying to sleep in a moving lorry on turning and twisting roads on a winter's night at Kohima or Mao, several thousand feet above sea level, and in a lorry with no windscreen or doors was, shall we say, not an enviable experience. Drivers got so tired that accidents were common. Driving in the hills, the twists and turns kept them awake, but once in the plain again they would fall asleep and the lorry would run off the road.

Vehicles from all the different companies in the area were part of a combined line of communication ('L of C') transport pool, managed by a civilian called Holmes who had been rapidly classified as a colonel to give him sufficient authority. He made an excellent job of it, setting up a rota system that kept the vehicles constantly moving day and night. The base to Tamu turn-round averaged about forty-eight hours. Drivers could take two breaks in twenty-four hours, of about twenty or thirty minutes each, at one of the few places on the road where they could get food. Apart from these and loading and unloading, there was no stopping. Drivers were allowed only twelve hours in lines between trips. That was strictly adhered to – drivers returning from a trip at twelve o'clock midnight were regularly again sent out at the following twelve o'clock midday. Most of the men, whose homes were one to two thousand miles away, did not get leave more than once during these two years. And incredible though it may seem, some of the same companies who had helped bring the Burma Army out were still working there, and most of them continued to do so. It didn't seem to have occurred to general headquarters that they might change places with others who had been doing comparatively light work in India.

Since the halting of the Japanese advance there had been a definite lessening of tension, and I was finally able to write more openly to Rex – and also I think to Chris – about where we were and what had been happening. I described the work of the Indian sepoys, whose vital contribution to the war effort ought, I felt, to be more widely recognised. I had seen a press report praising British transport drivers in Italy who, to keep the front line troops supplied, were working 'twelve and sometimes fourteen hours a day.' I compared this with work on the Manipur Road. 'What *these* men have been doing is, I guarantee, as hard work as any soldier, not excluding fighting troops, has done in this war – and on a gross pay of about eleven shillings a week. Their achievement, which has cost not a little in health and in accidents due to sheer fatigue, is beyond all praise. No British troops would or could have done it.'*

After about a month near Kohima we were moved again, this time to Milestone 108, a point on the road about twenty-five miles from Imphal, at the foot of the hills where the Imphal Plain begins. Here we exchanged our three-tonners for five-tonners, and a little later for big diesel-driven ten-tonners, and our lorries now began to do the whole run from Dimapur to Kalewa, over the Burma border on the bank of the Chindwin.

Our company was now for the first time stationed quite near others. Kannayan, Chandra Reddy and the others in our group were now also able to be in contact with men in the other units, and they found some who were interested in our ideas. Over the course of the last months we had at last begun to make quite rapid progress within our own section. Kannayan had won over a Malayali sepoy and in the course of it weaned him from religion. Chandra Reddy too was beginning to question his own religious ideas, partly as a result of discussions with me, though I was careful to let him draw his own conclusions. He was having considerable success in encouraging political consciousness among the Telegu-speakers, and we could not keep up with the requests for more Telegu literature. Even Damodaran was becoming steadier in his views – perhaps under the influence of his brother back in Kerala, now an experienced worker in the local Kisan Sabha (Peasant League).

We now had people working in all the three main language groupings – Tamil, Telegu and Malayalam-speakers. I decided it was now possible to arrange for a regular supply by post of the Communist Party weekly papers in Malayalam, Tamil, and Telegu – *Deshabhimani*, *Janasakti* and *Prajasakti*. At nights when I was orderly officer I started giving a basic course in Marxism-Leninism to Chandra Reddy and Kannayan. The study group gradually enlarged, and I noted at the time that there were now at least eight sepoys with whom I could talk on political themes quite openly. One of them was Ramunni Nair, the man whom I had scared so badly nearly two years earlier when I, so to speak, made a political pass at him at railhead.

With all the to-ing and fro-ing around Milestone 108, the Indian officers of the various companies began to get together and formed a sort of social circle of their own. I, of course, didn't belong to it, but since I was vouched for by Khan and Gopal Singh I was on friendly terms with them. Those I remember best were Lachman Singh, a Rajput from

Moving troops up to the front

Rajasthan, Harbans Singh, a Sikh from the Panjab, Quraishi from U P, and another whose name I can't remember who was a great joker and a teller of lewd stories much appreciated by his fellow Indian officers. My knowledge of Urdu was not yet adequate enough for me to understand most of these, but one I remember is that in response to a British officers' 'Cheerio!' he would reply *'Teri bhi chirio!'* which they took to be an Indian response of similar meaning. Actually it meant something like 'Up yours!' *Chirio* means 'split' and *teri bhi* means 'yours too' but in this context *teri* becomes 'your [arsehole]' – or in the case of a woman, 'your [cunt].' Whether I knew this at the time or whether someone explained it to me later I can't remember.

My chief memory of Quraishi is that on one of the rare occasions when some entertainment was provided for us, he was so smitten by the beauty of a dancer that he went around frantically trying to raise the money to pay her to share his bed for the night. I was puzzled – why did he think he *could* buy her for the night? The other officers to whom I put this question were equally puzzled by my question. Why on earth should I think this would be any problem? Of course she could be

314

bought. It was years later that I learnt that accomplished dancer and accomplished courtesan were almost synonymous terms.

Lachman Singh had developed a great reverence for Gandhi. I spoke critically of Gandhi and followed it up by suggesting that he should read R Palme Dutt's *India Today*. This he did, and it was a revelation to him. I would have liked to know what happened to his ideas after that, but he was posted to another unit soon afterwards and I lost contact with him.

The real surprise was Harbans Singh. He came over to my tent one day, probably looking for Gopal Singh or for Khan, and was startled to see Marxist books lying around. He asked if I didn't think it a bit risky to have such books. I knew that the obvious assumption for him to make was that this British officer was trying to trap people into declaring an interest in such ideas, only to expose them later. I explained that I was a communist, that army Intelligence already knew this and that there was therefore no need to conceal the books. He seemed satisfied and said no more then. But later he must have decided that I was trustworthy, and confided to me that he too was a Communist Party member.

I liked and respected Harbans Singh. He told me that he had enlisted with the Party's permission, so I assumed that both they and he had seen some political point in his doing so; and since he was the only Indian communist officer I had met, I was naturally curious to know how he interpreted his role. But it seemed that he had joined for largely personal reasons, which the Party had simply accepted as valid. The Party had never suggested that he do any communist work in the army, and the idea had never occurred to him. He was surprised to find that *I* was working in this way to influence the men under my command.

At about the same time I had a chance encounter with a British communist officer, the only one I met during all my years in Assam. In one of the companies passing by us towards the Burma border I recognised a man I had known slightly as a communist student in Cambridge, a year or two ahead of me. We had perhaps five minutes to talk before his company headed off along the road. I asked him whether he had learnt Urdu – an innocuous enough question if anyone should overhear it, but one that would indicate how he regarded his relationship with his men. He seemed scarcely to understand the question.

14

For years we had lived in a state of time suspended, all of us away from our 'real' lives, not knowing how long it would be before we could return. Meanwhile it was our life together that had become the real one; and now it seemed that this time might soon be ending.

In December 1944 the Fourteenth Army collected at Imphal began to move across the Chindwin River to begin the new offensive against the Japanese. In Europe, the Allied invasion of France had finally been launched in mid 1944. By January 1945 it was running into difficulties when Germany launched an unexpected, and initially successful, offensive in the Ardennes; but the Soviet Union began another offensive, bringing forward the date at the urgent request of Britain and the US, which turned the balance against Germany. Though no one knew how long the war might still drag on, there was now little doubt about an eventual Allied victory.

Knowing that our remaining time together might now be short heightened my awareness of the value of the relationships with the men around me. I remember about the time we moved to Milestone 108 there was a new arrival in our unit, a youngster called Krishnamoorthy. He was scarcely more than a boy, simple, ignorant, but very intelligent and far more straightforward than most. He was not a swaggerer but once roused he would stand up to anybody without being frightened. I made him my personal truckdriver and in all the hours of driving we got to know each other well. He was from Andhra and spoke pure Telegu but couldn't read and write a single letter – except his own name, and he only learned that because I refused to pay him out until he could sign for his pay. He was a peasant, or rather for some years since his father lost his land, a farm labourer.

I never failed to find him a refreshing contrast to the rest. If we were on convoy and I asked him whether I should drive or whether he wanted to, he would always give a definite answer. I once asked him just after I had had a bath why Indians do not bath naked, as we do. (No Indians, except a few Malayalis bath without a small pair of drawers or a loin cloth). He said that they were too modest, and that even when quite alone they would never bath naked. I said, 'Why? Have you got something in your drawers that no other man has got?' He grinned and said

'No, everyone's got it,' but wouldn't be persuaded. 'So,' I said, 'our way of going on is bad, is it?' and he at once replied 'Yes.' All this in an Indian is most unusual.

I often talked to him about my village and how people live and work there, and he said that he would like to come and work there after the war to see what it was like. I would very much have liked to take him and a few others back with me for a couple of months. But I knew very well that this would never be possible.

In February, with the end of the war almost in sight, my brother Wilfred was shot down over France. I felt more regret at his death than I had at my father's. Though we had not been close, since the time we had worked together in the fields and he had begun to develop communist sympathies, I had felt more interest in him, and had been hearing from Froude's letters about his subsequent development. I learnt from her later that he had never got past his fear of the danger of his work as a navigator in a bomber, each time hating the prospect of yet another flight. Many years later Froude's daughter visited Wilfred's grave in Belgium and found that someone, perhaps my mother, perhaps Froude, had had these words inscribed on it:

He always loved peace
And hated strife
But he did his duty.

I had always known that my mother loved him more than any of the rest of us, but I regret to say that I didn't have the imagination to think about what his death must have meant to her. I don't even know if I wrote to her about it.

The strain of two and a half years in difficult physical conditions was beginning to show, and not just on the drivers who had the really hard jobs. Though I am conveniently oblivious to most physical discomfort and tend not to notice – or remember – ill health, I do remember once registering the fact that I felt undernourished, and checking it with a test someone had told me about, looking at my tongue in the mirror and discovering that it was unnaturally smooth. Since there wasn't anything to be done about it, that was the last I thought about it. Then I fell – a very minor event – but for some reason the skin of my grazed left shin wouldn't heal. Then some odd skin complaint developed on my thigh. A patent remedy had no effect and when the condition worsened I eventually reported sick, but nothing the medical officer could supply made any difference.

By April 1945 I began to develop some new skin ailment on my waist and chest. The medical officer decided that I had some unidentified disease and sent me off to the hospital in Imphal. It was a pukka building, not a bamboo and thatch structure, but whether recently built at Slim's command or surviving from pre-war days I do not know. No one there had much idea what my skin disease was. They tried a new treatment, which seemed to help but took a long time. While I waited for it to heal I occupied myself by beginning to write a basic course in Marxism-Leninism for Chandra Reddy and Kannayan. Some sort of welfare visitor also tried to teach me to knit, but I simply couldn't get the hang of it, useful skill though I felt it to be (and I never have learnt). To my pleasure I discovered that the hospital had a small miscellaneous collection of books consisting, presumably, of those left behind by earlier patients. Two of them I read with great interest: Andre Gide's journal of his travels in Africa, which greatly modified my previous wholly hostile attitude to him, and volume one of Frances Parkman's *The conspiracy of Pontiac*. I knew of Parkman's classic, highly praised by Rex, *The Oregon Trail*, but had not heard of this book. Nor had I the least idea of who or what Pontiac was and what the conspiracy was all about. It is a fascinating story of an American Indian chief (Pontiac) who united Indian tribes from Canada right down to the mouth of the Mississippi to resist the westward expansion of the colonists. The library didn't have volume two, so I never learnt how the story ended.

Eventually I was allowed to return to my unit, but still my skin did not heal and problems began to reappear in new places, always in a slightly different form. It was soon obvious that I was going to be sent back to hospital; and this time, with the uncertainty of the war situation, it looked as if I might never return to 317 Company.

I left Milestone 108 in May 1945. I said goodbye to everyone and made such arrangements as I could for the future political welfare of my group, putting Chandra Reddy in touch with Harbans Singh.

From Imphal I was taken to Comilla, where the dermatologist's attempt at treatment with wet dressings of sulpha something made things infinitely worse, causing my skin to weep copiously. I was then flown out to a transit hospital in Calcutta, to be sent on by ambulance train to a big military hospital in south India. Before leaving Calcutta I managed to meet my Cambridge friend Indrajit Gupta, and prepared for him two thirty-page reports summing up my work in my unit since 1943. I also gave him the names and home addresses of all the men in my unit who had given active support to the Party and asked him to see to it that when they were demobilised the local units of the Communist

Party contacted them. He took the list, but told me not to expect that much would come of this.

It was a three days' journey from Calcutta to Trimulgharri, the military hospital just outside Secunderabad. Here for the first time I was in a part of the country that some of the men in my unit came from – Secunderabad more or less runs into Hyderabad, Chandra Reddy's home. The slow business of trying out treatments got under way – I counted at least nine, and as usual none of them seemed to make much difference. Meanwhile the weeks went by and still I was stuck in hospital, away from my unit.

I decided to occupy myself by acquiring the basic political vocabulary of modern Urdu. I managed to get hold of a rather inadequate Urdu dictionary, and with its aid read the Urdu translations of Marx's *Letters on India* and Stalin's *Foundations of Leninism*. The latter I took to pieces, interleaved and re-bound, making a cover from the blue paper in which rolls of cotton wool were packed. I also continued work on the basic course in Marxism-Leninism I had started in Imphal.

In May we heard the news that Germany had surrendered. In the east the war still dragged on, but the prospect of it coming to an end meant brought significant political changes in India. The British government had let it be generally understood that in return for taking India into the war it would consider the granting of independence once the war was over; and it was in any case now clear that Britain could not hold on to India indefinitely. Britian now had no choice but to begin a process of talks leading to eventual granting of independence; and that meant that the Congress leaders had to be released from jail to take part in the talks.

Now it was announced that British officers attached to the Indian army could claim repatriation after three and a half years in India. For me that meant only a month or so to go. For the first time in years I had to make some choices about my own future. The one clear thought that emerged was that I didn't want permanent repatriation. I had the option instead to apply for two months leave – dubbed LILOP, Leave In Lieu Of [re]Patriation. I would then return to India, and if possible get my discharge here after the war. I thought that I would like to spend at least a year more in India, for there was a lot I wanted to do that had been impossible in wartime conditions. Khan had been pressing me to spend some time with him in his home in the North-West Frontier Province, and so had Lachman Singh from Rajasthan and Harbans Singh from the Panjab. I very much wanted to accept their invitations – all of them! But most of all I did not want to lose touch with the men I had become close to in my unit, whom I had been with now for nearly two and a half years. I had become strongly attached to some of them; I wanted to see their villages and get a better idea of what their conditions of life were really like.

In early July my name was taken by the office as having completed my required time in India. The dermatologist put in a recommendation that my leave be speeded up. He said that I wasn't infectious, but with my skin as it was I couldn't be sent back to my unit; perhaps rest in a cooler climate would sort me out. Meanwhile I was allowed out for short periods – I had to be in bed when the doctors came on their rounds, but in the afternoons I could get up and out. I hired a bike from a cycle hire and repair shop near by, run by a young Marwari with a delightful little boy whom I used to talk with. And on my bike I went looking for the local organisation of the Party.

There were things about how things worked there that surprised and displeased me. The leading communist in Secunderabad was a man called Venkat Chari, and he seemed to be the 'only begetter' of communist work on every front. The party bookshop, the party organisation, peasant work, the trade union office – Venkat Chari was all of these, and if *he* wasn't there, apparently no one else seemed to have any overall grasp of what was going on in any of these fields. Except one. I was much impressed by a peasant comrade whose name I can't now remember. He was a Telegu-speaker and knew no English so we communicated in Urdu, though this too he spoke only with some effort. I remember a long ride with him cross-country, sitting on the carrier of his bike. He had come to communism via the unlikely route of the Arya Samaj, a militant Hindu communalist organisation which sought to match the egalitarianism of Islam with a similarly egalitarian version of Hinduism, 'purified' and allegedly 'restored' to a pristine purity which had been corrupted over the centuries. It was this egalitarianism that had appealed to him and had set him on the road towards communism. It struck me that *such* a man, an Indian through and through in a sense that no English-educated Indian is, was the kind whom one ought to encounter much more frequently in *leading* positions in the Indian party. But when I expressed some such idea to Venkat Chari he was surprised and, as it seemed to me, unable to grasp so novel an idea. To him the English speaking intellectuals alone were equipped for leading work.

Eventually word came through that my application for Leave in Lieu had been accepted. My instructions – received, as always, in the absurdly bureaucratic telegram style peculiar to the army – were that I was to proceed to Karachi, from where I would be flown to Britain. My leave was for sixty-one days. On my return I could expect at least another year of wartime service, for everyone believed that the Japanese

320

Cycle store owner & his son, Secunderabad

were likely to go on fighting a good long time yet.

I committed to Venkat Chari's care, to look after until I would return to reclaim it, a tin trunk with some of my things, mostly books – including the complete works of Homer that the vicar of Holme on Spalding Moor had presented to me, and which I had carried around India, fondly imagining I would have time to read it. Also the incomplete manuscript of my basic course on Marxism. I talked to Venkat Chari about Chandra Reddy, whose home address was in Gun Foundry, Hyderabad, virtually next door to Secunderabad, and asked if he would make contact with him when he came home.

I viewed the prospect of leaving India with mixed feelings. I should have felt happier if I had been sure that I could return to my own unit, but I knew there was only a slender chance of that. Nevertheless, I was gradually evolving a longer term plan. When the war eventually ended I would take my demobilisation here in India, and spend a year in the tutelage of the Communist Party of India. After that I would return to Britain with the hope of a job in the international department of the Party. Such a plan would of course require the sanction of both the British and the Indian parties, but I hoped I would be able to get that.

The journey from Secunderabad to Karachi proceeded by slow stages, moving from one military hospital to the next. I was on the last leg of the train journey to Karachi when the totally unexpected news of Japan's surrender came through. The war was over.

The practical implications for me were not immediately evident. I was still in the army, and not likely to be demobilised for a good while yet. It was well known that after the first World War a crisis had been created by demobilising all the armed forces too suddenly, with no jobs for people to go back to. We knew that this time the authorities would not repeat this mistake, so it might be months or even years before my turn came. I expected to be returning to India after my leave, as planned.

I left Karachi by a Dakota aircraft on 19 August, with troops seated along each side facing a mound of our kit in the middle of the plane. I don't remember much of the journey except that, I fear, I greatly irritated my companions during the first part of it by my continual helpless laughter at the exploits of *The Good Soldier Schweik* which I was reading. You don't realise just *how* funny this book is until you have been in the army and seen how amazingly close to reality the fantastic stories in it are.

I also remember a day or so's break in Tel Aviv, and bringing away from there a big basket of bananas to take home to a Britain where at that time many young children had never seen one. And then on 23rd August we reached England's green and pleasant land, and as we crossed the coast and looked down on the soil of our native land I realised keenly, and for the first time, how apt a description of England these words are.

For our return the army had thoughtfully equipped us with a 'Memorandum for Personnel of the Indian Services arriving in the United Kingdom', which included such essential survival information as which categories of officer were entitled to a post-war credit of six pence a day for each day's service rendered, how to obtain ration cards, and the circumstances in which we were and were not permitted to dispose of battle dress. Since I wasn't yet leaving the service most of this didn't apply to me, and the only order I had to follow for the next two months was to report to the Hospital for Tropical Diseases in London. Here the dermatologist started me yet again on the cycle of ineffective creams; but I don't remember being much bothered by my ailment, apart from the irritation of having to constantly bandage and unbandage my legs.

For official purposes I had given my address during my leave as Holme on Spalding Moor, but I was in no hurry to get back there. My first priority was to reestablish contact with my communist friends, and the first of these was Chris Freeman. His wife Peggotty was in London, and expecting a baby; Chris was still away, having been posted to Germany as part of the Allied occupation. I based myself in the house in London that they shared with another couple, and from there I set out to find other friends. One was Freddie Lambert. I had mixed feelings about Freddie. She was the one to whom in 1941 I had given my letter to the Central Committee, attacking its line of support for the government – a letter I thought she had probably never bothered to deliver. I also took a poor view of what I knew about her personal life. Her boyfriend from Cambridge days, John Vickers, had been taken prisoner at the very beginning of the war, and he was hardly gone before Freddie moved in with Ram Nahum. She too had been hit by the bombing raid that killed Ram; she was so badly injured that she had to have both legs amputated from below the knee. Now John had returned from the war, and they were married.

I tried to track down Bob Hone, whose friendship in my early months at Cambridge had rescued me from its oppressive upper class atmosphere. I went to his parents' house and found his sister and his father there. I learnt from them that Bob had married his Esthonian girl friend Aira, and that they had left for Esthonia in the summer of 1939. They had been there when the Red Army marched in in June 1940, and letters home from him described what he saw of the enthusiastic welcome it received.★ They fled when the Germans invaded in June 1941, and were on a ship that was sunk on its way to Leningrad, but survived. Later they were evacuated with the industrial plants moved to the Urals where they worked in the open air and in intense cold, and where Aira had a baby which died. They survived the war and returned to Esthonia. His mother, who wasn't there when I visited, wrote to me after my visit, 'He has had a truly dreadful time and we are very lucky to think he is still alive.' Bob had written that he was hoping to come and see his family; but his father said, 'Of course he won't. He's living in a socialist country, isn't he? Stands to reason he'll stay there.'

Letter writing was easier than it had been from India, so Chris and I were now back in frequent touch. He couldn't write much about the detail of what was going on in occupied Germany, but he felt he was doing a worthwhile job as part of an allied force that would hopefully make a resurgence of fascism impossible, and prepare the way for a democratic German government to emerge. Through his work he was brought into contact with German fellow communists and he valued their cooperation very much. Much later he told me that it made him feel quite distressed when he would see an SS man being arrested and watch him saying goodbye to his children and telling them that he'd soon be back when he knew he would not be, but that his German comrades who had suffered terribly at the Nazis' hands felt no such compunction. I admired both Chris's compunction and their lack of it.

Margaret Horton, the friend from Loughton days in whose garden Rex and I had discussed life, communism and everything, was on a brief visit to London and came to see me. I remember her contemplating with a puzzled air a photo of me, taken shortly before leaving India, that I was about to send to my sepoys. Then she smiled and said, 'I know what's wrong with this – your mouth is shut!'

The only other person from those years that I was still in touch with was Roper, the chaplain at Chigwell School who had been quietly and lovingly supportive of my developing independence, even though he didn't share my political concerns. He had now retired to a quiet rural parish near Lincoln. 'I suppose I'm of the kind to be happy in most places,' he wrote, 'but I do find life here with the leisureliness, pleasant country people and the garden to see to very good indeed.' And then added, with moving honesty, 'It is a relief to be away from the emotional strain of Chigwell.' When I wrote him a brief account of what I had been up to in India, he replied with characteristic understanding, 'Oddly enough you and Green seem to have made the best use of service that I have met, and you are quite different types. I'm afraid the average Chigwellians haven't got much out of it except a taste for magnificence with the possible addition of dissipation.'

Rex was still in the navy, and I went to see him when he was stationed at Plymouth. I remember being both disconcerted and pleased to be called 'dear' by a bus conductress. I later learned that *everyone* was called dear, just as in Yorkshire everyone is called 'love'. I remember too that Rex told me that he was in the habit of addressing his men as 'brother' in the style trade-unionists used to address one another, and once when he was on the phone overheard the person he was speaking to saying to one of his mates, 'It's brother Russell.'

It was years before I began to hear from him stories of what it was like being in the navy. His initial posting was on a destroyer doing convoy duty in the North Sea. For eleven months he and the other seamen worked four hours on and four hours off. When on duty he sat at an anti-aircraft gun looking out for German aircraft; when off duty he simply ate and slept. He remembers how fat he became – the only time he has ever been overweight – because there was no opportunity to exercise. But the most profound effect of the rigorous training was to make him simply a navy man and nothing else. Afterwards he was shocked to realise the changes this had produced in him, at the most personal level – it was as if he had found it difficult even to remember that he was a married man, with a wife towards whom he had responsibilities.

When he was finally taken off destroyers and sent to train as an officer, the one thing he was certain about was that he didn't want to go back. Near the end of their training when decisions were being made about where to send newly-fledged officers Mountbatten happened to visit. Tall, handsome, newly-appointed Chief of Combined Operations, he said, 'I am looking for men with a particular kind of courage.' Rex didn't know what exactly this meant (Mountbatten probably didn't either) but he instantly put up his hand. It turned out to mean that they needed men to be part of the preparations for the landing of Allied forces in France. From September 1942 to June 1944, just before D-day, he was with a small flotilla of landing craft, manned by about thirty men, who had worked closely together and got to know each other well. Then, in a typical exercise of armed forces idiocy, just before D-day the naval officers were suddenly replaced by Royal Marine officers.

In later years he spoke with indignation of the inefficiency and stupidity of his top-echelon commanders. At one point he was stationed at Loch Fyne, where he had to train soldiers to climb – in full equipment – down a net hung over the side of a ship, onto a floating platform and thence into a landing craft. It was a difficult operation and if the weather was rough could be a very dangerous one, for the platforms were in constant movement and could clash with great force against the side of the ship – sufficient force to kill a man who had slipped and lost his footing. On one accasion Rex considered the danger too great and refused an order to continue with the exercise. It took considerable courage to do so. He was lucky – the regulations were that action could be taken against an officer refusing an order only if the superior officer who had given it appeared in person and repeated it. But the weather was so rough that he couldn't get there to do so.

There were also some stunning incidents of self-interestedness. To increase the men's chances of safely negotiating the floating platforms, these were supposed to be covered with coconut matting. A lot of them weren't, and Rex complained. He subsequently discovered that the missing matting was furnishing the house of a senior naval officer. He had at one point seriously wondered if there were saboteurs among the senior officers; he came to the conclusion that with commanders like these the enemy didn't *need* saboteurs.

I had returned with my mind still full of my own political experiences during the years in India and on my return began almost at once to write it all up; but I found that no one was interested to read what I had written. I thought at the time that this showed a deplorable lack of communist spirit in them, but looking back in later years I realised that *I* hadn't shown any great interest in what *they'd* been doing either. I hadn't asked Rex about his experiences. I knew that John Vickers had been taken prisoner at the very beginning of the war, but I didn't ask him anything about what it had been like, either at the first meeting or later. Nor did I ever ask Freddie about her experiences, either while John was away or about what had happened when he returned from the prison camp. Even with Chris, my strong interest in what he was doing was entirely concentrated on the present. It did not occur to me to ask him about his army experiences over the last five years. I knew that he had been in a machine-gun regiment and that he had been in action, but it wasn't until years later that I thought to ask him what it had been like. He said, 'It's indescribable,' and left it at that.

I think there was a feeling in all of us that the war was over and done with and we wanted to look forward rather than back. I had been in no hurry to be reunited with my kin, apart from Rex. I had met Noel in London – once, briefly – for a drink at a pub near Baker Street. It was called 'The Volunteer' – I remember the name because when we fixed up our meeting over the phone I didn't hear the name clearly and Noel said, 'You know, worth ten pressmen.' The meeting went OK but nei-

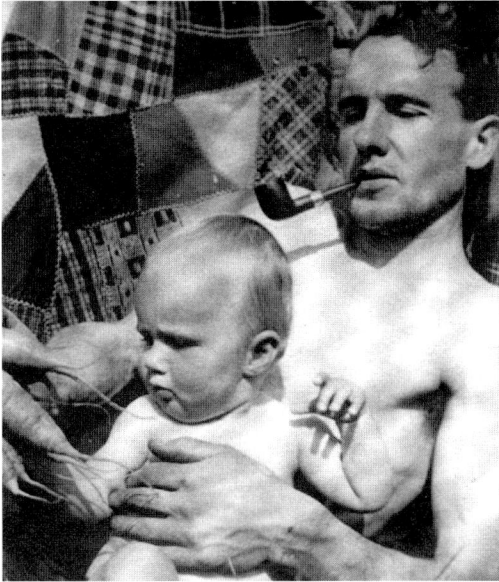

Looking forward rather than back: Rex (above) and Chris Freeman (below)

ther of us felt on the same wavelength, and there was no impetus to repeat it.

I felt much the same about my mother. I know from letters I received at the time that I did make a journey to Yorkshire early on in my leave, but it was probably very brief and I have no memory of being with my mother for any length of time. We had little in common, and I had never really felt that she took much interest in me, so I felt no obligation to spend much time with her. I now think my lack of consideration for her was inexcusable. It was two years since my father's death, and a year and a half since Wilfred's, and for years Noel, Rex and I had all been far away. Those must have been very lonely years for her. Yet it never occurred to me that I should feel any responsibility for her.

Froude was still in Holme, now with a young daughter, Kleta. Marie was no longer there – she had gone off to another part of Yorkshire when she married. But I went to see her sister Gertie in nearby Beverley, whose household I had enjoyed visiting in the days when my regiment had been stationed there. I was very happy now to be in contact with them again. Barbara was by now about sixteen and an attractive young woman. After all the years in India with no female company I enjoyed her willing encouragement of my attentions. I suspect that her parents secretly hoped that, now Marie was out of the picture, I might marry Barbara. I remember one night – possibly on a later visit – when Barbara was sitting on my lap and Frank and Gertie said they were going to bed. Barbara would be all right with me, wouldn't she? I wouldn't do anything to get her into trouble, would I? (hoping, I think, that I might very well do this and then she would 'have to' marry me.) To their great amusement Barbara said, 'It's all right, it's me bust he's after.'

The Hospital for Tropical Diseases had still neither identified nor cured my mysterious skin disease, and eventually they gave up on me and referred me to the Seamen's Hospital at Albert Dock. I wondered vaguely why a Seamen's Hospital would have a better chance than any other of finding out what was wrong. As I sat in the waiting room the sailors waiting alongside me were very jovial, asking such questions as, 'Did she sit on your knee, then?' It took me a while to realise that all of them were being treated for one or other sexually transmitted disease, and they assumed that I was too. Perhaps the dermatologists thought so too. But whatever they thought, all they did was to issue me with yet another cream.

Meanwhile, by the end of October my sixty-one days of leave were over; but the army had apparently not registered this and for two months more I heard nothing from them. I used part of the time to visit

Holme again, this time I spending a couple of weeks with my mother in her cottage. I remember that I was much less tolerant than I should have been. She had always had an infuriating habit of saying something and then two minutes later repeating exactly the same thing in exactly the same words, and this drove me up the wall. Once she said to me rather wistfully, 'Don't you like being at home, Ralph?' and I said 'No'. The fact that I remember this incident so clearly probably means that I realised even then that this had been unnecessarily cruel.

The thing that made most impact on me was what I heard from her about Wilfred. It seemed I had been right in thinking that in the years I had been away his values had been developing in a similar direction to mine. As part of his RAF training he had been sent to South Africa, and he had been horrified at conditions of life for black people. When he got back to Holme he had talked to my mother about it; pointing to a sort of garage-shed that we had at the back of our house, he told her that in South Africa that would have been a palace for most black people.

It was a time of waiting around, unable to move forward. My plans for the future now seemed to be in all probability unrealisable. My skin condition seemed finally to be clearing, but I thought that when the army did finally remember my existence, they would probably decide that I should not be sent back to India. And that is what happened. In December I finally heard that I was to appear before a medical board in early January 1946. When I did, a member of the board told me frankly that no one had yet any idea of what my disease was or whether it related to my being in India, but that they had decided that it had better play safe. It therefore categorised me in typical army speak as 'B(NT) 3/12' – NT meant Not fit for further Tropical service, and 3/12 meant for three months. But after the end of the three months, with no war being fought in India, it was unlikely that anyone would revise the decision. Within a month I was ordered to rejoin my parent unit in Beverley.

So it was finally clear. I was not going back to India.

∞

In the years that followed I thought often and often about my three and a half years in the army in India. I still have a strongly nostalgic feeling about it all. I remember the great natural beauty of some of the places where I was stationed – the canopy of the great tall trees in our jungle lines at Milestone Four, the clear sunshine of the Mikir Hills, and the almond blossom below Kohima. I thought I should probably never see all that again, and I never have.

329

With Froude and Kleta

For almost four years I had been been surrounded by a culture very different from my own – an experience I had not have thought to look for, but which in the event immeasurably enriched my understanding. Now the focus of my life was changing and I was having to reorient myself to what I might do with my life now that I was not going back. But I held still a store of vivid pictures of the life that for three years had been so absorbing. I had learnt about different ways of living, and of thinking – and that along with the differences there was much that was universal.

I was lucky to find, soon after my return to Britain, a means of continuing – and indeed deepening – that relationship with South Asian culture. The vehicle for that was my study of Urdu. The work I had done to become fluent in Urdu enabled me in 1946 to gain a studentship in Urdu at the School of Oriental and African Studies. After I had taken my degree I went on to teach Urdu there until my retirement in 1981, and thereafter for some years to a much wider group of adult learners in a number of British cities. My work for Urdu has taken me to India and Pakistan many times, and for several periods I have lived there for up to a year at a time, as part of Indian and Pakistani families. My closest colleagues for over fifty years have been Indian and Pakistani poets, writers or scholars of Urdu literature. This long and close involvement with Urdu speakers and their literature has brought unexpected pleasure and depth to my life, nurturing my abiding interest in South Asian ways of living and thinking, and contributing much to my own understanding of life, love and commitment. It remains the focus of my work till today.

Back in Britain, the aspect of my time in India that I looked back on with the greatest pleasure and satisfaction was my work as a communist. I was happy that even though I had been cut off from any possibility of collective action with fellow party members, I had been able to work on my own initiative; and through that work I greatly increased my understanding of what being a communist ought to mean. I was closer to the mass of the Indian people in those years than I have ever been since or am ever likely to be again, and I liked and admired men like Chandra Reddy and my other comrades of those years more than most Indians and Pakistanis I have met since. There is a lot that I learnt with them and from them, and I hope that those who are still alive remember me as I do them and feel the same about me as I do about them.

In the current state of the world, communism seems a lost cause to many people who did not live through the times I did; as it did also to many of my own generation who were once communists and then became disillusioned. I too went through a process of disillusionment, starting traumatically in 1946 and continuing with less force thereafter. The earliest indications of this had already happened in India, with my gradually dawning realisation that Party leaders did not take work among ordinary sepoys seriously. Those early tentative questionings turned into a traumatic experience of disillusionment within a year of my return to Britain, when I had the opportunity to see party leaders at work – a full decade before the 1956 revelations which were the decisive event for so many other communists. Some of them recorded their disillusionment in a once well-known book aptly entitled *The God that Failed*. But to me communism was never 'a god', and the basic beliefs which led me to become a communist in 1934 have not 'failed'. The political leaders I had assumed to be the most dedicated and principled people in the world had turned out to be very far from that, but while that taught me a much fuller understanding of the realities of the world and the people around me, it did nothing to change my commitment to the fundamental ideals that have inspired my for so many years. The way I have interpreted that commitment has gradually changed, partly through my own growing maturity, and partly in response to radically changing times and political contexts; the commitment itself remains constant. Looking back now over my whole life, I still feel that the political understanding I began to develop through my 'crisis' at the age of fifteen was essentially sound, and I am grateful to have come to adulthood at a time when those issues were so unmistakably clear. Young people growing up in subsequent decades have perhaps had a harder time finding things of value to guide their lives.

I was twenty-three when I arrived in India, twenty seven when I returned to Britain. For me, as for so many young men at the time, the war had cut across the critical years of young adulthood, changing us perhaps more fundamentally than it did men who entered the army with lives more formed. At a stage in life when our natural instincts would have been directing us to make plans, to choose a direction in life, we were put in the most passive of situations, where all we could do was go where we were sent. And the war caused a long postponement of the chance to fall in love and to move on from there to building a continuing loving relationship with one person.

By 1948 I was married. I had not found anyone who evoked the same sense of being deeply in love that Marie once had, and I did not expect to. All that had happened since had in any case changed me; I was thirty, and life was moving on fast – I wanted to be in a loving relationship with a woman and to have a family, and it did not seem sensible to wait for some possibly non-existent perfect partner. In the decades since then, experience has caused me to rethink many of my earlier assumptions about marriage, friendship, and love of all the many kinds that make up human experience. I have throughout my life been intensely interested in how people view their personal and sexual relationships, and how they formulate their own understandings of them, and I am continually struck by the fact that these central concerns of most people's lives remain the most difficult for them to talk about honestly.

Since earliest childhood I had had moments of vivid awareness of my capacity to love. Only much later did I try to put into words the feeling – which my study of Urdu poetry helped to clarify – that loving is fundamental to being human, and that in one sense it scarcely matters who you love or how much opportunity you have to express it; what matters is to love. It has been suggested to me, probably rightly, that in the years in India I learnt through force of circumstances to practise loving in a more diffuse way than might have happened if there had been no war and I had been left to follow a civilian life; and that perhaps part-ly because of the absence of women from my life, I learnt in my com-panionship with the men around me to value their sterling qualities and to find a reward in their warm response. It was through working in the fields in Holme-on-Spalding Moor, and then in the army in Northamp-ton, that I first realised I had the capacity to be warm and open with many different people, and in India I felt this ever more strongly. It is something I have carried with me and valued ever since.

These have been the three main strands of my life – the commitment to the fundamental values which made me a communist, the study of Urdu, and an awareness of love as the fundamental feature of true humanity. Most of my friends or colleagues, even those to whom I am closest, have connected with only one of these strands of my life, or at most two. My communist friends have known almost nothing about my Urdu work, and on the whole would not have been interested. To most of my colleagues in the world of Urdu studies, the fact that I am a com-munist hardly registers. In my family my son shares some of my interest in Urdu but my daughters never have and I see no reason why they should; all three have what I regard as sound political values, but my concern to constantly define my values and actions in communist terms is something of a puzzle to them, as it is to most of my friends, not excluding communist ones.

To me the three strands have always been inextricably inter-twined, each informing the other, and it is that interaction which has constituted the real story of my life.* My political convictions have fundamentally affected the way I have worked for Urdu, enabling me to understand things in Urdu literature and about the lives of Urdu speakers that would hardly have been possible otherwise. This in turn has had an effect on both my personal relationships and my under-standing of what it means to be a communist. And it has been through my personal experiences as much as through the pressure of world events that my concept of how to live as communist has changed.

People who, like myself, became communists in the thirties gener-ally entertained hopes that they would accomplish in their life-time far more than in fact it was possible for them to do. It doesn't follow that their efforts have been wasted. If you try to live according to your prin-ciples, and find wherever possible ways of putting your values into prac-tice, this moulds to some extent the lives of all who come into contact with you, and to that extent moulds many of the conflicting individual wills that make the future. And since that is the most that most of us can do, we should do it, and be content. I, and every true communist, would want no better judgement on their life than George Eliot's judgement on Dorothea's in the concluding words of *Middlemarch*:

> Her full nature, like that river of which Cyrus broke the strength, spent itself in channels which had no great name on the earth. But the effect of her being on those around her was incalculably diffusive: for the growing good of the world is partly dependent on unhistoric acts; and that things are not so ill with you and me as they might have been, is half owing to the number who lived faithfully a hidden life, and rest in unvisited tombs.

Notes and References

CHAPTER 1

p.11 There is a striking piece 'Young Adam Cupid' in Kenneth Grahame's *The Golden Age* (1895), in which he describes the infatuation of a young boy with the baker's wife – exactly the feeling I had for Eileen.

CHAPTER 2

p.21 Since I myself didn't quite know how best to describe a copper I consulted dictionaries. Two taken together yielded the information that it is 'a large boiler made of copper or often of iron, especially one in which clothes are boiled.' But I've never heard of one in which the boiler was made of anything other than iron, or one intended for any other purpose than boiling clothes.

p.22 Anton Rubenstein's 'Melody in F' (Op.3 No. 1). But there were words set to Mendelssohn's 'Spring Song' which my mother used to sing. They are supposedly sung by a man and ran

Put me upon an island where the girls are few
Put me among the lions and the tigers at the zoo
Put me upon a treadmill and I'll never, never fret
But for heavens sake don't put me with a suffragette.

p. 23 By George Manville Fenn, 1883.

p. 25 The poem appeared in *Punch*, 11th April 1928. The 1st verse is:

One Willingale of Loughton – blessed be his name
Stood beside a hornbeam, lopping of the same;
The lord of Loughton Manor bidding him begone,
Willingale said several things and Willingale went on;
And when I stand by Loughton Camp and look on Debden Slade
I think upon one Willingale and how his billhook played
For Willingale, a labourer, by lopping of a tree
Kept houses off the Forest, for men like you and me.

p. 30 In April 2000 Rex and I went to Holme and found that all three of the Ward sisters were still alive, aged 89, 87 and 85 respectively. We called upon Kathleen and later in July went and met all of them, when Kathleen had gathered them all together for the occasion.

p. 38 The communist historian Allen Hutt gives a vivid account of it in *The Post war History of the British Working Class* (1937) ch VI

p. 40 R M Ballantyne (1825–94). A remarkable writer whose adventure stories were often drawn from first hand knowledge. *The Cambridge Guide to Literature in English* (1993) tells us that *The Young Fur Traders* (1856) reflected his experience in Canada. He wrote *The Lighthouse* (1865) after spending three weeks on Bill Rock and *Fighting the Flames* (1867) after a short spell as a London fireman.

CHAPTER 3

p.49 Ian Bradley, in *The Penguin Book of Hymns* (1990), p.103, explains what it means.

CHAPTER 4

p.62 I only recently discovered in a copy of Benham's *Book of Quotations* (n.d. but post-1935) the correct version of this. It was the reply of La Place to Napoleon, when asked why he had not mentioned God in his 'Méchanique céleste,' and his actual words were, 'Sire, je n'avais besoin de cet hypothèse' – Sire, I had no need of this hypothesis (p.755b).

p.64 Rex Warner's translation, Penguin Books (1954) pp. 118-9.

p.65 It is amusing to compare what two editions of *The Oxford Companion to English Literature* have to say about this poem. The Sir Paul Harvey one (1932, fourth edition revised by Dorothy Eagle, 1967) calls it a 'fine poem.' The fifth edition, edited by Margaret Drabble, is more cautious and uses the neutral words 'celebrated' and 'much anthologised'.

p.66 *The Psalms for Modern Life*, interpreted with drawings by Arthur Wragg (1933).

p.67 Some people question the morality of this. I don't. The ban on members of the Communist Party was unjustifiable. People who were communists could have circumvented it by not joining the Party. Joining it and concealing their membership seems to me to amount to the same thing.

p.68 After the accession of the present occupant of the throne and in face of growing feeling that this sort of Kipling jingoism was no longer thought quite decent, this changed to 'For Queen and Commonwealth'. Later it dropped mottoes and observed a discreet silence rather than attempt any brief formulation of what it was for.

p.73(i) R Palme Dutt & Harry Pollitt, *Report on Organisation* (1922).

p.73(ii) From *Left Wing Communism* (1920), quoted by Stalin in *Foundations of Leninism* (1924). This quotation has an interesting history. In my early days in the Party it was both quoted and acted upon, at any rate in some Party organisations. It was still regularly quoted, but more and more selectively acted upon until about the early fifties. Then not even quoted any more. Another passage that made a great impact on me was a passage in Stalin's letter to Dmitriev, March 15, 1927, asserting that the Communist Party, unlike other parties, always says what it means and means what it says and can never, never, lie. The fact that I learnt much later that Stalin was already violating this principle has not altered my opinion of the value of his statement. The principle is one all true communist parties should always have observed.

p.73(iii) *Foundations of Leninism* (1924), ch. III, section 1, where the wording (but not the content) is a little different from this version.

p.74 *The Programme of the Communist International* (1929) p.24.

p.75 Letter of Feb 28th 1922, *Collected Works*, vol 36 p. 567, quoted with other statements by James Klugmann, 'Socialist Democracy', *Marxism Today*, May 1970, p.133.

p.82 Lenin, *Left Wing Communism* (1920) Ch X.

CHAPTER 5

p.86 In later days I often felt that 'this is where I came in,' for you could read exactly this kind of report in Maoist student papers.

p.93 In a letter to Hermann Schlucter, May 15, 1885, quoted in *Literature and Art* (Sydney 1949), a volume of selections from the writings of Marx and Engels.

p.96(i) *Inprecorr*, Vol 15, no 45, d. 17 September 1935, p. 1172. Here and elsewhere I have quoted the versions printed in *Inprecorr*, because it was these which I studied at the time. Later a series of 'verbatim official reports' was published, and the wording in these sometimes differs from that of the *Inprecorr* reports. But I have checked that the two accounts do not conflict where content is concerned.

p.96(ii) *Left Wing Communism*, chapter VIII.

p.98 *Letter to American Workers*, August 20, 1918.

p.100 I have read two reports of Dimitrov's closing speech, that included in Stella D Blagoyeva, *Dimitrov: a biography* [n.d., 1934?] and that included in *The Reichstag Fire Trial* (1934) – based on material collected by the World Committee for the Relief of the Victims of German Fascism – with an introductory chapter by Dimitrov. Neither includes in the text of the speech the incident of Dimitrov's confrontation with Goering. But Blagoyeva describes it fully on pp.69 ff, and there is a briefer reference to it in *The Reichstag Fire Trial*, p.203. And G K Chesterton has a poem and a footnote, signed GKC (1933) about this incident, in *Collected Nonsense and Light Verse* (1987), p.111. The footnote concludes, 'How anybody can see such lunacy dancing in high places, in the broad daylight of political responsibility, and have any further doubt about the sort of danger that threatens the world, is more than I can understand.' It was not until some years after this that anyone except the communists and others on the left were expressing such a view.

p.101 Clara Zetkin, pamphlet produced by International Publishers, the US communist publishing house.

p.103 Present day readers who are used to the picture (often a correct one) of communist satellite organisations as comprising only communists and crypto-communists may be surprised to learn that the League Against Imperialism in its day attracted important non-communists, of whom the best known is Nehru.

CHAPTER 6

p.116 This was George Barnard, later a Professor of Statistics at the University of Essex and then at Imperial College London.

p.119 In my subsequent experience of Eric Hobsbaum I felt this continued to be the case where work in the basic units of the Party was concerned. He may have thought that he could serve the Party better by concentrating on his work as a historian – and if he did I now think he was probably right.

p.120 Glover, *The Ancient World*, Cambridge University Press, 1935, & later Pelican, 1944.

p.123 Sanders, *A Short History of English Literature*, revised edition, 1996, p. 508.

p.125(i) Albert Axell, *Stalin's War* (1997) p.40.

p.125(ii) Keith Shephard, *International Relations, 1919–39*, Simon & Schuster Education (1987), p.32.

p.126(i) The pact was concluded on May 2nd 1935 but left unratified until February 1936, when 353 deputies voted for it, 164 against it, and 100 abstained.

p.126(ii) Keith Shephard, see above, 48 pages; in 'History Project' series, lst published in 1987, reprinted 1989, 1990, 1992, and possibly after that; but it is the 1992 reprint that I have.

p.126(iii) Axell, p.40.

p.126(iv) Axell, p.40.

p.127(i) Quoted in Axell, p.206.

p.127(ii) Preface to volume 1 of his history of World War II, *The Gathering Storm*.

p.128 *Inprecorr*, Vol. 15 No. 33, 15 August 1935, p. 913.

p.131 I think the parish itself was in the gift of St John's, though I did not know this at the time.

CHAPTER 7

p.141(i) This was an unusual lapse on Arnold Kettle's part – we generally worked together harmoniously. He later became a lecturer in English at Leeds University and author of a two volume work on the English novel.

p.141(ii) The best of their films were made in 1932/3, but I may also have seen some of the later ones, made in 1935 and 1937.

p.145(i) I have not heard of Winkler since, but Boris Ford later achieved fame as the editor of *The Pelican Guide to English Literature*.

p.145(ii) A truer appreciation of Dimitrov in due course became more common. I was delighted to learn only recently that one of the mandarins, Matthew Hodgart, used to describe himself as a Marxist-Leninist-Stalinist-Dimitrovist! – a notable uprgrading of Dimitrov's status – even I would not have ventured to add his name to that of the Great Four.

p.146 Claud Cockburn's autobiography, *I, Claud* (1957, revised edition 1967) pp. 262–264.

p.148(i) Axell, p. 205.

p.148(ii) There have been much publicised examples of Cambridge communists – Philby and others – who during the thirties, but before my arrival in Cambridge, tried to help the cause by joining the Soviet intelligence service. This too, of course, no one knew until many years later. As far as I know, none of my contemporaries at Cambridge were among them; but it is something which I consider they would have been justified in doing. I hope that people contemplating now the appalling conditions with which capitalism has replaced the much less appalling conditions of latter-day Soviet communism, may feel more sympathy than they would once have felt with the simple statement of the 87-year-old lady who was for years a Soviet agent, when she said, (reported in *The Guardian Weekly*,16–22 September 1999) 'I did what I did not to make money but to prevent the defeat of a new system which had, at great cost, given people food and homes which they could afford.'

p.149(i) There is a vivid account of this in Cockburn, pp. 170-171.

p.149(ii) Hobsbaum, *The Age of Extremes*, p. 143.

p.149(iii) Axell, pp 45-47.

p.154 A lot of highly intelligent people have written a lot of nonsense about the

Soviet–German pact. Arthur Koestler wrote in his contribution to the once celebrated book *The God that Failed* (1949) of,

'… the day when the swastika was hoisted upon Moscow Airport in honour of Ribbentrop's arrival and the Red Army band broke into the Horst Wessel Lied … That was the end; from then onward I no longer cared whether Hitler's allies called me a counter-revolutionary.'

What an extraordinary statement! It is on a par with thinking that two statesmen who shake hands and smile at each other are thereby expressing a genuine cordial friendship. If Koestler felt such loathing for Hitler why didn't he feel a comparable loathing for the powers without whose active help Hitler could never have been in a position to menace the world? Koestler, and most of the anti-Soviet chorus, wrote as though the pact was one of unconditional mutual assistance, and that the Russians were 'Hitler's allies'. We now know that up to a point this was true, but as far as we or anyone knew at the time, the Soviet–German pact was a non-aggression pact and nothing more than that. We communists were worried by only one feature of it. Previous pacts had included an 'escape clause', saying what circumstances would render it invalid, and this one did not. But this, we convinced ourselves, was of no great consequence. I recall now that Ram Nahum might have approved the secret provisions of the pact at the time if he had known of them. I remember him suggesting with a grin that a division of the world between Hitler and the Soviet Union might not be a bad idea. To me, such an idea was, and is, profoundly shocking.

p.156 Cockburn, p.215. Dimitrov's subsequent career was regrettably distinguished by (as far as we know) complete subservience to Stalin. A communist historian, Monty Johnstone, has told me that Stalin insisted that at the 7th World Congress of the Communist International there must be no criticism of the often disastrous line pursued in the years 1928–35. Dimitrov evidently silently accepted this total violation of communist principle, and for all I know may already have been doing so before the Reichstag trial. It is also possible that he may have known that he was not speaking the truth when he asserted there (in words which I have often quoted) 'Such a party [the Communist Party] cannot say one thing to its adherents and at the same time in secret do exactly the opposite. Such a Party does not go in for double book-keeping.'

But knowing this doesn't invalidate my conception of Dimitrov as a hero in the earlier phases of his life. Probably there has never been a hero who was 100% hero, but accounts, especially contemporary accounts, of such people never pay due attention to the contradictions in their character. Togliatti in 1956 said of Stalin that 'he combined the maximum good qualities with the maximum bad qualities', but I don't know of anyone who has not stressed one side of him to the virtual exclusion of the other. I have often asked myself how people who can face torture and death in their fight against the avowed enemies of communism cannot muster the courage to take a stand against the crimes of their fellow communists. I have never come up with an answer.

p.158 It was not until the 1990s that I encountered anything that shed light on this. In 1990 the transcripts of the Central Committee meetings of 25 September and 2-3 October 1939 were published in a book called *About Turn*. It was already clear that the British Party was now not quite in step with Moscow.

339

Palme Dutt, a leading member of the party's political committee, recommended that before formulating its policy the Party leadership should wait until it had 'established our contact with international comrades', by which he meant Springhall, the British party's representative in Moscow, then on his way back to London. Maurice Cornforth had at first spoken scathingly about this recommendation. 'What have we got a Central Committee for?' he asked, 'and if this is the way our leadership is working, how are we going to have a party with any authority in the country at all?' But in no time at all he had turned a 'political somersault', as he himself put it. He explained why he had done so. 'Perhaps it sounds rather silly in some ways to have oneself in the position where when the Soviet Union does something one is willing to follow what the Soviet Union is doing, but I must say that I personally have got that sort of faith in the Soviet Union, to be willing to do that, because I believe that if one loses anything of that faith in the Soviet Union one is done for as a Communist and Socialist.' Having so recently felt his own immortal communist soul to be in peril he no doubt felt he must make sure that we lower-ranking communists did not go along that path. And why must we not think of acting on the principle, 'turn the imperialist war into a civil war?' Because Dimitrov, as reported by Springhall, had told us not to. 'He [Dimitrov] stressed that in this task of unmasking the imperialist character of the war we would have to proceed cautiously at the beginning, not jumping in and speaking of turning imperialist war into civil war etc. At this stage we had to limit ourselves to the task of explaining patiently and unmasking the imperialist essence of the war and we could not go beyond that in the first stage.'

CHAPTER 8

p.169 In those days I never thought that anyone would dare to publish such songs, but in the late 1960s a paperback series, Sphere Books, did. I have four, entitled (inappropriately) *Rugby Songs*, *More Rugby Songs*, *Rugby Jokes* and *Son of Rugby Jokes*, and the last informs us that there is another collection, *What Rugby Jokes Did Next*. Presumably the title suggests that these were the songs rugby players used to sing after a game. No doubt they did, but I knew nearly all of them and I have never played rugby in my life. Similar books, and gramophone records, followed these.

p.171 I have since learnt that 'Bren' was a perfectly reasonable combination of the first two letters of Brno with the first two letters of Enfield, where it was then being manufactured.

p.176(i) *Inprecorr*, vol. 15, no. 67, 12 Dec. 1935, p. 1656. These words are taken from Dimitrov's reply to discussion on his report. For several pages (pp. 21ff) in the 'verbatim official report' he speaks of 'cadres', a word commonly used in communist writings to mean those dedicated, experienced and active Party members who form the core of the party. Dimitrov says (p. 21) 'the problem of cadres, one of the most important questions that confronts us, received practically no attention at this congress.' Whether he knew it or not, the reason for it soon became clear. His statement that the party does not value the man 'who always does only what other people tell him' was the exact reverse of the truth. It is precisely such people that the party leaders do value.

p.176(ii) *Left Wing Communism*, Chap VI.

p.180 Later Sir David Willcocks, musical director of the Bach Choir.

p.185 Soviet writers later pointed out that their retreating troops killed many more Germans than the British and French armies had.

CHAPTER 9

p.202 I later wrote an account of my Durban experiences for my Cambridge comrade Indrajit Gupta, who now, back in India, was working underground as a full-time Communist Party worker; but I didn't keep a copy of this.

p.207 The disguise succeeded to the extent that 'Dark Rosaleen' was included in *The Oxford Book of English Verse*!

p.208 There is a remarkably frank and even more remarkably modest account of all this by General William Slim (later Field Marshal) in *Defeat into Victory* (1956). He was given the unenviable task of trying to hold on to Burma in these conditions. He says that at one point he thought, 'If somebody brings me a bit of good news I shall burst into tears' – but he was never put to the test. (p. 82).

CHAPTER 10

p.231 Slim, p.107

p.232 Slim, p.139

p.235 Once, on a train journey in the old princely state of Hyderabad ('The Nizam's Dominions') I got talking to a South Indian who remarked sarcastically (and with a considerable degree of accuracy) that the British, extending their rule from South India northwards, had conquered new territory with South Indian soldiers and then declared them to be non-martial races.

CHAPTER 11

p.244 Slim, p.145: 'In 1943, for every man evacuated with wounds we had one hundred and twenty evacuated sick. The annual malaria rate alone was eighty-four per cent per annum of the total strength of the army.' An official history prepared for the South-East Asia Command, *The Campaign in Burma* (HMSO, London, 1946) says 'of all the British and Indian combat troops engaged since the outset only 12,000 marched into India. Of these barely a sixth were anything but sick.' p.26.

p.247 Each unit or section had about 30-35 vehicles, and 100 men: 1 officer (usually lieutenant, either British or Indian), 1 VCO, 2 Havildars, 6 Naiks, 13 Lance Naiks, about 65 sepoy-drivers, 2 cooks, 2 water carriers, 2 sweepers.

p.254 Hilary Spurling, *Paul Scott: A Life*, 1990, p. 145. Spurling says (p.119) that Scott 'could never understand why they [i.e. British people] should not treat Indians as equals.'

p.255 Nirad C Chaudhuri, *The Continent of Circe*, 1965, ch.6.

p.266 I knew of a few others who had challenged this orthodox view, for instance George Barnard, who I have been told was an exceptionally good convenor of shop stewards in a big factory.

CHAPTER 12

p.274 Pieter Keunemann, who later became General Secretary of the Communist Party of Sri Lanka and for a time a member of the Sri Lanka government.

p.277 I can't swear to it that the Indian party didn't have a policy on work in the armed forces and didn't give any guidance to party members who enlisted in them, but I have no evidence that it did, and my own experience gave clear indications that it did not.

CHAPTER 13

p.295 The Soviet Constitution provides a remarkable instance of the Soviet practice of presenting a detailed picture of things as they ought to be as though this was how they really were. The enthusiasm with which we studied it was not entirely misplaced. I still think that if ever a union of socialist republics (really socialist, really democratic, really strict in their observance of human rights) comes into being, its inhabitants would do well to study that constitution as thoroughly as we did in those days.

p.299(i) Slim had surprise checks done of whole units to see that mepacrine was being systematically taken by all the men. 'If the overall result was less than ninety-five per cent positive I sacked the commanding officer. I only had to sack three; by then the rest had got my meaning.' Slim, p.148.

p.299(ii) For instance his statement after the Soviet victory at Stalingrad that the Soviet Union was now the main enemy.

p.306 See Slim, ch.13 & 14.

p.307 Peter Ward Fay's *The Forgotten Army* (1993) tells the story from the viewpoint of the Indian National Army.

p.308(i) That the feeling was not confined to the less educated I discovered only recently through reading Nirad Choudhuri's book, *Thy Hand, Great Anarch* (1987), which describes how highly literate Bengalis rejoiced in Nazi victories.

p.308(ii) Slim, p. 257.

p.311 Ronald Lewin, *Slim the Standard Bearer*, Wordsworth Editions, 1999.

p.313 The effectiveness of this work was recognised by senior levels in the army. An official history, *The Campaign in Burma* (HMSO, 1946) quotes Field-Marshall Wavell, commander in chief of the British forces in India and Burma, 'The more I have seen of war the more I realise how it all depends on administration and transportation.' On the Manipur L of C it says: 'During the worst weather of the months of 1944, the truck drivers kept up a daily average of 77 miles from railhead to forward areas. They averaged nearly 28,000 miles per accident, though you would never believe it as you raced round those shelf-like roads with your wheels on the brink of a precipice. Working round the clock, the Sepoy drivers delivered 3,000 tons a day to the marching armies.'

CHAPTER 14

p.324 Extracts from these were later published in the Party-controlled periodical *Russia Today*, Dec. 1940.

p.334 Some of the material for Part 2 already exists in the form of separate pieces on particular topics. If you are interested to see them, or receive a 'Preview' of progress on Part 2, please contact me.

Index of Songs & List of Illustrations

SONGS

LIST OF ILLUSTRATIONS

SOURCES OF PHOTOGRAPHS

Frank Owen; *The Campaign in Burma*, HMSO, 1946; Jack Farmer, *Woodford as I knew it* (nd); Leila Ghosh & Dalia Roy, *Agra & Delhi*, IBH; Henry Hawkins, *London's Great Legacy: Epping Forest*, Thomas Mitchell, 1896; F.H. Headley, *Rambles in Epping Forest*, 1945; Durban Lacom, *The struggle for Trade Unions in South Africa*, Sached, 1986; Ronald Lewin, *Slim the Standard Bearer*, Wordsworth Editions, 1999; Charles & Karoki Lewis, *Delhi's Historic Villages*, Ravi Dayal, 1997; William Newton, postcard reproduction of a painting of Chigwell School; Oxfam Education Department, *India, Country & People*, 1977; Stephen Pewsey, *Epping & Ongar: a pictorial history*, Phillimore, 1997; Stephen Pewsey, *Chigwell and Loughton, A pictorial history*, Phillimore, 1995; W. G. Ramsey, *Epping Forest then and now*, Battle of Britain prints, 1986; *Staples Road School Centenary, 1988-1988*; Pavan K. Varma & Sondeep Shankar, *Mansions at Dusk: the Havelis of Old Delhi*, Spantech, 1992.